COLONIZATION OF
UNFAMILIAR LANDSCAPES

The process of familiarization with and adaptation to unfamiliar landscapes has been an integral part of colonization and settlement throughout human history. Yet the workings of this process – its social, psychological, and environmental components, the influence of the process on later history, and indeed the full extent to which humans can truly know their habitat – are not yet well understood.

This innovative and important volume presents the archaeological and anthropological foundations of the landscape learning process. The contributors apply the related fields of ethnography, cognitive psychology, and historical archaeology to the issues of individual exploration, development of trail systems, folk knowledge, social identity, and the role of the frontier in the growth of the modern world. A series of case studies examines the archaeological evidence for and interpretations of landscape learning from the movement of the first pre-modern humans into Europe, the peopling of the Old and New World at the end of the Ice Age, and the colonization of the Pacific, to the English colonists at Jamestown. The final chapter summarizes the implications of the landscape learning idea for our understanding of human history and sets out a framework for future research.

Understanding initial colonization is essential to addressing questions of how and why we live where we do. This significant and wide-ranging collection of work moves the theme away from the chronological curiosities of "firsts" and "oldests" towards a view in which it is a process with characteristics and lessons of its own.

Marcy Rockman is a Lecturer in the Department of Anthropology at the University of Arizona, Tucson. **James Steele** is a Lecturer in the Department of Archaeology at the University of Southampton.

Contributors: Atholl Anderson, David Anthony, Dennis Blanton, Stuart Fiedel, Reginald Golledge, Donald Hardesty, Lee Hazelwood, Robert Kelly, David Meltzer, Marcy Rockman, Wil Roebroeks, James Steele, Richard Stoffle, Christopher Tolan-Smith, María Nieves Zedeño.

COLONIZATION OF UNFAMILIAR LANDSCAPES

The archaeology of adaptation

Edited by
Marcy Rockman and
James Steele

Routledge
Taylor & Francis Group

LONDON AND NEW YORK

First published 2003
by Routledge
11 New Fetter Lane, London EC4P 4EE

Simultaneously published in the USA and Canada
by Routledge
29 West 35th Street, New York, NY 10001

Routledge is an imprint of the Taylor & Francis Group

Typeset in Garamond by
Bookcraft Ltd, Stroud, Gloucestershire
Printed and bound in Great Britain by
MPG Books Ltd, Bodmin

British Library Cataloguing in Publication Data
A catalogue record for this book is available from the British Library

Library of Congress Cataloging in Publication Data
A catalog record for this book has been requested

ISBN 0–415–25606–2 (hbk)
ISBN 0–415–25607–0 (pbk)

CONTENTS

CONTENTS

FIGURES

TABLES

CONTRIBUTORS

Atholl Anderson, Department of Archaeology and Natural History, Research School of Pacific and Asian Studies, Australian National University, Canberra, ACT 0200 Australia.

David Anthony, Department of Anthropology, Hartwick College, West Street, Oneonta, New York 13820-4020, USA.

Dennis Blanton, Center for Archaeological Research, College of William & Mary, PO Box 8795, Williamsburg, VA 23187–8795, USA.

Stuart Fiedel, Louis Berger Group, 1819 H Street NW, Suite 900, Washington, DC 20006.

Reginald Golledge, Department of Geography, University of California, Santa Barbara, Santa Barbara, CA 93106-4060, USA.

Donald Hardesty, Department of Anthropology / MS 096, University of Nevada, Reno, Reno, NV 89557, USA.

Lee Hazelwood, Department of Archaeology, University of Southampton, Highfield, Southampton SO17 1BJ, United Kingdom.

Robert Kelly, Department of Anthropology, University of Wyoming, Laramie, WY 82071, USA.

David Meltzer, Department of Anthropology, SMU, Dallas, Texas 75275-0336, USA.

Marcy Rockman, Department of Anthropology, The University of Arizona, Tucson, AZ 85721, USA.

Wil Roebroeks, Faculty of Archaeology, Leiden University, PO Box 9515, 2300 RA Leiden, The Netherlands.

James Steele, Department of Archaeology, University of Southampton, Highfield, Southampton SO17 1BJ, United Kingdom.

Richard Stoffle, Bureau of Applied Research in Anthropology, The University of Arizona, Tucson, AZ 85721, USA.

Christopher Tolan-Smith, 2 Home Farm, Newborough, Hexham, NE47 5HF, United Kingdom.

María Nieves Zedeño, Bureau of Applied Research in Anthropology, The University of Arizona, Tucson, AZ 85721, USA.

FOREWORD

I routinely evaluate everything I read in terms of its applicability to modeling the peopling of the New World. In the Americas, we acknowledge the importance of long-distance social networks for information transfer but presume that the primary information being transferred relates to environmental and demographic pressures, i.e. ultimately ecological issues. But what if the settling of the Americas, though constrained (not determined) by environmental factors, was a historical, social process driven by the social life and cultural constructs of lateglacial societies? After all, even in the harshest of circumstances, reactions to environmental changes are mediated by decisions of individuals.

For too long the environment has been treated as a backdrop to cultural developments – a physical stage one travels across. As the creators of this book well know, however, people do not travel across a landscape, they interact with it. Once archaeologists accepted the need to incorporate environment into archaeological interpretations, the question became how to do this. Can we identify the mechanisms that link cultures to their environments, as well as discern their archaeological correlates? What are the critical variables? What mediates the interaction? This volume offers a multiplicity of approaches to answering these questions and more. The common theme of the papers is the key linking mechanism of landscape learning, dealing with such questions as: What did they know? How did they learn it? When did they know it? Several examples – wide ranging in time and place, of initial explorers naming rivers, mountains, or other natural features – provide analogues of just how cultural knowledge is learned/created: from that first scout relying on prior knowledge to assign/name landscape features (and making, as landscape archaeologists would say, "the change from space into place") to the transmission of that knowledge to relatives left behind. After years of imagining hunger or cold or adventure as the driving forces behind the first Americans' trek from northeast Asia, it's intriguing how many of these papers refer to initial exploration as being sparked by the exile of individuals for various political and social reasons.

I've come to realize that much of the disagreement over the timing and mechanisms involved in the first peopling of the Americas derives from our inexact use of terms. By peopling do we mean "to supply or fill with people"?[1] Or do we refer to the very first explorers to set foot on new shores? An environment that might be passable to a transient ("passing through or by a place with only a brief stay") explorer ("a person who travels over (new territory) for adventure or discovery") may yet be incapable of supporting actual inhabitants ("those that occupy a particular place regularly, routinely, or for a period of time") who have migrated ("to move from one country, place, or locality to another") to, colonized ("to establish a colony in or on or of"), or settled ("to establish in residence; to furnish with inhabitants") a particular region. A tour through these definitions amply illustrates that colonization is a process, not an event. Though many of us acknowledge that fact, we have not often separated the variables according to which aspect of the colonization process we are studying. We must identify these stages as well as be explicit about which phenomena we are measuring and interpreting, which pertain to which stage of population movement. For example, contributors to this volume suggest that the initial phases of movement in unknown lands will be characterized by cultural homogeneity, and assemblages of a "generalized" nature, whereas the second phase of colonization would evidence a greater use of locally available raw materials, demonstrating the landscape learning process at work. Such clarification will allow us to move beyond such simple dichotomies as "no knowledge" versus "knowledge" during the landscape learning process. I see this as comparable to the initial perception of a switch from "ice" to "no ice" at the end of the Pleistocene, causing many altogether to overlook the dynamic transitional nature of the Pleistocene–Holocene transition and its implications for cultural adaptations.

The separate but complementary questions of how and why people move can be approached from either an ecological standpoint or an ideological standpoint, or both. The traditional ecological approach that sees migration as range expansion stresses physical parameters rather than social and ideological aspects of migration. Not that these aspects were completely denied, but they were relegated to secondary roles. In my own work (e.g. Mandryk 1992, 1993) I stress the importance of social variables to the biological viability of populations, arguing that social viability requires a minimum level of contact for exchange of mates. Strong social alliance networks in turn provide better environmental information and further contribute to biological robustness and societal stability.

The landscape learning process, as demonstrated by this book, is surprisingly similar, whether pertaining to gold miners on the western frontier, early British islanders, Polynesian voyageurs, mid-Pleistocene Neanderthals, or early American colonists. There are several especially tantalizing ideas in these essays. Anderson (Chapter 10), for example, finds lower rates of success for one-way versus return voyaging, and that physical barriers may result in discontinuous patterns of colonization. He suggests that low biomass levels might cause the colonization process to move faster. Blanton (Chapter 11) stresses the importance of the scouting stage of landscape learning, and provides some indication of how long this initial stage may take. Especially intriguing are Rockman and Steele's (Chapter 8) suggestions for exploring whether we can recognize the stages of the landscape learning process in the archaeological record through careful analysis of changes in patterns of mobility, types of terrain traversed, and lithic types used. To one grown accustomed to traditional "materialist" approaches to the process of colonization, this volume is a breath of fresh air.

This rich collection is the result of a collaboration between an American anthropologist (who coined the phrase "landscape learning") and a British archaeologist. It is fitting that most of the organizing and editing was carried out by Rockman and Steele in Britain, where it seems there has always been a deeper understanding of landscape as being far more than environmental background. Archaeologists in the United States seem less at ease with the word landscape than their colleagues in Britain and Canada. We've long gotten by by referring to "environment," a seemingly more solid, straightforward word. The value of the term "landscape," however, is that it is anything but straightforward, possessing many layers of meaning pertinent to our understanding of the relationships between people and the places they inhabit, as the chapters in this book ably demonstrate.

Carole Mandryk
Associate Professor of Archaeology
Harvard University

Note

1   Definitions from Merriam-Webster online (http://www.m-w.com/cgi-bin/dictionary)

References

Mandryk, C.A.S. (1992) "Paleoecology as Contextual Archaeology: Human Viability of the Late Quaternary Ice-free Corridor, Alberta, Canada," unpublished PhD dissertation, University of Alberta, Edmonton, Alberta.

Mandryk, C.A.S. (1993) "Hunter-gatherers Social Costs and the Nonviability of Submarginal Environments," *Journal of Anthropological Research* 49(1):39–72.

ACKNOWLEDGMENTS

There are many people who must be thanked for their contributions to this volume. First and foremost, we would like to recognize the tremendous creativity of all the contributors, including both those of the original symposium in Philadelphia and of this volume. Landscape learning was not the primary research focus of any of them when they were approached to contribute to this project. Yet each of them took the ideas and questions with which we presented them and returned works with results and significance we only dreamed of. In addition to the contributors of this volume, we would like to thank Clive Gamble, James McGlade, Eelco Rensink, Thembi Russell, and Todd Surovell for their participation in the original symposium.

We would like to thank the editors at Routledge Press, including Julene Barnes, Polly Osborn, Catherine Bousfield, and Richard Stoneman, as well as the initial reviewers who saw promise in all of this. To Julene Barnes, we know we still owe you cookies.

We would also like to thank the Department of Archaeology of the University of Southampton for its logistical support in collecting and preparing the manuscript for this volume.

Finally, Marcy would like to thank James for his unfailing support of this project and of her as a first-time symposium organizer and editor. Pursuing landscape learning as an actual field of study has been a long-held dream, but it is doubtful that it would ever have come to so substantial a form as this volume without his enthusiasm and encouragement. Thank you.

Marcy Rockman
James Steele
Southampton, England, July 2002

EDITORS' INTRODUCTION

Marcy Rockman and James Steele

The process of familiarization with and adaptation to unfamiliar landscapes has been an integral part of colonization and settlement throughout hominid history. Yet the workings of this process – its social, cognitive, and environmental components, its influence on subsequent occupation patterns, and the question of how fully humans can ever truly know their habitat – are not yet well understood. The objective of this volume is to define "landscape learning" as a research field. Part I presents a set of review papers that consider the place of knowledge within archaeological models of colonization, the cognitive psychology of human wayfinding, the anthropology of landscape knowledge, the evolution of trail systems, and the importance of landscape learning in the pioneer phases of historical colonizations. Part II presents a temporally and geographically diverse set of case studies. These include the pre-modern human entrance into Europe, Late Pleistocene, Neolithic, and historical American colonizations, and the peopling of the Pacific. Each study considers the presence of, absence of, and rate of acquisition of knowledge about natural resources among early populations and how their acquisition of environmental knowledge may be studied in the archaeological record. The final part of the volume summarizes these findings and sets out frameworks and agendas for future research in this field.

As editors, we came to be interested in this topic along very different routes – James Steele through the development of mathematical models of hunter-gatherer dispersals, Marcy Rockman through studying the geology and documentary records of nineteenth-century gold rushes in the American West. We therefore took as our starting point the suggestion that learning the landscape has been a factor in many instances of human colonization and settlement and must be considered across the full geographic and temporal scope of archaeological interpretation. We do not suggest that the traces of the landscape learning process are the same for all colonizations; rather, we expect that they vary by natural resource, geographic region, time period, and method of investigation, and in some instances may not be visible at all.

This volume began as a symposium for the 2000 Society for American Archaeology meetings in Philadelphia. Contributors were asked to think creatively about how the landscape learning process might apply to their particular area of expertise. In preparing this volume, we expanded and re-organized the original speaker list to include a balance of background theory, case examples, and summary and interpretation. We see this volume as a means of initiating discussion of the various ways in which landscape learning can be studied as a widespread phenomenon.

Interest in the process of familiarization with and adaptation to new landscapes has been growing of late, particularly with respect to classic initial colonizations such as the movement of Paleoindians into the Americas. We see publication of this collection of review papers and case studies as an opportunity to move even more firmly away from controversies over the "firsts" and "oldests" of colonization events and instead focus on the anthropological experience of colonization processes. With our combined efforts, we hope to generate some genuine and critical new approaches to the study of colonization and, since colonization necessarily underlies every subsequent occupation, perhaps some new ideas about long-term habitation as well.

The following is a brief overview of the ideas and organization of this volume. Part I provides an introduction to the concepts of landscape learning and the theoretical foundation for all of the papers of the volume. Rockman presents the introductory concepts of the relationships between environmental knowledge and adaptation, and working definitions of landscape, initial colonization, and the landscape learning process. She includes an overview of how knowledge is currently represented in colonization models and discusses how knowledge and learning may be explicitly incorporated into colonization studies, as well as the implications of the topic of knowledge for archaeological interpretation and application.

Golledge presents relevant concepts from the field of cognitive psychology. He discusses models of individual exploration and gives evidence for how environmental knowledge is acquired at its finest scale.

Kelly considers the information available in the ethnographic record about the processes of landscape familiarization and large-scale colonization. He notes the methodological paradox such that archaeology is essential to the study of initial colonizations but that in turn there is little ethnographic evidence upon which to base solid archaeological interpretations. Further, standard ethnographic categories such as group size, rate of movement, and mobility pattern may have been influenced by the landscape learning process, and therefore the landscape learning process should be acknowledged when assumptions about these categories are included in colonization models.

Zedeño and Stoffle assess the development of path systems using recent ethnographic and ethnohistorical research. They consider the initial development of path and track systems and the many social and geographic factors that can influence their pattern, orientation, and direction. They also describe how the initial layout of path systems can persist in social groups for at least several hundred years, thus illustrating the potential long-term effects of at least some portions of the landscape learning process.

Hardesty discusses landscape learning in the context of the mining rushes of the American West. He shows that different categories of knowledge are required to function in a landscape, including geographic knowledge, technical knowledge, and social knowledge. A given piece of knowledge or perspective or aspect thereof can influence many elements of material culture. He also demonstrates that landscape learning has played a role in the construction of the modern world, and thereby provides a link to other more present-oriented research fields.

Part II is an overview of the landscape learning process through space and time, examined through a range of case examples. Roebroeks presents the earliest case example, based on the initial peopling of Europe approximately 500,000 years ago. He suggests that at this time depth, landscape learning must be considered on the scale of glacial/interglacial cycles. Further, he notes that in terms of archaeological traces, at this high temporal and spatial scale, it may not be possible to distinguish the behavioral adjustments of landscape learning from the physical changes of human evolution.

Tolan-Smith looks at the hunter-gatherer recolonization of the British Isles following the end of the last Ice Age. He presents an interpretation of radiocarbon patterns in comparison to the landforms over which they are spread and presents some ethnographic evidence that may provide explanation for the progression of the lateglacial colonization. With his evidence, it appears that patterns related to landscape learning may be visible on scales of one to two millennia.

Steele and Rockman model the dispersal of early Paleoindian populations across the northern American Great Plains. This model is an effort to address the individual to small group exploration aspect of colonization. They show that prioritization of different resources or application of different rules of thumb for locating resources may have resulted in noticeably different paths of movement. Such alternative paths would have brought colonizers into contact with different ranges of resources, which in turn may have influenced the rate and direction of further dispersal movements. When considered alongside the paper of Zedeño and Stoffle, this model suggests that even fine-scale movements and small group sizes can have effects across later and much larger scales of time and space.

Fiedel and Anthony review the spread of Neolithic agriculturalists across Europe. They suggest that the primary pattern of movement for the agriculturalist populations is better described as a leap-frog pattern rather than the wave-of-advance pattern originally described by Ammerman and Cavalli-Sforza in 1984. They consider the many social factors that can contribute to the phenomenon of migration and the multiple avenues of information acquisition and transfer that subsequently occur. They propose a "Natty Bumppo" model of information acquisition and distribution, such that the primary source of environmental information for these agriculturalists may have been the frontiersmen who interacted with local hunter-gatherer populations along the internal frontiers of Europe.

Anderson discusses the colonization of the Pacific. He suggests that discovery and settlement of the Pacific islands was not a result of random sailing, but of astute recognition of the geographic patterns of island organization and island resource distribution. He tests this model against the radiocarbon and archaeological record of the Pacific and also examines the culture of colonization, such that exploration for new islands was propelled not by population pressure or resource depletion alone, but an ongoing colonizing spirit or culture of colonization.

Blanton presents a study of the early English colonists at Jamestown, Virginia. He looks at how this colonization effort almost failed because of the mental outlook of the colonists and their initial determination not to learn the environment. This example also provides a means of considering the implications of rapid translocation from origin to a significantly different unfamiliar environment. Blanton provides a model for identifying colonizations involving unfamiliar environments in the historical archaeological record.

In Part III, Hazelwood and Steele review continuum models of population expansions and explore the conditions for archaeological detection of the pioneer phase of a prehistoric colonization episode. Meltzer gives an overview of all of the papers in the volume. He interprets the broad themes and patterns presented throughout the volume and adds the particular perspective of his own very extensive work and experience with the initial colonization of the Americas.

DATING ABBREVIATIONS

BP   **years before present**   Dates given with this abbreviation have been reached by one of a number of dating techniques. This abbreviation does not imply calibration of radiocarbon date measurements.

rcbp   **radiocarbon years before present**   Dates given with this abbreviation have been derived from radiocarbon measurements. Unless specified by the individual author, this abbreviation does not imply calibration of the radiocarbon date measurements.

cal BC   **calibrated years** BC   Dates given with this abbreviation have been derived from radiocarbon measurements. These measurements have subsequently been corrected using a calibration curve.

kyr   **thousands of years**

mya   **millions of years ago**

Part I

CONCEPTUAL FRAMEWORKS

1

KNOWLEDGE AND LEARNING IN THE ARCHAEOLOGY OF COLONIZATION

Marcy Rockman

What does it mean to know an environment? In today's terms, what do we know about the spaces in which we live – about their resources, their unique characteristics, their limitations? How long did it take for us to learn them? How much of what we know comes from personal experience and how much is drawn from the experiences of others? When we leave an environment, what information do we take with us, and how and for how long do we apply that information in the new environments to which we go? And, from a material perspective, do the things we leave behind represent what we knew of our environments during our time in them?

The inspiration for asking these questions in this paper was a discussion by Bruce Trigger of V. Gordon Childe's work on the topic of knowledge and the environment. Childe, Trigger states, described knowledge as a "set of shared mental approximations of the real world that [permit] human beings to act upon it" Childe also noted that "human beings adapt not to their real environment but to their ideas about it, even if effective adaptation requires a reasonably close correspondence between reality and how it is perceived" (Trigger 1989: 261). This idea of effective adaptation is key. It underlines the question of what knowledge is absolutely necessary for people to exist and persist in an environment, and how knowledge about an environment accumulates and comes to reflect experiences in the environment over time.

The topics of adaptation and the development of human–environment interactions are therefore deeply linked to the archaeological study of colonization. Clive Gamble, in his work *Timewalkers: The Prehistory of Global Colonization* (1993: 182), notes that "the changes in behavior required to complete this process [of global colonization] are what made us human, even though that behavior had no such goal in mind. We were not adapted for filling up the world. It was instead a consequence of changes in behavior, an exaptive radiation produced by the cooption of existing elements into a new framework for action." Thus, it was changes in behavior that brought the human form into contact with new environments and, in turn, new environments that further enforced and encouraged the development of new behaviors. As such, there is a need for archaeology to consider deeply how it studies, understands, and interrelates the topics of colonization, behavior, and environmental knowledge.

Further, an archaeological response to the opening questions of this paper requires not only assessment of artifacts made and used in past environments and assessment of what effective adaptations to them might entail, but also a consideration of how humans shared information about those environments and how long it took for that shared information to generate an appropriate balance between perception and reality.

Over the years, archaeologists have constructed several models to describe past colonizations. Knowledge of and learning an environment are implicit in these models, but have not yet been examined as primary factors. I think they should be. The choice of whether or not to consider the issue of environmental knowledge when constructing or applying a movement model is itself based on assumptions of how environmental knowledge develops and functions in the interactions between people and the places they lived in and how environmental knowledge may have affected the traces of the people we study. The task taken here is a critical examination of these assumptions and a consideration of the questions above in terms of human colonization and adaptation. It is not yet clear whether the theoretical and methodological tools of archaeology are fine enough to complete the task. The purpose of this paper is to show that the topics of knowledge and learning are already so integral to our conceptions of how people come to be in places and how they live there once they arrive that it is important to make the attempt. This chapter discusses what is meant by knowledge of the environment and how such knowledge currently exists in our models of human movement, and gives suggestions on how the topic of knowledge and learning can address important questions relating to both the past and the present.

Environmental knowledge

Knowing the environment can mean many things. For the sake of clarity, I suggest three basic types of information:

- **Locational**   Locations and physical characteristics of necessary resources (e.g. the size of the lithic source outcrop)
- **Limitational**   Boundaries and costs of necessary resources (e.g. the harvesting potential of ripe vegetation, extremity of seasonal variation)
- **Social**   Attribution of names, meanings, and patterns to natural features; transformation of environment into a human landscape (see Basso 1996; Rossignol and Wandsnider 1992) (e.g. attribution of experiences to specific local landscape features).

Locational knowledge includes information relating to the spatial and physical characteristics of particular resources. For example, it includes the extent of a given plant community, the valley in which there is a particular lithic source, the topography of faunal migration routes. It also includes the ability to relocate such resources after their discovery. Locational knowledge is considered to be the easiest form of information to acquire. As Golledge (Chapter 2) shows, modern locational knowledge may be gathered rapidly, in the space of days, weeks, or months. Research by Brody (1981) among the Native Americans of the Dog River Reserve in British Columbia also suggests that hunter-gatherers are and were very acute to locational information and could gather large amounts in a similarly short timeframe.

This category should not be taken to suggest that all resources of a given area are identified instantaneously. In order for a resource to be located and relocated, it must be considered within the technology and economy of the identifying group. A number of historical situations are known in which the potential of particular resources was not recognized until a significant period after initial occupation of the region. For example, it took nearly 40 years for gold miners in Nevada to recognize gold deposits that varied from the "traditional" forms known from the Comstock Lode (Hardesty, Chapter 5; see also Rockman 2001, concerning a similar case in Wyoming). Some resources may be noted but may lie outside the technology of the group and its economy. Van Andel and Runnels (1995) note that Mesolithic populations of Greece do not seem to have used the upland plains, although these areas were later occupied by early Neolithic settlers.

Limitational knowledge refers to familiarity with the usefulness and reliability of various resources, including the combination of multiple resources into a working environment. For example, what are the seasonal variations in biotic resources? How workable and reliable are the lithic materials for the variety of stone tool tasks? How fertile is the soil for agriculture? How extensively can plants be harvested; how many people can be supported in the area? What is the range of game that inhabits the area, and how stable are those populations? Development of limitational knowledge depends upon the periodicity of the given resource and its intended use. For general purposes, I suggest that it most likely takes at least a generation to develop familiarity with resources: their fluctuations, their potentials, and their carrying capacity on a scale that influences human activity. For example, in their study of demic expansion of early Neolithic settlements in central Greece, van Andel and Runnels (1995) cite the output flow of the Pineios River in the Larisa basin of Thessaly. The main discharge of the river takes place over the winter months, with a total flow of $3,000 \times 10^6$ cubic meters. Measurements taken over a period of 35 years show that the annual variation in output is approximately one-fourth of the average annual flow. These measurements do not indicate whether even greater variations might be noted over a longer period of observation; nor do figures taken in the middle of the twentieth century necessarily represent the range of variation during the early Neolithic. What it does show is that it may have taken up to 35 years or more to develop a baseline familiarity with river behavior and the frequency and full extent of its flooding potential. Other periodicities, such as drought and temperature variation, would also affect full growing potential in the basin. The interplay among these variations may extend the time period needed for familiarization with them, or they may ultimately be beyond the range of human planning. (For full discussion of temporal dynamics and environmental process rates, see Dean 1988; Hopkinson 2001; Rockman 2002.)

Social knowledge is the collection of social experiences that serves as a means of transforming the environment or a collection of natural resources into a human landscape. There is currently an abundant literature on the archaeology of landscapes (see Rossignol and Wandsnider 1992; Ucko and Layton 1999) and a range of specific definitions. It is not the objective of this chapter to propose a new definition, but to emphasize the key theme of many of the definitions that landscapes are spaces in which a group of humans actively interact with a natural environment. In this sense, landscapes include natural topographic features, a range of built or modified features, and socially determined patterns of activity within and amongst these features (after C. Tolan-Smith 1998: 1). These patterns of activity are of particular interest here in the context of the knowledge and perceptions that inform them and the processes of their development and change through time.

Analyses of the oral traditions of native coastal and inland groups of northern Alaska by Minc (1986) and Minc and Smith (1989) provide a basis for characterizing social knowledge of landscapes and estimating the timeframes necessary for developing the information to a usable level. This work suggests that a group's stories and folklore encode mechanisms for coping with the different scales of environmental variation in the region. Different types of stories include different types of information and prescribe different types of mechanisms. The most extreme mechanism is that of abandonment. When abandonment is prescribed by ritual stories, it is under circumstances that environmental periodicities may produce in the order of once every several hundred years. Thus, more than one such cycle is necessary (e.g. up to twice the period of several hundred years) to develop the mythical structure of adaptation. For example, oral traditions of the Tareumiut and Nunamiut encode oscillations between environmental conditions that alternately favor marine or terrestrial fauna in the movement of animal spirits. One storyline notes that

> [w]hen wolves starve on land they go to their relatives in the sea and turn into killer whales; conversely, killer whales, when unable to find food in the sea, travel inland and become wolves. Similarly, mountain sheep are thought to wander down to the sea and become beluga. Thus, it is known that when there are plenty of beluga off the Arctic coast, mountain sheep will be scarce and when sheep are plentiful in the Brooks Range, beluga are absent in the adjacent coastal regions.
>
> (Minc and Smith 1989: 20)

In this way, myth and ritual provide an explicit example for human responses to failure of resources or famine: in the way that fauna take alternative forms and move between resource zones in times of need, human groups should also migrate and adopt alternative subsistence strategies when local resources fail. As these coping mechanisms for resource stress are founded on the behavior of animals during climatic cycles, it can be suggested that it should take as long as at least one full cycle to create such mechanisms. Paleoenvironmental data collected by Minc and Smith indicate that the temporal length of each fluctuation is 60–100 years, thus a full oscillation requires at least 120–200 years (1989: 17).

Such mechanisms/tales linking environmental information and social practice can be integral to a group's sense of place and to the creation of a cultural landscape. This is important for the archaeology of knowledge and colonization: the longer and more closely tied a group is to a particular bounded environment, the more likely it is that the various ways in which the group members consider it "their" landscape will affect the ways in which they use that landscape and, ultimately, the archaeological traces of that use. For example, Keith Basso, in his account of the language of the Western Apache of the US Southwest, eloquently describes the importance of topography in Apache relationships with the landscape and how children learn Apache lifeways. Apache children are regularly invited to travel, especially with people who will tell them about the places they see and visit. This mode of education, Basso says,

> rests on the premise that knowledge is useful to the extent that it can be swiftly recalled and turned without effort to practical ends. *A related premise is that objects whose appearance is unique are more easily recalled than those that look alike.* It follows from these assumptions that because places are visually unique (a fact marked and affirmed by their possession of separate names) they serve as excellent vehicles for recalling useful knowledge.
>
> (Basso 1996: 134; emphasis added)

This "useful knowledge" is the sets of stories and tales about past events and experiences of Apache ancestors. These stories are fable-like and embody lessons on views of life and on ways of interacting with family and others and with local resources. Many of the stories are so well known that the morals they encode can be invoked simply by stating the name of the place where the events described took place. The names themselves are in turn highly descriptive of the landscape and thereby firmly tie lifeways of the Western Apache to the surrounding environment, giving both a sense of history and of long-term occupancy.

Relationship between environmental knowledge and colonization

These three types of knowledge – locational, limitational, and social – are not exclusive. In fact, they may function as a feedback loop, each serving to reinforce the others. For instance, research among the Haiǁom bushpeople of Namibia shows that locational information is incorporated into daily life to a high degree, in large part due to what the ethnographer Thomas Widlok terms "topographical gossip." Successful hunting and gathering in the bush depends on successful navigation. Haiǁom hunters noted that "dead reckoning was possible because they had often observed others pointing to … places while talking about them" (Widlok 1997:321). Thus, the ubiquity of pointing and topographical gossip in Haiǁom communication suggests that orientation skills are not solely responses to environmental stimuli but are facilitated by social interaction and information-sharing that take place over an individual's lifetime. In turn, the social knowledge encoded in the stories recorded by Minc are a reflection of in-depth limitational knowledge. This is locational information informed by social information, which illustrates the interlinking nature of the various forms of environmental knowledge. It is unlikely that a human group would develop social knowledge of an environment without at least some locational information on critical resources; in turn, however, some of the social information may encode limitational-related experiences. So, in order to understand how each may contribute to Childe's (and Trigger's) "effective adaptation," I suggest that it is most productive to consider them first from the perspective of the initiation of human contact with an environment – in other words, from the point of colonization. The archaeology of colonization is therefore integral to our overall understanding of how humans know and use their environment.

Knowledge in current models of colonization

The topic of colonization, along with the associated phenomena of migration, diffusion, and dispersal (from Gamble 1993; Graves and Addison 1995), has a long and varied history in archaeology. In the early days of archaeology, these phenomena were used as explanations of culture change (Trigger 1989). They were generally unpopular during the rise of New Archaeology (see explanation in Chapman and Hamerow 1997). More recently, they have been redefined as more biogeographically based processes that are themselves in need of explanation and that should be investigated in their own right (Diamond 1976; Gamble 1993; Kelly 1999; Steele, Adams and Sluckin 1998; Turner 1984).

The consideration of knowledge in colonization given here does not attempt to follow a particular archaeological paradigm. Rather, it has developed along with and in response to a number of recent studies of colonization of various types and origins. Chapman (1997) notes in his review of the history of migration in archaeological explanation that interest in migration has varied throughout the twentieth century with fluctuations in real-life population movements and invasions. The re-emergence of migration-oriented research and, by extension, colonization-related research in archaeology in the late 1980s and early 1990s may be related at least in part to the political reorganizations and corresponding population movements in eastern and western Europe in the late 1980s (Chapman 1997: 18). Thus, this paper and the other papers in this volume may be indirectly related to these events. In a similar vein, my inspiration comes from work in the environmental movements of the early 1990s. These multiple origins emphasize the many potential applications of this chapter and underscore the wide range of examples and forms of explanation. This discussion is, in essence, the start of an inquiry.

An examination of the recent compilations of colonization theory (Anthony 1990, 1997; Chapman and Hamerow 1997; Clark 1994; Gamble 1993) and a multitude of case studies (e.g. Anderson 1990; Anderson and Gillam 2000; Beaton 1991; Hardesty 1985; Housley *et al.* 1997; Jochim *et al.* 1999; Kelly and Todd 1988; Meltzer 1995; O'Brien 1984; Webb and Rindos 1997) suggest that, at present, the issue of knowledge in archaeological approaches to colonization occurs in two primary aspects. The first lies in the motivations that are considered for colonization and the second in the actual physical orientations of movement presented in colonization models.

8

Motivations for colonization are clearly discussed by Anthony (1997) in terms of "push" and "pull" factors. Push factors are those conditions experienced by a given population that make occupation of a different area more attractive than staying as part of the originating population. They include conditions such as resource depletion (which may be specific to the given economy or technology), social regulations and primogeniture systems, shifting labor markets, and selective prestige systems. Pull factors are the conditions that make particular migration and colonization destinations viable options, such as knowledge of specific characteristics of a given destination or the costs of transport between the origin and destination. It is clear that information is essential to the pull side of migration and, further, that a flow of information from a migration destination may lower thresholds of resistance to the push factors. Knowledge and information, therefore, are integral to balanced push–pull analyses of colonization.

When considered in these terms, migration and colonization are inherently social strategies (Anthony 1997: 22). Working from modern and historical examples, Anthony notes that "[m]igrants often simply move to places that are familiar and offer social support, rather than moving to the place that would make the best economic choice" (1997: 25). Migration and colonization considered without analysis of push and pull factors tend to be described primarily as ecological strategies, particularly as responses to population crowding. In that crowding is a condition that makes population reduction via migration and colonization an attractive option, this is in fact an argument that focuses on a single push factor rather than the full range of pushes and pulls (after Anthony 1997: 23). It is, therefore, an incomplete explanation.

This is not to say that all colonization studies can identify or assess all push and pull factors. In fact, as developed by Anthony the push–pull analysis format is not yet complete, as it does not consider the chances of migrating in the absence of information or what the mechanisms behind initial movements might be when information is lacking. Furthermore, it does not indicate the particular types of information that are more likely to be transferred back to other potential migrants. The push–pull analysis is useful in the way it highlights the potential importance of knowledge in the colonization process and the way it forces researchers to consider what is and is not known about information flows in a given colonization situation. This has particular implications for the physical form of colonization models.

Patterns of colonization

The case studies of colonization mentioned above suggest that, regardless of the particular case of interest, the process of colonization tends to be visualized in one of two major patterns: as points connected by lines or arrows, or as a relatively smooth advancing front or wave.

The point and arrow pattern represents movement in which colonizers "stream" from known areas to new areas, leaving the areas in between uncolonized (Figure 1.1). The colonization process that the point and arrow pattern describes can include return migration (e.g. the arrows may go both ways; Anthony 1997) or may result in

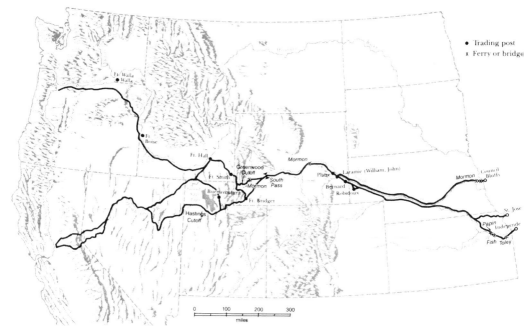

Figure 1.1 Example of the point-and-arrow or "streaming" colonization pattern: paths of the Oregon and California trail systems in the American West (from Unruh 1993: map 5). Copyright 1979 by the Board of Trustees of the University of Illinois. Used with permission of the University of Illinois Press.

isolation of a group in the newer area. Either way, the pattern suggests that what lies between the older and newer areas may not be completely explored or known until some time after initial arrival in the new area. The archaeological implication of this pattern is that sites a relatively short geographic distance apart in a newly colonized area may have been occupied during different phases of colonization. Such sites may therefore represent activities undertaken at different levels of environmental knowledge. Thus learning, when colonization is visualized in a point and arrow pattern, may be distinguished with appropriate dating and analytical tools.

The point and arrow movement pattern tends to be more commonly applied in situations in which social aspects of colonization movement can be described. Examples include the American gold rushes (see implications in Hardesty 1985) and Oregon Trail migrations (Unruh 1993), and recent studies of migrant workers in medieval Europe (Chapman and Hamerow 1997) and in the Mayan area (Anthony 1997). In other words, this pattern is often used by archaeologists studying the historical era, who have finer time control and often have additional documentary information about the social context of movement (but see Anderson and Gillam's [2000] proposal of streaming with respect to Paleoindians). Because of the availability of such detailed information, however, research attention tends to focus more strongly on the complex social issues at work rather than on issues of adaptation and environmental

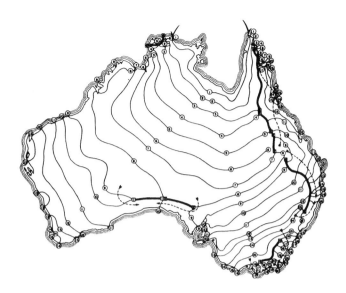

Figure 1.2 Example of advancing front colonization pattern: illustration of the initial peopling of Australia (from Birdsell 1957: Figure 2)

knowledge. Thus, while many of these colonization studies that apply the streaming model are well situated to study the learning process, they have not yet fully delimited its effects. (One exception is O'Brien [1984].)

In contrast, the advancing front pattern, perhaps best known from its use in the wave-of-advance demographic model (from Ammerman and Cavalli-Sforza 1984) (Figure 1.2), represents relatively regular movement over relatively short distances into areas directly adjacent to previously known ranges. The new area is explored and learned through a combination of short-distance wayfinding and substantial infilling before the next move is made. The initial implication of this pattern is that environmental learning is an additive process. Knowledge of the newer area is incorporated into the body of knowledge of the area already in use and does not tend to represent all that is known by human groups or individuals about the region in which they move. This pattern suggests that sites in a newly colonized area are not likely to differ strongly from each other in terms of the learning level that they represent. Therefore, learning – when it is conceived within an advancing front pattern – may be suggested to have a low-level effect on the archaeological record and to be effectively invisible.

The potential effects of landscape learning should not be disregarded in interpretations of an advancing front pattern, however, due to the problems of time, geographic scale, and archaeological resolution. Advancing front patterns have been used productively to study aspects of some colonizations, such as the Neolithic expansion of agriculturalists across Europe (such as Ammerman and Cavalli-Sforza 1984; but see counter-arguments in Chapter 9 of this volume). In other colonizations, however, although stream-like movements may have led to the peopling of a region, a loss or lack of intervening detail may result in an advancing front pattern being most apparent (compare Figures 1.2 and 1.3). In such cases, substantial differences in the represented levels of environmental knowledge may remain between sites in the colonized region and should be considered in site and regional interpretations. Therefore, I strongly suggest that any study of colonization, regardless of resolution, should examine the assumptions about the environmental learning process that are embedded in representations of colonization and the potential influences of the learning process on the remaining archaeological record.

Exactly what these influences might be and how they may best be examined is not yet completely clear. It has been noted that a primary contrast between these two major colonization model types – advancing front and point and arrow – is their respective emphasis on consistent process versus historical contingency (after Chapman and Hamerow 1997:1). Borrowing this terminology, I suggest that landscape learning is a consistent process that takes its form from contingent situations. In other words, it can be stated that many colonizations require some landscape learning. Thus, learning is a consistent part of the larger process of colonization. Also, learning itself takes place in stages, and so regularities in the sequence of learning may be identifiable. However, the aspects of landscape that require learning are contingent on the environment and circumstance of each historical or prehistoric case. Thus, the foci of learning and their archaeological representation may be unique in most or all instances.

Initial colonization and the landscape learning process

If the idea of a consistent process of learning in colonization situations is linked back to the main focus of this paper, namely the development of knowledge about an environment and the creation of a landscape, then it is useful to formalize the idea with the term "landscape learning process." It is defined here as the social response to situations in which there is both a lack of knowledge of the distribution of natural resources in a region and a lack of access to previously acquired knowledge about that distribution. The term landscape learning process refers to the means by which this knowledge is acquired and the period of time it takes to acquire the knowledge. It is possible, though by no means yet certain, that the landscape learning process may have distinctive characteristics that can be recognized archaeologically.

Lack of knowledge and lack of access to knowledge and thus landscape learning are most likely to occur in situations of initial occupation, such as the spread of Paleoindians into the Americas, the original peopling of Australia, and so forth (see Kelly and Todd 1988; Webb and Rindos 1997). However, in other situations colonizers encountered resident populations, and the transfer of information from the latter to the former cannot be assumed in its entirety. Some landscape learning may also have been necessary in these situations. It can be seen that these situations of lack of knowledge and knowledge access have occurred more frequently and more recently than the large-scale primary colonizations. Thus, if the phenomenon of initial occupation is re-oriented to include all situations in which the landscape learning process took place, a wide range of prehistoric and historical contexts can be included. Such an extension makes it possible to posit multiple "initial occupations" of a given area. When this possibility is combined with the potential for archaeologically distinctive patterns, the need more fully to understand the processes and patterns of initial occupations becomes an issue of deep archaeological significance.

Incorporating knowledge into archaeological approaches to the colonization of landscapes

There are several ways in which knowledge and landscape learning can be incorporated into archaeological investigations of colonization. The following discussion is not exhaustive by any means, but I hope that it illustrates the different ways we can address aspects of what is not yet known about landscape learning and how the development of the three types of landscape knowledge – locational, limitational, and social – may be included in a variety of different research designs (Table 1.1). These designs include landscape approaches, biogeographical approaches, ethnographic approaches, and resource modeling approaches.

Table 1.1 Matrix of knowledge types and landscape learning approaches

Learning approaches	Primary knowledge type	Supporting knowledge types
Landscape	Locational	Social
Biogeographical	Limitational	Locational, social
Ethnographic	Social	Locational, limitational
Resource	Locational/limitational/social	—

Landscape approaches

Landscape approaches emphasize the development of locational and social information. As noted above, there is a growing literature on the topic of landscape, its definition, and its application to archaeological topics. A useful simple definition of the term landscape is provided by C. Tolan-Smith (1998: 1): "[t]he landscape comprises, in addition to natural topographical features, a range of built features and patterns of land-use." Slightly modified for purposes here, a landscape may be considered a piece of topography bounded by its use by a given social group.

Such boundaries are defined and maintained by the practices of the group of interest. It is important to note that they may be created not only through operation of current practices, but also by adoption, adsorption, or re-use of the remaining traces of previous landscape occupants. A technique for assessing this is retrogressive analysis. In this analysis, research and interpretation move from well-known landscapes of the recent past back through a sequence of progressively earlier antecedent phases. The analysis is similar to an archaeological excavation in which recent layers are removed to reveal earlier deposits and contexts (C. Tolan-Smith 1998: 7).

An example of retrogressive analysis is a study of field boundaries and other physical features in Tynedale, northern England. The orientation and cross-cutting relationships of field boundaries and other physical features in Tynedale indicate a grain to agricultural use of the land that is truncated by the line of Hadrian's Wall. Thus, the modern landscape of Tynedale contains aspects of and can be seen to have been responding to features and practices established 2,000 or more years ago (M. Tolan-Smith 1997). Thus, with retrogressive analysis "[t]he continual re-use of features, far from being a drawback, can be turned to advantage. Once the grain of the landscape has evolved, continuity of use over subsequent centuries will, in many cases, ensure that the evidence is recoverable if the appropriate techniques are used" (M. Tolan-Smith 1997: 78). Similar situations may occur in regard to paths, as discussed in Chapter 4 of this volume.

Retrogressive analysis, and the landscape approaches of which it is a part, therefore are highly locational in nature. They deal with specific unique features and areas of topography and how those features and areas have been used and modified over time. With such use and modification come social practice. The decisions inherent in the re-use or disuse of features over time include documentation of how the resident groups adapted their practices to the given environment. The retrogressive form of the landscape approach is practicable primarily in situations of multiple documented colonizations. It does not presume transfer of information between previous and subsequent inhabitants, but rather assesses how the sequence of human use of a landscape can influence the learning process.

Biogeographical approaches

While landscape approaches deal primarily with the development of locational knowledge supported by social knowledge, biogeographical approaches address the acquisition of limitational knowledge, supported in turn by locational and social knowledge. Biogeography is the study of patterns and processes of plant and animal distributions at all levels (taxonomic, ecological, geological). It has a close relationship to the topic of human colonization of unfamiliar environments in terms of its emphasis on the relationship between present-day distributions of organisms and the distribution of suitable habitats. A biogeographical perspective does not take for granted that an organism will necessarily occupy all possible areas of a suitable habitat, but rather takes as a point of research how suitable habitats are distributed and how they are accessed by given organisms. The parallel in the study of human colonization and landscape learning is the relationship between knowledge and what humans recognize as suitable habitat. While it is obvious that at present humans have the capacity to live in many different environments, it cannot be shown or stated that all currently occupied habitats have been suitable habitats through all time and for all human systems and livelihoods. Rather, the process of adaptation, or learning how to live in the landscape, has taken place. The aspects of a given habitat that required adaptation or learning, or that may have for some period of time rendered a given area unsuitable, can be usefully likened to the biogeographical concept of barriers.

In biogeographical terminology, barriers are produced by unfavorable habitats. They can range from total barriers to filter barriers and from tight to loose filters and can serve to inhibit or completely to restrict movement from an area of suitable habitat to other potentially suitable areas. Barriers can be variously effective across different groups of organisms or, potentially, different human social groups. Barriers can change, develop, or dissolve over time. Thus, presently ineffective barriers may have been very effective in the past and vice versa (Brown and Gibson 1983: 208–11).

Since learning is the topic of interest here, the basis of comparison and fullest explication of variations on this approach is the barriers that may exist with respect to access to information for the colonizers, particularly with respect to the barriers that may develop or dissolve in relation to any previously resident populations. Certainly, other types of barriers are possible, particularly those resulting from combinations of environmental characteristics and social behavior (on behavioral barriers, see discussion in Gamble [1993: 95] on behavioral modifications that allowed the initial migration of *Homo erectus* out of Africa). To illustrate the barrier concept with respect to learning in colonization, I suggest three main types of barrier:

- **Population barriers**   Compatibility with resident population; considerations include both numerical population density and relations/compatibility with respect to economic system; limitations in terms of carrying capacity
- **Social barriers**   Resident population's defense of territories; information storage and transfer systems; limitations in terms of social, political, and economic structures
- **Knowledge barriers**   Existence of usable, previously collected information (inspired by Bogucki 1979); limitations in terms of absolute presence/absence of transferable information.

Population barriers refer essentially to the availability or unavailability of suitable physical landscape space and structural space in established economic systems. In sum, it refers to the availability of niche space. The inspiration for this barrier is a discussion by Lattimore in his work on the structure of frontiers (1962). He suggests several scenarios of colonization interaction, based on a comparison of the economic and population characteristics of the interacting groups:

> [i]f there is a great difference in social vigor and institutional strength, the weaker community may be simply subsumed by the stronger; but if the difference in strength is not so great, the result will be a new community not only larger in numbers and occupying a greater territory, but differing in quality from both of the communities by whose amalgamation it was created. In this connection it is well to note also that when an expanding community, in taking over new territory, expels the old occupants (or some of them), instead of incorporating them into its own fabric, those who retreat may become, in the new territory into which they spread, a new kind of society
>
> (Lattimore 1962: 469)

Thus, if physical and economic space exists, then the area may be readily recognized as suitable habitat, colonizing groups may be readily integrated into existing structures, and the flow of landscape information is greatly facilitated. If physical space is lacking altogether, or economic structures are highly incompatible, then the area may not be deemed suitable habitat or may be the subject of conflict (see Keeley 1996), regardless of its raw environmental characteristics, and so information for the area may not flow or be gathered at all. Various combinations in between, of availability of physical and economic space, will restrict or facilitate the flow of information.

Social barriers refer to impediments to information transfer between groups that cannot be directly related to physical proximity or structure of subsistence systems. Rather, they may be due to social organization factors such as language or kinship systems and the various mechanisms through which information may actually be transferred. Maddock (1976: 170) notes that there are two basic mechanisms through which information can be shared and that each has bearing on how useful the information may ultimately be to the group to whom it is passed. In the first case, information can be shared directly and overtly between groups, and in such cases information is often more accurate and specific. Alternatively, information can be absorbed indirectly through exposure of outsiders to tales and stories. This type of transfer may not be overtly recognized and so is subject to a greater range of error and misinterpretation. It seems relevant to note that in cases of later migrations to an area with a well-established existing population, information transmission may take place primarily through indirect absorption and consequently may more closely resemble situations of a fully initial colonization than those in which there is more ready communication between established residents and colonizers.

Knowledge barriers refer to whether or not useful environmental information has already been collected. For example, in a subsistence economy, an existing population may not have information that is particularly useful to the colonizing group, and therefore the colonizing group will have to gather its own information. Bogucki (1979) presents an example of the limitations that lack of knowledge can impose on settlement patterns in his study of the early Neolithic settlement of Poland.

It should not be expected that any one of these types of barrier by itself will result in an area being deemed as unsuitable. Rather, various combinations of all three should be considered, as illustrated in the following scenarios. The first scenario – the base or null condition – is that of no resident population. This is the situation encountered during initial colonizations. In such cases, the knowledge barrier is high, but the other barriers presented by resident groups do not exist (Figure 1.3a). Learning is therefore conditioned solely by the practices of the colonizing group.

Other scenarios include resident populations. When the colonizers have the same or similar economic system as the resident population, the knowledge barrier is lower, as necessary environmental information will already have been collected, but the colonizers will have to cope with social and/or population barriers (Figure 1.3b). If these are sufficiently high, some relearning may be required to function in the new area. Situations with high population or social barriers may require high levels of learning. Such colonization situations may closely resemble initial colonizations, even though the colonizers are not chronologically first (Rockman 2001).

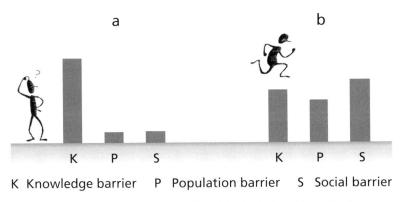

K Knowledge barrier   P Population barrier   S Social barrier

Figure 1.3 Knowledge barrier scenarios: (a) initial colonization; (b) colonization into area with a resident population

Ethnographic approaches

Ethnographic approaches emphasize the development of social knowledge, informed by both locational and limitational knowledge. Consideration of the knowledge barrier described above raises the question of how and how quickly colonizers learn aspects of a new environment when it is necessary for them to do so. Ethnographic evidence suggests that individuals gather environmental information from two sources that operate on different timescales. The first source is direct individual exploration and experience (after Brody 1981; also Binford 1980, 1983; analysis in O'Brien 1984). The second is knowledge incorporated into social practice, interaction, and lore (see Minc 1986; also Cruikshank 1981; Moodie *et al.* 1992; Widlok 1997). While to date no archaeologists have accompanied colonizers on extended migrations into unfamiliar areas, ethnoarchaeological fieldwork among a number of hunter-gatherer groups suggests that it is quite difficult for archaeologists to overestimate the abilities and acuities of such groups in matters of the natural environment (see Chapter 3 of this volume; also Binford 1980; Brody 1981; Kelly 1995). It is quite possible that in an area in the order of tens of thousands of square miles significant amounts of all three types of environmental information may be acquired by an individual in the course of a lifetime.

The development of socially and ritually preserved forms of environmental information may take substantially longer. Documentary evidence suggests that these forms can be compiled over 200–400 years or more (derived from Price 1983; see also Ingstad 1969), well above the span of an individual's lifetime experience. The work of Price (1983) with the oral traditions of the Saramaka of Suriname provides some evidence for how long it may take for origin myths to develop and is worth describing here. The Saramaka are descended from slaves who revolted against their Dutch masters in the mid-seventeenth century and made the rainforest of Suriname their new homeland. The events of the revolt and the subsequent establishment of the free Saramakan population have been maintained by older tribesmen as a body of oral tradition referred to as the First-Time. The events and people of the First-Time are held as sacred by the Saramakans, and it is currently the tradition of the storytellers that no one teller knows all of the stories. Through discussion with individual storytellers and careful comparison of information with Dutch documents describing the revolt, Price was able to document the evolution of the First-Time. This evolution includes the melding of individuals and re-ascription of activities to other individuals either through the loss of detail or error in the transmission of stories from one teller to another or deliberately, out of respect for the powerful status of the individuals.

While Price claims that First-Time "is not more 'mythologized' or less accurately recalled than the more recent past" (1983: 6), he also notes that knowledge of it is singularly restricted and guarded, and that knowledge of First-Time is the "fountainhead of collective identity" and contains "the true root of what it means to be Saramaka" (1983: 6). It is my interpretation that the process related by Price may be the development of an origin myth. At the time of Price's research, the events of First-Time had taken place approximately 200 years previously. Although sacred, First-Time is recognized as having a sense of historicity. Perhaps another 200 years will develop and meld the stories further to the point of their being detached in time. First-Time may, however, remain fixed in place. The work of Fowler with Native American traditions suggests that origin myths can maintain memories of place over potentially several thousand years and thousands of miles (in Echo-Hawk 2000).

This evidence is important for the archaeology of colonization as it highlights the point that in order to arrive at a new point, a colonizer must have come from somewhere else. Information is carried from that place, both in individual experience and in the stored collective social memory provided in origin and other stories. To return to Childe's descriptions quoted at the start of this chapter, these are the imported perceptions that meet the new realities. The degree of imbalance between the perception and reality depends in large part on the fourth major approach to learning in the archaeology of colonization: the combination of locational, limitational, and social information that allows assessment of natural resource variability and its relationship to the transferability of this information between environments.

Resource modeling approaches

The ability of colonizers to use information from an older area in a newer area depends on the similarity of necessary resources in terms of location and distribution, the limitations in terms of carrying capacity, and the social organization required to access them. Several researchers have suggested that subsistence systems based on large fauna are relatively transferable across long distances (e.g. Kelly 1999; Kelly and Todd 1988; Meltzer 1995). A knowledge perspective supports this suggestion. It is recognized that the larger the animal, the larger the range needed to support it (see Turner 1984; also Gamble 1995). Once social practices are in place to locate and access large faunal resources, only potentially low-level changes related to limitational aspects of faunal populations might be needed to continue previous behavior concerning faunal resources.

In other words, variations in climate may enhance or reduce the size of faunal populations, which in turn affect long-term hunting pressure that the faunal populations can sustain (after Kelly and Todd 1988).

Plant-related information may be less transferable because plants grow in fixed locations and ripen on seasonal schedules. Even small variations in climate and topography in newer areas may lead to substantial alterations in the location, distribution, and scheduling of plant resources, which in turn may require substantial alterations in social organization and knowledge.

Finally, information related to non-organic resources such as lithic materials may be the least transferable. While the geological associations of materials such as flint and chert are not random, the distribution and the material properties, often recognized as quality, of individual sources across a landscape are not even and are dependent on long-term geological and tectonic history. As such, non-organic natural resources must be encountered directly in order to be accessed and assessed. Thus, colonizers may need to acquire substantial locational knowledge and limitational knowledge (represented by material quality) effectively to use the non-organic resources of a newer area. Likewise, substantial social modifications may be necessary to establish new non-organic resource access patterns or maintain access to previously used sources (or both).

From this discussion, it is clear that the learning process will vary with the colonizing group, depending on each group's primary resource needs and established social structure. Archaeological traces of the learning process can be expected to vary accordingly. For example, in terms of a single resource, such as patchy lithic resources, it is possible that risk-reducing social strategies may be used to cope with the possibilities of not being able to locate necessary outcrops. In new areas where these resources are uneven or not abundant, outcrops or sources that do exist may not be located or brought into use concurrently with initiation of occupation of the region. This may explain the apparent preference of Paleoindian (Kelly and Todd 1988: 237) and northern European Magdalenian groups at the end of the last Ice Age (Barton and Roberts 1996: 260) for high-quality lithic raw material, particularly flint or chert, and the transport of this material over distances of up to several hundred miles.

Archaeological evidence for resource learning may also exist in the timing of colonization and in broad-scale patterns of movement. For example, work by Tolan-Smith (see Chapter 7) on the distribution and density of radiocarbon dates from lateglacial Britain suggests that the need to learn the many new resources and topographies – entailing new locations, new limitations, and new social organizations – of western maritime Britain may have restrained colonization there for up to 2,000 years. Anderson (Chapter 10) suggests that colonizers of the Pacific used the grain or geographic patterning of island distribution in combination with wind direction to enhance exploration. In so doing, the Pacific colonizers achieved a much higher rate of landfall than might be expected from random exploration. Locational knowledge was used to orient migration activity that in turn was powered not only by limitational knowledge of individual islands, but also by a strong social colonizing imperative.

Using knowledge approaches in archaeological interpretation and application

Using knowledge and the landscape learning approaches in studies of colonization requires careful fitting of archaeological tools to testable cases. Certainly, not all aspects of landscape learning occurred or can be detected in every colonization setting. Many case studies will likely raise more questions than they answer. One example is the work of Webb and Rindos on the colonization of Australia (Webb and Rindos 1997; Webb 1998). Their careful analysis of radiocarbon error ranges demonstrates that it is not possible to distinguish between competing models of slow versus fast colonization. What is clearly needed are multiple lines of evidence for given cases and assessment of the learning process through multiple cases (such as in this volume) and research designs that include, but are not limited to, the approaches discussed above.

Other questions and issues not discussed above but that are certainly relevant include the many components of modeling and resource evaluation. For instance, how can the theories of optimality be applied to instances of initial occupation? How might the situation of unfamiliarity have affected the recognition and calculation of environmental and behavioral costs and risks (after Kelly 1995: 97–8)? To what extent is non-optimization of resources recognizable archaeologically, and how might the costs and risks of incomplete environmental information compare with the costs of developing or re-organizing a social information infrastructure during and after colonization (after Moore 1981)?

As noted above, Chapman (1997) discusses how archaeologists' writings about the past are the product of many influences – academic, non-academic, intellectual and emotional, social and personal. He cites R. G. Collingwood's observation that every archaeological problem "ultimately arises out of 'real' life" (quoted in Chapman 1997: 11). Chapman also suggests that the influence exists not only at the level of individual work, but also in the ebb and flow of archaeological thought. His example demonstrates that the popularity of various migration models and archaeological interpretations of colonization events over the course of the twentieth century mirror the migration experiences of Western countries.

Likewise, the research questions contained in and presented by the landscape learning process and case examples of global colonization hold particular resonance for the late twentieth and early twenty-first century Western world. In his work *Wilderness and the American Mind* (1983), Roderick Nash documents the history of the relationship between European perspectives on the natural world and the environment of the North American New World. Originally considered by early settlers as something to be tamed and beaten back, it was not until approximately the past 100 years that natural uncultivated spaces were considered worthy of appreciation and preservation. As a case in point, the first United States national park, Yellowstone, was established on 1 March 1871. By the mid-nineteenth century, prevailing attitudes toward the natural world were characterized by a frontier paradox, such that unknown or empty places were the places one went to to retreat from the pressures and strictures of society. In turn, however, it is the process of civilizing the wild – in other words, making a living in and from the unknown wilds – that man (as a proxy for American society) made himself (Worster 1991: 8; also Limerick 1987; Limerick *et al.* 1991). Learning about how these recent wilds were learned – or not learned – can provide invaluable information on how the Western world came to be how it is today.

Thus, the questions posed and answered by the landscape learning process lie at the interface of archaeology and contemporary society and modern conceptions of the capacity of the global environment. Again, the recent historical colonization of the American West is a useful final example. In Chicago in 1893, historian Frederick Jackson Turner declared that, as of the information in the 1890 census, the American frontier had closed (Turner 1932). Much controversy has existed ever since as to whether this closing date was correctly placed at 1890 or whether it should be adjusted earlier or later. Recent work by Western historians suggests instead that the modern American West far more closely resembles the themes of the older "ended" West than it does a distinct period. Thus, the modern American West is much better served if it is understood in terms of its ties to the earlier settlement phase – in short, the frontier never ended (Limerick 1987; Limerick *et al.* 1991). Popular culture, however, has so thoroughly enmeshed the term frontier with images from the nineteenth century that a still-open frontier is a difficult concept to accept (Limerick 1994). It is also difficult to use. I suggest that re-assessment of occupation in the American West in terms of learning – our understanding of its resources, their potentials, and their limitations – provides a much better platform from which to integrate further archaeologically and historically identified practice with current patterns. It will also ultimately serve to illustrate that the modern world is neither exempt nor unique in the knowledge it needs to live in the natural world.

Acknowledgments

I am most grateful to the reviewers who have helped this work on its journey from idea to conference paper to chapter in a book: Dale Brenneman, Hortensia Caballero, Beth Kangas, Steve Kuhn, Laura Mazow, Jacqueline Messing, Janneli Miller, Gillian Newell, Kerry Sagebiel, Rebecca Waugh, and Nieves Zedeño. Any remaining faults are, of course, my own.

References

Ammerman, Albert J. and L. L. Cavalli-Sforza (1984) *The Neolithic Transition and the Genetics of Populations in Europe*, Princeton: Princeton University Press.

Anderson, David G. (1990) "The Paleoindian Colonization of Eastern North America: A View from the Southeastern United States," *Research in Economic Anthropology* 5:163–216.

Anderson, David G. and J. Christopher Gillam (2000) "Paleoindian Colonization of the Americas: Implications from an Examination of Physiography, Demography, and Artifact Distribution," *American Antiquity* 65(1):43–66.

Anthony, David W. (1990) "Migration in Archaeology: The Baby and the Bathwater," *American Anthropologist* 92:895–914.

—— (1997) "Prehistoric Migration as Social Process," in John Chapman and Helena Hamerow (eds) *Migrations and Invasions in Archaeological Explanation*, British Archaeological Reports International Series 664, Oxford: Archaeopress.

Barton, R. N. E. and A. J. Roberts (1996) "Reviewing the British Late Upper Palaeolithic: New Evidence for Chronological Patterning in the Lateglacial Record," *Oxford Journal of Archaeology* 15(3):245–65.

Basso, Keith (1996) *Wisdom Sits in Places: Landscape and Language among the Western Apache*, Albuquerque: University of New Mexico Press.

Beaton, John M. (1991) "Colonizing Continents: Some Problems from Australia and the Americas," in Tom D. Dillehay and David J. Meltzer (eds) *The First Americans: Search and Research*, Boca Raton, FL: CRC.

Binford, Lewis (1980) "Willow Smoke and Dogs' Tails: Hunter-Gatherer Settlement Systems and Archaeological Site Formation," *American Antiquity* 45(1):4–20.

—— (1983) *In Pursuit of the Past: Decoding the Archaeological Record*, New York: Thames and Hudson.

Bogucki, Peter (1979) "Tactical and Strategic Settlements in the Early Neolithic of Lowland Poland," *Journal of Anthropological Research* 35(2):238–46.

Brody, Hugh (1981) *Maps and Dreams: Indians and the British Columbia Frontier*, Vancouver: Douglas & McIntyre.

Brown, J. H. and A. C. Gibson (1983) *Biogeography*, St Louis: C. V. Mosby Company.

Chapman, John (1997) "The Impact of Modern Invasions and Migrations on Archaeological Explanation," in John Chapman and Helena Hamerow (eds) *Migrations and Invasions in Archaeological Explanation*, BAR International Series 664, Oxford: Archaeopress.

Chapman, John and Helena Hamerow (1997) "On the Move Again: Migrations and Invasions in Archaeological Explanation," in John Chapman and Helena Hamerow (eds) *Migrations and Invasions in Archaeological Explanation*, British Archaeological Reports International Series 664, Oxford: Archaeopress.

Clark, G. A. (1994) "Migration as an Explanatory Concept in Paleolithic Archaeology," *Journal of Archaeological Method and Theory* 1(4):305–43.

Cruikshank, Julie (1981) "Legend and Landscape: Convergence of Oral and Scientific Traditions in the Yukon Territory," *Arctic Anthropology* 18(2):67–93.

Dean, Jeffrey S. (1988) "A Model of Anasazi Behavioral Adaptation," in George C. Gumerman (ed.) *The Anasazi in a Changing Environment*, New York: Cambridge University Press.

Diamond, Jared M. (1976) "Colonization Cycles in Man and Beast," *World Archaeology* 8(3):249–61.

Echo-Hawk, Roger C. (2000) "Ancient History in the New World: Integrating Oral Traditions and the Archaeological Record," *American Antiquity* 65(2):267–90.

Gamble, Clive (1993) *Timewalkers: The Prehistory of Global Colonization*, Stroud, Gloucestershire: Alan Sutton.

—— (1995) "Large Mammals, Climate and Resource Richness in Upper Pleistocene Europe," *Acta Zoologica Cracova* 38(1):155–75.

Graves, Michael W. and David J. Addison (1995) "The Polynesian Settlement of the Hawaiian Archipelago: Integrating Models and Methods in Archaeological Interpretation," *World Archaeology* 26(3):380–99.

Hardesty, Donald (1985) "Evolution on the Industrial Frontier," in Stanton W. Green and Stephen M. Perlman (eds) *The Archaeology of Frontiers and Boundaries*, New York: Academic Press.

Hopkinson, Terry (2001) *The Middle Palaeolithic Leaf Points of Europe: an Ecological Geography*, unpublished PhD thesis, University of Cambridge.

Housley, R. A., Gamble, C. S., Street, M., and P. Pettitt (1997) "Radiocarbon Evidence for the Lateglacial Human Recolonisation of Northern Europe," *Proceedings of the Prehistoric Society* 63:25–54.

Ingstad, Helge (1969) *Westward to Vinland: the Discovery of Pre-Columbian Norse House-sites in North America*, New York: St Martin's Press.

Jochim, Michael, Herhahn, Cynthia, and Harry Starr (1999) "The Magdalenian Colonization of Southern Germany," *American Anthropologist* 101(1):129–42.

Keeley, Lawrence H. (1996) *War Before Civilization*, New York: Oxford University Press.

Kelly, Robert L. (1995) *The Foraging Spectrum: Diversity in Hunter-Gatherer Lifeways*, Washington, DC: Smithsonian Institution Press.

—— (1999) "Hunter-Gatherer Foraging and Colonization of the Western Hemisphere," *Anthropologie* 37(2):143–53.

Kelly, Robert L. and Lawrence C. Todd (1988) "Coming into the Country: Early Paleoindian Hunting and Mobility," *American Antiquity* 53(2):231–44.

Lattimore, Owen (1962) "The Frontier in History," in *Studies in Frontier History: Collected Papers, 1928–1958*, London: Oxford University Press.

Limerick, Patricia Nelson (1987) *The Legacy of Conquest: The Unbroken Past of the American West*, New York: W. W. Norton & Company.

—— (1994) "The Adventures of the Frontier in the Twentieth Century" in James R. Grossman (ed.) *The Frontier in American Culture*, Los Angeles: University of California Press.

Limerick, Patricia Nelson, Milner, Clyde A. II, and Charles E. Rankin (eds) (1991) *Trails: Toward a New Western History*, Lawrence, KA: University Press of Kansas.

Maddock, Kenneth (1976) "Communication and Change in Mythology," in Nicolas Peterson (ed.) *Tribes and Boundaries in Australia*, Atlantic Highlands, NJ: Humanities Press.

Meltzer, David J. (1995) "Clocking the First Americans," *Annual Review of Anthropology* 24:21–45.

Minc, Leah D. (1986) "Scarcity and Survival: The Role of Oral Tradition in Mediating Subsistence Crises," *Journal of Anthropological Archaeology* 5:39–113.

Minc, Leah D. and Kevin P. Smith (1989) "The Spirit of Survival: Cultural Responses to Resource Variability in North Alaska," in Paul Halstead and John O'Shea (eds) *Bad Year Economics: Cultural Responses to Risk and Uncertainty*, Cambridge: Cambridge University Press.

Moodie, D. Wayne, Catchpole, A. J. W., and Kerry Abel (1992) "Northern Athapaskan Oral Tradition and the White River Volcano," *Ethnohistory* 39(2):148–71.

Moore, James A. (1981) "The Effects of Information Networks in Hunter-Gatherer Societies," in Bruce Winterhalder and Eric Alden Smith (eds) *Hunter-Gatherer Foraging Strategies: Ethnographic and Archaeological Analyses*, Chicago: University of Chicago Press.

Nash, Roderick (1983) *Wilderness and the American Mind*, 3rd edition, New Haven: Yale University Press.

O'Brien, Michael J. (ed.) (1984) *Grassland, Forest, and Historical Settlement: An Analysis of Dynamics in Northeast Missouri*, Lincoln, NE: University of Nebraska Press.

Price, Richard (1983) *First-Time: The Historical Vision of an Afro-American People*, Baltimore: Johns Hopkins University Press.

Rockman, Marcy (2001) "The Landscape Learning Process in Historical Perspective," in J. Gillespie, S. Tupakka, and C. de Mille (eds), *31st Annual Chacmool Conference Proceedings*, pp. 493–509, Calgary: Archaeological Association of the University of Calgary.

—— (2002) *A Palaeolithic Perspective on Historical Colonization: The history of the landscape learning process and a dynamic scalar approach to human migration and "new" environments*, paper presented at the 35th Annual Conference on Historical and Underwater Archaeology of the Society for Historical Archaeology, Mobile, Alabama, 8–12 January.

Rossignol, Jacqueline and LuAnn Wandsnider (1992) *Space, Time, and Archaeological Landscapes*, New York: Plenum Press.

Steele, J., Adams, J., and T. Sluckin (1998) "Modelling Paleoindian Dispersals," *World Archaeology* 30(2):286–305.

Tolan-Smith, Christopher (1998) "Radiocarbon Chronology and the Lateglacial and Early Postglacial Resettlement of the British Isles," in B. V. Eriksen and L. G. Straus (eds), *Quaternary International* 49/50, 21–7.

Tolan-Smith, Myra (1997) "The Romano-British and Late Prehistory Landscape: the Deconstruction of a Medieval Landscape," in Christopher Tolan-Smith (ed.) *Landscape Archaeology in Tynedale*, Newcastle upon Tyne: Department of Archaeology, University of Newcastle upon Tyne.

Trigger, Bruce G. (1989) *A History of Archaeological Thought*, Cambridge: Cambridge University Press.

Turner, Alan (1984) "Hominids and Fellow Travellers: Human Migration into High Latitudes as Part of a Large Mammal Community," in Robert Foley (ed.) *Human Evolution and Community Ecology: Prehistoric Human Adaptation in Biological Perspective*, New York: Academic Press.

Turner, Frederick Jackson (1932) *The Significance of the Frontier in American History* (eds. Max Farrand and Avery Craven), New York: H. Holt and Company.

Ucko, Peter J. and Robert Layton (eds) (1999) *The Archaeology and Anthropology of Landscape: Shaping Your Landscape*, London: Routledge.

Unruh, John David (1993) *The Plains Across: the Overland Emigrants and the Trans-Mississippi West*, Urbana, IL: University of Illinois Press.

Van Andel, Tjeerd H. and Curtis N. Runnels (1995) "The Earliest Farmers in Europe," *Antiquity* 69:481–500.

Webb, R. Esmée (1998) "Problems with Radiometric 'Time': Dating the Initial Human Colonization of Sahul," *Radiocarbon* 40(2):749–58.

Webb, R. Esmée and David J. Rindos (1997) "The Mode and Tempo of the Initial Human Colonisation of Empty Landmasses: Sahul and the Americas Compared," in C. Michael Barton and Geoffrey A. Clark (eds) *Rediscovering Darwin: Evolutionary Theory and Archaeological Explanation*, Arlington, VA: American Anthropological Association.

Widlok, Thomas (1997) "Orientation in the Wild: The Shared Cognition of Hai‖om Bushpeople," *Journal of the Royal Anthropological Institute* 3(2):317–32.

Worster, Donald (1991) "Beyond the Agrarian Myth," in Patricia Nelson Limerick, Clyde A. Milner II, and Charles E. Rankin (eds) *Trails: Toward a New Western History*, Lawrence, KS: University of Kansas Press.

2

HUMAN WAYFINDING AND COGNITIVE MAPS

Reginald G. Golledge

Wayfinding refers to the ability to determine a route, learn it, and retrace or reverse it from memory. Wayfinding is universal to all cultures. It is involved in a myriad of daily and longer-term episodic activities ranging from a search of local areas for food sources to the large-scale and long-term international migrations that first populated the world. Fundamental scenarios in which wayfinding takes place include (a) wandering in search of, then finding and settling in, a new home environment; (b) situations where the ultimate intent is to return home after traveling; (c) episodic food searches; and (d) travel from and to home to achieve a specific purpose (e.g. health, safety, recreation, socialization, communication, and interaction). For the successful completion of a wayfinding trip, people must acquire and use environmental knowledge.

When interacting with an environment, the most pervasive choice to be faced is how to travel in that environment. Making inadequate or incorrect decisions about travel results in being lost and suffering psychological and physiological discomforts. The use of recorded representations of environments (e.g. maps) appears to be of particular importance when one has to follow a complex new route involving many segments and many turns. But, throughout history, humans appear to have been capable of successful wayfinding by learning spatial characteristics – whether on the route itself or in a distant environment – using only information perceived and memorized while traveling. This ability is evidenced by the fact that vision-impaired or blind people can successfully wayfind by memorizing and recalling route segment sequences or by following auditory, touch, or smell markers which are used in lieu of visual landmarks (Loomis *et al.* 1992).

Most human behaviors (at least according to Simon [1957]) are best described as "satisficing" or "boundedly rational" rather than rational or optimizing. In accordance with this general principle, wayfinders are often satisfied with the act of reaching a destination while paying little heed to how effective or efficient they have been in pursuing the wayfinding task. Since wayfinding occurs so frequently, this is probably a reasonable coping strategy. Today, human wayfinding is most often confined to specific networks laid down by national agencies, and researchers have developed mathematical models to find optimal routes through these network systems that depend on specific path-selection criteria. Despite this, humans most often choose routes that are "good enough," "seem simple," or "get me there anyway." And, given the modern-day experience of using vehicles (private and public) within these networks, there is less and less incentive to pay attention to observing and learning the environment as one passes through it. This is diametrically opposite to wayfinding needs throughout history.

To return to an origin after traveling away from it, travelers must have (a) learned the structure of the route by rote and have developed a capacity for reversing it; (b) been able to move generally from landmark to landmark or choice point to choice point along a traverse; or (c) been able to move by direct short-cutting to the home base. All these involve deliberate mental activities, but can be supplemented by reference to external aids. While hard-copy or digital cartographic maps are the supplement of choice today, in earlier times travelers used knowledge of star patterns, sun angles, wind or wave direction, terrain visualization, or other environmental features as those supplements.

There has been much speculation on whether these former abilities are still extant in humans despite radical changes in information and technology. Sholl (1987) conducted experiments to show that even today humans can point successfully to unseen but familiar locations – a classic gesture-based representational mode for communicating about the location of unseen places or objects. Although this experiment was undertaken on humans living in what we call advanced Western societies, pointing has been regarded as an essential orientation process that has been part of human environmental knowing throughout history and prehistory. The ability to recall the direction of a given place from where one is currently located is perhaps the most fundamental principle involved in wayfinding. People in many cultures can point in the direction of features they know are several days' journey away, thus directing a traveler who is unfamiliar with the environment in such a way as to increase their chances of successfully arriving at that destination. Complementing this pointing gesture with verbal or graphic explanations of choice points or landmark features along the way provides additional evidence that could help the wayfinding process.

A second tenet of wayfinding, stated by Worchel (1951), is that human travelers have a constant veering tendency, a result verified by Klatzky *et al.* (1990) when they compared the abilities of sighted and blind or vision-impaired people to walk straight lines under conditions of lack of sight. They showed that uncorrected veering produced a path that diverged from a straight line by an average of 18 degrees. This tendency to veer has been anecdotally reported by professional explorers and talented amateurs when exploring featureless environments such as deserts or dense forests. The result of uncorrected veering is that, on an extended journey, the traveler may follow a spiral path, eventually returning to the vicinity of the origin.

A third fundamental tenet of wayfinding is the ability to undertake travel planning. Travel planning may involve acts as simple as selecting a sector or corridor of space to constrain movement that would allow for obstacle avoidance without unduly diverting the traveler from a general direction to a target destination. Travel plans must be flexible, because of a lack of knowledge of possible events that could disrupt travel (e.g. a flash flood). Thus, travel plans often include rules for implementing alternative strategies if the original plan becomes impossible. These alternatives might include delaying travel, choosing an alternative destination, choosing an alternative route, or changing the purpose of travel.

It is conceivable that, in many primitive cultures, "self to object" was the primary mode of orientation and direction giving. As opposed to this process, cultures that have developed advanced means for assisting wayfinding have relied more on "object-to-object" specification. The former represents an egocentric arrangement of environmental information and is perspective-dependent. The latter represents an understanding of the inter-object geometry and is independent of perspective.

With this overview of wayfinding behind us, I now discuss the mental processes that are involved in wayfinding and the nature of the basic cognitive mapping process used universally as the dominant mode of wayfinding, examine the extent to which environmental awareness has been supplemented by external representations, and acknowledge the fundamental errors and biases in environmental knowing that have plagued wayfinders throughout history.

The processes involved in wayfinding

We learn about the everyday environment by interacting with it. In this process, the locations of objects are noticed; place-to-place differences are recognized; ways of interacting between locations or between places are constructed and become identifiable paths; concepts of distance, proximity, and direction are developed; local and global frames of reference that provide orientation and relational information about locations and places are developed; and classes of similar places (i.e. groupings or clusters of places) are identified and stored in memory as schemata. As the need arises, incidentally and intentionally noticed information is recalled into working memory and manipulated as part of a problem-solving (travel-planning) procedure. Throughout history (and still today), most of our environmental knowledge is gained "incidentally": we "notice" things when we travel for different purposes or we "hear about" things before or during travel. This represents "naive" or "common-sense" environmental knowing and is usually fuzzy, spatially inaccurate, and prone to error. "Intentional" knowledge is deliberately taught and learned and is usually less error-prone. Intentionally gained knowledge usually differentiates experts from novices. Intentional environmental knowledge is acquired through deliberate manipulation of the spatial concepts embedded in stored information. Manipulation procedures are frequently taught and emphasized in a culturally defined learning process. Environmental knowledge may be stored in the memory of elders or other experts (e.g. school-teachers) or may (as of nowadays) be recorded in written, cartographic, animated, or other hard-copy or electronic form. Intentional knowledge about wayfinding, for example, may be acquired by reading books or taking classes about navigation.

The critical difference between these two procedures of knowledge accumulation is that incidentally acquired knowledge does not always transfer to different situations. For example, a person may (via repetition) use rote learning to lay out a path from home to work and become efficient at traveling it. But, unless the underlying concepts of wayfinding are understood, the knowledge so gained may not transfer to a new and different environment, and inefficient search and learning procedures may have to be initiated anew. This ability to transfer knowledge through comprehension of wayfinding principles defines the successful explorer who, used to finding a way in the open wood-lands of one environment, is then placed in a dense forested environment or on a seem-ingly interminable and featureless flat plain and can solve a wayfinding problem.

In general, it is argued that one of two processes is involved in successful wayfinding: homing or piloting. Homing, often called "path integration," is a person-based proce-dure whereby the traveler constantly updates position with respect to a home base by automatically integrating time and motion as a journey proceeds. Under these circum-stances the traveler, at any point on a route, should be able to turn and point in the direction of home base and to estimate the straight-line distance that must be traveled to get there. No detailed record of the track or route that has been followed is necessary to solve this problem, for position of the home base is maintained via spatial updating.

Spatial updating occurs moment by moment. Evidence for this type of wayfinding process has been shown in much research on animal and insect behavior (e.g. Müller and Wehner 1988; Etienne *et al.* 1999; Judd *et al.* 1999; Wiltschko and Wiltschko 1999; Gallistel 1993). Although many species appear to demonstrate an ability to take short-cuts and to perform homing via path integration, at times the homing vector is an approximate one and has to be supplemented by reference to a critical landmark near the home base or by local search to find the appropriate location and entrance (see Judd *et al.* 1999). Alternatively, when exploring an intervening area, given a known but non-perceivable destination (e.g. a destination obstructed by topography or distance), the traveler may use a strategy involving movement between known intervening places or landmarks – a strategy known as "piloting" (Figure 2.1). Here, landmarks act as environmental cues that may be perceived in sequence rather than simultaneously in a configurational structure. In air and sea navigation by humans, spatial updating is called "piloting" or "geocentered dead reckoning." In this process, the current position is known and observed landmarks are integrated into a represen-tational self-referencing system. In a familiar environment, travel over specific routes is traced onto the cognitive map, thus allowing route retrace, route learning, and route reversal to take place.

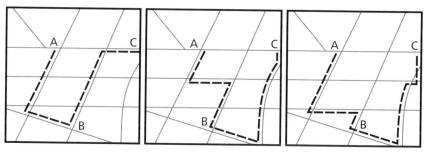

Figure 2.1 Piloting: landmark-to-landmark piloting can result in quite different path selections
to achieve the same goal

In addition to path integration and piloting, a third process used in wayfinding is that of "chunking" (Allen 1982). This involves subdividing or chunking known, planned, or experienced routes to aid memorization and recall. Sometimes landmarks are used to identify places where routes can be subdivided; sometimes particular directional changes provide such an opportunity. When a significant directional change occurs, or after a particular landmark has been reached, a new chunk might be identified with its own distinct landmarks and route traces. A reasonably long or circuitous route can therefore be subdivided into a number of manageable chunks which allow an individual to develop a parsimonious memory structure to define a complex route. Within chunks, some departure from following the path can take place, depending on things such as local topography or network structure.

A fourth process is described in terms of using a template or schema developed from knowledge of other settings to help wayfinding. In many domains it is clear that human intellectual behavior is supported by structured generic knowledge of the world. These structures are called schemata, frames, templates, scenes, and scripts. The contribution of such knowledge to wayfinding has been largely unexplored, but researchers such as Brewer and Treyens (1981) and Mandler (1984) have suggested that schemata are used for memorizing "objects in context" in everyday environments. Other researchers, such as Axia *et al.* (1991), suggest that use of schemata is a fundamental part of environmental cognition. Schemata used for wayfinding must be able to compensate for the lack of information beyond the immediate perceptual domain. It has also been anecdotally suggested that navigators in previous millennia used schemata to compensate for incomplete cognitive maps or inaccurate navigational techniques, particularly in featureless environments such as oceans (e.g. the Etak of the Puluwat Islands of the South Pacific) (Gladwin 1970; Lewis and George 1991).

But knowledge about environmental structure is not of course limited to featureless environments. Recently, Lawton (1996) has suggested that travelers use three dominant factors of wayfinding: orientation, route memorization, and configuration development. For example, exploring a building such as a hospital involves recognizing the generic layout or (building) schema, including the number of floors and the pattern of room numbers. She suggested that participants in her experiments, when traveling in unfamiliar settings, used such generic knowledge (or schemata) about buildings in general to find locations such as exits, elevators, stairs, and toilet facilities. Although developed in natural rather than built environments, environmental schemata based on slopes, gradients, and watercourses may have been used by many successful explorers to build a configurational or layout picture of the environment through which they traveled. Thus, in the past, wayfinders probably used such schemata to generalize from environmental knowledge gained in one area to conditions in other areas. Researchers into the use of schemata argue that these structures can compensate for incomplete environmental knowledge or incomplete spatial representations of environments in long-term and working memory. As such, it can be suggested that wayfinding activities must be explained by representations of spatial relationships, environmental knowledge, and schemata that help wayfinders "close" partial representational knowledge structures in the absence of complete information.

Evolutionary psychologists and some anthropologists (e.g. Tooby and Cosmides 1992) claim that male–female differences have existed throughout time because of the traditional historical role of men as explorers and hunters of game in distant areas, as opposed to women, whose traditional role was gathering and child minding. Hunting often took men to very distant, unfamiliar places that required macroenvironmental knowledge acquisition to facilitate return to home base in a reasonable timeframe. It was assumed that women, because they needed to care for children, usually undertook shorter forays for gathering purposes. This perspective also argues that women are more likely to gain extremely detailed knowledge of their immediate environment, while men are more likely to garner knowledge of distant places. This is reflected today in research that indicates that women and pre-teenage girls appear to know more precise information about their neighborhoods than do boys and men, while the latter know more geographic-scale information that extends beyond neighborhood boundaries and (in the case of adult men) extends across substantial areas of urban environments (Gale *et al.* 1985). There is also some feeling that women use more of a landmark-based approach to wayfinding (i.e. piloting) and are less concerned with comprehending general layout or establishing frames of reference such as recognizing cardinal directions (Lawton *et al.* 1996).

Cognitive maps and cognitive mapping

"Cognitive map" is a term used to describe one's internal representation of the external world. Most researchers agree that it is a hypothetical construct or is used metaphorically to describe the process of recreating stored spatial information in working memory. There is as yet no evidence that humans do or do not store spatial information in a map-like manner in the brain, but it is most generally accepted that they do not. Recent neurobiological research (O'Keefe and Nadel 1978; Nadel 1999) has indicated that representations of objects are stored in what are termed "place cells," and that these same cells "fire" any time an object is experienced or perceived. But the arrangement of such cells has not yet been deciphered, so there is no clear evidence that memory representations of objects or features are stored in particular spatial arrays. What the term cognitive map does imply, however, is that there is deliberate and motivated encoding of environmental information so that it can be used to determine where one is at any particular moment, where other specific perceived or encoded objects are in surrounding space, how to get from one place to another, or how to communicate spatial knowledge to others. The specifics of the representational format are not yet known, but it is assumed that bringing information from long-term memory into working memory for problem-solving activities is dependent on the particular cultural and social experiences and habits and procedures of a person or group. Consequently, in most cultures, manipulation and analysis of information brought into working memory depends largely on the training and experiences of the culture – particularly in terms of the mathematical, topological, or geometric principles conventionally used to arrange and interpret spatial information.

Cognitive maps as wayfinding tools

Throughout history, a variety of guidance instruments and materials have been available for assisting wayfinding. Regardless of the variety and range of technical aids available then and now, throughout the greatest part of human history, and even for the greatest number of trips today, people tend to use cognitive maps and cognitively stored, processed, and recalled information more than anything else to assist in wayfinding. This is partly because most trips are made in familiar or partly familiar environments. Many trips are habitual behaviors, so there is no expressed need constantly to check current position with respect to an external representation – e.g. a traditional cartographic or strip map of a route (Figure 2.2).

When new to an environment, however, most people tend to use information obtained from an external source to assist in wayfinding. In the past, this probably involved querying local inhabitants (when possible), interpreting the structure or "spatial syntax" of a perceived environment, or using celestial, magnetic, or environmental schemata to specify location, orientation, or travel direction. These sets of information usually focus on commonly recognized important features (significant landmarks).

Maps are "summary representations" of an environment. Many early maps were hardly more than informed sketches and differed from maps intended to show

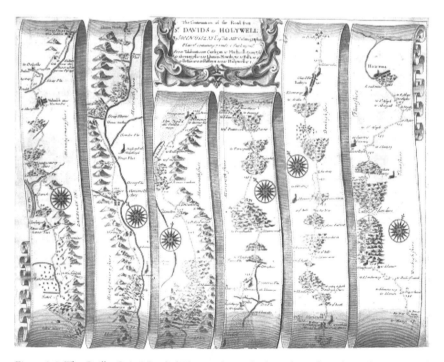

Figure 2.2 The Ogilby Strip Map (1675), covering a trip through north Wales in the seventeenth century (courtesy Bill Norrington)

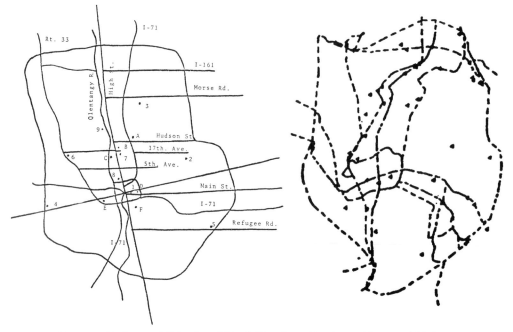

Figure 2.3 Real map of Columbus, Ohio (left) and a resident's cognitive map (right)

matching between real-world and represented features; problems of interpretation arise because of the need to understand scale transformations required to interpret maps or because of the mental or physical rotations needed to match a sketch or map-like representation with features and directions in the real world (the "alignment" process).

Most cognitive maps are incomplete, are often distorted because of incomplete information, and require mental rotation, alignment, and matching as well as scale transformation when being used in travel planning or in actual wayfinding (Kitchin 1994; Portugali 1996). Figure 2.3 shows a lack of metric fit between a cognitive map and a real map, but it also shows that topology (sequences and adjacencies) is preserved, making the cognitive map a useful wayfinding tool (albeit that inter-point distances are recorded inaccurately). But humans are often able successfully to complete wayfinding tasks, even if they do it inefficiently and ineffectively.

Using cognitive maps in a wayfinding context

Cognitive maps are designed to provide answers to questions such as: Where am I? How do I return home? Where is the place for which I am searching? How do I get there? How do I get to the next place on a route, given my current location? What characteristics indicate when I'm lost? What strategies or heuristics do I use to regain locational knowledge? What guidelines or rules influence decision making at choice points? How do I determine distance and direction between specific places or land-marks? Answering these questions relies on understanding and using one or more of

32

the different types of wayfinding discussed earlier. Cognitive maps are not built instantly. They emerge over time as more correct spatial information is accumulated. They are almost never "complete" but are dynamic entities that change as information changes and as the environment changes. A skeletal working framework of locations and paths often develops quickly (e.g. in a few days). A few critical places anchor this structure (e.g. home, place of work, a food source). Over time, more places ("land-marks") are added, more connections (links or paths) connect the places, and a cogni-tive map evolves from a linear, route-based system to a layout-based system. In the course of this evolution, specific "areas" develop around the landmarks and paths (e.g. "home range," "hunting/foraging area," etc.). There are substantial differences between people in the speed at which cognitive maps emerge, based on variations in spatial abilities and variations in personal confidence in being able to solve spatial problems. In earlier societies, "scouts" and "trackers" must have developed high spatial abilities and high levels of spatial confidence.

Spatial primitives needed in wayfinding

In many Western civilizations where it is a basic part of educational experience, Euclidian geometry serves as a template onto which environmental structure is "mapped." Information in working memory is mined for quantitative concepts such as distance, direction, orientation, magnitude, shape, pattern, object class, connec-tivity, hierarchy, and so on. In cultures where formal mathematical training is less universal, more qualitative expressions of spatial characteristic dominate. "Place" replaces absolute "location"; exact distances and directions are replaced by fuzzy spatial concepts such as nearness, proximity, similarity, enclosure, partition, and so on. While the language and teachings of Western culture have, over time, increasingly emphasized the need for precision in comprehending spatial relationships (which then become tied to very specific technical terms), other cultures have had less need for precision and work in a more topological or fuzzy metric domain. In advanced Western cultures, therefore, fundamental geometric components such as points, lines, edges, and districts are described by terminology such as landmarks and reference nodes, roads or routes, districts, regions, neighborhoods, and communities, and spatial limits are defined by exact boundaries (such as by political boundaries).

However, regardless of their levels of social, cultural, economic, or educational development, humans experience and learn about features and places: their names or identities, their location, their size, magnitude, or frequency of occurrence, their temporal domain or times of existence, and their use potential (Golledge 1995). The details associated with any of these primitives of spatial knowledge are constrained by the way of knowing and the type of experiences by which knowledge is acquired. In any particular area, the degree to which one or another of these primitives dominates is influenced by the legibility of the environment and the familiarity that a resident or transitory population gains of that environment.

Environmental legibility

The legibility of an environment is dominated by two dimensions. The first, identified by Lynch (1960), concerns the clarity of spatial representations of one's surroundings and focuses on both physical characteristics and spatial relations. In this view, one's representation of an external environment is structured to be as isomorphic as possible vis-à-vis the surrounding physical world – a view emphasized by Kosslyn (1975). This approach argues that environments are examined for coherent structure. A legible environment is one where the spatial structure is relatively obvious. In these cases, legibility depends on an ability to organize the complexity of the surrounding environment, the ease of differentiating its particular components, and its visual perceptual form. Thus, legible environments allow for object clustering and feature characterization as well as hierarchical ordering of phenomena. Legibility becomes the degree of distinctiveness that enables viewers to comprehend their surroundings.

A second interpretation of legibility focuses on behavior, particularly on travel. Weisman (1981) suggested that legibility is essentially the facility with which travelers can find their way through an environment. While again this concept is based on the quality and complexity of the surrounding spatial structure, this interpretation focuses more on the ease with which humans can manipulate spatial information to assist in moving between particular origins and destinations. In this situation, a legible environment is one where destinations can be directly observed or estimated and where travel can be guided by directly viewing elements of the surrounding space. Spatial concepts (such as distance and direction) partly determine environmental legibility. Thus, two environments that are approximately the same size can have different levels of legibility if one is complex and difficult to move through while the other is complex but where travel is relatively unimpeded.

In recent years a third dimension of legibility has been stressed that combines both spatial and functional characteristics of the surroundings. This approach emphasizes the sociocultural meanings of the surroundings, incorporating qualitative and emotional characteristics with the physical and spatial. In this view, emotional, spiritual, or religious facets of particular surroundings have more or less significance to different social and cultural groups, making the environment more or less legible to them. Symbols that are not directly perceivable may replace physical form as the major differentiating characteristic that facilitates environmental knowing. This approach allows elements of an environment to be imbued with significance and to be elevated to the status of landmarks even where they are not distinctly different in physical form or appearance from their surroundings (e.g. in a row of terrace houses, the particular house in which George Washington slept). The approach underlies the definition of "idiosyncratic landmarks." These may be significant for a single individual or a particular sociocultural group but may have little meaning to other people. Such landmarks facilitate within-group communication, particularly of information relevant to travel, whereas they are much less meaningful if used in communication between different sociocultural groups. To people outside the group, travel directions based on such idiosyncratic information are often incoherent. Overall, this approach argues that legibility is tied to behavior and is interpreted in terms of communicable information that is particularly relevant for wayfinding.

Legible environments, therefore, include features with strong symbolic meanings (Appleyard 1969). These meanings are used to elaborate a region's landmark structure, and they provide the pieces for organizing spatial characteristics of both the physical and sociocultural layout of environmental representations and cognitive maps. In a previous paper (Golledge 1978) I used the term "anchor point" to reflect designated meaningful, physical, or functional elements of an environment, and described how a local environment may be hierarchically structured around these anchor points (Figure 2.4).

Environmental legibility can, therefore, consist of three forms: physical or spatial relationships made obvious by characteristics such as shape, size, color, dominance of visual form, proximity, and hierarchical dominance; sociocultural characteristics such as religious, spiritual, aesthetic, functional, or historical factors; and behavioral legibility, which is tied to ease of travel or ease of imparting communicable information about how to move within specific environments. Legibility thus appears to have physical, spatial, social, or cultural markers as well as behavioral dimensions, and in any given setting one or more of these can dominate. Maurer and Baxter (1972) showed that different cultures exposed to a similar environment create different representations of it. They compared Afro-American and Anglo-American sketch maps of a particular place and showed, firstly, that the Afro-American sketches were less spatially accurate than those of the Anglo-Americans and, secondly, that different sets of landmark features appeared to dominate the representations of each group. Ramadier and Moser (1998) also showed differences when comparing African and European students' representations of Paris. Students from Africa produced a more propositional or spatial objective view of the city, whereas European representations emphasized value and historical meaning as key identifiers of places and relations. Ramadier and Moser use the terms "surroundings" and "settings," respectively, to refer to these different ways of representing environments.

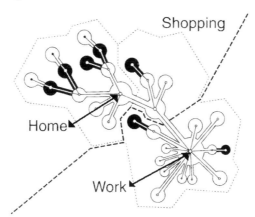

Figure 2.4 Anchor point theory of spatial knowledge acquisition

According to Gärling *et al.* (1984), environmental legibility goes through three stages: exploratory, adaptive, and abstract. Exploratory representations are dominated by visual experience gained through travel and are essentially concrete (i.e. spatial/ geographic). Spatial products (i.e. external representations of stored knowledge) tend to be dominated by route-map structures rather than survey or configurational structures. Knowledge is accumulated to facilitate travel and to allow individuals and families to establish daily activity patterns. In the adaptive stage, social and cultural meanings and symbolic interpretations of place become more prominent. These cultural codings and physical signs increase the legibility of an environment by focusing attention on specific features and relationships. In the abstract stage, a "survey"-type representation is built. This allows for travel plans to be developed prior to movement between unfamiliar places by providing an overlaying frame of reference and giving positional information with respect to the layout of distant features. Once this stage is reached, individuals can more easily explore an environment and visit unknown places. Legibility is thus a function of time of exposure and familiarity. Environments of different complexity either help or hinder transition through these stages. There is no standard "rate" of environmental learning. Some people learn all they "need to know" in 2–3 weeks; others still have incoherent environmental mappings after 2–3 years.

Components of legibility: landmarks

Perhaps the most fundamental pieces of spatial information used for both environmental knowing and wayfinding purposes are identifiable locations that can be represented as points. Referred to in the literature as "reference nodes" or "landmarks," these act as location identifiers or as organizing concepts for local or more global representations. They allow identities to be associated with specific places, and they allow the objects at those places to be used as constant and communicable referents in wayfinding and navigation. Sometimes these points are specifically associated with the need to make a choice (e.g. where to cross a water body, or a point identifying which valley facilitates travel into a mountainous region). Landmarks also act as origin and destination points and occur either on a route or as an off-route referent point that helps in orientation and decision making.

Landmarks acting as identifiers or choice points can be linked in sequence to create routes. Distant off-route landmarks provide orientation and frame of reference information and, while not necessarily determining a specific path, provide a heading vector or help define a general sector or corridor of travel (e.g. "towards a notch in a distant range," or "towards the tallest building in the downtown area"). And, finally, landmarks or other point-related features often act as primers: for example, seeing a specific rock formation may signal the presence of a nearby water hole.

Landmarks also act as regional differentiating features. Differentiation can occur because of changing physical characteristics (e.g. the place where sand desert changes to rock or "gibber" desert), changing geology, the presence or absence of water bodies (e.g. a desert oasis or Niagara Falls), and, of course, built additions to the environment, such as residences or unique human constructed artifacts (the Statue of Liberty, the Eiffel Tower, the Kremlin, or the Sydney Opera House).

Landmarks may be regarded as strategic foci towards or away from which one travels. They may act as intermediate foci on courses and routes that assist in spatial decision making by priming decisions or making decision making place-specific. The objects that are defined as landmarks can be significant physical or biotic features, can be built by human action, or may be natural features that accrue cultural significance (e.g. the tree that locals recognize as "the hanging tree"). People often give salience to objects or features that allow them to be differentiated from their surroundings. Landmarks can be culturally created (the Golden Gate Bridge) just as they may occur naturally as outstanding natural features (the Victoria Falls). However, landmarks used as wayfinding aids are often remembered because of the dominance of their visible form. Since they can be perceived and recognized from a distance, uniqueness accrues from the peculiarity of their shape, size, or structure, or because of social, cultural, or religious significance. Important unique natural features or deliberately created ones are called "common" landmarks, and they are usually part of the cognitive maps of large groups of people. But other landmarks are personally "created" and are called "idiosyncratic"; they are more specific to individuals or small groups such as families (e.g. one's personal residence or place of work). Thus, some places accrue salience for individuals or small groups but are not part of the common geographic knowledge structure of larger population groups. The salience of the idiosyncratic landmark for a given individual, however, can be at a level equivalent to that of the common and most widely known and recognized landmarks. But it is on the basis of the commonly recognized and identifiable landmarks that group activities and group communications usually take place. If features are salient enough to be recognized by group members in common, then they are usually distinct enough to impart to an alien group as a signifier or symbol of a boundary or edge between adjacent territories or as key wayfinding information.

Another characteristic of landmarks lies in their role as "organizing features." Whether they are individual idiosyncratic features or commonly recognized features or places, landmarks act as anchor points for organizing other spatial information in the surrounding area (Couclelis *et al.* 1987). They are often used as centroids or edge markers for spatially differentiating regions or territories, and as the major orienting features when in the process of giving verbal or other types of directions (e.g. "Go towards the Mission and turn right three blocks before it.").

Paths and networks as components of legible environments

Points are connected by lines of travel. The most primitive of these are called tracks or paths, and may be imprecisely defined, may wander, and, depending on the presence or absence of environmental obstacles, may be more or less imprinted on the landscape. Whether formed by animals or humans, these paths facilitate repeated travel. Repeated travel by volumes of travelers over periods of time imprints paths and tracks on the environment by destroying vegetation, compacting soil, and leaving a line of travel discernable to the naked eye. But, in circumstances where the environment is unimpeded by major obstacles (e.g. flat plains or deserts), it is not necessary to follow the same path on each trip. Free ranging can occur over an area provided the destination is known (i.e. stored in memory) or can be perceived in the distal environment. Under free-ranging conditions with limited obstructions, paths can more closely approximate "shortest path" or "crow-fly" distances. In any particular cultural area, paths or tracks can be linked to form networks that provide simple and easy ways to interact between places within those areas.

While landmarks and choice points are linked in sequence to form a mental route structure that guides wayfinding actions, since the earliest times humans have tried to externalize route-based information in simple graphic representational format. The earliest modes for doing this are now known as "strip maps." In ancient Egypt, influential people were buried with strip maps indicating the way the soul had to travel to reach its heavenly destination. In ancient China, scroll strip maps depicted route segments, landmark features, and even flora, fauna, or human cultural features along a way. Many cultures embodied wayfinding knowledge in folklore and tales and legends. Norse sagas focused both on the heroic acts of humans and identified routes and places to which heroes traveled when performing their legendary deeds. Some of the earliest great literature in the English language focused on people as they traversed long and difficult routes – as in *The Pilgrim's Progress* and *The Canterbury Tales*. Australian Aboriginals embed and include environmental and route information in song and dance to represent features and places experienced while on walkabout. But all these representations are one-dimensional and linear. As travel became more common, single routes had to be linked to others. The integrated set of paths is termed a network. Just as selections of locations or places were combined to form configurations, so have individual routes been combined to form networks. Networks are developed to formalize connections between multiple places in an environment.

Routes and networks make environments "legible" in the sense of organizing and facilitating travel. In more primitive or less developed settings, "networks" are simple,

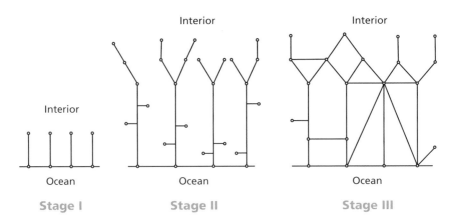

Figure 2.5 Development of network complexity

linear, and have few cross-route links. As development advances, networks become more complex, with increasing numbers of connections between places (Gould 1959). Figure 2.5 gives an example of how this complexity develops over time.

Frames of reference and configurational understanding as components of legibility

Configurations of locations and places are learned with respect to frames of reference and orienting schemata. During wayfinding, specific places are constantly referred to a surrounding reference frame so that direction and heading can be determined and maintained. Problems arise when reference landmarks are mistaken or when frames of reference become rotated (i.e. facing in the wrong direction) or obscured, as might be the case during inclement weather conditions, for example.

Specific environments are made legible by defining boundaries around a particular area, integrating the individually learned routes within this area into a network, and comprehending the layout of features and routes as if viewed from a bird's-eye vantage point. This is conventionally referred to as "configurational" understanding or "layout" understanding and represents the formal metric knowledge about an environment. It facilitates abstract spatial thinking and mental geometry and is presumed to be the highest metric level of spatial knowledge (Hart and Moore 1973; Siegel and White 1975). In the absence of constructed representations such as maps, this occurs as an internal (cognitive) process which could be facilitated by overviewing the area from a height (e.g. a hilltop), a process often used by early land-based explorers. Later, obtaining such an overview was facilitated using a constructed representation of the area, such as a map, diagram, or picture. Route knowledge is sequential in nature and can be metrically quite inaccurate but topologically correct (i.e. interpoint distances can be in error, but sequences of landmarks may be correct). Configurational or layout information formalizes the entire set of geometric relations among all elements of an environment and allows "mental geometry and mental trigonometry" to be used in wayfinding tasks. A "bird's-eye" or "survey" procedure unpacks spatial relations embedded in both the real world and as mentally stored information, including things such as identification of nearest neighbors, adjacencies, hierarchies based on magnitude, connective centrality, distances separating places, and directions with respect to external reference frames as well as with respect to where an individual is currently located.

In the communication of information about potential travel, routes may be adequately described using only ordinal or sequential information, whereas layouts or configurations are best described using some form of metrically structured information that requires an ability to comprehend interpoint distances and directions, linkages, boundaries, patterns, and concepts of scale. This configurational or layout knowledge may not be mentally represented in a uniform type of metric and is often a mix of qualitative (non-metric) and quantitative (metric) characteristics, depending on different levels of familiarity with parts of the environment in question.

Summary

There is convincing evidence that humans and other animals do not develop instantaneous, complete, and precise spatial knowledge of any given environment. Such knowledge traditionally accrues during and after wayfinding. Researchers such as Stea *et al.* (1996) hypothesize that activating processes of ecological macroenvironmental thinking and behaving requires both cognitive and external mapping. Macroenvironments are so vast and complex that they ordinarily cannot be observed as a whole from any single earthbound vantage point – although we currently have the ability to observe significantly large parts of the global surface from satellites or space stations. In the absence of this ability, however, our perception, cognition, and planning of travel behavior in macroenvironments call for distinctive actions. Historically, one of these has been the making of material maps or map-like pictures, diagrams, or models that facilitate comprehension of the layout of features that normally cannot be observed from a single vantage point.

Throughout history, cognitive maps and material maps have played a vital part in our ability to deal with, orient ourselves in, and travel through large-scale places or macroenvironments. This capacity and need lie behind the hypothesis that cognitive maps and material maps are cultural universals and that humans have natural or innate abilities to engage in data collection, map construction, map representation, and map interpretation – even from a very early age. If this is true, then recognizable mapping behavior should be in evidence everywhere, regardless of geographic place or culture. If the ability emerges early in life, it should be apparent in children's representation of geographic landscapes through the media of play with toys or interactive games (e.g. hide-and-seek or war games). Environmental knowledge should also be one of the more common themes in temporary or permanent children's art, as it should be in the adult art of specific societies and cultures. There is substantial evidence that ecological adaptation was facilitated by recording information on maps or map-like representations in the distant past of human history. Stea *et al.* (1996) have reviewed literature from art, archaeology, anthropology, and history to support their contention that forms of map use have been an integral part of recorded human history. More explicitly, Stea *et al.* have shown that US, Puerto Rican, Mexican, and South African children can interpret aerial photos of their own and other environments, clearly differentiating routes that would be taken by a bird as opposed to a car between particular places. While there is as yet no specific proof that mapping was coincident with, predated, or postdated the development of linguistic ability, it is reasonable to assume that the ability to represent spatial information in pictorial, gesture, or other material modes has been a temporal constant that facilitates travel behavior (Stea *et al.* 1996). Woodward and Lewis (1998) provide an extensive review of the various practices of traditional societies in Africa, pre-European North America, the Arctic, Australia, and the Pacific Islands with respect to the development of maps and map surrogates (e.g. rock art, mud maps, stick and shell navigation charts, and sand sketches) as a means of representing environmental information.

The accumulation of environmental knowledge is usually partial and is error-prone. Errors can consist of:

- mis-specifying locations;
- mismatching cognized or recalled layouts in real-world phenomena;
- incorrectly encoding distances or directions;
- failing to integrate overlapping paths into a structured network in an accurate manner;
- mis-specifying self-to-object relations;
- incorrectly encoding or decoding object-to-object relations;
- spatially updating poorly as one travels through an environment over time;
- falsely perceiving landmarks or anchors because of changing viewing perspectives;
- misplacing landmarks or anchors in their appropriate regions of space; and
- mis-specifying an appropriate sequence of links and turns when creating a memory trace of a successfully followed path.

Nevertheless, and despite this propensity to commit errors, these same humans (and other animals) can successfully complete wayfinding tasks by finding a destination or returning to a home base in a timely manner.

In many settings, different people give different saliencies to different features and base their cognitive representations on idiosyncratic, as much as commonly recognized, anchors. Thus, when asked to reproduce or report on environmental knowledge gained about a specific setting, different people may construct substantially different spatial representations. It appears that some people are more prone to directional errors than to distance errors, while for others the reverse is the case (Loomis *et al.* 2002). Some groups find the greatest problems in establishing, encoding, and recording absolute locations and prefer to treat locational information in the looser and fuzzier relative terms that are typical of fuzzy spatial prepositions ("near" the church, "behind" the shopping center, "to the right of" the Mission: Landau and Jackendoff 1993; Tversky and Taylor 1998).

While wayfinding behavior may be somewhat redundant in today's information technology-dominated societies, it is still important to understand how it takes place. This knowledge is important for understanding how the earth was peopled and how today's cultures and societies were spatially delineated. We need to understand the wayfinding process that facilitated colonization in the past, just as this knowledge will be required if humans ever travel to the stars and explore new uncharted worlds.

References

Allen, G. L. (1982). "The organization of route knowledge." *New Directions for Child Development* 15:31–9.

Appleyard, D. (1969). "Why buildings are known: a predictive tool for architects and planners." *Environment and Behavior* 1:131–56.

Axia, G., Peron, E., *et al.* (1991). "Environmental assessment across the life span." In T. Gärling and G. W. Evans (eds), *Environment, Cognition and Action: An Integrated Approach.* New York: Oxford University Press: 221–4.

Brewer, W. F. and Treyens, J. C. (1981). "Role of schemata in memory for places." *Cognitive Psychology* 13:207–30.

Coulclelis, H., Golledge, R. G., Gale, N. D., and Tobler, W. R. (1987). "Exploring the anchor-point hypothesis of spatial cognition." *Journal of Environmental Psychology* 7:99–122.

Etienne, A. S., Maurer, R., *et al.* (1999). "Dead reckoning (path integration), landmarks, and representation of space in a comparative perspective." In R. G. Golledge (ed.), *Wayfinding Behavior: Cognitive Mapping and Other Spatial Processes.* Baltimore and London: Johns Hopkins University Press: 197–228.

Gale, N. D., Doherty, S., Pellegrino, J., and Golledge, R. G. (1985). "Toward reassembling the image." *Children's Environments Quarterly* 2(3):10–18.

Gallistel, C. R. (1993). *The Organization of Learning,* 2nd edition. Cambridge, MA: MIT Press.

Gärling, T., Böök, A., and Lindberg, E. (1984). "Cognitive mapping of large-scale environments: the interrelationship of action plans, acquisition, and orientation." *Environment and Behavior* 16:3–34.

Gladwin, T. (1970). *East is a Big Bird: Navigation and Logic on Pulawat Atoll.* Cambridge, MA: Harvard University Press.

Golledge, R. G. (1978). "Representing, interpreting and using cognized environments." *Papers and Proceedings, Regional Science Association* 41:169–204.

—— (1995). "Primitives of spatial knowledge." In T. L. Nyerges, D. M. Mark, R. Laurini, and M. J. Egenhofer (eds), *Cognitive Aspects of Human–Computer Interaction for Geographic Information Systems.* Dordrecht: Kluwer Academic Publishers: 29–44.

Gould, P. (1959). *Transportation in Ghana.* Evanston, IL: Department of Geography, Northwestern University (Studies in Geography).

Hart, R. A. and Moore, G. T. (1973). "The development of spatial cognition: a review." In R. M. Downs and D. Stea (eds), *Image and Environment: Cognitive Mapping and Spatial Behavior.* Chicago: Aldine: 246–88.

Judd, S. P. D., Dale, K., and Collett, T. S. (1999). "On the fine structure of view-based navigation in insects." In R. G. Golledge (ed.), *Wayfinding Behavior: Cognitive Mapping and Other Spatial Processes.* Baltimore and London: Johns Hopkins University Press: 229–58.

Kitchin, R. M. (1994). "Cognitive maps: what are they and why study them?" *Journal of Environmental Psychology* 14(1):1–19.

Klatzky, R. L., Loomis, J. M., Golledge, R. G., Cicinelli, J. G., Doherty, S., and Pellegrino, J. W. (1990). "Acquisition of route and survey knowledge in the absence of vision." *Journal of Motor Behavior* 22(1):19–43.

Kosslyn, S. M. (1975). "Information representation in visual images." *Cognitive Psychology* 7: 341–70.

Landau, B. and Jackendoff, R. (1993). "'What' and 'where' in spatial language and spatial cognition." *Behavioral and Brain Sciences* 16:217–38.

Lawton, C. A. (1996). "Strategies for indoor wayfinding: the role of orientation." *Journal of Environmental Psychology* 16(2):137–45.

Lawton, C. A., Charleston, S. I., and Zieles, A. S. (1996). "Individual- and gender-related differences in indoor wayfinding." *Environment and Behavior* 28(2):204–19.

Lewis, D. H. and George, M. (1991). "Hunters and herders: Chuchi and Siberian Eskimo navigation across snow and frozen sea." *Journal of Navigation* 44:1–10.

Loomis, J. M., Klatzky, R. L., and Golledge, R. G. (1992). *Analysis of Navigation without Sight*. Santa Barbara, CA: University of California Santa Barbara (Final Report, Grant 7022 from the National Eye Institute).

Loomis, J., Lippa, Y., Klatzky, R., and Golledge, R. (2002). "Spatial updating of locations specified by 3-D sound and spatial language." *Journal of Experimental Psychology: Learning, Memory, and Cognition* 28(2):335–45.

Lynch, K. (1960). *The Image of the City*. Cambridge, MA: MIT Press.

Mandler, J. M. (1984). *Stories, Scripts, and Scenes: Aspects of Schema Theory*. Hillsdale, NJ: Lawrence Erlbaum Associates.

Maurer, R. and Baxter, J. (1972). "Images of neighborhoods among black, anglo, and Mexican-American children." *Environment and Behavior* 4:351–88.

Müller, M. and Wehner, R. (1988). "Path integration in desert ants, Cataglyphis Fortis." *Proceedings of the National Academy of Sciences of the United States of America* 85:5287–90.

Nadel, L. (1999). "Neural mechanisms of spatial orientation and wayfinding: an overview." In R. G. Golledge (ed.), *Wayfinding Behavior: Cognitive Mapping and Other Spatial Processes*. Baltimore and London: Johns Hopkins University Press: 313–27.

O'Keefe, J. and Nadel, L. (1978). *The Hippocampus as a Cognitive Map*. Oxford: Clarendon Press.

Portugali, J. (ed.) (1996). *The Construction of Cognitive Maps*. Dordrecht: Kluwer Academic Publishers.

Ramadier, T. and Moser, G. (1998). "Social legibility, the cognitive map and urban behaviour." *Journal of Environmental Psychology* 18(3):307–19.

Sholl, M. J. (1987). "Cognitive maps as orienting schemata." *Journal of Experimental Psychology: Learning, Memory, and Cognition* 13(4):615–28.

Siegel, A. W. and White, S. H. (1975). "The development of spatial representation of large scale environments." In H. W. Reese (ed.), *Advances in Child Development and Behavior*, vol. 10. New York: Academic Press: 9–55.

Simon, H. A. (1957). *Models of Man*. New York: John Wiley & Sons.

Stea, D., Blaut, J. M., and Stephens, J. (1996). "Mapping as a cultural universal." In J. Portugali (ed.), *The Construction of Cognitive Maps*. Dordrecht, Boston, and London: Kluwer Academic Publishers: 345–60.

Tooby, J. and Cosmides, L. (1992). "The psychological foundations of culture." In J. Barkow, L. Cosmides, and J. Tooby (eds), *The Adapted Mind: Evolutionary Psychology and the Generation of Culture*. New York: Oxford University Press.

Tversky, B. and Taylor, H. A. (1998). "Acquiring spatial and temporal knowledge from language." In M. J. Egenhofer and R. G. Golledge (eds), *Spatial and Temporal Reasoning in Geographic Information Systems*. New York: Oxford University Press: 155–66.

Weisman, G. D. (1981). "Evaluating architectural legibility: Wayfinding in the built environment." *Environment and Behavior* 13(2):189–204.

Wiltschko, R. and Wiltschko, W. (1999). "Compass orientation as a basic element in avian orientation and navigation." In R. G. Golledge (ed.), *Wayfinding Behavior: Cognitive Mapping and Other Spatial Processes*. Baltimore and London: Johns Hopkins University Press: 259–93.

Woodward, D. and Lewis, G. M. (1998). *The History of Cartography*, vol. 2, book 3: *Cartography in the Traditional African, American, Arctic, Australian, and Pacific Societies*. Chicago: University of Chicago Press.

Worchel, P. (1951). "Space perception and orientation in the blind." *Psychological Monographs: General and Applied* 65:1–27.

3

COLONIZATION OF NEW LAND BY HUNTER-GATHERERS

Expectations and implications based on ethnographic data

Robert L. Kelly

Nearly all of the world was initially colonized by people equipped with a foraging adaptation. How hunter-gatherers adapt to "empty" land masses, therefore, is a question that is essential to understanding an important segment of human history. It is a frustrating question, however, for there are no easy analogies. We have no cases of ethnographically known hunter-gatherers moving into terra incognita.[1] Yet too often it is assumed that the first prehistoric foragers to occupy a region fit an ethnographic model, one based on only one or two ethnographic cases that serve as simple ethnographic analogies. In recent decades, it has been the Ju/'hoansi (the !Kung, San, Basarwa, or Bushmen), or some amalgam of Arctic groups (Kelly 1996). But it is clear that such analogies are not always useful even when examining later Holocene foragers (Kelly 1995). How much less so for colonizing populations that faced environmental and social circumstances that would have been foreign to ethnographically known foragers?

The purpose of this volume is to move toward a better understanding of how humans initially occupy large land masses about which nothing was known, about which nothing could have been encoded into oral history or folklore, about which the accumulated wisdom of grandparents and great-grandparents was silent. This chapter's contribution is to ask what ethnographically known hunter-gatherers have to contribute to this venture. Since there are no analogies to call upon, our effort is aimed at looking at how ethnographically known hunter-gatherers "know" their landscape and what this might suggest about foragers entering unoccupied continents. It is most likely that different land masses were occupied differently, depending on a number of variables such as population density, the particular environment (e.g. the Australian desert versus the Siberian taiga), and the adaptation that the colonizers brought with them to the new land. But in writing this paper I must admit that in the back of my mind is the colonization of the western hemisphere.

Landscape knowledge: the ethnographic record

Some years ago, Lawrence Todd and I argued that some facets of North American Paleoindian archaeology might be accounted for by the fact that Paleoindians may not have known their landscapes very well (Kelly and Todd 1988). We took some flak for this claim from several individuals who pointed out that "all hunter-gatherers know their landscape well." This is, of course, true enough for ethnographically known hunter-gatherers, people who have lived someplace for a long time. I would be surprised if they did not know their landscape very well.

But there is some variability in how well hunter-gatherers *have* to know their landscape as well as in how well they *can* know it. Ethnographically known Arctic foragers, for example, can draw fairly accurate, detailed maps of large parcels of land. The Central Eskimo drew maps for Boas that covered some 650,000 km^2 (Boas 1888: 234–40). The Aivilingmiut (Iglulik) could map Southampton Island – some 52,000 km^2 (Carpenter 1955), and the Bering Strait Eskimo could also make accurate maps of long stretches of coast (E. Nelson 1899: 197). Inuit in Greenland could carve long, accurate maps of the coastline from wood (Petersen 1984). Groups in the tropics live in much smaller territories (Kelly 1983, 1995), although they also know large tracts of land. Silberbauer (1981: 95) notes that "few G/wi [of the Kalahari Desert] have any knowledge of geography beyond a radius of 250 km [about 196,000 km^2] and the personal experience of most is limited to a range of about 80 km [about 20,000 km^2]." The latter is still, nonetheless, a large area. Silberbauer relates several accounts which show that the G/wi do know this area extremely well and can orient their current location to known places. Likewise, Holmberg (1950: 120) noted that, although the lowland Bolivian Siriono have only two cardinal directions (east, where the sun rises, and west, where it sets), "most adults have an excellent knowledge of the geography of the area in which they wander. No matter how meandering his course, the Indian never gets lost in the jungle and is able to return directly to the spot from which he started."

How do foragers know and communicate these large landscapes? First, hunter-gatherers know their landscape as cognitive maps, an internalized representation of spatial information (Golledge 1999: 15). These maps may occasionally be physically constructed through images scratched in the sand, or carvings, but these are temporary. Instead, landscapes are memorized and based on experience, rather than learned through an iconic projection; geographers refer to these two modes of acquiring a cognitive map as route-based and survey knowledge (Golledge 1999). Second, hunter-gatherers, like members of most small-scale societies, know their landscape in terms of specific named localities rather than in general terms (Fowler 1999). These place names often refer to specific characteristics of a place, as when the Toedökadö Paiute (cattail-eater Paiute) refer to a spring as *padici yibiwinni*, "place-where-water-bubbles-up" (Fowler 1992: 27). And places may often be related to mythical events of the past. The Australian Dreamtime is the best example (see e.g. Tonkinson 1978: 90), but there are others: the G/wi for example (see Silberbauer 1981: 96), or the Toedökadö Paiute, who referred to an enormous sand dune in their territory (now known as Sand Mountain) as $K^w azi$, referring to the snake who inhabited it and who formed the dune's sinewy "backbone" (Fowler 1992: 40).

Places may also be remembered in terms of events in the recent past that have meaning to the speakers. The Toedökadö referred to one place as *nimiʔoho*, "people's bones," referring to a place where many people died when the Carson River was allegedly poisoned in the 1880s. Among California's Atsugewi "every small hill or flat seems to have had a name of its own," names that were sometimes descriptive and sometimes related to mythical events (Garth 1953: 195). Relying on her experience with the Ju/'hoansi, Biesele (1993: 55–6) argues that dramatic stories retain information better than other mnemonic devices. She shows that new stories are inventive retellings that incorporate new experience, and thus that oral traditions must be flexible to serve as a way to memorize information, including that of landscapes.

Sometimes places acquire names that are handed down but whose associated stories are not. Silberbauer (1981: 97) notes that there were several pans with names for which no one knew the origin; there was even one name for which no one knew the literal meaning. While I was in southwest Madagascar with the Mikea (Kelly *et al.* 1999; Poyer and Kelly 2000) I came to know a stretch of forest as "Antaitsoavaly," meaning "place of horse feces." There are no horses in the area today, and although young men knew the place and used its name, they had to ask the village's elder for its story (it had to do either with a horse-mounted foreigner who was looking for gold or silver [personal fieldnotes], or with the horses used when a footpath was widened to accommodate oil exploration [B. Tucker, personal communication, 2001]).

A landscape as a remembered surface of named places may become more important and prevalent as the land becomes more and more geographically monotonous. Returning to southwest Madagascar, the landscape there is thick, tangled forests with no significant topography. I once traveled with some Mikea along a 40 km stretch of forest trail that crossed named places every 2–3 km (data collected by Jim Yount). Most of these places were singularly undistinguished (to me), or referenced ephemeral things that no longer existed, such as a particularly large tree that was long since cut down.

Hunter-gatherers have terms to refer to compass directions, although these can vary from as few as two, normally east and west (e.g. the Siriono [Holmberg 1950: 120] or the Californian Shasta [Holt 1946: 343]) to as many as twenty-two (the Chukchee [Bogoras 1904]). However, as is true for other small-scale societies, foragers tend not to use compass directions when talking about location (Brown 1983). Most of the time direction is relational, given with reference to geographic features, as among the G/wi (Silberbauer 1981: 98), the Tanana (McKennan 1959: 113), the Ingalik (Osgood 1936: 102), and the Kutchin (R. Nelson 1986: 184). Distance, too, is relational and is measured in terms of how long it takes to travel from one place to another under different conditions rather than in specific terms. Thus, distance varies depending on whether a person is traveling alone or with children; burdened or unburdened; in good or bad weather; across steep or flat terrain; with dog-assisted transport or not (e.g. Silberbauer 1981: 98; Carpenter 1955: 133; Holmberg 1969: 122; Osgood 1959: 56; Honigmann 1949: 213; Garth 1953: 196). In sum, for hunter-gatherers (as well as for any persons who do not use printed maps) landscapes are sets of named and/or "storied" places. These are generally made into a cognitive map, not necessarily as a two-dimensional map but as a relational set: one place is known as being a certain distance (or time) and direction from another place.

There are two factors to remember here. The first is that it takes time to learn landscapes. Learning a landscape begins with children (Tonkinson 1978: 31) and can take many years. Men tend to travel further and cover more terrain than women do, either through hunting or through trading, visiting, or wife-seeking trips that take them to other bands a long distance away. Boys learn the landscape by accompanying their fathers on hunting trips. In the Arctic, this does not happen until the boys are 12 years of age or so (e.g. Murdoch 1892: 417). While it would seem that younger boys could accompany their fathers in less severe climates, this is only sometimes true. Kutenai informants recalled that boys accompanied their fathers by the age of six (Turney-High 1941: 117). Although Klamath boys received their first bow by age six, they did not accompany their fathers until "several years later" (Pearsall 1950: 343). Neither Ju/'hoansi nor Australian Aboriginal boys accompany their fathers until they are about 12 years old (Marshall 1976: 322; Berndt and Berndt 1964: 133). This is important, because learning the environment takes some amount of time, and the earlier a child starts, the more he or she will learn. Nelson (1986: 184) states that a Kutchin man's familiarity with an environment takes many years:

> A man learns to find his way around in an area after a couple of years, but it takes much longer to become highly efficient as a hunter-trapper. Knowledge of the landscape is almost as important to successful exploitation of the boreal forest environment as knowledge of hunting and trapping techniques.

And since the landscapes are learned as a set of places that are connected to or exist as "remnants" of secular stories or sacred, mythical "adventures" of the past, one has to know not just simple geography but also extensive folklore and/or religious information as well.

Second, some kinds of terrain are easier to learn than others. R. Nelson (1986: 184) makes this point in talking about hunting and trapping among the Alaskan Kutchin:

> An old Kutchin said that he could trap successfully far up the Black River even though the terrain is unfamiliar, because in that mountainous country it is easy to find the way. It is undoubtedly less difficult to learn to orient oneself by the configurations of a few dozen mountains than by an infinitude of local forest configurations.

The same difference exists in the tropical deserts of Africa, where the broken hill country of the Hadza is apparently easier for children to learn than the monotonous, rolling sand hills of the Ju/'hoansi's territory (Blurton Jones et al. 1994). Among the Inuit, Nelson (1986) notes that indicators of cardinal directions, such as the position of the sun and stars, and wind direction, are used for orientation, while the Athapaskans in the northern forests use topography – trails, lakes, meadows, and rivers. The simple reason is that on the Arctic ice and tundra there are fewer topographic indicators; these cardinal directions and their relationship to wind and the common direction of weather, such as snowstorms, are especially important for sea-faring Inuit. (One can see this in some of the terms used. For example, according to Boas [1888: 235] the Central Eskimo term for east-northeast, the direction from which snow comes, is *qanara*: "is it snow?")

I have experienced these differences myself. I have spent a fair amount of time in the outdoors, and pride myself on not getting lost. But I have spent most of my time in mountainous country, where direction is easier to reckon. In southwest Madagascar, however, I experienced the unfamiliar, and frightening, feeling of disorientation several times. For example, on one foraging trip with a Mikea man I was shocked when after a few hours we suddenly emerged from a thicket into the camp that we had left. We had completed a circular route when I thought we had been walking all the while in a straight line out from camp.

Landscape learning

Geographers recognize at least six different ways that humans "wayfind" (Allen 1999: 48–50). This categorization was developed, understandably, with urban or suburban dwellers in mind, or, at least, without hunter-gatherers in mind. Likewise, it was developed, again understandably, in terms of an individual's immediate behavior rather than in terms of the data of archaeology, where we see patterns that document not individual behavior but the aggregate result of the behavior of many individuals. Even when dealing with living individuals it is often difficult to sort out which wayfinding strategy is being used (Allen 1999: 50). I suspect there might be even more overlap when considering ancient peoples who did not use printed maps.

In thinking about the wayfinding issues that confront foragers, and especially those who were exploring new terrain or traveling to novel destinations, it seems that the development of a cognitive map of some area is most critical. In developing that map for an unknown region foragers would have to rely on oriented search, using information gathered during forays as a way to find their way home (keep the forest on your left, then, when you return, keep the forest on your right). Such trips would also undoubtedly involve some level of what geographers call path integration, in which a forager takes his or her ever-changing speed and direction into account to calculate where they are on a grid and use that information to calculate a new direction home rather than follow the outbound path (I walked at a constant speed over level terrain into the morning sun for two hours, then with the sun to my right or above me for two hours, so if I now walk with the late afternoon sun ahead of me and to my right I should be home in a bit under three hours [by walking the hypotenuse of the right triangle and assuming that time equals distance in this case]). Finally, a forager would certainly pilot between landmarks, using rivers or mountains, for example, to help locate him- or herself and return home. The less familiar a forager is with an area, the more prominent those landmarks would have to be. Following river systems is perhaps the simplest case, because if one goes upstream on the way out, one simply has to go downstream to return home.

The ease with which a landscape can be learned and converted into a cognitive map is related to the geography of the landscape itself as well as the amount of time available to a person to learn it. What strictly geographic factors might influence the ease with which a landscape could be learned? From the above discussion, two factors stand out. The contrast between the Hadza and Ju/'hoansi suggests that the presence of topographic relief aids in landscape negotiation, and possibly memorization. Landscapes that are flat and monotonous are more difficult to navigate and memorize. To an extent, this will be corrected for through keener perception that picks out more subtle topographic features for navigation. For example, at the 1990 International Conference on Hunting and Gathering Societies (CHAGS) in Alaska I was listening to a paper on northern Scandinavia. The slide that was projected had been taken from a boat facing the shoreline, and it showed a wide expanse of water with a very low terrestrial horizon that I perceived as "flat." Two Inuit from northern Canada entered the session after the speaker had been introduced and, after looking at the slide a few moments, asked me if the paper was about a particular place on the north Canadian coast. When I replied no, one commented to the other that the hill in the photo looked just like a particular place near the MacKenzie Delta. I had to look again at the slide to see, indeed, a slight rise in the middle of the photo that to me was meaningless as a topographic marker. Nelson's account above also suggests that in such situations non-topographic factors such as wind direction and sun position (both of which could vary, depending on the season) will be used to determine direction and the relative positions of places on a landscape. Still, it seems to me that the initial learning of a landscape would be more difficult where navigation required the use of subtle geographic features, or the use of those features in combination with atmospheric or solar patterns, than in places where topography was more dramatic and differentiated.

But too much topography, or topography with no larger pattern, may create its own problems. Ernest Shackleton and members of his failed Imperial Trans-Antarctic Expedition learned this lesson as they (eventually successfully) piloted their way across the uncharted mountainous interior of South Georgia Island in 1916. They had repeatedly to backtrack and try other routes to find a way across glaciers and arretes. In that case, the topography also presented a problem by requiring enormous physical effort to traverse it.

Badlands may not require such heroic effort to cross, but they are an example of a case where the topography has no larger plan to it, and where one could easily get lost until acquiring familiarity with it. Compare such badlands with the mountains of the Great Basin in the western USA, where all the ranges are linear, with normally a single spine running north–south, and all canyons running either to the west or to the east. People entering a new continent may have avoided areas where the local topography could not be connected to some larger topographic scheme. In this regard, linear mountain chains (or their foothills), major rivers, and coastlines might provide the easiest topography to navigate and to relate to other known places: "Just follow the coast north and you can't miss it" would be good, usable advice. Languages of Oceanic peoples, in which directions are commonly given in terms of "seaward" or "sea-side" and "inland" or "mountain-side" (see Hill 1997), demonstrate this approach to the construction of cognitive landscape maps.

Vegetation might also make some landscapes more difficult to negotiate by obscuring prominent topographic features that could be used for piloting. Of course, this could be compensated for by simply climbing a tree (something everyone who has spent time doing archaeological survey in forested areas has done). But if heavy vegetation were combined with flat topography, then I would expect that major geographic features, especially rivers, would become the primary way of constructing a cognitive map. Harrison (1949: 135) asked a group of Penan foragers in Borneo – a tropical forest environment, albeit one with considerable relief – to construct a map of their territory with twigs and leaves for the purpose of tracking their annual settlement system. His rendering shows that rivers form the major feature of their cognitive map. In more open terrain, smoke from a camp's fires would also provide foragers with an easy way to locate themselves and find their way back to camp.

A second issue for colonizing foragers concerns the effect of having sufficient time to learn an environment. What if individual foragers do not have sufficient time to learn a landscape? What if, by the time a boy reaches 12, an age at which he can accompany his father on hunting and landscape-learning forays, his band shifts their territory to someplace new, where even his father is a novice? Nelson (1986: 275–6) gives us a clue by contrasting the landscape knowledge systems of the Inuit and the Kutchin:

> The Eskimo devotes a lifetime to learning more and more about the habits of the animals and about the mobile sea ice on which he hunts, whereas the Kutchin spends a lifetime learning more and more about the landscape. The key to success in the high Arctic is knowledge of the game, current, ice, and weather – the major factors influencing resource availability; but in the boreal forest the key to success in hunting and trapping is knowledge of the landscape. The Indians must know where to find the trails, lakes, hills, valleys, forests, and meadows and the most stable concentrations of edible plants and game.

From this astute observation one might gather that where an adaptation forces movement into new terrain the ability to gather knowledge would be limited, and people would have to rely on a generalized and transferable system of knowledge of weather, animal behavior, and ecological relations that could be extrapolated from one area to another, rather than on region-specific knowledge. My guess is that in these circumstances people might very well develop cognitive maps that cover vast areas, but with only a few prominent landmarks and several major paths defined by geography – rivers, most notably. Within this landscape, my guess is also that a few known places would be used repeatedly, not necessarily because they are the best places, but simply because they are known and use of them reduces the risk that would be entailed in trying to locate critical resources, for example sources of raw material for stone tools. Risk reduction might be a more relevant factor for colonizing groups in new landscapes than for groups in known landscapes (Meltzer 2001).

Testing ideas about the effect of landscape learning against archaeological data is difficult. Most archaeological sites, especially those of ancient foragers, record long spans of time: we cannot see the first years of occupation without their effects being blotted out by the archaeological effects of later adaptations. Thus, we need to ask how landscape learning might affect large-scale patterns in the archaeology of a colonizing population. Two areas that may be useful here are studies of group size and mobility.

Group size

How many foragers does it take to learn an environment? In entering new land, it would obviously be useful to have as many people as possible out gathering information. Ethnographically known hunter-gatherers tend to live in groups of about 25 persons, or perhaps a bit larger. There could be a number of reasons for this (see Kelly 1995: 209–13), but Winterhalder's (1986) discussion of reducing the risk associated with foraging probably provides the most accurate explanation. Assuming that foragers share their food resources, Winterhalder argues that the greater the number of active foragers, the lower the risk of anyone going hungry, because someone will bring home something. But, of course, the more people there are, the more rapidly an environment is depleted of food, the lower the return rates of the foragers, and the higher the frequency of residential mobility. At some point, a balance has to be struck between reducing the risk associated with foraging and the rate of local resource depletion.

Using simulation, Winterhalder shows that even at high levels of variance in individual foraging rates there is not much reduction in post-sharing return rates after a group contains 7–8 foragers. When children and the elderly are accounted for, a group containing 7–8 active foragers translates into a residential group of about 25–30 persons (Kelly 1995). The so-called "magic number" of 25 appears to be grounded in the reality of foraging.

But this sets up another problem. A group of 25 is fine for foraging, but not for reproduction; it is probably too small to be demographically viable (Wobst 1974, 1976). Hunter-gatherers solved this problem by customs that ensured extensive social contacts (e.g. marriage practices that forced people to look elsewhere for mates, and seasonal aggregations where mates could be found). However, a colonizing hunter-gatherer population would in all likelihood be small, and individual foraging groups might be spread far and wide across the land. MacDonald (1998) argues that this is precisely the situation that would have resulted in long-distance social networks and mating distances for Folsom peoples (not a colonizing population, but certainly one that existed at a very low population density). Indeed, using ethnographic data MacDonald shows a strong inverse correlation between population density and mating distance: as population density declines, mating distance increases.

But wide social networks might have been very difficult to maintain under conditions of low population density and territorial shifting (see below), where the landscape may not be known well enough to permit accurate long-distance travel. This is a particular problem, because any such travel requires that foragers be able to predict what group will be where. Ethnographically known foragers can make such predictions because they have more-or-less redundant settlement patterns; members of a particular group can always be found at a particular spring or water-filled pan during the dry season, for example, or at a particular seed-gathering locality in the late summer, a stand of willows in the winter. They are not hard to find. But this may not have been possible for colonizing populations. Although colonizing foragers may have been more residentially mobile than later foragers (Surovell 2000), and hence may have increased the probability that they would run into one another, that seems too risky. Small groups who relied on chance for encountering other groups in which they could find mates may very well have found themselves alone and have become extinct. One way to reduce that risk would be to live in larger groups than are commonly recorded ethnographically. These larger residential groups may also have assisted with the landscape-learning issue by increasing the number of people searching a region at any one time. Some might even have been specialized information collectors. But this response to the demographic problem creates a problem alluded to above. The rate of local resource depletion would have increased and thus increased the need to move – into unknown territory at times, which would have started the process all over.

So, perhaps it is more likely that people lived in sets of small groups that were not spread far across a landscape and so could have remained in close social contact without placing such a strain on local foraging. I suspect that this pattern would be more likely than having groups of, say, 60 to 100 individuals living together, because those large groups would have lowered the immediate, i.e. daily, return rate of foraging, which in turn would have increased the social tensions that among ethnographically known foragers often lead to group fissioning. Small but socially linked sets of foraging groups would also have helped create a shareable knowledge base about the landscape.

However, this approach might assume that groups were moving as coordinated sets. If one small group ventured alone into new territory it would run the risk of extinction. But such coordinated movements seem unlikely, unless there were some process at work at a higher scale. Perhaps Beaton's (1991) notion of "megapatches" is useful here, in which foragers adapt to gross environmental categories and learn enough about the nature of animal and plant behavior in these environments to be able to transfer that knowledge and push migration along them. These environments might include such gross categories as coasts, rivers, mountains, plains, or deciduous forest. Clearly, at times, people moved into new environments, but perhaps that was a secondary adaptation. If this were how humans compensated for the landscape learning conundrum of colonization, then there should be some clear implications in terms of geographic patterns and dating of movements, as well as the geographic distribution of artifact styles.

Mobility

How mobile would a colonizing population be? The above hypothesis about group size has implications for mobility, for a larger group would more rapidly deplete local resources and require a higher degree of residential movement. Such movement would make it more difficult to acquire knowledge of a landscape and negate the use of previously acquired knowledge. In such a case, there might be less of a premium on acquiring landscape knowledge and more on resource knowledge. Elsewhere, in discussing the specific case of the colonization of North America I have suggested that residential mobility would have been high and that territories would have shifted frequently (Kelly and Todd 1988; Kelly 1996, 1999). This was a function of a hunting-adapted people moving into an environment that was more similar across larger areas than today's biomes, and with a fairly high animal biomass that was naive of human predators. Under such circumstances, we could expect hunters to move fairly quickly across a continent as a combination of hunting-related pressures and the late Pleistocene environmental changes (which almost certainly played a role in the extinctions) that conspired to reduce animal biomass locally and make hunting in virgin territory more attractive than remaining in place and accepting lower return rates. But, if this reconstruction is correct, the lifeway it depicts is partly a product of the particular historical circumstances surrounding the colonization of the western hemisphere – namely, that the colonization was by an Arctic-adapted people who had no choice but to move quickly into the lower forty-eight United States. Serious questions are now being raised about the timing of the opening of the ice-free corridor, and we now know that the west coast of North America was free of ice earlier and more extensively than previously thought, perhaps making the latter a more viable route than the former. But in either case, people would have moved along a fairly narrow geographic passage into an environment south of the ice sheets that would have been significantly different from the Arctic they had just left.

In cases elsewhere in the world, people may have moved into environments that were more similar to the one they were leaving, and they could have moved into them more slowly. The colonization of western Beringia was very slow compared with that of the western hemisphere (Kelly 1996, 1999). The colonization of Australia, as another example, would have entailed migration of people from New Guinea who would have moved between roughly similar environments and been able to make a slow transition to the deserts and other environments of Australia. Likewise, the movement from New Guinea to northern Australia would not have seemed such an "all-or-nothing" affair as it may have for the colonizing population moving south of the ice sheets in North America. Not all colonizing populations confront the same landscape learning, mobility, or demographic problems.

However, it is likely that most colonizing populations would have experienced relatively high population growth, as Surovell (2000) has argued for North American Paleoindians. Such high growth would certainly not be out of line with that of other organisms that find themselves occupying an empty niche in new lands. Such growth would promote a continuous colonizing push across a continent by placing demographic pressure upon a local food base. So, in any case, we can expect a colonizing population to find itself moving into unknown terrain and to need to adapt itself to that circumstance. A key factor here, of course, is what sorts of constraints this places on a population. What do foragers need to know about their landscape and what do they have to do to get information?

Conclusions

The rate of colonization is critical because, if it were fast, and it does appear to have been so in some cases, people would not have been able to learn their landscapes, since learning requires personal experience that is gathered from a very early age and that is encoded in folklore that requires some time depth for its development. If the environment cannot be learned, then people will need to rely upon a more generalized knowledge, resulting in a more regionally uniform, and perhaps less "optimal," adaptation (see Webb and Rindos 1997).

As an aside, the lack of a knowledge system rooted in geography would also result in a lack of geographically based ritual (and, I suspect, a lack of rock art) and the lack of a geographically based esoteric knowledge system. That is, a landscape mnemonic such as the Australian Dreamtime would not have been present in a rapidly moving colonizing population. (There's much more to Dreamtime theology than its function as a mapping device, but the point is that a theology could not contain a landscape component if sufficient time did not exist to permit development of landscape-based stories.) I would also expect that logistical mobility would provide a more rapid way to acquire landscape knowledge, since it is most likely that men would not be burdened with children and could therefore move faster and farther, and take more risks – as when they might try to return to camp by dead-reckoning their way from a river across a mountain range.

Regions that presented especially difficult landscape learning challenges may have been avoided if the risk associated with them was perceived as higher than some other area or the current "megapatch." My best guess, then, is that large-scale movements would be along easily traceable geographic features – rivers would be the most obvious one (see Anderson and Gillam 2000), but also linear mountain chains, or clear ecological zones, Beaton's "megapatches." But in addition to expecting colonizers to move along environment "corridors" whose resources were known, we might also expect them to move where the landscape is more easily internalized into a cognitive map. This means, coincidentally, that the nature of the adaptation brought with a colonizing population will have a strong influence over the initial choices made.

But if some areas are not considered habitable to a colonizing population because of perceived landscape learning impediments, then this also means that a colonizing population will have a smaller area of land available to it than might otherwise appear to be the case. If, for example, a colonizing population had a coastal adaptation, it might consider movement into the interior to be too risky if that interior presented (or appeared to present) relatively large landscape learning problems. Consequently, that population could be expected to move fairly rapidly, because they have for all intents and purposes relatively little land at their disposal.

It is difficult to rank environments on a simple scale of landscape learning difficulty. In general, I would expect land without significant topographic relief or substantial waterways to be difficult places to learn initially (this doesn't mean that they can't be learned – obviously people did in places like Australia's Western Desert – it just means that, given a choice and holding other factors constant, people would turn away from such environments in favor of another). Heavy forest cover might make such flat landscapes even more difficult. But at the same time I would expect places with too much topography or places without any obvious "scheme" to their topography also to be avoided. Again, heavy forest cover could make this sort of topographic situation worse.

Weather and seasonality would also condition the ease with which a landscape could be learned and cognitive maps generated. Arctic environments, for example, are not very forgiving; misjudgments might have severe results. Less seasonal environments, on the other hand, might tolerate greater error and permit one to move into an environment with less knowledge of it. This could mean that migration would be faster in tropical environments than in Arctic environments. But water will be another major conditioning variable. One can go without food for some time, but not for very long without water or some viable plant substitute, such as melons or water-engorged tubers. Extreme deserts could have been perceived by a colonizing group as entailing too much risk, and may have been colonized later, through demographic pressure, but also more slowly, as they are explored (whether this would be detectably slow using the chronometric scales of archaeology is hard to tell).

In closing, let me bring up a problem that Meltzer (2001) deals with in greater detail. In this paper we have treated landscape learning as a problem at the level of the individual standing before a vast prairie or mountain chain that he or she knows nothing about. We have asked, how would such individuals behave? What choices would they make? There is, perhaps, no other way to ask the question; or perhaps the fear (or excitement) that such a situation might generate leaves us too exhilarated to think of it in any other way. And even though the archaeological record is the conglomerate product of individual behaviors, it is not clear whether that record reflects those decisions or whether it reflects some other level of behavior – simple return-rate maximization or risk-minimization approaches, for example. Maybe landscape learning is a relevant problem, but it is not one that can be studied from archaeological data. Other chapters in this volume will take up that torch.

Acknowledgments

Marcel Kornfeld, David Meltzer, Marcy Rockman, James Steele, and Todd Surovell provided comments on previous drafts of this paper. They are not responsible for any of its shortcomings, but they have increased my knowledge of the landscape of hunter-gatherers and colonizing populations.

Note

1 Actually, Tindale (1974: 87) offers a brief account of the Nakako, who moved into an area that had been abandoned for some time. Unfortunately, all Tindale says of this group is that 'they found themselves unable to find mining places for new stone. They had, therefore, been compelled to glean old implement stone pieces from archaeological campsites and remake them...'

References

Allen, G.L. (1999) "Spatial Abilities, Cognitive Maps, and Wayfinding: Bases for Individual Differences in Spatial Cognition and Behavior," in R.G. Golledge (ed.) *Wayfinding Behavior: Cognitive Mapping and other Spatial Processes*, Baltimore: Johns Hopkins University Press.

Anderson, D.G. and J.C. Gillam (2000) "Paleoindian Colonization of the Americas: Implications from an Examination of Physiography, Demography and Artifact Distribution," *American Antiquity* 65:43–66.

Beaton, J.M. (1991) "Colonizing Continents: Some Problems from Australia and the Americas," in T.D. Dillehay and D.M. Meltzer (eds) *The First Americans: Search and Research*, Boca Raton, FL: CRC Press.

Berndt, R. and C. Berndt (1964) *World of the First Australians*, Chicago: University of Chicago Press.

Biesele, M. (1993) *Women Like Meat: The Folklore and Foraging Ideology of the Kalahari Ju/ 'hoan*, Bloomington, IN: Indiana University Press.

Blurton Jones, N., Hawkes, K., and P. Draper (1994) "Foraging Returns of !Kung Adults and Children: Why didn't !Kung Children Forage?" *Journal of Anthropological Research* 50:217–48.

Boas, F. (1888) *The Central Eskimo*, Washington, DC: Bureau of American Ethnology (Annual Report 6).

Borgoras, W. (1922) "Chukchee," in F. Boas (ed.) *Handbook of American Indian Languages, Part II*, Washington, DC: Bureau of American Ethnology (Bulletin 40).

Brown, C.H. (1983) "Where do Cardinal Direction Terms Come From?" *Anthropological Linguistics* 25:121–61.

Carpenter, E.S. (1955) "Eskimo Space Concepts," *Explorations* 5:131–45.

Fowler, C. (1992) "In the Shadow of Fox Peak: an Ethnography of the Cattail-Eater Northern Paiute People of Stillwater Marsh," US Department of the Interior, Fish and Wildlife Service, Region 1, Cultural Resource Series No. 5, Washington, DC: US Government Printing Office.

—— (1999) "Ecological/Cosmological Knowledge and Land Management among Hunter-Gatherers," in R.B. Lee and R. Daly (eds) *The Cambridge Encyclopedia of Hunter-Gatherers*, Cambridge: Cambridge University Press.

Garth, T.R. (1953) "Atsugewi Ethnography," *University of California Anthropological Records* 14(2):129–212.

Golledge, R.G. (1999) "Human Wayfinding and Cognitive Maps," in R.G. Golledge (ed.) *Wayfinding Behavior: Cognitive Mapping and Other Spatial Processes*, Baltimore: Johns Hopkins University Press.

Harrison, T. (1949) "Notes on Some Nomadic Punans," *Sarawak Museum Journal* 5:130–46.

Hill, D. (1997) "Finding your Way in Longgu: Geographical Reference in a Solomon Islands Language," in G. Senft (ed.) *Referring to Space: Studies in Austronesian and Papuan Languages*, Oxford Studies in Anthropological Linguistics, Oxford: Clarendon Press.

Holmberg, A. (1969) *Nomads of the Long Bow: The Siriono of Eastern Bolivia*, Garden City, NY: Natural History Press.

Holt, C. (1946) "Shasta Ethnography," *University of California Anthropological Records* 3(4):299–349.

Honigmann, J. (1949) *Culture and Ethos of Kaska Society*, New Haven: Yale University Press (Publications in Anthropology 40).

Kelly, R.L. (1983) "Hunter-Gatherer Mobility Strategies," *Journal of Anthropological Research* 39:277–306.

—— (1995) *The Foraging Spectrum: Diversity in Hunter-Gatherer Lifeways*, Washington, DC: Smithsonian Institution Press.

—— (1996) "Ethnographic Analogy and Migration to the Western Hemisphere," in T. Akazawa and E. Szathmary (eds) *Prehistoric Dispersals of Mongoloid Peoples*, Tokyo: Oxford University Press.

—— (1999) "Hunter-Gatherer Foraging and Colonization of the Western Hemisphere," *Anthropologie* 37(1):143–53.

Kelly, R.L., Rabedimy, J.-F., and L.A. Poyer (1999) "The Mikea of Southwestern Madagascar," in R.B. Lee and R. Daly (eds) *The Cambridge Encyclopedia of Hunter-Gatherers*, Cambridge: Cambridge University Press.

Kelly, R.L. and L.C. Todd (1988) "Coming into the Country: Early Paleoindian Hunting and Mobility," *American Antiquity* 53:231–44.

Marshall, L. (1976) *The !Kung of Nyae Nyae*, Cambridge, MA: Harvard University Press.

MacDonald, D.H. (1998) "Subsistence, Sex, and Cultural Transmission in Folsom Culture," *Journal of Anthropological Archaeology* 17:217–39.

McKennan, R. (1959) *The Upper Tanana Indians*, New Haven: Yale University Press (Publications in Anthropology 55).

Meltzer, D. (in press) "Modeling the Initial Colonization of the Americas: Issues of Scale, Demography, and Landscape Learning," in G.A. Clark and M. Barton (eds) *Pioneers on the Land: the Initial Human Colonization of the Americas*, Tucson, AZ: University of Tucson Press.

Murdoch, J. (1892) *Ethnological Results of the Point Barrow Expedition*, Ninth Annual Report of the Bureau of American Ethnology for the Years 1887–1888. Washington, DC.

Nelson, E. (1899) *The Eskimo About Bering Strait*, Bureau of American Ethnology Annual Report for 1896–1897, Vol. 18, No. 1. Washington, DC.

Nelson, R. (1986) *Hunters of the Northern Forest*, 2nd edition, Chicago: University of Chicago Press.

Osgood, C. (1936) *The Distribution of the Northern Athapaskan Indians*, New Haven: Yale University Press (Publications in Anthropology 7):3–23.

Osgood, C. (1959) *Ingalik Mental Culture*, New Haven, MA: Yale University Press (Publications in Anthopology 16).

Pearsall, M. (1950) *Klamath Childhood and Education*, Berkeley, CA: University of California Press (Anthropological Records 9):339–51.

Petersen, R. (1984) "East Greenland Before 1950," in D. Damas (ed.) *Handbook of North American Indians. Volume 5: Arctic*, Washington, DC: Smithsonian Institution Press.

Poyer, L. and R.L. Kelly (2000) "Mystification of the Mikea: Constructions of Foraging Identity in Southwest Madagascar," *Journal of Anthropological Research* 56:163–85.

Silberbauer, G. (1981) *Hunter and Habitat in the Central Kalahari Desert*, Cambridge: Cambridge University Press.

Surovell, T. (2000) "Early Paleoindian Women, Children, Mobility, and Fertility," *American Antiquity* 65:493–508.

Tindale, N. (1974) *Aboriginal Tribes of Australia*, Berkeley: University of California Press.

Tonkinson, R. (1978) *The Mardudjara Aborigines*, New York: Holt, Rinehart and Winston.

Turney-High, H.H. (1941) *Ethnography of the Kutenai*, Washington, DC: Memoirs of the American Anthropological Association 56.

Webb, R.E. and D. J. Rindos (1997) "The Mode and Tempo of the Initial Human Colonization of Empty Landscapes: Sahul and the Americas Compared," in C.M. Barton and G.A. Clark (eds) *Rediscovering Darwin: Evolutionary Theory and Archeological Explanation*, Archeological Papers of the American Anthropological Association No. 7, Arlington, VA.

Winterhalder, B. (1986) "Diet Choice, Risk, and Food Sharing in a Stochastic Environment," *Journal of Anthropological Archaeology* 5:369–92.

Wobst, H.M. (1974) "Boundary Conditions for Paleolithic Social Systems: A Simulation Approach," *American Antiquity* 39:147–78.

—— (1976) "Locational Relationships in Paleolithic Society," *Journal of Human Evolution* 5:49–58.

4

TRACKING THE ROLE OF PATHWAYS IN THE EVOLUTION OF A HUMAN LANDSCAPE

The St Croix Riverway in ethnohistorical perspective

María Nieves Zedeño and Richard W. Stoffle

> For untold thousands of years we travelled on foot over rough paths
> and dangerously unpredictable roads, not simply as peddlers or commu-
> ters or tourists, but as men and women for whom the path and road
> stood for some intense experience: freedom, new human relationships,
> a new awareness of the landscape. The road offered a journey into the
> unknown that could end up allowing us to discover who we were and
> where we belonged.
>
> J. B. Jackson, "Roads Belong in the Landscape," 1994

In his elegant essay "Roads Belong in the Landscape" geographer J. B. Jackson (1994: 189–205) observes that, in the evolving Western notion of space, the path and the road became increasingly neglected and outclassed by the prestige of private space and the comfort of permanent settlement. Whereas before medieval times the road implied food and freedom, and the wanderer had a rightful place in the social order, modernity has imposed on our society a view of the road as "an unsightly, elongated and crooked space," whose only role is to take us from one safe place to another, the road itself being dangerous and unwieldy. Moreover, those who belong on the road by choice or need – the transient and the homeless – have been set in a social class apart from, and incompre-hensible to, the house dweller. Only recently have geographers and historians of the landscape begun to recognize that the road and the path are places in their own right, with unique activity, social intercourse, and material culture associations.

Anthropological studies of human–land interactions and social space, too, have favored the settlement over the pathway (e.g. Pearson and Richards 1994; Roberts 1996). However, well-developed road systems such as the Roman roads in Italy (Laurence 1999), the Inca roads in South America (Beck 1979; Hyslop 1984), the Chaco Canyon roads in the US Southwest (Gabriel 1991; Kincaid 1983), or the

Mesoamerican causeways (Santley 1991; Trombold 1991) have received some attention. These studies analyze the form, function, extent, and spatial organization of roads to reconstruct the evolution of transportation systems vis-à-vis the development of wealth, sociopolitical complexity and, to a lesser extent, hierarchical religious systems. Studies of American Indian trail systems, on the other hand, address trade (e.g. Davis 1961; Riley and Manson 1991) and warfare (e.g. McClintock 1923; Myer 1928). Yet, the main analytical unit, the pathway, is frequently treated as a functional and convenient means to an end, such as the movement of information, goods, and armies, rather than a central integrative feature in the development of human landscapes. Some exceptions are the classic American Indian thoroughfare surveys (Hulbert 1900, 1902), the modern landscape studies of scenic rural roads in North America (e.g. Copps 1995), and the phenomenological recreation of prehistoric landscapes in Europe (e.g. Tilley 1994).

Here we highlight the role of the pathway in the opening of unfamiliar lands and its evolution from newly cut trail to social and political tool of resource control among mobile or transhumant societies. The central argument is that pathways (trails, roads, waterways, portages, and thoroughfares) organize the ways in which humans use and modify nature; in this process humans develop characteristic social relations that are tied to, influence, and are influenced by the surroundings (e.g. Kidder 2000: 16–20). Elsewhere, Zedeño (2000) has suggested that human landscapes may be analyzed through progressive contextualization (after Vayda 1983) – that is, beginning with one activity or resource type, and progressively documenting connections between that activity or resource and other activities or resources. We apply this approach to pathways to document how people develop attachments with the surroundings and how these attachments, in turn, constrain and enhance social spaces and social relations among mobile or transhumant groups, with especial attention to the Ojibway of the western Great Lakes. First, we briefly discuss pathway development and potential landmark associations. Next, we draw on comparative ethnographic and historic literature to investigate the kinds of behaviors and meanings associated with pathway uses. And last, we illustrate the discussion with the archaeology, history, and ethnography of the St Croix Riverway of Wisconsin and Minnesota.

Rootedness, pathways, and learning

There was a time in American anthropology when mobile or transhumant groups were not considered to be attached to any particular piece of land. Julian Steward, for example, invested a great deal of effort to document transhumant patterns among the Western Shoshone and Paiute groups of Nevada and California (Steward 1938). Even though Steward described how geographically distinct bands returned to the same places year after year and followed the same paths, he was convinced that these repeated moves were dictated by kinship ties rather than by attachment to place. The far-reaching impact of this anthropological view of transhumance is best illustrated in a statement made by Justice Black in Shoshone Indians *v.* United States (324 US 335, 357, 1945, cited in Barney 1974: 14):

Ownership meant no more to them than to roam the land as a great common, and to possess and enjoy it in the same way that they possessed and enjoyed sunlight and the west wind and the feel of spring in the air. Acquisitiveness, which develops a law of real property, is an accomplishment only of the "civilized."

Thus absence of settled life, of homogeneous and bounded territories, and of property was often interpreted as rootlessness. Indeed, transhumance often required flexible territorial boundary maintenance strategies wherein geographically, politically, and ethnically diverse groups were able to access the resources found in joint-use areas; but as Kroeber (1925: 981) observed, the manner in which these strategies shaped ownership of, attachment to, or what we call "rootedness" in a place escaped the anthropologists of that time. Data collected since have changed the ways in which anthropologists conceptualize human–land interactions, but it is only with some difficulty that we accept the challenge of incorporating non-Western worldviews of land use into research design or data interpretation.

The concept of rootedness, as used here, denotes a process whereby individuals or groups develop relationships of interdependence with places and resources; such relationships, in turn, require the accumulation of landscape knowledge, the sociocultural sanctioning of specific human–land interactions borne out of that knowledge, and the sharing or transmission of knowledge and sanctions. Thus, rootedness encompasses spatial, cultural, and historical dimensions of land and resource use. We suggest that because the pathways of transhumant groups are spatially confined, are traversed time after time, and often are associated with specific social sectors and activities, they constitute a material manifestation of these dimensions.

Pathways may be conceived of as material links in spatial networks that connect people to places, resources, and objects. Pathway networks constitute the spaces humans devote to communication (Whittlesey 1998: 24) with other humans, with nature, and with the supernatural. Pathways order human–land interactions in two ways: first, they link places, resources, and objects sequentially and hierarchically; and second, they determine the confines wherein humans can engage repeatedly in particular experiences and activities (Feld 1996: 103; Pandya 1990; Tilley 1994: 30). Through repeated use and continued development of pathway networks humans accumulate knowledge and experiences that generate a sense of attachment to fixed places and resources, even though these are not located, in the strictest sense, within the bounded, exclusive, and homogeneous polygon frequently referred to as "territory" (Zedeño 1997).

Not all pathway networks determine the same behaviors or may be used for all activities, and not everyone can take the same pathway. Therefore, pathway networks vary in formal properties, in behavioral and cultural associations, and in specific life histories. An analysis of the historical, formal, and behavioral variability of pathways can expand our understanding of the processes and mechanisms through which humans learn about, set roots in, and transform the natural landscape.

Pathway development

Before modern means of communication formalized and permanently prescribed routes and transportation modes, just about every activity that took people away from their familiar environment brought along the opportunity for landscape learning (see Chapter 1). In that context, pathway networks likely developed in tandem with exploratory or scouting activities. In his survey of Indian thoroughfares in the North American Midwest, Hulbert (1902: 14) observed that animal trails offered the most visible and easily accessible exploratory or scouting routes. The American elk, for example, open least-resistance trails along escarpments or through heavily vegetated areas; such trails could save the hunter or the scout some travel time and effort. Longer and wider least-resistance paths made by the roaming buffalo were not only used by Indian hunters and explorers but also defined the territorial identity of historic tribes like the Plains Cree (Milloy 1991). Famous buffalo roads such as the Big Bone Lick in Kentucky and the French Lick and South Fork roads in Tennessee were followed every year by diverse tribes who flocked to the springs to make salt. According to Myer (1928: 741–3), these buffalo roads determined the routes of seasonal movement, pilgrimage, trade and transportation, migration, and, ultimately, the location of Indian and non-Indian settlements.

In addition to accessibility and visibility, animal trails offered important landscape learning opportunities, including the mapping of wildlife ranges, water sources, potential camping locales, and potential land-use competitors, human or animal. Furthermore, by following animal trails and observing animal behaviors, people could learn about the properties of unfamiliar plants. For example, the Ojibway, who have a vast botanical knowledge that goes back numerous generations, learned to distinguish edible and medicinal plants by watching what sick or wounded animals eat and how they interact with plants (Zedeño *et al.* 2001b). The Ojibway, as well as other Algonquian-speaking groups, think of animals as consummate "plant doctors" and landscape teachers in general, and thus they observe and follow their actions very closely, especially if they find themselves in an unfamiliar environment. Valuable knowledge learned from animals extends to the role played by active environment modifiers, like beaver, on the preservation of dry potages and navigable water levels (Mann 1998), among other trail features.

Alternatively, or in complement to animal trails, the natural topography provided access routes. Old Indian trails usually followed canyons and washes, valleys, mountain passes, or navigable rivers (Hinsdale 1931). Hulbert (1902: 14–23) observed that Indian trails were primarily located on high ground, following hilltops and ridges, where the water was most quickly shed, the wind swept off the snow in the winter and the leaves in the summer, and the forest suffered the least from annual fires. These trails also afforded visibility and safety from enemy parties, who could easily hide and set an ambush in lower, more densely forested areas. Low-lying trails were the available option on flat terrain, and these were far more circuitous than high-ground trails because of the need to avoid swamps and other obstacles. In the woodlands of the upper Midwest, navigable waterways formed a complex pathway network that served as the principal mode of long-distance communication in warm seasons. In the winter months, when the secondary and tertiary waterways were frozen, people used land trails that paralleled the waterways as closely as the topography would allow; sometimes winter trails also crossed thick ice. The key was to know which trail to use during each season. Ojibway pathway-use behaviors suggest that the mobile Indian groups could easily alternate between water and land trails.

Among historic transhumant groups such as the Ojibway, exploration and scouting were a customary part of the annual cycle. Task and family groups moved across as broad an area as was required to participate in traditional subsistence economies, the fur trade, social obligations, and war; distances of as much as 600 miles (960 km) of waterway could be covered in a seasonal journey (e.g. from the Red River, Minnesota to Lake Huron, Michigan [Tanner 1994: 30–40]). Exploratory activities associated with the annual cycle resulted in the addition of "fallback" or potentially useful land to the group's land base that might or might not have been exploited or colonized at a later time. As explained in the case study below, fallback areas increased in importance in the eighteenth century, when the Ojibway bands began to expand west and south of Lake Superior because of war and the development of the fur trade (Warren 1984: 126).

Although known trails may have traversed fallback areas, complex and localized pathway networks did not develop until new areas were colonized or incorporated into the group's land base and traffic increased in tandem with regular resource use. Heavily trafficked pathways were maintained and upgraded: stones, cairns, petroglyphs, trail-marker trees, stepping stones on canoe landings, rope and hand-and-foot rails, and wooden bridges were sometimes placed along land and water trails (Hinsdale 1931: 3, 12; Ritzenthaler 1965). Paths that were used regularly and for long periods of time tended to increase in width and depth or even move slightly away from their original location. The resulting trail track was distinct from its surroundings by being clear of trees, compacted, and lower than the rest of the ground (Hulbert 1902: 21). Many of the old trails were eventually widened to allow wagon and motorized vehicle traffic. Some of these trails served as blueprints for railroads as well. A feature associated with the heavily trafficked pathways that is also observable today along modern roads and railroads is the vegetation that characteristically colonizes soils on the disturbed, but not hardened, edges of trail tracks.

The transformation of water bodies into waterways followed a behavioral rationale similar to the development of land trails, but the former shaped prehistoric and historic land-use strategies and modified social spaces in unique and far-reaching ways. First, waterways facilitated long-distance travel in a relatively short time; second, they allowed entire families with small children to move about with ease; and third, they permitted travel parties to carry larger loads than would have been possible by foot travel. Horses were brought into the upper Midwest by European trading houses early in the historic period, but the dense, wet woodlands were not easily traversed on horseback. Thus, waterways were the preferred mode of transportation in this and other regions irrigated by navigable rivers. Waterways presented the traveler with great challenges, which the Jesuit Fathers who first canoed the Mississippi River tributaries described on many occasions: shallow waters in some seasons and thin ice in others, precipitous rapids, whirlpools, and treacherous crossings (Verwyst 1886). On the other hand, waterways naturally facilitated life on the path by providing fast travel and ready access to food and shelter. Not surprisingly, the flow of the fur trade was sustained, for the better part of three centuries, primarily by the voyageurs whose livelihood largely depended on the ability of the Indian scouts and trade partners to negotiate the waterways (Nute 1969).

Of the numerous features that waterway networks possess, three were the most important for the canoe traveler: portages, or the land bridges between water bodies or around impassable rapids; landings, or accessible banks where canoes and loads could be pulled off the water and onto dry ground; and river crossings, which were placed at points of shallow water or where accumulated sediment would slow down the force of the current, thus allowing canoers, pedestrians, or pack animals to move safely across the river (Hulbert 1902). Portages, in particular, deserve special attention both for their strategic value in trade and territorial politics and for their cosmological meaning in aboriginal society. For example, Mann (1998) observes that the portage between the Maumee and Wabash Rivers in Indiana not only permitted the flow of people and goods, but was also considered the home of spirit beings that controlled access to the portage route and the resources around and beyond it. For the historic Miami Indians, this was a holy, "glorious portal," where their main village stood and from where they could access both the Great Lakes and the Mississippi River. The Miami had rituals specifically designed to harness the power of the portage spirits in order to obtain safe passage to the Maumee-Wabash riverway. Among Europeans and Americans, portages had yet another practical use: they were strategic locations for controlling trade and human traffic. Consequently, portages were selected as the sites for building forts and posts (Kidder 2000). The act of building these facilities on ancient portages, in turn, carried strong messages of ideological and political control.

In addition to portages, landings, and crossings, each waterway had its own landmarks, including rapids, waterfalls, caves and crevices, ledges, dalles, islands, narrows, and old channels, most of which had geographic, behavioral, and symbolic associations. Landmarks found on waterways traversed during subsistence and other cyclical activities were systematically used for long periods of time; the Ojibway occupational history of the interior Rainy River and Lake systems dividing Minnesota and Ontario provides excellent examples of this pattern (e.g. Hickerson 1967; Richner 1992). The Great Lakes waterways, on the other hand, offered a different kind of travel and experience. The cosmopolitan canoe trail that followed the south shore of Lake Superior, from the Sault Ste Marie in the east to Fond du Lac in the west, linked important villages, burial grounds, ceremonial sites, trading houses, missions, and forts, and also incorporated outstanding topographic features. In fact, the significance of this trail was formalized by the Ojibway in their origin and migration traditions and was depicted in the sacred bark scrolls of the Midewiwin medicine society (Dewdney 1975: 86). Nevertheless, differential use patterns of specific landmark types, such as dunes, islands, or cliff faces, along the lakeshore canoe trail mirrors those patterns recorded on the interior riverways (Zedeño 1999).

Life on the path: behavioral and cultural variability

While topography certainly influenced the physical layout and landmark associations of pathways, and availability of natural resources justified efforts of opening or traversing them, the uses that humans made of the paths in turn influenced their inter-actions with, and transformations of, different portions of landscape through time. There are myriad reasons why people would take particular paths, but these may be classified into four broad behavioral categories: (1) movement, or the sequence of short-term, seasonal, cyclical, and multidirectional, everyday-life activities under-taken at spatially discrete locations; (2) journey, or prolonged, multipurpose travel; (3) pilgrimage, or bi-directional, single-purpose travel; and (4) migration, or unidirec-tional and permanent relocation. These categories are not mutually exclusive; on the contrary, they may combine sequentially, spatially, or functionally according to the specific strategies for exploration and colonization used by a given group.

Everyday pathtaking

Networks used for everyday activities are a criss-cross of trails traversed frequently and for relatively short distances, or seasonally and for longer distances. Activities range from water fetching to gardening, and from hunting and plant collecting to social gathering. Movement creates strong place attachments and stable social relations; because everyday and cyclical activity pathways are used regularly and repeatedly, they define the confines of used spaces, the behaviors allowed in those spaces, and the iden-tity of the users. For example, in Death Valley, California, people normally used path-ways for every kind of activity; families and even individuals owned their trails and had to ask for permission to use other people's trails.[1] Among the Pintupi of Australia, kin groups who descend from a common ancestor own waterholes and the trails that connect to them; the trail, in this particular case, symbolizes the tie to the ancestor. Pintupis, too, expect to be asked for permission to use their trails (Myers 1986). Trail ownership may not develop until an area has been colonized by a particular group. Yet, ownership may shape colonization of already occupied areas in two ways: first, by defining use rights between "old settlers" and "newcomers," and, second, by predeter-mining areas available for resource exploitation or colonization by newcomers. In both cases, ownership may curtail the process of landscape knowledge acquisition by individuals or groups that plan to migrate or expand their land base.

Journeys

Journeys are the most complex and varied of all categories. Journeys may be under-taken by individuals, gender-specific groups, age-specific groups, heterogeneous groups, or specialists (e.g. traders, doctors, priests, or runners). In terms of duration, journeys tend to last from a few weeks to months or even years and may take people great distances from their homelands. Therefore, journeys are infrequent, ranging from once-in-a-lifetime to annual occurrences. Pathway networks associated with journeys are far reaching. They may be either circuitous or longitudinal and frequently combine several means of travel, including water, land, and even altered-state dreaming (Brody 1998). Regardless of frequency of occurrence or duration, all journey types furnish valuable opportunities for acquiring landscape knowledge, for identifying potential areas for future exploitation or colonization, and for expanding social networks.

Once-in-a-lifetime journeys are those that mark changes in the individual's life cycle. Among the Sault Ste Marie Ojibway, a boy would take the vision quest path at the time of his initiation. This path ended at a high point, usually on a dune or ridge, overlooking Lake Superior. There the boy would build a seclusion hut where he would spend some time trying to envision his purpose in life (Zedeño *et al.* 2001b). A male seclusion hut still stood on Au Sable Dunes, now in Pictured Rocks National Lakeshore, Michigan, in the mid-1800s (Gilman 1836). Contemporary Australian Aborigines of the Western Desert may extend the coming-of-age journey over several years during which they build social networks, acquire landscape knowledge, and develop place attachments that last a lifetime (Myers 1986). Other individuals may undertake journeys at different times in their lives; for example, Ojibway medicine men prescribe medicinal plants and water from distant sources, so that the patient must travel far to find medicine. The rationale is that healing power is in the journey as much as in the medicine. An important individual journey that cross-cut ethnic groups was that of runners, who were in charge of recording events and transferring information over long distances.

Individual journeys have special landmark associations and often involve leaving offerings on inconspicuous places along the path, such as rock crevices, ledges, or caves. Chemehuevi runners of the Mojave Desert had their own trails and sites, marked by the knotted string design in rock art that denotes event recording (Laird 1976). The Southern Paiute and Hualapai Salt Song Trail, a funerary chant with clear geographic referents, takes the soul of the dead across the Colorado River and the Mojave Desert of California before leading it to heaven (Laird 1976). The trail connects prominent landmarks on both sides of the river, and in historic times it fostered political alliances and economic cooperation between these ethnic groups. Landmarks may also denote pathway ownership or use rights, as is the case of certain Southern Paiute ceremonial and runner trails.

Gender- or task-specific journeys, such as the warpath, usually involved long-distance travel that could take months or even years. The warpath afforded an opportunity for males to hunt, scout, and trade, as well as avenge offenses or harass their enemies (Tanner 1994). In historic times, the warpath took pressure away from marginally productive areas where Indians had been forced to settle and farm, as occurred in the overpopulated Pawnee villages of Nebraska during the early 1800s (Wishart 1985). Characteristic features of the warpath were hiding places (caves, crevices); message-carrying petroglyphs, pictographs, and bark scroll caches; sweat lodges; dance circles; and warrior burial and scalp-hanging scaffolds (Bray 1967; Adams 1961; Tanner 1994). Hulbert (1902) distinguished warpaths from other trails because they pointed in the direction of enemy territory; yet, most of these paths doubled as scouting, journeying, and migrating routes during peacetime.

In the Great Lakes, group or family journeys took people away from population centers, particularly during epidemics. These journeys, too, were useful for networking and scouting, as indicated in Ojibway pictographic narratives of travel incidents (Densmore 1979: 180). Yet another type of journey involves dreaming or out-of-body traveling. Both North American and Australian groups recognize dream trails as having a physical reality equal to that of land or water trails; importantly, dream trails have landmark associations that range from old trees to rock formations and from animal tracks to rock art sites (e.g. Brody 1998; Myers 1986; Stoffle *et al.* 1995).

Attachment to place may derive from experiences lived during individual and group journeys. Encountering strange people, animals, or spirits, witnessing unusual natural phenomena, or simply learning new landscape features are experiences that form the fabric of traditional oral history and cultural memory. As Basso (1996) documents for the Cibecue Apache of Arizona, places or landmarks contain information on experiences lived while moving along and settling the land, moral lessons, and rules of everyday behavior that teach people how to live well and become wise. Therefore, landmarks connected to specific journeys complement and expand the cultural geographic referents accrued through everyday or cyclical movement and, altogether, help generate and maintain a sense of rootedness. The simple act of traversing the same path the ancestors once took and looking at the same landmarks the ancestors saw during their journeys helps contemporary people recapture their landscape-based history, knowledge, and cultural identity even though they may no longer live in the ancestral lands or follow traditional ways.

Pilgrimages

In contrast to journeys, pilgrimages constitute a very narrow behavioral category. Pilgrimages are unique in that they target a single destination, usually a holy place, and the pilgrim aims to attain some type of spiritual enlightening, pardon, or blessing. Pilgrimage pathway networks are structurally distinctive in that paths radiate in all directions from the locus of pilgrimage. These paths tend to be long and tortuous, fitting into the sacrificial demands of pilgrimaging (Stoddard 1997: 57). Pilgrimage pathways have unique landmarks, including shrines, sanctuaries, springs, and rock art, associated with specific activities pilgrims must engage in during their journey. Pathways to holy places may be owned or used by geographically or ethnically distinct groups. For example, the Zuni Salt Lake in New Mexico is a holy place for several ethnic groups (Ferguson and Hart 1985). Each ethnic group has its own pilgrimage trail, liturgical order, and landmarks associated with salt gathering. Similarly, pilgrimage pathways led diverse people to the pipestone (catlinite) quarries in western Minnesota. So sacred was this place for Woodland and Plains tribes that during wartime a truce was maintained so that pilgrims could safely access the quarries (Carver 1956: 99).

Migration

Finally, migration is a unidirectional journey that results in permanent relocation. In brief, migration is an informed, target-oriented strategy that presupposes at least partial (Anthony 1997: 24) or very detailed and specific (Ammerman and Cavalli-Sforza 1984) knowledge of the paths or routes that lead to attractive destinations and social settings as well as of the environmental conditions to be found in the new homeland. Such prior knowledge is crucial for the success of migration: consider, for example, how many illegal immigrants die each year while crossing the Sonoran Desert along the US–Mexico border because they lack basic knowledge of environmental conditions and safe routes. Therefore, migrants tend to follow pathways previously scouted by individuals or task groups and preferably target fallback areas. While long-distance travel routes help channel a stream of migrants moving from one place to another, the shorter pathways used in everyday and cyclical movement allow migrants to accumulate new landscape knowledge – provided, that is, that these paths are open to newcomers.

Migration responds to push and pull factors (Anthony 1997). In traditional societies, war was one of the strongest pushes for migration. The Iroquois wars of seventeenth-century North America, for example, displaced entire ethnic groups as far as 700 miles (1,100 km) from the main battle fronts around Lakes Erie and Ontario (Tanner 1986), thus permanently changing the geo-demographic structure of aboriginal societies in the Great Lakes and beyond. In peacetime, drought, disease, or lack of economic or social standing were important push factors. Pull factors, on the other hand, usually entailed real or perceived promise of progress, and ranged from economic gain to messianic visions of salvation (e.g. Cameron 1995; Kopytoff 1987; Kristiansen 1989). As discussed by Anthony (1997) and Kopytoff (1987), among others, push and pull factors may affect whole groups as well as specific sectors thereof, such as young male adults, unemployed adults of either sex and various ages, or disadvantaged families. The composition of the migrating population as well as the number of individual migrants, in turn, may influence the selection of routes to be taken as well as the appropriate mode of transportation.

Migration rarely replaces an old homeland with a new one. Rather, it contributes to an expansion of rootedness by allowing people to incorporate a whole new landscape learning experience in to the one they already have. This dynamic interaction is evident in origin and migration traditions that evolve as people add landscape knowledge to the original story in order to legitimize their "right-of-being" at a particular place, but without rescinding their roots in the ancestral homelands. For groups who are or were transhumant in a recent past, the incorporation of landscape references – ranging from general environmental descriptions to explicitly named landmarks – into an origin story is the highest expression of rootedness, because it helps to establish a god-given birthright to that land. At the same time, the retention of former homeland knowledge may serve to preserve the group's right to return should the migratory effort fail.

It is obvious from this brief narrative that attempting to devise a linear, causal relationship between the development of pathway networks and progressive attachment to place is simplistic at best, given that numerous activities conducted contemporaneously and sequentially along different pathways may generate rootedness. Yet, to understand better the role of pathways in the evolution of human landscapes one may begin by recognizing that, like the Ojibway who colonized the St Croix Riverway, people whose livelihood depended on movement and travel must have frequently stumbled onto a pass, a track, or a waterway never encountered before but nonetheless full of potential learning and living experiences.

Life history of a path: the St Croix Riverway

In the winter of 1661, the French *coureur du bois* Pierre Esprit Radisson and his party crossed the St Croix River to meet the tribes inhabiting the region to the west, the *Nadouecioux* or Dakota Sioux. Radisson's pioneer incursion into the Mississippi headwaters marked the opening of this remote country to the influence of European colonization. He described in some detail the regional tribes and assessed the potential for incorporating them into the fur trade system (Adams 1961). Almost twenty years later, Daniel Greysolon Sieur du Luth set out to explore this region, becoming the first white man to navigate the Bois Brulé–St Croix Riverway, from Lake Superior to the Mississippi River (Kellog 1917: 331). This trail was the shortest route connecting these major waterways, with a portage of only seven miles of marsh between the headwaters of the Brulé River and the upper St Croix Lake (Figure 4.1). By building a supply post on the portage in 1683, du Luth correctly anticipated that the St Croix River would figure prominently in the fur trade system; in 1695, Pierre Charles Le Sueur built another fort on Prairie Island (then Peleé Island), at the mouth of the St Croix, to protect the route and maintain the peace among the region's tribes (Nute 1930: 385; Wedel 1974: 159). Numerous winter posts manned by agents from the main French, English, and American trading houses flourished on the St Croix watershed at the turn of the nineteenth century. Beginning in 1837 the waterway was used for the transport of timber from the interior mills to the Mississippi River.

In addition to its crucial role in travel and transportation for native and European peoples, the St Croix River loosely corresponded to an early historic boundary between the Indian tribes inhabiting the forests to the northeast, those inhabiting the prairies and valleys to the southwest, and those located in the highlands and Mississippi headwaters to the northwest. This location not only made the St Croix watershed a place for intertribal rendezvous, as Radisson had observed in 1661, but also the central stage of a century-long tribal war. War centered on the struggle for the area's vast natural resources, in particular game, fur-bearing animals, and extensive wild rice beds; this event illustrates the role and significance of waterway access and control in the colonization of hinterlands by an expanding mobile group.

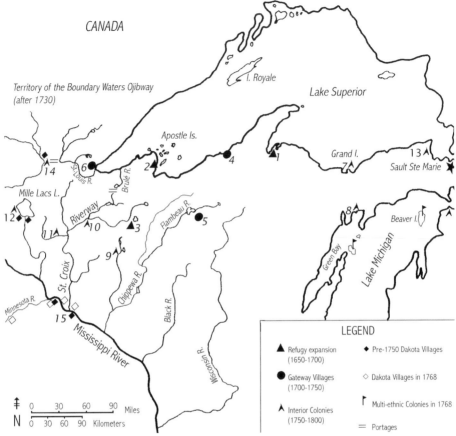

Figure 4.1 Ojibway colonization of the Mississippi headwaters region, 1660–1800: (1) Keweenaw Bay; (2) La Pointe; (3) Lac Courte Oreilles; (4) Ontonagon; (5) Lac du Flambeau; (6) Fond du Lac; (7) Grand Island; (8) Bay de Noc; (9) Cedar Lake; (10) Yellow River; (11) Snake River (Pokegama Lake); (12) Ysatis (Dakota) and Mille Lacs (Ojibway); (13) Whitefish Bay; (14) Sandy Lake; (15) Prairie (Peleé) Island (sources: Warren 1984; Tanner 1986).

Aboriginal occupants of the riverway

The diverse topography and geomorphology of the St Croix watershed, which encompasses 11,550 km², is the result of at least four different glacial epochs, but the present Brulé–St Croix channels represent the action of the final ice-melt overflow from terminal Pleistocene lakes that formed in the Lake Superior basin, particularly Lake Duluth. It is not known when the river became navigable; however, the presence of late Paleoindian materials and animal remains in the Sucices Site, near the Brulé–St Croix portage in Douglas County, Wisconsin, along with two other contemporary sites (one containing bones of *Bison occidentalis*) near tributaries on both sides of the middle St Croix (Mason 1997), suggests that the portage and waterway may have been open to traffic as early as 8,000 years ago. Occupation during the Archaic and early Woodland periods was ephemeral in the St Croix hinterlands. In contrast, the relative abundance of middle and late Woodland period sites dating between *c.*800 BC and AD 1400 indicates the development of a regional land-use pattern that emphasized riverine and lacustrine exploitation of wild rice and other resources; the summer aggregation/winter dispersion seasonal cycle required access to huge hunting grounds as well. Burial mound construction, plant manipulation, and marginal cultivation where possible were broadly incorporated during this period, but the regional land-use patterns were diverse in the Mississippi headwaters, corresponding to the landscape diversity found along the woodland-prairie ecotone (Johnson 1969; Stevenson *et al.* 1997). It appears that the late prehistoric inhabitants of the headwaters region and the St Croix watershed, in particular, had little contact with Mississippian groups other than through long-distance exchange of regionally available resources such as galena and catlinite. Thus, the regional land-use patterns continued undisturbed throughout the protohistoric period (AD 1400–1600). The connection between prehistoric inhabitants and protohistoric Dakota Sioux has been difficult to pinpoint archaeolog-ically; yet in the Mille Lacs area to the west of the St Croix River there is evidence of continuity in material culture and subsistence strategy until the mid-1700s (Birk and Johnson 1992). In the lower St Croix and upper Mississippi Rivers, aboriginal land use strategies of the Dakota Sioux continued into the nineteenth century (see Figure 4.1).

Two characteristics of the regional land-use pattern point to the use of the St Croix River as a thoroughfare since prehistoric times and possibly by more than one group. The first characteristic is the lack of population concentration along the riverway per se, except at numerous camps located just below the mid-river dalles and rapids, which are ideal fishing grounds (C. Clark, personal communication, 2001). Large semi-sedentary settlements, such as Ysatis, were located near the interior lakes and on the numerous navigable tributaries on either side of the river. The focus was, therefore, on the control of resources on the St Croix hinterland, even though a similar range of resources was available on the main valley. It is likely that the aboriginal inhabitants needed to be in close proximity to the shallower tributaries and lakes, where the fish would spawn and the rice beds would thrive, while keeping a relative and safe distance from, but still in close connection to, the riverway. The second characteristic is the presence of pictographs on caves or cliff faces on prehistoric sites along the middle and lower St Croix. Pictographs on interior waterways frequented by Indian travelers were noted by the Jesuit Fathers (Verwyst 1886), by Carver (1956), and by Nicollet (Bray 1967), among other explorers. Conway (1993) recently surveyed and recorded numerous pictographs along the boundary waterways. Early explorers also described the ritual significance of the pictographs for the Indian travelers of various ethnicities, who placed offerings of copper and other valuables on the water right below the pictographs to ensure safe passage. Thus, these landmarks and corresponding behav-iors seem to be of great antiquity.

Ojibway exploration and colonization of the St Croix Riverway, 1750–1836

The southwestern Ojibway, as a group with a more or less defined social, ethnic, and cultural identity, are entirely the result of early historic demographic processes that forced autonomous and highly mobile Algonquian-speaking bands to integrate through the migration and colonization of the Lake Superior shores early in the seventeenth century (Schenk 1997: 4, 17). Pushed west by the Iroquois War, the Ojibway readily took upon the exploration of potential hunting and fishing grounds beyond their core area or the village at Sault Ste Marie (*Bawating*) at the east end of Lake Superior. By the late 1600s they had already taken over the Apostle Islands fisheries on the south-central shore of this lake and were maintaining seasonal gardens at the village of La Pointe (Birmingham 1984). Seventeenth-century historical accounts, particularly Radisson's, place the Ojibway in northern Wisconsin, at Lac Courte Oreilles (then a predominantly Ottawa and Huron refugee settlement east of the St Croix River) by 1661 (see Figure 4.1). These were small groups of Ojibway hunters, fur trappers, and scouts that opportunistically joined French parties and Indian refugees in their explorations of the interior regions.

Ethnohistorian Harold Hickerson (1962: 34) noted that the rise of permanent villages and concomitant adoption of sedentary life was an overarching characteristic of the historic Ojibway development. Yet, his discussion of the land-use behaviors of southwestern Ojibway bands suggests that village placement was closely related to their expansion. They typically placed gateway colonies along the lake shores, near the mouths or headwaters of the navigable rivers; this strategy increased, rather than decreased, their ability to move about freely and safely, and to control the movement of other groups. In fact, in little more than a century (1660–1768) they had placed, in addition to the Sault Ste Marie, three main villages at key locations along the south shore of Lake Superior, from east to west: Keweenaw Bay, near the headwaters of the Menominee River; La Pointe, which later moved to Madeline Island; and Fond du Lac, at the mouth of the St Louis riverway. Smaller but nonetheless strategically located settlements were present near Lake Michigan by 1768 (Warren 1984: 128–30; Tanner 1986, map 13).

It cannot be said, strictly, that the Ojibway perceived the St Croix watershed to be an unfamiliar landscape or an unoccupied area at the time they founded their first community there. Rather, the progression of their colonization of the Mississippi headwaters and the historical junctures that surrounded it strongly suggest that the Ojibway had scouted and identified the region as a fallback area. Thus, this case is an excellent example of the long-term effects that landscape learning opportunities brought about by hunting, trading, and warfare, among other activities that required travel, may have on the decision-making processes that lead to migration and colonization.

In 1697 the Ojibway made a trade agreement with the Dakota Sioux, who would welcome Ojibway hunters and trappers into the Mississippi headwaters in exchange for European goods. This agreement lasted 40 years, placing the Ojibway in the enviable position of middlemen whose ability swiftly to cover great distances was unsurpassed (Hickerson 1962: 65). So influential was their presence that the Ojibway or

Chippewa language soon became the lingua franca of the Great Lakes tribes (Carver 1956: 414). Having established themselves as middlemen and free of threat, the Ojibway bands began to encroach upon the interior woodlands between Green Bay and the Mississippi headwaters. As the next colonizing step, the Ojibway from La Pointe founded after 1760 one colony in Lac Courte Oreilles – the old refugee village – and another in Lac du Flambeau, at the headwaters of the Chippewa and Wisconsin Rivers respectively. Both colonies were connected by land trails to Lake Superior. The first Ojibway colony on the Yellow River tributary to the east of the St Croix appeared soon thereafter (Tanner 1986; see Figure 4.1). From this vantage point the bands succeeded at displacing smaller tribes in northern Wisconsin and at monopolizing the regional fur trade. However, their efforts to follow this same strategy to the west of the St Croix River, in eastern and central Minnesota, were met with great resistance by the Dakota Sioux, their former trade partners.

Throughout this exploration and encroachment period, the St Croix Riverway continued to be free of permanent occupation or control by any one group, except for a loosely kept pattern whereby the lower St Croix was utilized by the Dakota and the upper St Croix–Brulé River area by the La Pointe Ojibway. The aboriginal land-use pattern remained focused on the hinterlands, and it was there where the war was fought – of the more than 50 battlegrounds recorded by William Warren in Minnesota, fewer than ten are located along the St Croix, and these, in turn, concentrate on the middle to lower portions of the river (Winchell 1911). Nicollet's account of his exploration of the St Croix watershed in 1836, which includes a description of pictographs of scalping events, suggests that the riverway was most likely navigated by war parties of both ethnic groups (Bray 1967). The lack of evidence of sustained battle also suggests that the St Croix remained an open thoroughfare, and that it may have been used by different people to access the Mississippi River and Lake Superior trading posts.

Importantly, during the height of the Dakota–Ojibway War (1740–1825), both warring sides allowed their allies, the Winnebago and Menominee, to hunt along the St Croix watershed and toward the Mississippi headwaters (Coues 1895: 341). This observation supports the notion that passage through the riverway may have been subject to a truce similar to that maintained on regional trade centers such as Prairie du Chien. Such a truce would have allowed people to go about their trading business even though they were still struggling to gain or maintain the land base devoted to subsistence activities and to commercial fur trapping. This was not the case for other navigable rivers on either side of the St Croix (Carver 1956: 60, 99). An additional indicator of this open use pattern around the turn of the nineteenth century is the location of Northwest Company and XY Company posts on the main tributaries of the upper and middle St Croix – the Snake and Kettle Rivers, in Minnesota, and the Yellow River in Wisconsin (Gates 1933; Nute 1930). These posts would have been inoperable without safe and open passage through the riverway.

By the traders' accounts, at the turn of the nineteenth century the Ojibway had already "settled" the upper and middle St Croix (Gates 1933). However, Zebulon Montgomery Pike's description of the population of the St Croix and Chippewa

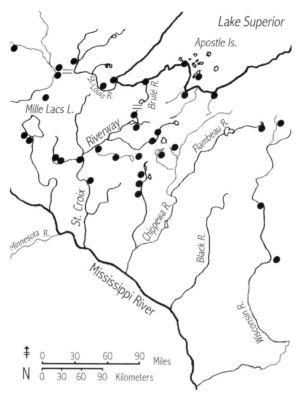

Figure 4.2: Distribution of Ojibway villages on the St Croix River watershed and vicinity, *c.*1830. Not plotted are 16 Ojibway villages along the boundary waters to the northwest and five villages west of Mille Lacs Lake (source: Tanner 1986, maps 27 and 28).

Rivers in 1804 refers to the Ojibway as "the roving bands." Pike's demographic figures for this area – 50 lodges and 689 "probable souls"(Coues 1895: 346) – indicate a rather dense, albeit seasonal, use pattern and decreasing Dakota resistance to Ojibway colonization. No true settlement of the riverway took place until after the war of 1812, but by 1815 the Ojibway were well established in the upper St Croix, whereas the Dakota were grudgingly moving west toward the plains. Even though war was renewed, and a measles epidemic decimated the Lake Superior Ojibway in 1820, their colonies were flourishing in hinterlands on either side of the river; furthermore, the appearance of the first permanent villages located right along the riverway, at the mouths of its upper tributaries (Tanner 1986, maps 27 and 28) (Figure 4.2), suggests that the character of the aboriginal thoroughfare was undergoing a radical change (Zedeño *et al.* 2001a).

The peace treaty between the Dakota and the Ojibway was signed at Prairie du Chien in 1825. The treaty divided the riverway between the two groups, with the dividing line crossing the St Croix River at the point named Standing Cedar, near Cedar Bend, Osceola, at the site of an ancestral Dakota pictograph (Dunn 1979: 13). This treaty did not end the war but only encouraged the Ojibway to fill in vacated land. By the time Henry Rowe Schoolcraft undertook his expedition to the source of the Mississippi River in 1832 and navigated the St Croix, the regional Ojibway population, despite war and disease, numbered around 900 souls (Mason 1958: 85–9). At a broader scale, Schoolcraft's 1832 census data indicate that the Ojibway population of the interior waterways was more than triple that of the lakeshore villages, even accounting for seasonal movement. His figures illustrate the sweeping power of Ojibway colonization of the upper Mississippi landscape. Ironically, the land the Ojibway had fought so long to possess was ceded to the United States only twenty-two years after the signing of the peace treaty at Prairie du Chien.

Following paths by circumstance and design

Almost 400 years have passed since a European first reported the existence of a populous Indian village strategically located at the Sault Ste Marie in upper Michigan (Butterfield 1898). Indeed, when Etienne Brulé reached the south shore of Lake Superior in 1618, the *Saulteur* Indians he met at that village had yet to become the historic Ojibway or to expand beyond the Sault. Yet, the exploration and colonization strategies that the Ojibway later applied on Lake Superior and on the St Croix were already in place at that time. These strategies, with an emphasis on the control of waterway junctions, portages, and trail heads, offer a good example of how the paths that lead people to explore new lands may also serve as blueprints for appropriating and transforming the landscape after the initial exploration period. Most Ojibway villages, even those built as late as the nineteenth and early twentieth centuries, followed the ancestral blueprint to the extent allowed by European and American political forces. The case illustrates the timing of expansion of a mobile group, given strong push and pull factors; it took the Ojibway less than 150 years (approximately six generations) to expand across 1,000 km of occupied and defended territory.

The Ojibway land-use history also reveals how the blueprint furnished by exploratory pathway networks may transcend effective land-use behaviors and go on to shape a people's social memory and ethnicity. Although the archaeological identity of the Ojibway ancestors who colonized the east end of Lake Superior some time before European contact is speculative at best, the oral history, and particularly the origin and migration stories, offer some clues as to the ways in which the ancestors acquired landscape knowledge and subsequently developed land-based social and cultural sanctions. When the migration story that Warren recorded in the nineteenth century (Warren 1984) is compared with the archaeological and historic records of Ojibway expansion, it becomes clear that the Ojibway added landscape learning experiences to their ancient origin myth as they moved west and south of the Sault Ste Marie, following the Lake Superior waterway, and then advancing toward the interior wilderness through a network of land and water trails. Plant, animal, landform, and even material culture allegories progressively enriched the oral history and pictographic repertoire as their environmental knowledge grew in tandem with expansion and colonization (Densmore 1979; Dewdney 1975). The Ojibway's dynamic oral traditions, which include several places of origin, also evolved through intergenerational transmission; and, as they shaped and reshaped Ojibway identity as "a people," the traditions helped individual bands to establish rights-of-being in lands colonized as recently as the nineteenth century.

In the case of the St Croix River Ojibway, both traditional history and effective land use have lent a sense of rootedness and legitimacy, even though this band has clear memories of the recent colonization of the riverway and continues to acknowledge its descent from the mother villages of Lake Superior (Zedeño *et al.* 2001a). The Ojibway further trace their roots back to the ancestral lands and through the many waterways they have followed since time immemorial – from their primordial origin place, the Atlantic seaboard, to the St Croix River. Contemporary Ojibway, regardless of their residential status, still see themselves as transhumant; most people traverse the old pathways for seasonal hunting, fishing, ricing, sugar-making, and drumming, on the occasion of a life-cycle change or an illness, or when the times call for a feast or a pilgrimage. Granted, motorized boats have replaced the birch bark canoes, paved roads now parallel the foot trails, modern towns and parks thrive near the old landings, and the crossings and portages are best left to backpackers. But for the most part the Ojibway are a people for whom the true significance of learning about and interacting with the landscape reveals itself in the act of taking the path.

Acknowledgments

This paper is based on research funded by the National Park Service. Regional ethnographer M. J. Evans from the Midwest Region, cultural resource specialist J. Schaeppi from the St Croix National Scenic Riverway, Wisconsin, and archaeologist C. Clark were especially helpful during the research process. R. C. Basaldú, G. Dewey-Hefley, A. Eisenberg, K. Hamm, F. Pittaluga, and M. Porter assisted in various stages of the research and contributed to the production of technical reports. A. Carroll provided editorial and substantive reviews of an earlier draft. The volume editors offered invaluable and constructive criticism throughout the preparation of the manuscript.

Note

1 This information was collected as part of the authors' ongoing Indian History Project, funded by the US Air Force's Nellis Air Force Base and Range Complex, Nevada.

References

Adams, Arthur T. (1961) *The Explorations of Pierre Esprit Radisson.* Minneapolis: Ross and Haines.
Ammerman, A. J. and L. L. Cavalli-Sforza (1984) *The Neolithic Transition and the Genetics of Populations in Europe.* Princeton, NJ: Princeton University Press.

Anthony, David W. (1997) "Prehistoric Migration as a Social Process." In J. Chapman and H. Hamerow (eds) *Migrations and Invasions in Archaeological Explanation*, BAR International Series 664, Oxford: Archaeopress.

Barney, Ralph A. (1974) "The Indian Claims Commission." In D.A. Horr (ed.) *American Indian Ethnohistory Series*. New York: Garland Publishing.

Basso, Keith (1996) *Wisdom Sits in Places*. Albuquerque: University of New Mexico Press.

Beck, Colleen (1979) "Ancient Roads on the North Coast of Peru," PhD dissertation, Department of Anthropology, University of California, Berkeley.

Birk, Douglas and Elden Johnson (1992) "The Mdewakanton Dakota and Initial French Contact." In *Calumet and Fleur-de-lys*, J. A. Walthall and T. E. Emerson, (eds), Washington, DC: Smithsonian Institution Press, pp. 203–40.

Birmingham, Robert A. (1984) "Dogtown: A Historical Study of a Late Historic St. Croix Chippewa Community," *The Wisconsin Archaeologist* 65(3):183–300.

Bray, Martha Coleman (1967) *Journals of Joseph N. Nicollet*. St Paul: Minnesota Historical Society Press.

Brody, Hugh (1998) *Maps and Dreams*. Prospect Heights, IL: Waveland Press.

Butterfield, Consul W. (1898) *History of Brulé's Discoveries and Explorations, 1610–1626*. Cleveland, OH: Heldman and Taylor.

Cameron, Catherine (1995) "Migration and the Movement of Southwestern Peoples," *Journal of Anthropological Archaeology* 14(2).

Carver, Jonathan (1956) *Travels Through the Interior Parts of North America, in the Years 1766, 1767, and 1768*. Minneapolis, MN: Ross and Haines.

Conway, Thor (1993) *Painted Dreams*. Minocqua, WI: Northword Press.

Copps, D. H. (1995) *Views from the Road*. Washington, DC: Island Press.

Coues, Elliott (ed.) (1895) *The Expeditions of Zebulon Montgomery Pike*, vols I–III. New York: Francis P. Harper.

Davis, James T. (1961) *Trade Routes and Economic Exchange among the Indians of California* (Reports of the University of California Survey 54).

Densmore, Frances (1979) *Chippewa Customs*. St Paul, MN: Minnesota Historical Society Press (Reprint of Bureau of American Ethnology Report no. 86, 1929).

Dewdney, Selwyn (1975) *The Sacred Scrolls of the Southern Ojibway*. Toronto: University of Toronto Press.

Dunn, James Taylor (1979) *The St. Croix: Midwest Border River*. St Paul, MN: Minnesota Historical Society Press.

Feld, Steven (1996) "Waterfalls of Song: An Acoustemology of Place Resounding in Bosavi, Papua New Guinea." In S. Feld and K. Basso (eds) *Senses of Place*, pp. 91–137. Santa Fe, NM: School of American Research Press.

Ferguson, T. J. and R. Hart (1985) *A Zuni Atlas*. Norman, OK: University of Oklahoma Press.

Gabriel, Kathryn (1991) *Roads to Center Place*. Boulder, CO: Johnson Books.

Gates, Charles M. (1933) *Five Fur Traders of the Northwest: Being the Narrative of Peter Pond and the Diaries of John Macdonell, Archibald N. McLeod, Hugh Faries, and Thomas Connor*. Minneapolis, MN: Minnesota Society of the Colonial Dames of America, University of Minnesota Press.

Gilman, Chandler R. (1836) *Life on the Lakes: Being Tales and Sketches Collected During a Trip to the Pictured Rocks of Lake Superior*, vols I and II. New York: George Dearborn.

Hickerson, Harold (1962) "The Southwestern Chippewa: An Ethnohistorical Study," *American Anthropologist* 64(3): part 2.

—— (1967) "Land Tenure of the Rainy Lake Chippewa at the Beginning of the 19th Century," *Smithsonian Contributions to Anthropology*, vol. 2.

Hinsdale, W. B. (1931) *Archaeological Atlas of Michigan*. Ann Arbor, MI: University of Michigan Press. (Michigan Handbook Series 4.)

Hulbert, Archer Butler (1900) *Red-Men's Roads*. Cleveland: Arthur H. Clark.

—— (1902) *Historic Highways of America. Vol. 2: Indian Thoroughfares*. Cleveland: Arthur H. Clark.

Hyslop, John (1984) *The Inka Road System*. Orlando, FA: Academic Press.

Jackson, John B. (1994) *A Sense of Place, a Sense of Time*. New Haven: Yale University Press.

Johnson, Elden (1969) "Preliminary Notes on the Prehistoric Use of Wild Rice," *The Minnesota Archaeologist* 30(2):31–43.

Kellog, Louise P. (1917) *Early Narratives of the Northwest 1634–1699*. New York: Charles Scribner's Sons.

Kidder, Tristram R. (2000) "Making the City Inevitable: Native Americans and the Geography of New Orleans." In Craig E. Colten (ed.) *Transforming New Orleans and its Environs*, pp. 9–21. Pittsburgh: University of Pittsburgh Press.

Kincaid, Chris (ed.) (1983) *Chaco Roads Project Phase I: A Reappraisal of Prehistoric Roads in the San Juan Basin*. Albuquerque: Bureau of Land Management.

Kopytoff, Igor (1987) "The Internal African Frontier: The Making of African Political Culture." In I. Kopytoff (ed.) *The African Frontier*. Bloomington, IN: Indiana University Press.

Kristiansen, Kristian (1989) "Prehistoric Migrations: The Case of the Single Grave and Corded Ware Cultures," *Journal of Danish Archaeology* 8:211–25.

Kroeber, A. L. (1925) *Handbook of the Indians of California*. Washington, DC: Smithsonian Institution Bureau of American Ethnology Bulletin 78.

Laird, Carobeth (1976) *The Chemehuevis*. Banning, CA: Malki Museum.

Laurence, Ray (1999) *The Roads of Roman Italy*. London: Routledge.

McClintock, Walter (1923) *Old Indian Trails*. Boston: Houghton Mifflin.

Mann, Robert (1998) "'That Glorious Gate': The Maumee-Wabash Portage as a Miami Indian Sacred Space." Paper presented at the annual meeting of the American Society for Ethnohistory, Minneapolis, Minnesota.

Mason, Philip P. (1958) *Schoolcraft's Expedition to Lake Itasca: The Discovery of the Source of the Mississippi*. Lansing, MI: Michigan State University Press.

Mason, Ronald J. (1997) "The Paleo-Indian Tradition," *The Wisconsin Archaeologist* 78(1/2):78–110.

Milloy, John (1991) "Our Country: The Significance of the Buffalo Resource for a Plains Cree Sense of Territory." In *Aboriginal Resource Use in Canada*. Winnipeg: University of Manitoba Press.

Myer, William E. (1928) "Indian Trails of the Southeast." In *Bureau of American Ethnology Annual Report* 42:727–857.

Myers, Fred R. (1986) *Pintupi Country, Pintupi Self*. Washington, DC: Smithsonian Institution Press.

Nute, Grace Lee (1930) "Posts of the Minnesota Fur-Trading Area, 1660–1855," *Minnesota History* XI(4):355–90.

Nute, Grace Lee (1969) *The Voyageurs' Highway: Minnesota's Border Lake Land*. St Paul, MN: Minnesota Historical Society Press.

Pandya, Vishvajit (1990) "Movement and Space: Andamanese Cartography," *American Ethnologist* 17(4):775–97.

Pearson, M. Parker and Colin Richards (eds) (1994) *Architecture and Order*. London: Routledge.

Richner, Jeffrey J. (1992) *Archeological Survey and Testing at Voyageurs National Park: 1985–1991.* Midwest Archeological Center Technical Report. Lincoln, NE: United States Department of the Interior, National Park Service, Midwest Archeological Center.

Riley, Carroll and Joni Manson (1991) "The Sonoran Connection: Road and Trail Networks in the Protohistoric Period." In C. D. Trombold (ed.) *Ancient Road Networks and Settlement Hierarchies in the New World.* Cambridge: Cambridge University Press.

Ritzenthaler, Robert E. (1965) "Trail Marker Trees," *Wisconsin Archaeologist* 46(3):183–9.

Roberts, Brian K. (1996) *Landscapes of Settlement.* London: Routledge.

Santley, Robert S. (1991) "The Structure of the Aztec Transport Network." In C. D. Trombold (ed.) *Ancient Road Networks and Settlement Hierarchies in the New World.* Cambridge: Cambridge University Press.

Schenk, Theresa M. (1997) *The Voice of the Crane Echoes Afar.* New York: Garland Publishing.

Stevenson, K. P., R. F. Boszhardt, C. R. Moffat, *et al.* (1997) "The Woodland Tradition," *The Wisconsin Archaeologist* 78(1/2):140–201.

Steward, Julian (1938) *Basin-Plateau Aboriginal Sociopolitical Groups.* Washington, DC: Smithsonian Institution Bureau of American Ethnology Bulletin 120.

Stoddard, Robert H. (1997) "Defining and Classifying Pilgrimages." In Robert H. Stoddard and Alan Morinis (eds) *Sacred Places, Sacred Spaces, the Geography of Pilgrimage*, pp. 41–60. Baton Rouge, LA: Louisiana State University Geoscience and Man Series no. 34.

Stoffle, R. W., L. Loendorf, D. Austin, D. Halmo, A. Bullets, and B. Fulfrost (1995) *TUMPITUXWINAP (Storied Rocks): Southern Paiute Rock Art in the Colorado River Corridor.* Tucson, Arizona: Bureau of Applied Research of Anthropology, University of Arizona.

Tanner, Helen Hornbeck (1986) *Atlas of Great Lakes Indian History.* Norman, OK: University of Oklahoma Press.

Tanner, John (1994) *The Falcon: A Narrative of the Captivity and Adventures of John Tanner During Thirty Years Residence Among the Indians in the Interior of North America.* New York: Penguin Books.

Tilley, Christopher (1994) *A Phenomenology of Landscapes.* London: Berg.

Trombold, Charles D. (1991) "Causeways in the Context of Strategic Planning in the La Quemada Region, Zacatecas, Mexico." In C. D. Trombold (ed.) *Ancient Road Networks and Settlement Hierarchies in the New World.* Cambridge: Cambridge University Press.

Vayda, Andrew (1983) "Progressive Contextualization: Methods of Research in Human Ecology," *Human Ecology* 11:265–81.

Verwyst, Chrysostom (1886) *The Missionary Labors of Fathers Marquette, Menard and Allouez in the Lake Superior Region.* Milwaukee, WI: Hoffman Brothers.

Warren, William W. (1984) *History of the Ojibway People.* St Paul, MN: Minnesota Historical Society Press (previously published by Ross and Haines, Inc., 1885 and 1957).

Wedel, Mildred M. (1974) "Le Sueur and the Dakota Sioux." In E. Johnson (ed.) *Aspects of Great Lakes Anthropology*, pp. 157–72. St Paul, MN: Minnesota Historical Society Press.

Whittlesey, S. (1998) "Archaeological Landscapes: A Methodological and Theoretical Discussion." In S. Whitlessey, R. Ciolek-Torrello, and J. Altschul (eds) *Vanishing River.* Tucson, AZ: SRI Press.

Winchell, Newton H. (1911) *The Aborigines of Minnesota.* St Paul, MN: Minnesota Historical Society.

Wishart, David J. (1985) "The Pawnee Claims Case, 1947–64." In Imre Sutton (ed.) *Irredeemable America,* pp. 157–86. Albuquerque: University of New Mexico Press.

Zedeño, M. Nieves (1997) "Landscape, Land Use, and the History of Territory Formation: An Example from the Puebloan Southwest," *Journal of Archaeological Method and Theory* 4(1):63–107.

—— (1999) "Ojibway Land Use in the Western Great Lakes," paper presented at the annual meetings of the Society for Applied Anthropology, Tucson, Arizona.

—— (2000) "On What People Make of Places: A Behavioral Cartography." In Michael Schiffer (ed.) *Social Theory in Archaeology*, 97–111. Salt Lake City: University of Utah Press.

Zedeño, M. Nieves, Christopher R. Basaldú, Kathryn Hamm, and Amy Eisenberg (2001a) *Ethnographic Overview – St. Croix National Scenic Riverway,* draft report. Tucson, AZ: Bureau of Applied Research in Anthropology, University of Arizona.

Zedeño, M. N., R. Stoffle, F. Pittaluga, G. Dewey-Hefley, C. R. Basaldú, and M. Porter (2001b) *Traditional Ojibway Resources in the Western Great Lakes: An Ethnographic Inventory in the States Michigan, Minnesota, and Wisconsin,* final report. Tucson: Bureau of Applied Research in Anthropology, University of Arizona.

5

MINING RUSHES AND LANDSCAPE LEARNING IN THE MODERN WORLD

Donald L. Hardesty

Archaeological landscapes of the last 500 years, a period of time often called the modern world, offer numerous opportunities to document the transformation of nature into culture through the process of learning. The archaeological record of the modern world documents the actions and consequences of biological, social, and technological forces that transformed human lifestyles and environments on a global scale. Population growth, urbanization, and industrialization brought about the transformation. The time period also is marked by large-scale social systems integrated by networks of economic exchange, production, and communication embedded within capitalistic world economies. Such systems effectively correlated or linked together local and regional ecosystems into world systems. Global population movements in the modern world introduced exotic plants, animals, diseases, technologies, and beliefs throughout the world. Such movements greatly increase the chances of the global migrants encountering completely new environments with no prior knowledge of the natural resources that occur there.

Historical archaeology takes the archaeological study of the modern world as its domain. In recent years, some of the key research topics in historical archaeology have included cultural identity, ethnicity, and assimilation. Environmental archaeology is another emerging research interest within historical archaeology (e.g. Deagan 1996). What is the relationship of landscape learning to these topics? Landscape learning involves the interplay between specific landscape patterns, elements, or components and the "meaning" that it has within specific historical, social, or cultural contexts. Environmental archaeology plays a role in documenting, analyzing, and interpreting the elements of past modern-world landscapes. Such elements include land-use patterns, vegetation patterns, landforms, circulation networks (e.g. roads and footpaths), boundaries, buildings and structures, clusters, and small-scale components such as mining claim markers. The methods of environmental archaeology, such as remote sensing, geographic information systems, geoarchaeology, palynology, plant macrofossil analysis, and zooarchaeology, clearly are needed to study archaeological landscapes. At the same time, archaeological studies of landscape learning go beyond this traditional approach by focusing more upon history and the assignment of social

1

and cultural meaning to landscape elements. Landscape learning, for example, involves the development of historical models of the transformation of nature into culture, which allies the approach with historical ecology, "the study of past ecosystems by charting the change in landscapes over time" (Crumley 1994: 5–6). Historical ecology explores the study of archaeological landscapes as the cumulative material expression of the history of human–environmental relations and takes into account the agency (decisions and actions) of individuals. The approach also considers the multiple time and space scales in which environmental events and processes operate and explore the constantly changing geographical boundaries and organizational structures in anthropogenic ecosystems.

Landscape learning also involves the process of assigning meaning to landscape elements, but this is more than just the transfer of the symbols of cultural identity through the study of ethnicity, assimilation, acculturation, and social appropriation. Some of the meaning of landscape features comes from the projection of symbols of cultural identity. Landscape meaning, however, also comes from new knowledge gained from the experience of interacting with other people and from exposure to landscape elements such as landforms or vegetation. Yet other meanings come from what some call the process of "glocalization" or the interplay between the global and the local. Certainly archaeology is well equipped to document a global presence at localities in the form of globally distributed knowledge and commodities. But it all too often stops there. Archaeologists also need to explore how global knowledge and commodities are locally interpreted or transformed into new meanings. Cultural anthropologist Daniel Miller's (1998) studies of Coca-Cola in Trinidad, for example, show that the homogenization of commodities so often assumed as a consequence of globalization is counteracted quite effectively by social and cultural interpretation at the local level.

Mining colonization in the modern world

The global mining rushes in the modern world following new discoveries of precious metal deposits provide a good illustration of how prior knowledge and learning transformed the landscapes of the modern world. Mining rushes are considered to be episodes of colonization because they involve the establishment of colonies or groups of people in places distant from their homeland and previously unknown to them. Mining colonies typically are short-lived and made up of individuals who do not expect to live permanently in the new environment. In this sense, they are "sojourners," even though some of them end up staying for the rest of their lives. The scale, intensity, and magnitude of the mining rushes varied. Each, however, left behind distinctive mining landscapes that constitute a significant material expression of these "colonization" events. Mined resources are often similar to icebergs in that most of the resource is buried and not directly observable. As a result, the process of landscape learning continues throughout the life of the mining colony. How did such landscape learning influence the history and patterns of mining-related colonization? One expression, for example, may be settlement history and the evolution of settlement patterns. The architecture of buildings and structures is another possibility. The key question is how to identify the steps or stages of the learning process as reflected in these pathways. Are there distinctive characteristics of each step or stage that can be recognized? How are they expressed in the archaeological record? Both prior knowledge and learning transformed landscapes in the new environments that the mining rushers encountered. Such knowledge falls into three categories: geological knowledge, technological knowledge, and social knowledge.

Patrick Kirch's (1980) evolutionary model of adaptation to new environments suggests one possible model of how these three categories of knowledge are learned during colonization. Three stages are involved in the learning process. The first stage is the introduction of prior knowledge about natural resources brought by the first miners to the new discovery. The initial colonization stage reflects knowledge about the previously unknown geology and other natural resources of the new environment that is based on cultural tradition, myth, published reports, and the like. It also reflects the introduction of a traditional miner's tool kit and other existing technological knowledge carried by the colonists, such as methods for extracting precious metals from rock. Finally, the first stage of learning reflects traditional concepts of social relations and cultural identities brought by the miners to the new environment. All three categories of prior knowledge at this point are likely to be relatively standardized and invariable. The second stage of learning involves the diversification of the three categories of knowledge through geological discoveries, technological innovation, information exchange among local groups, both indigenous and migrants, living in the mining colony, and the transfer of knowledge from the outside such as new technologies or geological concepts. Finally, the third stage of learning reflects the selection and use of the accumulated prior and learned knowledge to assign meaning to landscape elements in the new environment. In the case of technological knowledge, for example, the variability of effective knowledge within the mining colony or island is generally reduced through a process that selects those technologies that work most effectively to locate, extract, or process the ore body.

Perhaps the earliest precious metals mining rush in the modern world was the Appalachian gold rush in the 1790s. The Amazonian gold rush occurred as recently as the 1980s (MacMillan 1995). Most of the great mining rushes of the modern world, however, occurred between 1849 and 1929 (Fetherling 1997; Paul 1963). The 1849 California gold rush and the Klondike stampede that began in 1897 are the best known of the mining rushes. Others around the world included the great Australian gold rush in 1852, the New Zealand gold rush in 1861, the Main Reef strike on the Rand in the Transvaal region of South Africa in 1886, and the 1906 cobalt rush in the northern Ontario of Canada.

Most of the great global rushes, however, took place in western North America. Geographically, western North America extends from the Rocky Mountains westward to the Pacific Ocean and includes the major US regions of the Pacific Northwest, California, the Southwest, the Great Basin, and the Rocky Mountains. The time-frame of the western mining rushes begins with early Spanish exploration in the 1500s in search of El Dorado, but the 1849 California gold rush is the first bona fide mining

Figure 5.1 Malakoff Diggings State Park, California, showing the landscape created by hydraulic mining in the mid-nineteenth century

rush in the American West. The discovery of gold at Sutter's Mill near Sacramento and the subsequent search for the "mother lode" in the Sierra Nevada mountains attracted an estimated 80,000 migrants from around the world in the first year. Migrants of diverse ethnicities and nationalities came mostly from Mexico, South America, China, Europe, Australia, and the eastern United States. Three other global mining rushes followed on the heels of the California gold rush. The discovery of gold in British Columbia in 1858 on the Fraser River brought 30,000 miners by the end of the year. In the same year, the discovery of gold on Cherry Creek in Colorado led to the famous "Pike Peak or Bust" rush, with at least 10,000 people taking part by the following year. At the same time, the discovery of silver on the Comstock Lode in what is now western Nevada in 1859 led to the "rush to Washoe," with more than 25,000 people arriving within a short time. Many global migrants to this rush originated in England and Ireland, but large numbers also came from China, Mexico, and the eastern United States. Among other things, the Comstock miners established the world's first system of industrial mining. Other mining rushes followed. Among the most famous of these is the 1862 Cariboo gold rush in British Columbia, which attracted large numbers of Europeans, Australians, and eastern Canadians. In the same year, the discovery of silver near north-central Nevada's Reese River created another rush, and yet another rush in the "silver state" began in 1867 at Treasure Hill. Elsewhere in the American West, the discovery of gold in the Black Hills of South Dakota led to Custer's last stand and the murder of Wild Bill Hickock in Deadwood in 1876. Miners found silver in 1877 at Leadville, Colorado, setting in motion another famous mining rush. Yet another began in 1892, also in Colorado, with the discovery of gold at Cripple Creek. What is perhaps equal only to the California gold rush in fame, although certainly smaller in size, followed the discovery of gold in 1896 on the Klondike River in Alaska. The Klondike stampede peaked in 1898. Finally, the discovery of gold at Tonopah, Nevada, in 1900 and the Goldfield strike in 1902 brought another global rush of miners (Elliott 1966). In addition to these well-known rushes are a large number of smaller mining rushes, such as the "rush to Baldy Mountain" in New Mexico in 1867 (Loosbrock 1999).

Geological knowledge

Colonizing miners brought with them a body of geological knowledge about the location, distribution, and characteristics of the ore bodies that contained metals and minerals. Such prior knowledge originated in the personal experiences and beliefs of miners, in the knowledge accumulated from learning in other mining regions, and in existing scientific or folk concepts. Mining rushes typically followed the discovery of new ore bodies about which little was known. The gold found in the stream bed at Sutter's Mill in California, for example, offered few clues about its origin. Contemporary beliefs in a "mother lode," however, strongly patterned where the first miners taking part in the rush searched for gold. The mother lode was thought to be a "great master vein, occupying the central fissure in a system" and having "a continuous outcrop for 60 miles" (Raymond 1869: 11 [Raymond questioned this common belief at the time]). Likewise, the "rush to Washoe" after the discovery of the Comstock Lode in 1859 began with the erroneous idea that the ore body followed the pattern of narrow quartz ledges dipping at well-defined angles, found by the California "49ers" in the Sierra Nevada mountains (Lord 1959: 43–4). The first Comstock miners set up rules governing the location and development of mining claims accordingly, assigning mining claims in lengths up to 300 feet that followed the ledge downward wherever it went. Unfortunately, the numerous rock outcrops around which the claims were defined turned out to be part of the same lode that inclined at an angle of 45 degrees eastward, eventually creating innumerable acts of violence and lawsuits.

In the same way, the process of learning on the Comstock Lode preconditioned the miners' expectations about the geological distribution of ore bodies elsewhere in the American West. Tingley *et al.* (2000), for example, note that prospectors in Nevada searched for ore bodies that followed the Comstock model of "true fissure veins" or "lodes" and that occurred within 500 feet of the surface for several decades after the Comstock discovery. The geographical distribution of early post-Comstock discovery mining camps is associated only with ore bodies that followed this geological model. Miners during this period completely overlooked the vast gold deposits situated in a quite different geological context, which did not have veins. The deposits occurred in silica ledges weathered to orange, red, and black knobs. Not until the 1902 discovery of gold at Goldfield in south-central Nevada did prospectors realize this new truth. The discovery set off a new generation of mining rushes to gold fields with this set of geological characteristics and structured a new settlement pattern.

Technological knowledge

Technological knowledge involves the tools and techniques for extracting the ore and for separating the metals or minerals from their rock matrix. Mining rushes typically begin with pre-existing mining technologies introduced by the first miners to arrive at the new discovery. The beginning of the modern world brought with it a mining technology that had become more or less standardized in Europe by the sixteenth century and that was exported worldwide with European global colonization. Early modern-world miners built simple pumping, hoisting, transport, and grinding machines from the gear trains, cams, pistons, cylinders, and other devices in common use at the time. German miners, for example, developed a system of wheeled carts and tracks for moving ore through the mineshafts, larger and deeper underground shafts, and hydraulically powered pumping systems (Grandemange 1990). The standardized European mining tool kit included basic knowledge of the process of mercury amalgamation for recovering gold and silver from ores. This technology later evolved into the arrastra and patio yard amalgamation processes in the Spanish colonial silver mines in Mexico and the Andes, the Freiberg barrel amalgamation process in the

Figure 5.2 Ceramic representation of a mine using a windlass hoist, part of the technological pattern associated with the sixteenth-century European mining "adaptive radiation." German Mining Museum, Bochum

Figure 5.3 "Giant" water nozzles used for hydraulic mining in the mid-nineteenth century, Malakoff Diggings State Park, California

Saxony region of Germany, and pan amalgamation on the Comstock. The landscapes of the earliest global mining rushes in the modern world clearly reflect the "adaptive radiation" of European mining technology that took place in the sixteenth century.

The learning of technological knowledge about mined natural resources typically goes through the sequential stages of mine exploration, mine development, and mine production. Mine exploration includes all the activities involved in the discovery of mineral deposits. Mine development involves activities that define and create access to the ore body. Finally, mine production is the systematic extraction of the ore body. These three stages structure the learning of technological knowledge about how to extract the ore body. Mine exploration typically involves the application of low-cost technology that is powered by humans or animals and that typically is associated with small, shallow mineral deposits less than 300 feet deep. The methods include "rat-hole" underground mining that follows an ore body, surface vein mining, small-scale open pit mining, and mining of shallow placer gravels. Mine development and production more often involves the application of expensive and high-power technologies to extract large mineral deposits more than 300 feet deep. Such technology used powerful and expensive engines or other machines run by steam, fossil fuels, or electricity in the everyday activities of underground excavation, haulage, ventilation, drainage, and mine maintenance – for example large hoisting engines, pumps, air compressors, blowers, and mechanical rock drills.

After extraction, the mineral typically must be concentrated and separated from its rock or other matrix. A variety of processing technologies are used for this task, ranging

Figure 5.4 A Scott furnace, used to extract mercury in the early twentieth century, at the Mariscal Mine, Big Bend National Park, Texas

Figure 5.5 Virginia City, Nevada, the "Queen of the Comstock"

from simple mechanical concentration to chemical methods such as mercury amalgamation, chlorination, and cyanidation. Examples of the technologies associated with processing technology are arrastras, mercury retorts, rotary kilns, Scott furnaces, dry washers, sluice boxes, stamp and concentration mills, amalgamation mills, cyanide mills, flotation mills, smelters, mill tailings, slag dumps, and assay houses.

The success or failure of prior knowledge about technology, subsequent technology transfers, and innovations depend upon the economic, political, scientific, engineering, social, and cultural contexts of that knowledge (Hughes 1983, Pfaffenberger 1992). The existing literature in the history of technology argues for several principal reasons for accepting or rejecting a technological transfer or innovation, including the availability of capital, the size of the firm making the decision to innovate or not, the availability of knowledge about the innovation, the extent to which the workforce is unionized, and the environment. Of these, the size of the mining company is considered to play the most significant role in whether technological transfers or innovations are accepted. Small mining companies, for example, live too close to the margin to take risks, and the "corporate culture" of large mining companies typically prevents risk taking. Moderate-sized companies, on the other hand, are considered to be the most innovative and willing to take the greatest risks with a new mining technology. Janice Wegner's (1995) study of the mining technology used between 1885 and 1915 at the Croydon goldfield in Australia's north Queensland, however, found evidence to the contrary. In this case, technology transfers or innovations occurred independently of company size. Wegner's study suggests that two factors played much more important roles in bringing about technological change: the ability of mining companies to acquire capital, and the geological and chemical characteristics of the ore body. The characteristics of the ore body, for example – especially its variability – largely determined the need to develop innovative methods for extracting or processing ore.

The history of the Comstock provides a dramatic illustration of the importance of the role of learning about the ore body in technological change. Mining on the Comstock began with the discovery of gold on the Carson River plain in 1850 and continued into the early years after the discovery of the Comstock Lode in 1859. Placer mining in the 1850s used hand tools, long toms, and arrastras, mostly introduced by Mexican miners to mine and mill the gold-bearing gravels. The earliest mines on the Comstock lode continued to use the same technology. The miners dug open "glory hole" and shallow shafts down to a depth of 100–200 feet to reach the lode. They then dug "ratholes," a traditional practice in Spanish colonial Mexican and South America, to follow the ore body. They carried ore and waste rock out of the underground mines in bags on their backs by climbing up ladders or walking up inclines. Or the miners used hand-operated windlasses or animal-powered whims to hoist themselves and materials in and out of the mines.

The first Comstock miners used a variety of prior technologies to mill ores in the early years. The miners experimented with a variety of technologies. The Little Gold Hill mines at the south end of the Comstock Lode, for example, successfully used animal-powered arrastras to crush ores. Miners coming from California brought with them stamp mills based on a Cornish machine and modified during the California gold rush. The California stamps crushed the ore, which was then passed over a mercury-covered copper plate or caught on blankets for amalgamation. Likewise, the mines at the north end of the lode, such as the Ophir, Mexican, and the Gould and Curry, experimented with the Freiberg barrel process. This process, exported from Saxony, used California stamps (based on a Cornish machine) to crush the ore, chloridizing the ore by roasting with salt in ovens, and then amalgamating with mercury in small revolving barrels or tubs. Mills using the Freiberg process, such as the Gould and Curry, also experimented with patio yards, transferred from the Mexican and Peruvian silver mines, during the last step in the process. The Freiberg process recovered up to 80 percent of the ore's silver but left behind much of the gold and was very expensive. Non-European participants in the mining rushes introduced other prior mining technologies. Perhaps the best example is the Chinese pump, introduced by Chinese participants in the California gold rush. The Chinese pump, a series of bucket bailers on an endless chain driven by an undershot waterwheel, was based on traditional irrigation technology in south China. Chinese pumps, which were powered mostly by people and animals but also by water and other inanimate sources of power on a small scale, soon became part of the standard tool kit for gold rush miners.

The initial period of applying prior technological knowledge is followed by learning and adapting to the local conditions of the new environment. On the Comstock, the "industrial revolution" soon transformed Comstock mining practices. Mining was among the last of the American industries to industrialize, and the Comstock played a key role in bringing about the change. The Comstock pattern of deep industrial mining, developed in the 1860s and 1870s, was exported around the world to provide a standardized global technology that is still being used. The greatest incentives for industrialization on the Comstock came from deep underground mining and the need for low-cost milling. Pre-industrial milling technologies, for example, gave way to the highly mechanized and steam-powered Washoe process of pan amalgamation. The "factory system" was introduced into the workplace of precious metals milling. To work well, the Washoe process had to be capable of processing large amounts of ore per unit of time, resulting in a total silver yield that was higher than that given by the competing Freiberg and other processes. Mass production through industrialization proved to be the solution. Power was the key to the underground industrial revolution. As the Comstock mines deepened, the hand-operated windlasses and animal-powered whims no longer provided the power needed to hoist miners and materials in and out of the mines. Large steam engines were the solution. The first steam engines used at the Ophir mine generated only about 15 horsepower but were followed rapidly by enormous engines generating hundreds of horsepower. Their fuel was cordwood cut from the forests of the nearby Sierra Nevada and the Lake Tahoe basin. Contemporary photographs of clear-cut forests – one newspaper account observes that nothing larger than a toothpick was left – dramatize the impact of industrial mining on the landscapes of the Comstock. Steam engines powered hoists, pumps, stamp mills, and air compressors, which operated blowers for ventilation and mechanical rock drills. The Yellow Jacket mine introduced the first Burleigh drills to the Comstock in 1872, and they soon became a standard fixture of industrial mining.

Social and cultural knowledge

Mining colonists also transform landscapes by assigning social and cultural meaning to landscape elements. The recursive relationship between meaning and landscape includes representations of prior social and cultural identities and learned knowledge needed to live in the new environment. Consider, for example, domestic architecture. Mining landscapes often include the archaeological remains of specific buildings or structures that reflect the interplay. Neville Ritchie's (1993) study of the domestic and landscape architecture of migrant Chinese settlements in the goldfields of southern New Zealand offer a good example. He found that the buildings typically followed pre-existing Western models and reflected adaptation to local environmental conditions but also retained some traditional Chinese elements. For example, they used locally available construction materials (e.g. turf, mud bricks and puddled mud, forest trees, canvas, corrugated iron sheets, cobblestones) and sites (e.g. rock shelters) and often took advantage of abandoned buildings. Although they did not have the typical "high culture" Chinese architectural elements of upturned eaves, decorative eave brackets, tile roofing, and fretwork patterns on fascia boards, the buildings often retained some elements of traditional Chinese rural architecture, such as being windowless and having hut shrines, door inscriptions, and a chopping block placed just outside the door.

The landscapes of mining rushes reflect and document changing knowledge of beliefs and world views. Global migrants to the rushes brought with them a wide variety of belief systems. Consider, for example, the nineteenth-century Chinese migration into the mining districts of the American West. Chinese miners or workers in the mining industry brought with them principles stipulating the ideal relationships between people and nature. *Feng shui*, for example, is "an esoteric set of theories and practices grounded in indigenous philosophies and human experiences … used in China to probe the landscape and to discern from the irregularity and asymmetry of mountains and waters appropriate locations for specific human occupancy" (Fan Wei 1992: 35). It includes orienting buildings to the south, calm water in front, placement at the confluence of streams but not a branching stream, square town plans and dwellings, and alignment of buildings on a north–south axis. Ritchie (1993) found that the principles of *feng shui* played a role in building and landscape architecture in some cases in New Zealand. These include the avoidance of doorways that faced one another, the avoidance of flat and unwatered places as building sites, building in places that overlooked water sources and that backed onto terraces or sloping ground, building at the confluence of streams, and the avoidance of settlement patterns in straight lines. In general, however, the extent to which Chinese migrants applied the principles of geomancy in practice probably varied enormously and depended on local conditions and expediency. Existing buildings were often re-used, for example, and the placement of buildings often depended as much upon economic and political or social constraints, and opportunities as *feng shui*. Chinese settlements in nineteenth-century California, for example, were often found either in areas with low land prices or on the outskirts of towns where they were forced by the dominant white population to reside (Greenwood 1993). Thus, learned knowledge about social competition shaped the meaning of the landscape for the local Chinese populations.

In addition, the landscapes of mining rushes provide images of and information about the cognitive world of miners as representations of knowledge. Mining landscapes contain symbolic representations of knowledge about mining and, among other things, cultural concepts of settlement. Peebles and Gardin (1992) describe the recognition of such representations as a key problem in archaeology and suggest some solutions. In a similar vein, Ezra Zubrow (1994) applied the concept of "figure ground," developed by linguists, to the representation of Iroquoian settlement patterns on the Niagara frontier in the Great Lakes region. Figure ground focuses on the linguistic, visual, and geographic conceptions that relate an object (the "figure") to its context (the "ground") or a part to a whole. In developing settlement pattern models, for example, Zubrow explores one figure ground in which settlements (the figure) track trade routes (the ground). Another model explores how the geometric designs found on wampum belts determine settlement pattern. Yet another model explores the way in which the geometric image of the Iroquoian long-house floor plan determines settlement pattern. By using relational rules, the figure ground concept allows the development of complex data structures simulating cognitive models of settlement patterns. Geographic Information System (GIS) technology provides the means to fit models of settlement patterns (such as the trade route, wampum belt design, and long-house models) to archaeological data about settlement locations.

The figure ground concept suggests several possibilities for using archaeological inventories of mining districts as sources of information about miners' knowledge and cognitive world. Stone cairns and other markers of mining claims, for example, which often occur in archaeological inventories of mining districts, represent not only miners' knowledge of where ore bodies should occur but also a legal concept in mining law. In this case, the claims outlined by the markers are the "figures" and the ore bodies are the "ground" to which they are being referenced. Another example comes from the geographical distribution of settlements, buildings, and structures on mining landscapes. The distribution reflects some combination of cultural concepts of settlement and community and physical determinants such as topography, water availability, transportation routes, and mine locations. Thus, miners coming from the eastern United States typically carried with them cultural concepts of settlements laid out in a grid pattern (Reps 1979). Consider, for example, the settlement of Shermantown during the Treasure Hill mining boom of the late 1860s (Hardesty 1998). Major Edwin Sherman, a Civil War veteran and entrepreneur attracted to Nevada by earlier mining rushes, planned the settlement as a land development intended to "mine" the pockets of miners attracted to the Treasure Hill mines. He laid out the town to correspond with the image of the New England gridded town. Archaeological and documentary images of the evolution of the town, however, show that it developed along quite different lines, reflecting adaptations to local terrain and mining technology. Similarly, miners coming from China carried cultural concepts of *feng shui* as the key determinant of settlement pattern. Both cognitive concepts, however, were played out on a real-world stage that created a wide variety of actual settlement patterns on mining landscapes. Archaeological inventories of settlements and their environments provide the opportunity to explore the interplay between the "ideal" and the "real," the relational rules underlying the variation.

Conclusion

The landscapes and archaeological record associated with global mining rushes in the modern world are a potentially significant source of analogs for the general archaeology of colonization. Understanding of the formation processes of mining landscapes comes not only from the archaeological record but also from its interplay with the independent sources of documentary accounts and oral testimony. Perhaps even more important, mining landscapes in the modern world represent an enormous variety of colonization events, ranging from short to long in duration, from small to large in geographical scale, and from small to large in population size. These landscapes offer a "cookie jar" of analogs that are useful in the interpretation of the archaeological record of early colonization.

What are the implications of prior knowledge and landscape learning for the development of future research designs in historical and mining archaeology? Clearly, the theoretical framework within which questioning takes place is important. One framework within which knowledge and learning about natural resources can be understood is evolutionary ecology. Optimal foraging theory, for example, is one approach to help us understand the environmental decisions and movements of miners in the American West (Hardesty 1985). Within this framework, miners can be conceptualized as "industrial foragers" who colonize new places by moving from ore patch to ore patch. Charnov's "marginal value theorem" is one principle that helps explain the pattern of movement. The theorem states that "the optimal predator should stay in each patch until its rate of intake (the marginal value) drops to a level equal to the average of intake for the habitat" (Krebs and Davies 1978: 43). Ore patches can be viewed as landscapes with meanings (e.g. economic value as a commodity) that change within a global marketplace and with harvesting costs that vary with available technologies of transportation (e.g. railroads) and extraction (e.g. mechanized open-pit mining). The model predicts patterns of ore patch colonization, abandonment, and re-colonization. How miners colonize and re-colonize ore patches also reflects, among other things, their prior knowledge and learning of mining geology and technology, the individual knowledge of prospectors and other miners, and the existing "state of the art" of knowledge of how ore bodies are formed. Key research questions about how the process of learning geological, technological, and social knowledge affects decision making and subsequent patterns of mobility follow from this theoretical framework. The archaeological data needed to answer such questions would include information about the geographical distribution of mining technology sites during the initial, early, and later stages of colonization that shows changing ideas about the distribution and characteristics of the ore body.

References

Crumley, C. (ed.) (1994) *Historical Ecology*, Santa Fe, NM: School of American Research Press.

Deagan, K. (1996) "Environmental Archaeology and Historical Archaeology," in E. Reitz, L. Newsom, and S. Scudder (eds) *Case Studies in Environmental Archaeology*, New York: Plenum Press.

Elliott, R. (1966) *Nevada's Twentieth-Century Mining Boom*, Reno, NV: University of Nevada Press.

Fan Wei (1992) "Village *Feng shui* Principles," in R. Knapp (ed.) *Chinese Landscapes: The Village as Place*, Honolulu: University of Hawaii Press.

Fetherling, D. (1997) *The Gold Crusades: A Social History of Gold Rushes, 1849–1929*, revised edition, Toronto: University of Toronto Press.

Grandemange, J. (1990) *Les mines d'argent du duché de Lorraine au XVI siècle: Histoire et archéologie du Val de Liepvre (Haut-Rhin)*, Paris: Documents d'Archéologie Française No. 26, Editions de la Maison des Sciences de l'Homme.

Greenwood, R. (1993) "Old Approaches and New Directions: Implications for Future Research," in P. Wegars (ed.) *Hidden Heritage, Historical Archaeology of the Overseas Chinese*, Amityville, NY: Baywood Publishing Company.

Hardesty, D. (1985) "Evolution on the Industrial Frontier," in S. Green and S. Perlman (eds) *Frontiers and Boundaries*, New York: Academic Press.

—— (1998) "Treasure Hill and the Archaeology of Shermantown," *CRM* 21(7):53–6.

Hughes, T. (1983) *Networks of Power*, Baltimore: Johns Hopkins University Press.

Kirch, P. (1980) "The Archaeological Study of Adaptation," in M. Schiffer (ed.) *Advances in Archaeological Method and Theory*, vol. 3, New York: Academic Press.

Krebs, J. and N. Davies (1978) *Behavioural Ecology*, London: Blackwell.

Loosbrock, R. (1999) "Managing a Gold Rush: Mining on the Maxwell Land Grant, New Mexico 1867–1920," *The Mining History Journal* 6:1–7.

Lord, E. (1959) *Comstock Mining and Miners* (reprint of the 1883 edition), Berkeley, CA: Howell-North.

MacMillan, G. (1995) *At the End of the Rainbow? Gold, Land, and People in the Brazilian Amazon*, New York: Columbia University Press.

Miller, D. (1998) "Coca-Cola: A Black Sweet Drink from Trinidad," in D. Miller (ed.) *Material Cultures*, Chicago: University of Chicago Press.

Paul, R. (1963) *Mining Frontiers of the Far West, 1848–1880*, New York: Holt, Rinehart, and Winston.

Peebles, C. and J. C. Gardin (1992) *Representations in Archaeology*, Bloomington, IN: Indiana University Press.

Pfaffenberger, B. (1992) "The Social Anthropology of Technology," *Annual Review of Anthropology* 21:491–516.

Raymond, R. (1869) *Mineral Resources of the States and Territories West of the Rocky Mountains*, Washington, DC: Government Printing Office.

Reps, J. (1979) *A History of Frontier Urban Planning*, Princeton, NJ: Princeton University Press.

Ritchie, N. (1993) "Form and Adaptation: Nineteenth Century Chinese Miners' Dwellings in Southern New Zealand," in P. Wegars (ed.) *Hidden Heritage, Historical Archaeology of the Overseas Chinese*, New York: Baywood Publishing Company.

Tingley, J., T. Lugaski, and A. McLane (2000) "History of the Discovery of Mining Camps in South Central Nevada," paper presented at the 11th annual conference of the Mining History Association, Tonopah, Nevada.

Wegner, J. (1995) "Croydon: Technology Transfer on a North Queensland Goldfield, 1885–1915," unpublished doctoral dissertation, James Cook University of North Queensland, Australia.

Zubrow, E. (1994) "Knowledge Representation and Archaeology: A Cognitive Example Using GIS," in C. Renfrew and E. Zubrow (eds) *The Ancient Mind*, Cambridge: Cambridge University Press.

Part II

CASE STUDIES

6

LANDSCAPE LEARNING AND THE EARLIEST PEOPLING OF EUROPE

Wil Roebroeks

Biologists have huge advantages over palaeolithic archaeologists when it comes to the theme of how animals learn the landscape. They can, for instance, attach transponders to such tiny creatures as honeybees and actually document the orientation flights of these animals by using harmonic radar (Capaldi *et al.* 2000). Honeybees are able to find their small nests from distances as great as 10 km, probably as a result of a progressive process of orientation behaviour, with bees taking multiple orientation flights before becoming foragers (bees that return to the hive with nectar or pollen) in order to visit different, and larger, portions of the landscape around the hive. And there is a striking ontogeny to these honeybee orientation flights: with increased experience, bees hold trip duration constant but fly faster, so later trips cover a larger area than earlier trips. Orientation flights provide honeybees with repeated opportunities to view the hive and landscape features from different viewpoints, suggesting that bees learn the local landscape in a progressive fashion.

There are, of course, many differences between honeybees and the first occupants of Europe. For one thing, we know more about the behaviour of bees, for instance about important aspects of their social life: that they live in colonies with up to tens of thousands of workers, several hundreds of drones and a queen; that they start to forage for pollen at an average age of 14 days; and that they are central place foragers, operating out of what archaeologists might call base camps – all aspects of behaviour for which we have no unambiguous information as far as the largest part of the Palaeolithic is concerned.

And the main difference within the context of this volume is, of course, that we can study the behaviour of honeybees within timeframes infinitesimally finer than those that archaeologists of the Palaeolithic have to work with, especially in the period at stake here. But even in the later phases of the Palaeolithic it does not seem feasible to study the occupation history of an area as large as Europe with minimum chronological units finer than a few thousand years. This is nicely illustrated by recent discussions on inferring late Middle Palaeolithic and Upper Palaeolithic range contractions and expansions from radiocarbon dates, e.g. in the case of the demise of the Neandertals (see Pettitt and Pike 2001 versus Bocquet-Appel and Demars 2000), as well as in a recent review of the archaeology of the Gravettian (Roebroeks *et al.* 2000; Pettitt 2000). Housley *et al.*'s (1997) attempt to use a large series of accelerator mass spectrometry (AMS) and conventional radiocarbon dates to model the movements of people into northern Europe after the Last Glacial Maximum has been criticized in terms of the degree of resolution obtainable with carbon-14 dates, as discussed by Blockley *et al.* (2000). However, if we tune our questions to the degree of resolution obtainable within the various periods (see below), we can distil information on long-term developments in range extension and contraction of hominid species that no other 'fine-grained' discipline can yield. I will try to do that here using the earliest occupation of Europe as a case study. I see at least two reasons why the relatively small subcontinent of Europe can provide us with a case study relevant to larger questions about hominid adaptability and the dynamics of expansion and contraction of geographical ranges. Firstly, Europe is large enough to display ecological differences from south to north and from west to east, which may be of use in charting possible ecological barriers or problems during range expansion (cf. Gamble 1986). Going from the Mediterranean to the north of Europe, distances between resource patches tend to increase, and the same applies when moving from its Atlantic coast into its central and eastern parts. Distances between feeding patches must have been critical for mobile hominids, who may have encountered fewer problems in the highly diverse environments of, for instance, Mediterranean Italy (Mussi 1995) than in the north-ernmost areas of their range. And secondly, the long history and high intensity of Palaeolithic research in Europe has yielded a dense distribution of archaeological sites that enables us to chart hominid presence and absence within the various parts of Europe during the last million years or so.

In this chapter I will first discuss the chronology of the earliest occupation of Europe and present some arguments on the adaptations of the earliest Europeans, particularly from about half a million years ago onwards. Then, following Aiello (1998), I will try to limit the space of the possible social and foraging adaptations of these Pleistocene hominids by focusing on data and ideas from a range of disciplines dealing with life history strategies and dietary constraints of hominids (cf. Roebroeks 2001). This contextualization approach yields a crude and basic profile of the first Europeans, which I will relate to trends in the Palaeolithic record in the final part of the chapter.

Earliest Europe

The last decade has seen a heated debate over the age and the character of the earliest occupation of Europe (see e.g. Bonifay and Vandermeersch 1991; Roebroeks and van Kolfschoten 1994, 1995, 1998; Carbonell *et al.* 1995a, 1995b, 1999 Dennell and Roebroeks 1996; Turq *et al.* 1996; Villa 1996, 2001; Turner 1999; Oms *et al.* 2000; Roebroeks 2001). This ongoing debate has resulted in a kind of consensus view that the European archaeological record changed significantly around 500 to 600 kyr bp, with an increasing number of sites probably indicating a more substantial occupation than in the period before (e.g. Roebroeks and van Kolfschoten 1994; Dennell and

Roebroeks 1996; Dennell 1998; Bermúdez de Castro *et al.* 1999; Villa 2001). Most authors also agree now that north of the large mountain chains of the Pyrenees and the Alps the first unambiguous traces of human occupation date from about half a million years ago, from the Mauer-Miesenheim-Boxgrove time horizon, probably equivalent to oxygen isotope stage (OIS) 13 (see various papers in Roebroeks and van Kolfschoten 1995). The Mediterranean witnessed some earlier human presence than the more northern areas, though the exact age difference between the southern and more northern parts of Europe remains to be established (Roebroeks 2001).

Despite all the advances in relative and absolute dating methods for the Lower and Middle Pleistocene, much ambiguity still surrounds the age of many of the key sites of earliest Europe. This can easily be illustrated by the debate over the age of Isernia, Italy, which on the basis of palaeomagnetic and K/Ar data was originally published as a late Lower Pleistocene site. According to some palaeontologists the fauna from the site was considerably younger, and after two decades of discussion the site has recently been situated in the earlier part of the Middle Pleistocene, at around 600 ka (Coltorti *et al.* 2000). Likewise, the dating of another important site, Boxgrove, in England, remains problematic, in that the variety of the various chronometric methods used have given varying results, ranging from 175 kya to more than 350 kya, i.e. from OIS 6 to OIS 11, while the biostratigraphical evidence suggests a correlation to OIS 13 (Roberts and Parfitt 1999b). In view of the fact that application of various techniques yields varying results, and in view of the error terms on some absolute dating techniques and the imprecision of biochronological methods, for the time being it is probably best to work with large blocks of time and to develop scenarios that do not depend on fine chronological positioning of sites.

There are better possibilities for assigning hominid presence to specific stages within warm-temperate phases, even if the ages of these warm-temperate phases themselves are unclear. Palynological and faunal studies, for instance, sometimes enable us to pinpoint archaeological assemblages to specific pollen zones within an interglacial and hence to estimate whether hominids were present during the beginning, middle or final phase of a warm-temperate period. This is especially the case where floral and faunal analysis can be combined.

Within the presumed equivalent of OIS 13 and the next cold phase, hominids seem to have been present over large areas of Europe except for its easternmost parts, and in quite a wide range of environments, from temperate woodland conditions, as at Boxgrove (Roberts and Parfitt 1999a) and at Miesenheim in Germany, to colder steppe-like settings, as known from the Kärlich loess sequence in the German Neuwied Basin (Roebroeks *et al.* 1992). We encounter their traces in various types of landscapes, from dissected limestone valley systems in southern Europe to the loess plains of northern France and the Mittelgebirge of Germany and to the coastal plains at Boxgrove.

However, the case of the Gravettian, referred to above, reminds us that within this long period population density may have been extremely low, and that 'centres' of occupation may have shifted from north to south and from west to east, as seen within time slices of a few thousand years in the Gravettian (Mussi *et al.* 2000). But there are absolutely no indications for such movements of demographic centres in the period considered here, because of the resolution problems. Instead of the Upper Palaeolithic image of presence and absence of human occupation within specific time slices, of data pertaining to low population densities, of small trips from refugia into areas largely deserted during the last glacial maximum of around 20,000 BP (Street and Terberger 1999) and of possible pioneer and residential phases in the Magdalenian (Housley *et al.* 1997), we have a palimpsest of 100,000 years of trial and error, of exploratory movements, of possibly thousands of years of continuous presence in one region and a contemporaneous on-and-off ephemeral presence in another. How can we distil information about landscape learning from such a huge palimpsest? What, if anything, can we do?

I want to try here to obtain some information on this issue in an indirect way, by discussing the implications of the virtually continuous presence of hominids in Europe for at least 500,000 years. As detailed elsewhere (Roebroeks 2001), the European record shows that Middle Pleistocene hominids were present in a large range of environments, over large (but not all) parts of Europe, from about half a million years ago, and we have many sites from the middle parts of the Middle Pleistocene onwards (Roebroeks *et al.* 1992; Gamble 1995). Combining this with the genetic data on Neandertals (Krings *et al.* 1997; 1999) and using the Neandertalization model, with its focus on the development of European endemicity (e.g. Arsuaga 2000; Arsuaga *et al.* 1997; Hublin 1998), I suggest that from about half a million years ago Europe saw a continuous occupation by – occasionally very small and rather isolated – groups of hominids (Roebroeks 2001). From about half a million years ago, Europeans (as represented by the Mauer and Boxgrove fossils) gradually developed into early Neandertals, such as those from the Sima de los Huesos in Spain, and ultimately to the 'classic' forms from the last glacial.

The absence of Lower and early Middle Pleistocene sites north of the Pyrenees and Alps suggests that even if hominids were around the Mediterranean perimeter from the late Lower Pleistocene onwards, significant changes in their behaviour would have been needed to take them north, across the many inland barriers of Europe (Dennell and Roebroeks 1996). At the same time, the evidence from outside Europe suggests that other factors may have been involved in the colonization of Europe. Work in Atlantic Morocco indicates that there, too, a marginal hominid ('Acheulean') presence just prior to the Brunhes-Matuyama boundary was separated from a more substantial occupation in the second half of the Middle Pleistocene (Raynal *et al.* 1995). The similarity to the European pattern suggests that more was at stake than adaptations to northern latitudes per se. Potts' variability selection hypothesis offers an interesting perspective here, as it relates both African and European developments to the increasing amplitude in environmental fluctuations apparent from deep sea records and terrestrial regional records, especially from the Middle Pleistocene onwards (Potts 1996, 1998). Potts has pointed to the temporal correlation between these environmental changes and the spurt in hominid brain expansion at around half a million years ago (see below). In his view, this temporal correlation is one expression of the evolution of complex anatomical, cognitive and social factors capable of processing and responding to intricate and variable environmental conditions – in short, the evolution of the kind of adaptive flexibility indicated by the various types of environments documented in the European Lower Palaeolithic record.

What can this inferred continuous presence tell us about the behaviour of these early Europeans and thus, indirectly, about the issues at stake in this volume? For a first answer to this question I turn to the archaeological record of Europe north of the large mountain chains.

North of the mountains: hunters

While making their way through Europe, the first settlers were confronted with environments with shorter and shorter growing seasons as they went north, and they had to deal increasingly with the problem of the temperate zone: the winter halt in productivity of the environment. In such an environment hunting would have been a strategy that increasingly served an omnivorous primate (Geist 1978; Binford 1981). Until recently, these theoretical predictions simply lacked an empirical base, though, and in the last two decades northern hominids prior to the appearance of modern humans have been depicted, in many behavioural scenarios, as at least part-time scavengers, to a large extent surviving on the leftovers of large predators or on natural deaths. Although this scavenging model dominated discussions in the 1980s and the first half of the 1990s, a series of recent studies along the lines developed by Binford's research now unambiguously demonstrates that (late) Middle Pleistocene and Upper Pleistocene hominids were very capable hunters of large mammals (Marean and Assefa 1999). Middle Palaeolithic prey animals included reindeer, from the south of France to Salzgitter-Lebenstedt in the north of Germany (Gaudzinski and Roebroeks 2000); bovids, at sites such as Biache-Saint-Vaast (Auguste 1995), Coudoulous, La Borde and Mauran in France (e.g. Jaubert *et al.* 1990; Farizy *et al.* 1994) and Wallertheim in Germany (Gaudzinski 1999); and also woodland rhinoceros, hunted in the last interglacial (OIS 5e) forested environments of Central Europe (Bratlund 1999). The environmental settings of these sites are highly variable, from 'cold' to warm-temperate, from open, subarctic types of environments to full interglacial wooded habitats (Roebroeks *et al.* 1992). Studies of the stable isotopes from Neandertal skeletal remains strongly suggest that they were top-level carnivores, animal protein constituting a very large part of their diet (Bocherens *et al.* 1999; Richards *et al.* 2000, 2001). A recent study by Sorensen and Leonard (2001) indicates that if Neandertals indeed had the high activity levels implied by their skeletal robusticity, they would have required foraging efficiencies within the range observed among modern humans.

The evidence for hunting in the Lower Palaeolithic is not as clear cut as for the Middle Palaeolithic, though it remains to be established whether this difference really reflects behavioural differences or whether we are simply dealing with sample biases and processes of preservation, as strongly suggested by the evidence from Schöningen in Germany (Thieme 1997, 1999). The Schöningen site has become well known through the discovery of a series of wooden spears, dating to about 300,000 to 400,000 years ago, which were found amidst the remains of approximately 20 horses, with almost no other species present (Thieme 1997, 1999). The faunal remains are probably even more exciting than the spears, as they yield precious evidence on subsistence strategies of the earliest Europeans unknown from any other Middle Pleistocene site. An ongoing study by B. Voormolen (Leiden) shows that a large number of horse bones display unambiguous traces of cut marks, and that many bones have been processed for marrow extraction. The Schöningen evidence shows that the hominids who produced this assemblage were in all likelihood capable hunters of large mammals. The Schöningen finds were recovered over an area of approximately 1,000 square metres, along the edges of a former lake, which the hominids may have used to 'disadvantage' the horses before killing them at close range with the spears (L.R. Binford, personal communication, 2000). This environment, which had a high and steady sedimentation rate, enabled a perfect preservation of hominid activities. Schöningen is very clearly an exception, but in this subsistence discussion such a taphonomical exception carries more behavioural weight than the 'normal' type of Lower Palaeolithic sites, such as the ones available when Binford compiled his 'look at the northern temperate zone' (1985).

If, as I believe, one can generalize the Schöningen evidence to the whole of Europe around 400,000 years ago, this implies that the mid-Middle Pleistocene occupants of Europe were capable and active hunters of large mammals. At least, by the time we see the first occupants of Europe north of the Pyrenees and Alps, these hominids must have solved the overwintering problem of the temperate zone by hunting and eating animals that had solved this overwintering problem long before the arrival of the first Europeans (Geist 1978).

This evidence of Middle Pleistocene hunting should not distract us from the fact that these hunting activities probably took place within settings considerably different from those in the Upper Palaeolithic (Gaudzinski and Roebroeks 2000: 517–18). For instance, the absence of indications for a structured (architecturally) use of space until the end of the Middle Palaeolithic (Kolen 1999) and the long-term stability in stone tool technology and typology in the Lower and Middle Palaeolithic are striking when compared with the Upper Palaeolithic record. A recent study of stable isotopes from Neandertals and from mid-Upper Palaeolithic humans indicates a significant broadening of the resource base in the Upper Palaeolithic, brought about by an increase in the exploitation of aquatic resources and quick terrestrial small game, possibly caused by Upper Palaeolithic human population growth (Richards *et al.* 2001).

Hunting in context

But what can we do with these assessments in the context of a focus on landscape learning? What kind of information might we distil from these subsistence data on former learning processes and their social context? What kind of inferences can we draw from these data on the hunting activities of the first Europeans? I suggest five possible paths of further exploration of the hunting data, by conceptualizing within the findings of other disciplines (Aiello 1998).

Size of ranges

Hunting must have had important consequences for many aspects of the lives of the first settlers of Europe, including the size of their home ranges. For instance, among primates higher-quality diets tend to be associated with larger home ranges, while carnivores have much larger ranges than herbivores and omnivores. And carnivore ranges are larger in high altitudes than in lower ones (Geist 1978, passim; cf. Gamble and Steele 1999). Ethnographic data on hunter-gatherers likewise show a general increase in the area of land exploited as dependence on hunting increases: closer to the poles, resources tend to become more spatially segregated along a gradient of decreasing temperature, and the average distance moved per residential move of hunter-gatherers tends to increase with decreasing temperature (Kelly 1995: 128–30). As hunting becomes more important towards the poles and most mammals need larger territories to support themselves in colder latitudes, the total area exploited generally increases. This suggests that the first Europeans north of the large mountain chains were hunters who operated over large areas. There is, unfortunately, no archaeological evidence on the specific size of these areas (Gamble and Steele 1999). The small amount of data we have for raw material transfers in the European Lower Palaeolithic (Féblot-Augustins 1997) indicates that movements of raw materials were generally short and can only provide minimum estimates of the areas over which early hominids operated. The database is somewhat better for the early phases of the Middle Palaeolithic, where we see transportation of lithics connect such different regions as the northern European plains with the German Mittelgebirge from at least OIS 6 onwards, with stone artefacts being moved over distances of more than 120 km as the crow flies at around 200,000 years ago (Roebroeks *et al.* 1988). Concerning the earlier phases of the Middle Palaeolithic, some authors stress that the recurrences of provenances of raw materials over significant periods of time indicate transmission of shared knowledge relative to particular landmarks over many generations (e.g. Féblot-Augustins 1999; Roebroeks and Tuffreau 1999).

Physiological changes and sexual role differentiation

The 'expensive tissue hypothesis' (Aiello and Wheeler 1995; Aiello 1998) provides us with an interesting social contextualization of the hunting data. This hypothesis focuses on the large brains of humans and states that study of the metabolic cost of the brain can be very informative about the evolution of the human niche. Human brains constitute on average only 2 per cent of total body weight, but they use about 20 per cent of all the body's energy. Aiello and Wheeler (1995) posit that humans can maintain these costly, large brains without also having high basal metabolic rates simply by reducing the size of one of the other expensive tissues, the gastrointestinal tract. This is only possible by adopting a higher-quality diet, which would release the constraints on encephalization by producing a smaller gut and thus balancing the metabolic costs of the brain (Aiello and Wheeler 1995). As detailed by Aiello (1998), the relationship between the energy requirements for brain growth and a high-quality diet 'is likely to have had additional profound implications for hominia life-history and social behaviour and, therefore, for the human niche'.

One such implication was in gender relationships. Women paid a high price for the increase in brain size, becoming increasingly dependent on the help of others – grandmothers, males – in the procurement of high-quality food for themselves and their offspring (O'Connell *et al.* 1999). The marked increase in brain size after 500 kyr bp would have put both females and juveniles under increased energy stress, and it is around this time that cooperation among caring females and provisioning of high-quality food by males increase, as predicted by the hypothesis. It is also around this time that the archaeological record contains the first evidence for hunting of large mammals, as illustrated by the Schöningen evidence.

The predictions of the expensive tissue hypothesis concerning female–male cooperation are not easy to test, though. Recent statistical analysis of the rich Middle Pleistocene hominid material from the Sima de los Huesos at Atapuerca (Arsuaga *et al.* 1997) can be interpreted as confirming the predictions, as it shows that the degree of sexual dimorphism in this group of about 30 'Neandertal' individuals is similar to that in modern human populations (Arsuaga 2000). While the Sima de los Huesos material dates from about 300 kyr bp, more specific information relating to the sexual division of labour comes from studies of Late Pleistocene Neandertals only, and even there the evidence is very limited. Analysis of Neandertal humeri suggests that males and females used their arms differently, with males often engaged in activities that required considerable strength in their right arms (Ben-Itzhak *et al.* 1988). Differences between male and female Neandertals in traumas of the upper body and head form another possible signal of a sexual division of labour (Berger and Trinkaus 1995).

Food sharing

While the expensive tissue hypothesis (which has not remained uncontested: see Hladik *et al.* 1999) offers a valuable tool for contextualizing the hunting evidence and interpreting it in terms of the social behaviour of the early Europeans, Tooby and DeVore (1987) have likewise developed an interesting behavioural ecology perspective on the social setting of hunting. Hunting of large game is a boom-or-bust activity. Variability in hunting success and the fact that meat comes mostly in chunks too large for an individual capturer to consume indicate that there must have been a strong evolutionary selection for 'food sharing, food exchange and risk sharing through deferred reciprocation among the larger social group' (Tooby and DeVore 1987: 224). In Winterhalder and Smith's view it was only with the evolution of reciprocity or exchange-based food transfers that it became economical for individual hunters to target large game (2000: 60). Hunting made food sharing necessary, while food sharing made hunting feasible.

A knowledge base for hunting

Active cooperation among individuals also seems to be indicated by the hunting activities themselves. Compared with most other hunting animals, humans are slow-moving omnivores and are equipped with limited olfactory and auditory capacities; humans cannot outrun most game, and have to outsmart prey. As discussed at length by Geist (1978: 308–10 and passim), modern hunters are successful by virtue of knowing the animals and the various traces they leave behind in the landscape and by using this knowledge of animal behaviour as a 'tool'. It is obvious that knowledge of animal behaviour must have likewise played a key role in the successful hunting of large mammals in the Palaeolithic, especially with the limited technologies at stake. Even if experiments suggest that the Schöningen throwing spears were superb hunting weapons, usable up to a distance of about 25 m (Steguweit 1999; Rieder 2000), the most important 'tool' must have been an extensive knowledge of a wide range of animal behaviour. Combined with a keen insight into a variety of other factors, such as diurnal changes in wind directions, that knowledge enabled hunters to get close enough to a large mammal, considerably less than 25 m, for some certainty of a hit. As stressed by Guthrie (1997), such stalking activities are much more difficult out in the open, away from stands of trees in the forest or at the forest edge. The difficulties and complexities of hunting have been much emphasized (e.g. Geist 1978: 308–10 and passim; Frison 1991, 1998). Though no systematic study has been made yet of the informational requirements for large mammal hunting by prehistoric people with limited technologies, most agree that hunting the variety of species that we now know was present in the Lower and Middle Palaeolithic, in a variety of situations, "required considerable experience, quality education, and years of intensive practice. From what we know about hunting today, we can see that such hunting was very difficult" (Guthrie 1997: 107; see also Geist 1978). This suggests that there was a strong evolutionary stimulus to cooperation and to the sharing of information between the older members of a group and the young – an increasing social interaction in which the transcendence of the 'here and now' played a key role. The quality education that was required to become an expert Pleistocene hunter probably needed a form of active (intergenerational) transmission of information from adult to young individuals, and may have taken the form of active tutoring. Furthermore, judging from the evidence on their life history pattern, these hominids had a prolonged pattern of maturation similar to that of modern humans (Bermúdez de Castro *et al.* 1999), while a recent study of the Boxgrove tibia suggests that Middle Pleistocene adults may have reached a higher age than is commonly inferred (Streeter *et al.* 2001).

The development of language

The last context is the social origin of language, based on comparative morphology and the ethology of primates, which fits well with the implications of the archaeological evidence for hunting in the Middle Pleistocene as discussed above – though I do not see how the origin of language could actually be tested in the archaeological record. Dunbar's (1992) research has pointed to the clear relationships between the relative size of the neocortex of the brain of primates, their 'cognitive group' size (Dunbar 1998) and the time they invest in physical contact, in grooming. The relationship between neocortex size and group size holds up in at least four other mammalian taxonomic groups, important supporting evidence for what has become known as the 'social brain hypothesis' (Dunbar 1998), according to which primates' relatively large brains arise from the information-processing demands of their complex social systems. Starting from the relationships between the relative size of the neocortex, group size and time invested in individual contact, Aiello and Dunbar (1993; cf. Dunbar 1996) suggest that, by the time of the appearance of the genus *Homo*, groups had become so large that a non-physical form of social contact – language – became necessary for maintenance of the group's social cohesion. While early *Homo* may have had a rather rudimentary language, the Middle Pleistocene encephalization mentioned above would indicate a group size similar to that seen in modern humans. Using the human neocortex size ratio and extrapolating a value for human group size from the primate equation produces a value in the order of 150. This number agrees well with actual observations of the number of people that individual humans tend to associate with. As Dunbar (1998) stresses, among modern humans these larger groups are not (or only very rarely) conspicuous as physical entities, but they do have important social connotations for the individuals concerned: 150 is the number of individuals most people know on a personal basis, the definition used with other primates (Dunbar 1998; see also Steele 1996). The observed number of 150 also fits very well with the results of Wobst's (1974) computer simulations to determine the minimum size of a viable human breeding population, which suggest that biological survival is dependent on a minimum group size of 175. The actual size of such 'cognitive' groups and prehistoric breeding populations must have varied widely, in various complex ways, determined by environmental factors, amongst others (Kelly 1995: 210). The key point here, though, is that there are good arguments to infer a 'cognitive' group size of around 150 individuals by the middle part of the Middle Pleistocene. Following Aiello and Dunbar (1993), with such a group size it is impossible to influence other members' behaviour through physical contact only. Group integration cannot be performed on the basis of personal contact alone, and a new way of 'grooming' – vocal grooming, or language – must by then (i.e. about half a million years ago) have emerged for the development and maintenance of stable social relations. According to the social brain hypothesis, language came into existence as a kind of social glue that enabled displacement in both place and time.

Conclusions

Combining these various strands of evidence, data and ideas, one can construct a basic profile of the first Europeans north of the large mountain chains: highly mobile, omnivorous primates, adapted to a wide range of landscape settings, and competent hunters of large game whose hunting success, given the limited technology, must have been based to a large degree on a detailed knowledge of animal behaviour. This knowledge was probably updated and transmitted through intergenerational information exchange and through individual contacts within the larger 'cognitive' group, which had a size of about 150 individuals. The individual members of such loose larger groups collected information on the whereabouts of other individuals and smaller groups and the availability of food resources as they roamed the landscape and pooled this information with other members of the larger 'cognitive' group. Language may have made such exchange of information about resources and the coordination of foraging activities possible. Intensive, language-based cooperation between individuals of both sexes and between local small groups seems to have become a standard ingredient of the behaviour of these hominids by the middle part of the Middle Pleistocene, at the latest.

This profile is not unproblematic, though, for at least two reasons. First, it is clear that some of its dimensions are more observable than others: the various types of landscapes settled are archaeologically very visible, as are data on hunting activities, no matter how ambiguous the information from some of the important early sites. Dunbar's estimates of group size are difficult, if not impossible, to test with archaeological data, because the archaeological visibility of any group size of Palaeolithic hunter-gatherers is problematic. Recent studies of some Upper Palaeolithic sites that were thought to reflect the aggregation of smaller groups into larger ones, e.g. Dolni Vestonice and Pavlov in Slovakia (Verpoorte 2000), Mal'ta in Siberia (Vasil'ev 2000) and Oelknitz (S. Gaudzinski, personal communication, 2000) have shown that such interpretations are not unproblematic and that small groups may have reoccupied the same locations over many years, leading to the accumulations of large amounts of material. Furthermore, following Dunbar, I have opted here for a 'linguistic' form of information exchange between individuals, while Donald (e.g. 1999) has pointed to the possibility of complex forms of behaviour without the need for linguistic representations, i.e. with refined imitative and mimetic skills.

Second, apart from problems with its individual building blocks, this profile might suggest that we are dealing with extremely versatile, flexible hominids who could do almost anything, their landscape learning embedded in key aspects of social behaviour, indissolubly linked with high-quality diets, hunting and resulting range size and mobility. The archaeological record shows that this was clearly not the case. During the first half of the Middle Pleistocene hominids did not learn the landscape of large parts of Europe, as can be deduced from the distribution of human occupation in the Middle Pleistocene (see various contributions in Roebroeks and van Kolfschoten 1995), such as in Scandinavia or, until about 300,000 years ago, the Russian plains (Praslov 1995). The time discrepancy between eastern Europe and western and central Europe is in the order of 200,000 to 300,000 years, somewhat comparable to the age difference between the first traces of occupation in the Mediterranean and the area at stake here. Although here we face the problem that we archaeologists cannot in fact differentiate between a successful adaptation (without problems) to a given new area and a range extension that required the stretching of all capacities to their limits, the chronology of occupation of the various European regions may convey an ecological message, as one can relate the history of colonization to the variations in key resources observed within Europe (Gamble 1986). As nicely illustrated by the large transport distances of lithics in the Middle Palaeolithic of central Europe (Roebroeks *et al.* 1988; Féblot-Augustins 1999), the more continental, harsher conditions there increased the size of areas over which groups had to forage and hence the spatial scale of the networks that these hominids maintained. As these omnivorous hunting primates familiarized themselves with unfamiliar landscapes, their range extensions were limited by the spatial extension of their networks, by the physical distribution of the individual members of the 'cognitive group' over the landscape. The chronology and the ecology of the colonization of the various European regions (Roebroeks 2001) suggest that the size and the scale of these loose networks were subject to changes over a very long term, of a magnitude far greater than those we know from later range extensions, especially those of *Homo sapiens sapiens*. Although these first Europeans were successful hunters who colonized a wide range of environmental settings, the long-term stability of their archaeological distribution over major areas of Europe again suggests that in key aspects of their behaviour they were very different from Upper Palaeolithic humans. And the long-term stability in geographical range extension documented in Europe – provided the pattern is a valid one, and not significantly biased by differences in research intensity between western and eastern parts of Europe – is paralleled by the long-term stability in other domains, especially in stone tool technology and use of space, both referred to above.

It is difficult to draw meaningful inferences from this on the issue of landscape learning, apart from the very general – superficial – ones I have made above. The long-term stability in various domains, and especially in the geographical distribution of Lower and Middle Pleistocene hominids, is certainly a key issue that needs to be addressed, as it is so strikingly different – as far as one can deduce from later range extensions – from later ways of learning the landscape. The similarities between the European Lower and Middle Pleistocene record reviewed here and developments in northern Africa mentioned above suggest that the limiting factors may have been of a more general, possibly genetic, character.

References

Aiello, L.C. (1998). 'The "expensive tissue hypothesis" and the evolution of the human adaptive niche: a study in comparative anatomy.' In: J. Bailey (ed.), *Science in Archaeology: An Agenda for the Future*, 25–36, London: English Heritage.

Aiello, L.C. and R.I.M. Dunbar (1993). 'Neocortex Size, Group Size and the Evolution of Language', *Current Anthropology* 34:184–93.

Aiello, L.C. and P. Wheeler (1995). 'The Expensive Tissue Hypothesis: the brain and the digestive system in human and primate evolution', *Current Anthropology* 36:199–221.

Arsuaga, J.L. (2000). 'Les premiers peuplements européens et les Néandertaliens.' Paper presented at the CNRS Conference *Les Hominidés et leurs environnements. Histoire et Interactions*. Université de Poitiers, Poitiers (France), 18–20 September 2000.

Arsuaga, J.L., J.-M. Bermúdez de Castro, and E. Carbonell (eds) (1997). Special Issue: The Sima de los Huesos hominid site, *Journal of Human Evolution* 33:105–421.

Auguste, P. (1995). 'Chasse et charognage au Paléolithique moyen: l'apport du gisement de Biache-Saint-Vaast (Pas-de-Calais)', *Bulletin de la Société Préhistorique Française* 92:155–67.

Ben-Itzhak, S., P. Smith and R. Bloom (1988). 'Radiographic study of the humerus in Neanderthals and *Homo sapiens sapiens*', *American Journal of Physical Anthropology* 77:231–42.

Berger, T.T. and E. Trinkaus (1995). 'Patterns of trauma among the Neanderthals', *Journal of Archaeological Science* 22:841–52.

Bermúdez de Castro, J.-M., A. Rosas, E. Carbonell, M.E. Nicolas, J. Rodríguez and J.L. Arsuaga (1999). 'A modern human pattern of dental development in Lower Pleistocene hominids from Atapuerca-TD6 (Spain)', *Proceedings of the National Academy of Sciences USA* 96:4210–13.

Binford, L.R. (1981). *Bones: Ancient Men and Modern Myths*, Orlando, FL: Academic Press.

—— (1985). 'Human ancestors: changing views of their behavior', *Journal of Anthropological Archaeology* 4:292–327.

Blockley, S.P.E., R.E. Donahue and A.M. Pollard (2000). 'Radiocarbon calibration and Late Glacial occupation in northwest Europe', *Antiquity* 74:112–21.

Bocherens, H., D. Billiou, A. Mariotti *et al.* (1999). 'Palaeoenvironmental and palaeodietary implications of isotopic biogeochemistry of last interglacial Neanderthal and mammal bones in Scladina Cave (Belgium)', *Journal of Archaeological Science* 26:599–607.

Bocquet-Appel, J.-P. and P.Y. Demars (2000). 'Neanderthal contraction and modern human colonization in Europe', *Antiquity* 74:544–52.

Bonifay, E. and B. Vandermeersch (eds) (1991). *Les Premiers Européens*. Paris: Editions du CTHS.

Bratlund, B. (1999). 'Anthropogenic factors in the thanatocoenose of the Last Interglacial travertines at Taubach (Germany).' In: S. Gaudzinski and E. Turner (eds), *The Role of Early Humans in the Accumulation of European Lower and Middle Palaeolithic Bone Assemblages*, 255-62. Bonn: Habelt.

Capaldi, E.A., A.D. Smith, J.L. Osborn *et al.* (2000). 'Ontogeny of orientation flight in the honeybee revealed by harmonic radar', *Nature* 403:537–40.

Carbonell, E., J.-M. Bermúdez de Castro, J.L. Arsuaga *et al.* (1995a). 'Lower Pleistocene hominids and artifacts from Atapuerca-TD6 (Spain)', *Science* 269:826–9.

Carbonell, E., M. Mosquera, X. Pedro Rodriguez and R. Sala (1995b). 'The first human settlement of Europe', *Journal of Anthropological Research* 51:107–14.

Carbonell, E., M. Esteban, A.M. Nájera *et al.* (1999). 'The Pleistocene site of Gran Dolina, Sierra de Atapuerca, Spain: a history of the archaeological investigations', *Journal of Human Evolution* 37:313–24.

Coltorti, M., S. Corrado, D. Di Bucci *et al.* (2000). 'New chronostratigraphical and palaeoclimatic data from the "Isernia la Pineta" site.' In: Subcommission on European Quaternary Stratigraphy (SEQS) meeting, *The Plio-Pleistocene Boundary and the Lower/Middle Pleistocene Transition: Type Areas and Sections. Abstracts,* Bari, Italy, 25–29 September 2000.

Dennell, R.W. (1998). 'Grasslands, tool making and the hominid colonization of southern Asia: a reconsideration.' In: M.D. Petraglia and R. Korisettar (eds), *Early Human Behaviour in Global Context: The Rise and Diversity of the Lower Palaeolithic Record*, 280-303, London/ New York: Routledge.

Dennell, R. and W. Roebroeks (1996). 'The earliest colonization of Europe: the short chronology revisited', *Antiquity* 70:535–42.

Donald, M. (1999). 'Preconditions for the evolution of protolanguages.' In: M.C. Corballis and E.G. Lea (eds), *The Descent of Mind: Psychological Perspectives on Hominid Evolution*, Oxford and New York: Oxford University Press, 140–55.

Dunbar, R.I.M. (1992). 'Neocortex size as a constraint on group size in primates', *Journal of Human Evolution* 22:469–93.

—— (1996). *Grooming, Gossip and the Evolution of Language*, London and Boston: Faber and Faber.

—— (1998). 'The Social Brain Hypothesis', *Evolutionary Anthropology* 6:178–86.

Farizy, C., F. David and J. Jaubert (1994). *Hommes et bisons du paléolithique moyen à Mauran (Haute-Garonne)*, Paris: CNRS.

Féblot-Augustins, J. (1997). *La circulation des matières premières au paléolithique*, Liège: ERAUL.

—— (1999). 'Raw material transport patterns and settlement systems in the European Lower and Middle Palaeolithic.' In: W. Roebroeks and C. Gamble (eds), *The Middle Palaeolithic Occupation of Europe*, 193–214. Leiden: Leiden University.

Frison, G.C. (1991). 'Hunting Strategies, Prey Behavior and Mortality Data.' In: M.C. Stiner (ed.), *Human Predators and Prey Mortality*, 15–30, Boulder/San Francisco: Westview Press.

Frison, G.C. (1998). 'Paleoindian large mammal hunters of the plains of North America', *Proceedings of the National Academy of Sciences USA* 95:14576–83.

Gamble, C.S. (1986). *The Palaeolithic Settlement of Europe*, Cambridge: Cambridge University Press.

—— (1995). 'The earliest occupation of Europe: the environmental background.' In: W. Roebroeks and T. van Kolfschoten (eds), *The Earliest Occupation of Europe*. Proceedings of the European Science Foundation Workshop at Tautavel (France), November 1993, 279–95, Leiden: Leiden University Press.

Gamble, C.S. and J. Steele (1999). 'Hominid Ranging Patterns and Dietary Strategies.' In: H. Ullrich (ed.), *Hominid Evolution. Lifestyles and Survival Strategies*, 396–409, Berlin: Edition Archaea.

Gaudzinski, S. (1995). 'Wallertheim Revisited: a Re-analysis of the Fauna from the Middle Palaeolithic Site of Wallertheim /Rheinhessen/Germany), *Journal of Archaeological Science* 22:51–66.

Gaudzinski, S. and W. Roebroeks (2000). 'Adults only. Reindeer hunting at the Middle Palaeolithic site Salzgitter Lebenstedt, Northern Germany', *Journal of Human Evolution* 38:497–521.

Geist, V. (1978). *Life Strategies, Human Evolution, Environmental Design. Toward a Biological Theory of Health*, New York, Heidelberg, and Berlin: Springer Verlag.

Guthrie, R.D. (1997). 'Fossil fat – a forensic key to understanding life in the Late Paleolithic of northern Eurasia.' In: M. Patou-Mathis (ed.), *L'alimentation des hommes du paléolithique. Approche pluridisciplinaire*, 93–125, Liège: ERAUL (ERAUL 83).

Hladik, C.M., D.J. Chivers and P. Pasquet (1999). 'On Diet and Gut Size in Non-human Primates and Humans: Is There a Relationship to Brain Size?', *Current Anthropology* 40:695–7.

Housley, R.A., C.S. Gamble, M. Street and P. Pettitt (1997). 'Radiocarbon evidence for the Lateglacial human recolonisation of northern Europe', *Proceedings of the Prehistoric Society* 63:25–54.

Hublin, J. (1998). 'Climatic changes, paleogeography, and the evolution of the Neandertals.' In: T. Akazawa, K. Aoki and O. Bar-Yosef (eds), *Neandertals and Modern Humans in Western Asia*, 295–310, New York: Plenum Press.

Jaubert, J., M. Lorblanchet, H. Laville, R. Slott-Moller, A. Turq and J.-P. Brugal (1990). *Les Chasseurs d'Aurochs de la Borde. Un site du Paléolithique moyen (Livernon, Lot)*, Paris: Editions de la Maison des Sciences de l'Homme.

Kelly, R.L. (1995). *The Foraging Spectrum. Diversity in Hunter-Gatherer Lifeways*, Washington and London: Smithsonian Institution Press.

Kolen, J. (1999). 'Hominids without homes: on the nature of Middle Palaeolithic settlement in Europe.' In: W. Roebroeks and C. Gamble (eds), *The Middle Palaeolithic Occupation of Europe*, 139–75, Leiden: Leiden University.

Krings, M., A. Stone, R.W. Schmitz, H. Krainitzki, M. Stoneking and S. Pääbo (1997). 'Neandertal DNA Sequences and the Origin of Modern Humans', *Cell* 90:19–30.

Krings, M., H. Geisert, R.W. Schmitz, H. Krainitzki and S. Pääbo (1999). 'DNA sequence of the mitochondrial hypervariable region II from the Neandertal type specimen', *Proceedings of the National Academy of Sciences USA* 96:5581–5.

Marean, C.W. and Z. Assefa (1999). 'Zooarchaeological evidence for the faunal exploitation behavior of Neandertals and early modern humans', *Evolutionary Anthropology* 8:22–37.

Mussi, M. (1995). 'The earliest occupation of Europe: Italy.' In: W. Roebroeks and T. van Kolfschoten (eds) (1995). *The Earliest Occupation of Europe*. Proceedings of the European Science Foundation Workshop at Tautavel (France), November 1993, 27–49. Leiden: Leiden University Press.

Mussi, M., W. Roebroeks and J. Svoboda (2000). 'Hunters of the Golden Age: an introduction.' In: W. Roebroeks, M. Mussi, J. Svoboda and K. Fennema (eds), *Hunters of the Golden Age. The Mid Upper Palaeolithic of Eurasia 30,000 – 20,000 bp*, 1–11, Leiden: Leiden University.

O'Connell, J.F., K. Hawkes and N.G. Blurton Jones (1999). 'Grandmothering and the evolution of *Homo erectus*', *Journal of Human Evolution* 36:461–85.

Oms, O., J.M. Parès, B. Martínez-Navarro *et al.* (2000). 'Early human occupation of Western Europe: paleomagnetic dates for two paleolithic sites in Spain', *Proceedings of the National Academy of Sciences USA*, 97:10666–70.

Pettitt, P.B. (2000). 'Dating the Mid Upper Palaeolithic: the radiocarbon evidence.' In: W. Roebroeks, M. Mussi, J. Svoboda and K. Fennema (eds), *Hunters of the Golden Age. The Mid Upper Palaeolithic of Eurasia 30,000–20,000 bp*, 21–30: Leiden: Leiden University.

Pettitt, P.B. and A.W.G. Pike (2001). 'Blind in a cloud of data: problems with the chronology of Neanderthal extinction and anatomically modern human expansion', *Antiquity* 75:415–20.

Potts, R. (1996). *Humanity's Descent: The Consequences of Ecological Instability*, New York: Morrow.

—— (1998). 'Variability selection in hominid evolution', *Evolutionary Anthropology* 7:81–96.

Praslov, N.D. (1995). 'The earliest occupation of the Russian Plain: a short note.' In: W. Roebroeks and T. van Kolfschoten (eds), *The Earliest Occupation of Europe*. Proceedings of the European Science Foundation Workshop at Tautavel (France), November 1993, 61–6, Leiden: Leiden University Press.

Raynal, J.-P., L. Magoga, F.-Z. Sbihi-Alaoui and D. Geraads (1995). 'The earliest occupation of Atlantic Morocco: the Casablanca evidence.' In: W. Roebroeks and T. van Kolfschoten (eds) (1995). *The Earliest Occupation of Europe*, 255–62, Leiden: Leiden University Press.

Richards, M.P., P.B. Pettitt, E. Trinkaus, F.H. Smith, M. Paunovic and I. Karavanic (2000). 'Neanderthal diet at Vindija and Neanderthal predation: the evidence from stable isotopes', *Proceedings of the National Academy of Sciences USA* 97:7663–6.

Richards, M.P., P.B. Pettitt, M.C. Stiner and E. Trinkaus (2001). Stable isotope evidence for increasing dietary breadth in the European mid-Upper Palaeolithic. Proceedings of the National Academy of Sciences USA 98, 6528–32.

Rieder, H. (2000). 'Die altpaläolithischen Wurfspeere von Schöningen, ihre Erprobung und ihre Bedeutung für die Lebensumwelt des *Homo erectus*', *Praehistorica Thuringica* 5:68–75.

Roberts, M. B. and S. A. Parfitt (eds) (1999a). *A Middle Pleistocene hominid site at Eartham Quarry, Boxgrove, West Sussex*, London: English Heritage.

Roberts, M. B. and S.A. Parfitt (1999b). 'Biostratigraphy and summary.' In: M. B. Roberts and S.A. Parfitt (eds), *A Middle Pleistocene hominid site at Eartham Quarry, Boxgrove, West Sussex*, 395–415, London: English Heritage.

Roebroeks, W. (2001). 'Hominid behaviour and the earliest occupation of Europe: an exploration', *Journal of Human Evolution* 41:437–61.

Roebroeks, W. and T. van Kolfschoten (1994). 'The earliest occupation of Europe: a short chronology', *Antiquity* 68:489–503.

Roebroeks, W. and T. van Kolfschoten (eds) (1995). *The Earliest Occupation of Europe*. Proceedings of the European Science Foundation Workshop at Tautavel (France), November 1993, Leiden: Leiden University Press.

Roebroeks, W. and A. Tuffreau (1999). 'Palaeoenvironment and settlement patterns of the Northwest European Middle Palaeolithic.' In: W. Roebroeks and C. Gamble (eds), *The Middle Palaeolithic Occupation of Europe*, 121-38, Leiden: University of Leiden.

Roebroeks, W. and T. van Kolfschoten (1998). 'The earliest occupation of Europe: a view from the north.' In: E. Aguirre (ed.), *Atapuerca y la evolucion humana*, 155–68, Madrid: Fundación Ramón Areces.

Roebroeks, W., J. Kolen and E. Rensink (1988). 'Planning depth, anticipation and the organization of Middle Palaeolithic technology: the "archaic natives" meet Eve's descendants', *Helinium* 28:17–34.

Roebroeks, W., N.J. Conard and T. van Kolfschoten (1992). 'Dense Forests, Cold Steppes and the Palaeolithic Settlement of Northern Europe', *Current Anthropology* 33:551–86.

Roebroeks, W., M. Mussi, J. Svoboda and K. Fennema (eds) (2000). *Hunters of the Golden Age. The Archaeology of the Mid Upper Palaeolithic of Eurasia 30–20 Kyr bp*, Leiden: Leiden University.

Sorensen, M.V. and W.R. Leonard (2001). 'Neandertal energetics and foraging efficiency', *Journal of Human Evolution* 40:483–95.

Steele, J. (1996). 'On predicting hominid group sizes.' In: J. Steele and S. Shennan (eds), *The Archaeology of Human Ancestry*, 230–252, London: Routledge.

Steguweit, L. (1999). 'Die Recken von Schöningen – 400.000 Jahre Jagd mit dem Speer', *Mitteilungsblatt der Gesellschaft für Urgeschichte* 8:5–14.

Street, M. and T. Terberger (1999). 'The last Pleniglacial and the human settlement of Central Europe: new information from the Rhineland site Wiesbaden-Igstadt', *Antiquity* 73:259–72.

Streeter, M., S.D. Stout, E. Trinkaus, C.B. Stringer, M.B. Roberts and S.A. Parfitt (2001). 'Histomorphometric age assessment of the Boxgrove 1 tibial diaphysis', *Journal of Human Evolution* 40:331–8.

Thieme, H. (1997). 'Lower Palaeolithic hunting spears from Germany', *Nature* 385:807–10.

—— (1999). 'Altpaläolithische Holzgeräte aus Schöningen, Lkr. Helmstedt. Bedeutsame Funde zur Kulturentwicklung des frühen Menschen', *Germania* 77:451–487.

Tooby, J. and I. DeVore (1987). 'The reconstruction of hominid behavioral evolution through strategic modelling.' In: W.G. Kinzey (ed.), *The Evolution of Human Behavior: Primate Models*, 183–238, Albany, NY: State University of New York Press.

Turner, A. (1999). 'Assessing earliest human settlement of Eurasia: Late Pliocene dispersions from Africa', *Antiquity* 73:563–70.

Turq, A., B. Martinez-Navarro, P. Palmquist, A. Arribas, J. Agusti and J. Rodriguez-Vidal (1996). 'Le Plio-Pleistocene de la région d'Orce, province de Grenade, Espagne: bilan et perspectives de recherche', *Paléo* 8:161–204.

Vasil'ev (2000). 'The Siberian Mosaic: Upper Palaeolithic adaptations and change before the Last Glacial Maximum.' In: W. Roebroeks, M. Mussi, J. Svoboda and K. Fennema (eds),

Hunters of the Golden Age. The Mid Upper Palaeolithic of Eurasia 30,000 – 20,000 BP, 173–195, Leiden: Leiden University.

Verpoorte, A. (2001). *Places of Art, Traces of Fire. A contextual approach to anthropomorphic figurines in the Pavlovian (Central Europe, 29–24 kyr b.p.)*, Leiden: Leiden University (Archaeological Studies 8).

Villa, P. (1996). 'The First Italians. Le Industrie litiche del giacimento paleolitico di Isernia La Pineta' (book review), *Lithic Technology* 21:71–9.

—— (2001). 'Early Italy and the Colonization of Western Europe.' In: O. Bar Yosef and L. Straus (eds), special issue: Out of Africa in the Pleistocene, *Quaternary International* 75:113–30.

Winterhalder, B. and E.A. Smith (2000). 'Analyzing Adaptive Strategies: Human Behavioral Ecology at Twenty-Five', *Evolutionary Anthropology* 9:51–72.

Wobst, M. (1974). 'Boundary Conditions for Paleolithic Social Systems: A Simulation Approach', *American Antiquity* 39:147–78.

7

THE SOCIAL CONTEXT OF LANDSCAPE LEARNING AND THE LATEGLACIAL–EARLY POSTGLACIAL RECOLONIZATION OF THE BRITISH ISLES

Christopher Tolan-Smith

Although anatomically modern humans had established themselves in the British Isles at the latitude of 53N several millennia before the maximum stage of the last glaciation (Bocquet-Appel and Demars 2000; Jacobi and Pettitt 2000), the onset of extreme glacial conditions around 20,000 years ago led to the abandonment of this part of northwest Europe. By the time recolonization got under way, following on from deglaciation, there had been a hiatus of at least 7,000 years during which knowledge of these northern landscapes is likely to have lapsed. Although claims have been made for the extreme longevity of landscape traditions in the context of origin myths (Echo-Hawk 2000), from the practical perspective of the people involved the deglaciated landscapes of the British Isles were terra incognita in the most literal sense of the term, while even half-remembered and distorted myths were of no use in northern Britain and Ireland, which entered the realm of human settlement for the first time during the early postglacial. Knowledge had to be acquired anew, and the lateglacial and early postglacial settlement of the British Isles offers a classic case of the 'landscape learning process' in the context of remote antiquity.

The date and rate at which the formerly glaciated and periglacial areas of Europe north of latitude 50N were settled during the late Pleistocene and early Holocene has been well established by several hundred radiocarbon dates (Smith and Openshaw 1990; Gob 1991; Charles 1996; C. Smith 1997; Housley *et al.* 1997; Tolan-Smith 1998; Tolan-Smith and Bonsall 1999; Blockley *et al.* 2000a, b; Housley *et al.* 2000). The chronometric details of this process need not be gone into here, though it should be noted that the data do not appear to document an even rate of demic expansion across the areas studied. Housley *et al.* (1997) have argued that while the bulk of the dates appear to document a consistent picture of early human settlement, in some areas these dates are preceded by a number which are significantly earlier. They suggest that these early dates might represent what they call a 'pioneer' phase that preceded the main phase of 'residential settlement', which often occurred several centuries later. This interpretation of the data has been questioned by Blockley *et al.* (2000a, b), both on the basis of the statistical method used and on the grounds that Housley *et al.* used uncalibrated radiocarbon dates. I have consistently used uncalibrated radiocarbon dates (Smith 1997; Tolan-Smith 1998; Tolan-Smith and Bonsall 1999) and will continue to do so until a universally accepted calibration curve is available for the period in question. At present Blockley *et al.*'s statistical argument has more to recommend it, and I remain unconvinced that it is possible to identify a distinct 'pioneer' phase as opposed to the establishment of permanent 'residential' settlement. In any case, what is significant in terms of the recolonization process is the development of a situation in which communities can maintain themselves in their chosen locale more or less permanently. The Older Dryas plateau in the radiocarbon calibration curve also makes it difficult to interpret dates falling within this period (Kitagawa and van der Plicht 1998; R. Barton 1999: 76). While recent debate has focused mainly on the initial establishment of settlement in the formerly glaciated and periglacial areas of northwest Europe, the interesting issue of the apparent variability in the rates of expansion, beyond that which can be accounted for by compressions in the calibration curve, has received less attention.

Several papers published in the volume edited by Larsson (1996) provide details of evidence for the initial settlement of Scandinavia. In particular Thommessen refers to a number of radiocarbon dated records of a human presence in the far north of Norway in the centuries either side of 10,000 BP (Thommessen 1996: 237). With settlement established in southern Scandinavia by 12,600 BP, a human presence 2,000 km to the north 2,600 years later requires an expansion rate of 0.8 km per year, which compares well with the rate of 0.68 km per year estimated by Housley *et al.* (1997: 49).

Turning to the British Isles by way of comparison, the radiocarbon data document a human presence well established at about latitude 54N by 12,400 BP. Housley *et al.* (1997: 49) proposed a rate of expansion into Britain from adjoining parts of continental Europe of 1.54 km per year. On this basis the most northerly parts of mainland Britain should have been occupied within a further 650 years. Present radiocarbon evidence suggests that these northerly regions were not occupied, in any form, until the eighth millennium BP, a span of 5,000 years for humans to cover a distance of 500 km, or a rate of 0.1 km per year. Clearly there is a massive discrepancy between the two regions considered. This anomaly can be accounted for by a 'standstill' in the spread of settlement into and across the British Isles that occurred between 11,000 BP and 9000 BP which is not paralleled in the Scandinavian case. In assessing the duration of this phase it is necessary to take account of compressions in the radiocarbon calibration curve, in particular those identified in the tenth millennium (Becker *et al.* 1991). However, even the most significant of these compressions affects only a few centuries of calendar time, and speculations on the nature and significance of the 'standstill' phase in terms of the landscape learning process form the main focus of this chapter.

Landscape learning as a social process

From the perspectives of archaeology and palaeogeography a number of processes are implicated in the colonization of formerly uninhabited regions. First, there is the natural tendency of species to expand to fill their ecological niche. Second, human communities adapted to life in the boreal-tundra transitional zone are likely to have moved north with that zone as a policy designed to maintain a successful adaptation. Third, population growth will have provided a stimulus to expansion into unoccupied areas. In an important paper drawing on data from an ethnographic study of recent hunter-gatherer communities dependent on terrestrial animals, Binford (1999: 8) has suggested that a critical threshold is reached at 1.57 persons per 100 km^2 (0.0016/km^2), at which point structural changes take place that may involve a diversification of subsistence or the budding off of the surplus component in the population to found new communities. Population displacement caused by rising sea levels will have had the same effect by creating population increases in areas not subject to inundation. Although it may be a principle of ecology that species expand to fill their niche, in the case of humans this is not a random process but the result of decisions taken by individuals to venture into new, and at times unfamiliar, areas. Any deviation from the normal annual cycle is likely to have been a significant social event. The ability to find new hunting grounds or sources of raw materials may have been an additional social cachet to that of being a successful hunter, while the skill to help the group maintain a traditional way of life in the face of often rapid environmental change probably brought similar benefits to the individual concerned, as would the ability successfully to negotiate social relations within the context of a rising population. The benefits to the individuals concerned are likely to have been a stimulus to expansion, and the possibility of an 'ethos' of expansion and colonization is worth considering, particularly as this was a time when significant environmental changes were occurring within the span of a single generation. One of the most significant features – perhaps the most significant feature – in any group's environment is other groups, and considerations that apply at the level of the individual also apply to the co-residential, or local, group. Those groups best fitted to coping with the pressures presented by a dynamic environmental and social arena are likely to be those with strongly cohesive but flexible social relations. Of crucial importance in this social arena is the acquisition and dissemination of knowledge about the natural and social environment, and landscape learning must be viewed as a social matter as well as a process of ecological adjustment.

In considering this social arena attention needs to be paid to both within-group social organization and to the kinds of organization – or the lack of them – found to exist between groups. A number of within-group kinds of social organization have been proposed.

Binford's (1980) 'residential forager/logistic collector' model has as its prime focus the way in which communities map their economic strategies onto the pattern of resource availability. However, the ability to recruit and deploy logistically specialist task groups implies a level of social organization that is unnecessary in the case of a community of residential foragers.

A more overtly social approach is taken by James Woodburn in his 'immediate and delayed return' model (1980). Unlike in the Binford model, the social content of Woodburn's model is explicit in that communities, or 'societies', to use Woodburn's term, pursuing an immediate return economic strategy, are usually found to be more egalitarian than the complex hierarchical societies that have adopted delayed return systems.

A third example is Jack Ives' (1990) explicitly social 'local group alliance formation/ local group growth' model. In a study of Northern Athapaskan societies in prehistoric and historic times Ives focused on the principles which underlie group formation and found two broad patterns. In the first, kinship structures promoting exogamy regulated the size of local groups and led to the formation of extensive alliance networks, with the higher levels of social organization functioning at the level of the regional group. In the alternative case, endogamy was promoted, leading to growth of the local group and the emergence of social complexity within the group.

There are striking similarities between these models. Immediate return societies are usually residential foragers and have kinship systems which limit local group size and promote the formation of alliance networks, while delayed return societies are usually logistic collectors and have kinship rules which promote local group growth and, axiomatically, social complexity.

Whereas the acquisition and dissemination of knowledge about the landscape can be seen to be promoted by patterns of residential foraging focused on relatively immediate returns and conducted within the context of wide-ranging alliance networks, the converse applies in the alternative case. The deployment of parties of logistic collectors implies extant, pre-existing knowledge about the landscape, while the investment entailed in delayed return systems is not conducive to speculative expansion. Similarly, the endogamous tendency leading towards local group growth promotes the formation of inward-looking, socially isolated groups unlikely to share their knowledge.

Turning to the role of social relations found to exist between hunter-gatherer groups, I have suggested, on the basis of a review of ethnographic and ethnohistorical sources, that they can be characterized as lying on a continuum between amity and enmity (Tolan-Smith, in press). This applies both at the regional scale of mutually unintelligible language groups but also within these groups.

One of the classic contexts in which to review these issues is the well-documented relations between Arctic-dwelling Inuit groups and the Athapaskan- and Algonquin-speaking groups who occupied the tundra and boreal forest transitional zone, such as the Kutchin, Chipewyan and Cree, and the records are replete with detail on the relations observed to exist between them (Barger 1979; Bishop 1984; Janes 1973; Krech 1979; MacGregor 1998; Ray 1984; J. Smith 1976a, b; Smith and Burch 1979). The picture shown by these sources is a gloomy one, in that the relations that were observed to exist were normally those of animosity and often outright hostility. Let it not be thought that this situation was a product of European intervention, with indigenous peoples competing for favour and trade goods. The traders specifically sought to suppress conflict in order to develop trade. The groups concerned all had long oral histories of animosity and conflict. Even the names they gave each other are normally derogatory, and in the case of Athapaskan relations with Inuit the former considered the latter to be barely human (Smith and Burch 1979: 88).

The groups cited occupied vast areas and led different ways of life, but even with groups following essentially similar ways of life within ecologically similar zones social relations are often found to be characterized by animosity. One of the best-studied such groups are the Cranes, a band of Algonquin-speaking Ojibwa living south of Hudson's Bay and studied for many years by Mary Black-Rogers and Edward Rogers (1983). Records exist of the Cranes' relations with their neighbours over most of the past 200 years, and these are characterized by animosity and hostility. In fact the boundaries of the Cranes' territory can be mapped by documenting those points in the landscape where they came into conflict with other groups.

Within this broad picture some researchers have drawn attention to the fact that these groups did, nevertheless, trade with each other, swap marriage partners and occasionally cooperate (Janes 1973). However, this evidence cannot be advanced to contradict the broader picture of animosity. As Keeley (1996) has pointed out, such apparently amicable relations are often the cause of animosity and the flash-point for hostility when trade obligations are not honoured, bride payments not made and in-laws perceived to behave badly. Where amity exists it is usually fragile and qualified.

The specific point along the amity–enmity continuum at which a group finds itself will vary both temporally and spatially. For example, in the simplest case tension between two groups can be relieved by the expansion of one or both into unoccupied areas. This represents a fairly easy option in a relatively homogeneous landscape. However, such expansion is more difficult in cases where the group or groups involved have to confront a range of unfamiliar circumstances, such as the transition between major ecological zones. In such situations the ability to acquire knowledge about the new landscape, and to apply that knowledge effectively, becomes an important factor in the management of tension between groups. In cases where expansion is precluded, either temporarily or because the limits of possible expansion have been reached, groups resolve their tensions by management. Ethnographically, the most commonly encountered form of management is the adoption of a policy of avoidance. The policy of groups avoiding each other, either spatially or temporally, is likely to have inhibited the spread of landscape knowledge and may even have invested it with a privileged status.

The lateglacial and early postglacial recolonization of the British Isles

In a series of publications (Smith and Openshaw 1990; Smith 1997; Tolan-Smith 1998; Tolan-Smith and Bonsall 1999) I have proposed that the spatial and temporal distribution of the radiocarbon dated records of an initial human presence in the British Isles allows three broad phases of settlement to be identified. The first I regard as the phase of initial colonization. This began around 12,500 BP, towards the end of the Lateglacial Interstadial (Dryas Ib, Ic and II), and was marked by the rapid and widespread dispersal of human groups into the lowlands of central, southern and eastern England (Figure 7.1). The second phase, corresponding to the Loch Lomond

Figure 7.1 The first phase of recolonization of the British Isles, beginning *c.*12,500 BP

Figure 7.2 The second phase of recolonization of the British Isles, dating from *c.*11,000–9,000 BP: an episode of consolidation with little further spread of settlement

Figure 7.3 The third phase of recolonization of the British Isles, *c.*9,000–7,000 BP: a rapid expansion of settlement

Stadial (Dryas III) and the Preboreal (Godwin Zone IV), and dating from *c.*11,000 to 9000 BP, was an episode of consolidation with little further spread of settlement (Figure 7.2). This is the 'standstill' phase referred to in the introduction. The third phase, from *c.*9000 to 7000 BP, witnessed a rapid expansion of settlement that involved most of the rest of the British Isles, including Ireland (Figure 7.3). The mechanisms behind each phase of this process are likely to have been different.

During the initial phase people moved into Britain overland from adjoining areas of the North European plain. The world they encountered in southeast and central Britain differed little from the one they were familiar with, consisting mainly of rolling plains and broad river valleys. It is unlikely to have presented many challenges. Existing landscape knowledge could be applied in landscapes that were effectively replicated over half a continent. One area in which unfamiliarity may have exerted a premium is in the availability of raw materials. As groups moved into unfamiliar territory, it may have taken some time before a full appreciation of raw material availability was achieved, which would have led to a tendency, during the initial stages of occupation, for raw materials to be transported over long distances (Kelly and Todd 1988: 237–8). In a recent analysis of Late Upper Palaeolithic material from southern Britain, Barton and Dumont (2000: 155) have noted that their initial phase of settlement, dated to the middle part of the Lateglacial Interstadial and termed by them the 'Creswellian', is characterized by the use of non-local (>160 km distant) sources of raw material. This phase can be viewed ecologically as a case of a population expanding to fill its niche and socially as an example of the simple demic expansion case in the 'amity–enmity' model (Tolan-Smith (in press)). The radiocarbon dates for a human presence across the North European plain from the shores of the Baltic to the English Midlands, a spread of 12 degrees of longitude, are barely distinguishable but at the range of two standard deviations span a millennium. The spread of communities throughout this area need have involved no more than a barely perceptible adjustment of annual hunting ranges of 20 km per generation. Simulation studies by Surovell (2000) of the North American case have shown that regions can be populated very rapidly as a result of the accumulation of numerous small-scale moves by 'residential foragers'. Such a process is likely to have been enhanced by a policy of seeking more-or-less immediate returns, while the maintenance of wide-ranging alliance networks would have facilitated the dissemination of landscape knowledge. Support for this interpretation is provided by the archaeological record for the Late Upper Palaeolithic in southern Britain, which is characterized by the generalized nature of the assemblages recovered and by widespread cultural homogeneity.

The second, or consolidation, phase is one during which little further expansion occurred and population growth was accommodated by the infilling of areas already occupied and the development of strategies for the management of the resulting social tensions. Archaeologically this is reflected regionally by an increase in the evidence for a human presence in southern Britain (Tolan-Smith 1998: 23–5 and figures 2b and 3a) and on a site-by-site basis by a greater interest in the use of locally available raw materials (Barton and Dumont 2000: 157). Following Kelly and Todd (1988), the latter is precisely what would be expected as communities became familiar with the resources of a newly occupied region and provides a classic example of the landscape learning process at work.

Why did the process of recolonization stop in Britain at the end of the Lateglacial Interstadial, around 11,000 BP? Although the explanation is, at least in part, environmental or ecological, in practice it was limitations of the social structures and practices of the groups involved that actually called a halt to expansion. The groups were confronted with two adverse sets of circumstances. First, by the beginning of the twelfth millennium BP the climate in northern Europe had begun to deteriorate, with the onset of the Dryas III cold stage; in Britain this was represented by the return to glacial conditions in much of the north. At just the time when groups were beginning to extend their ranges west and north, conditions in those areas began to deteriorate. Second, even without the problems presented by a deteriorating climate, the way of life that had developed during the lateglacial on the North European plain had reached its geographical limit in the west and north. The people that had so successfully extended that way of life became confronted with very different and unfamiliar landscapes in the moorlands and mountains of western and northern Britain and on the shores of the Atlantic Ocean. These were terra incognita in the most literal sense, and landscape knowledge acquired during the phase of expansion across the North European plain was of limited use. These groups had hitherto pursued a way of life focused on the exploitation of terrestrial resources, and evidence of their response to some of the new opportunities is provided by the analysis of stable isotope ratios of lateglacial and early postglacial hominid fossils from the British Isles. Analyses of $\delta^{13}C$ and $\delta^{15}N$ ratios have shown that even those living within a relatively short distance (<20 km) of the contemporary coastline nevertheless had diets dominated by terrestrial resources (Richards *et al.* 2000). Acquiring, and then applying, knowledge about the potential of the new circumstances would not have occurred overnight. Within the social arena a policy of residential foraging aimed at producing immediate returns and operating within the context of wide-ranging alliance networks had proved a successful adaptation within the context of the human expansion across the relatively homogeneous North European plain. Landscape learning took place within an open social arena which facilitated the dissemination of knowledge.

Throughout this consolidation phase, continued population growth placed an ever-higher premium on the ability to expand into unoccupied areas, but for the first time in millennia such expansion involved coping with the diverse and unfamiliar uplands, mountains and shores of the Atlantic. I take the view that the reason for the standstill in the lateglacial and early postglacial colonization of the British Isles was that the prevailing pattern of socio-economic relations was unable to respond fully to the new opportunities, and progress would only be made once a new pattern had emerged. The process of landscape learning needs to be viewed within this dynamic social context.

In relatively uniform ecological zones such as those of the North European plain landscape knowledge would be accessible to most mature adults, and each member of the community could make a valued contribution to the success of the group. In more diverse circumstances this is less the case and landscape knowledge becomes increasingly the realm of specialists. This applies whether it is the capacity to hunt on the high moors, cross mountain ranges, settle offshore islands or exploit the marine biomass. At the frontier of settlement expansion, with pressure from hostile groups increasing, such specialist knowledge becomes highly valued, and those individuals and groups with access to it come to occupy privileged positions.

The potential for social differentiation implied by these developments and the role of specialists in prosecuting particular economic activities are both typical of the kind of socio-economic organization in which economic activity is increasingly focused on delayed returns supplied by logistically deployed task groups. From an archaeological perspective the activities of such task groups can be recognized from the occurrence in the archaeological record of specialized sites such as shell middens, hunting camps and lithic procurement sites, while the emergence of social differentiation can be documented in cemeteries. As indicated above, the deployment of specialist task groups implies a sophisticated level of landscape knowledge which affords a privileged position to groups with access to such knowledge. Such systems of socio-economic organization tend to have kinship systems that promote growth of the local group through endogamy and communities that seek to establish and maintain access to restricted resources through social isolation and hostility to outsiders.

A clear example of this process at work is provided by the switch to the exploitation of marine resources (other than the collection of shellfish) and the occupation of offshore islands. Both are activities involving high levels of investment in equipment such as fish traps, nets and, most expensive of all, boats. The high status of boat owning and handling is well documented ethnographically, and coastal hunter-gatherers provide some of the best examples of delayed return systems. The ethnographic record also reveals these groups to be some of the socially most complex to be found among hunter-gatherers and among the most hostile to their neighbours.

When expansion did resume after 9000 BP it was rapid, with communities being established in the north of Ireland and throughout the length of western Scotland and most of the Hebridean archipelago by the mid-eighth-millennium BP. This should be seen to have occurred within a social context in which groups had learned what the newly encountered landscapes had to offer and had developed a pattern of socio-economic organization capable of responding to opportunities the landscapes presented.

It is unlikely to be a coincidence that this further phase of expansion occurred at a time of fundamental ecological changes along the Atlantic shores of the British Isles. The role played in the development of the climate, and indirectly the biomass, by the migrations of the Polar Front is well established (Lowe and Walker 1987; Jones and Keen 1993; Smith 1997; Tolan-Smith 1998). During the tenth millennium BP the Polar Front migrated from the latitude of Galicia to that of Iceland (Figure 7.4). This brought the warm and biologically productive waters of the North Atlantic Drift to the shores of northern and western Britain and is likely to have encouraged the development of maritime-based economies. The early postglacial settlement of northwest Britain seems to have been mainly a maritime venture, and the stable isotope data document a virtually exclusively maritime diet among the groups involved (Richards

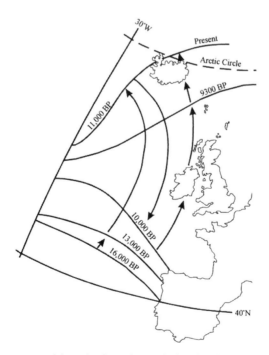

Figure 7.4 The migration of the polar front during the lateglacial and early Holocene period

and Mellars 1998; Richards and Hedges 1999a, b). This, and the fact that most of the earliest radiocarbon dates for the presence of humans in the area come from the Inner Hebridean islands of Islay, Jura, Ulva, Rum and Skye, suggests that settlement may have been accomplished by movement along the island chain, with occupation of the nearby mainland occurring as a secondary process. Such an 'island-hopping' scenario would certainly explain the rapidity with which the region was occupied and can be paralleled elsewhere in the world during many different periods.

At the beginning of this chapter I drew attention to the apparent inconsistency in the rates of colonization when those proposed for the British Isles are compared with those proposed for Scandinavia. I believe this inconsistency can be explained by the fact that, although the lateglacial colonization of northern Scandinavia was a mainly maritime venture similar to that which occurred in western and northern Britain, the Scandinavian colonization preceded the British by more than a millennium. In Scandinavia the limits of terrestrial expansion were reached in the eleventh millennium, when further advances were blocked by the continuing presence of the Weichselian ice sheet. If expansion was to continue, this had to be a maritime venture. In deglaciated Britain communities expanding across from the North European plain were confronted not by an impenetrable ice sheet but by the uplands and mountains of the north and west. It was only after the capacity to cope with these unfamiliar landscapes had been developed that the even more challenging circumstances of the Atlantic coasts had to be confronted. In both Scandinavia and Britain groups of terrestrially oriented hunter-gatherers had to learn about new and different landscapes. In the British Isles, gaining knowledge about the new landscapes was a two-stage process, but in both areas it was necessary for the communities involved to develop patterns of socio-economic organization that would enable them to deploy their newly acquired knowledge to advantage.

Conclusion

Any consideration of the landscape learning process needs to take account of the social context in which that learning process occurred. Humans are social actors, and the acquisition and dissemination of specialist knowledge about the landscape can, in certain circumstances, afford a privileged status to the individuals and groups with access to such knowledge. Within the context of the lateglacial and early postglacial recolonization of the British Isles, it is possible to consider how the process of landscape learning and the acquisition and dissemination of landscape knowledge may have operated within contrasting ecological zones and, by implication, social arenas.

Acknowledgments

I should like to acknowledge the contribution to my thinking on this matter of Jack Ives, of the Provincial Museum of Alberta, Edmonton, who first suggested to me the notion of an 'ethos' of expansion or colonization. I am also grateful to Mike Richards for discussion of the stable isotope studies and for allowing me to quote work in advance of publication.

References

Barger, W.K. (1979) 'Inuit-Cree Relations in the Eastern Hudson Bay Region' *Arctic Anthropology* XVI (no. 2):59–75.

Barton, N. and S. Dumont (2000) 'Recolonisation and settlement of Britain at the end of the Last Glaciation', in *L'Europe Centrale et Septentionale au Tardiglaciare*, Table-ronde de Nemours, 13–16 mai 1997, Mémoires du Musée de Préhistoire d'Ile de France, 7, 2000, 151–62.

Barton, R.N.E. (1999) 'Colonisation and resettlement of Europe in the Late Glacial: a view from the western periphery' *Folia Quaternaria* 70, Krakow, 71–86.

Becker, B., B. Kromer and P. Trimborn (1991) 'A stable-isotope tree-ring timescale of the late glacial/Holocene boundary' *Nature* 353:647–9.

Binford L.R. (1980) 'Willow smoke and dogs' tails: hunter-gatherer settlement systems and archaeological site formation' *American Antiquity* 45:4–20.

—— (1999) 'Time as a Clue to Cause?' *Proceedings of the British Academy* 101:1–35.

Bishop, Charles A. (1984) 'The First Century: Adaptive Changes among the Western James Bay Cree between the Early Seventeenth and Early Eighteenth Centuries', in Shepard Krech III (ed.) *The Subarctic Fur Trade: Native Social and Economic Adaptations*, Vancouver: University of British Columbia Press.

Black-Rogers, Mary and Edward S. Rogers (1983) 'The Cranes and their neighbours, 1770–1970: Trouble case data for tracing WE-THEY boundaries of the northern Ojibwa', in William Cowan (ed.) *Actes du Quatorzième Congrès des Algonquinistes*, Ottawa: Carleton University.

Blockley, S.P., R.E. Donahure and A.M. Pollard (2000a) 'Radiocarbon calibration and Late Glacial occupation in northwest Europe' *Antiquity* 74:112–21.

—— (2000b) 'Rapid human response to Late Glacial climate change: a reply to Housley *et al.* (2000)' *Antiquity* 74:427–8.

Bocquet-Appel, Jean-Pierre and Pierre Yves Demars (2000) 'Neanderthal contraction and modern human colonization of Europe' *Antiquity* 74:544–52.

Charles, Ruth (1996) 'Back into the North: the Radiocarbon Evidence for the Human Recolonisation of the North Western Ardennes after the Last Glacial Maximum' *Proceedings of the Prehistoric Society* 62:1–18.

Echo-Hawk, Roger C. (2000) 'Ancient History in the New World: Integrating Oral Traditions and the Archaeological Record' *American Antiquity* 65(2):267–90.

Gob, Andre (1991) 'The early Postglacial occupation of the southern part of the North Sea Basin', in N. Barton, A. Roberts and D.A. Roe (eds) *The Lateglacial in north-west Europe*, London: Council for British Archaeology.

Housley, R.A., C.S. Gamble, M. Street and P. Pettitt (1997) 'Radiocarbon evidence for the Lateglacial Human Recolonisation of Northern Europe' *Proceedings of the Prehistoric Society* 63:25–54.

Housley, R.A., C.S. Gamble and P. Pettitt (2000) 'Reply to Blockley, Donahue and Pollard' *Antiquity* 74:119–21.

Ives, John W. (1990) *A Theory of Northern Athapaskan Prehistory*, Calgary: University of Calgary Press.

Jacobi, R.M. and P.B.Pettitt (2000) 'An Aurignacian point from Uphill Quarry (Somerset) and the earliest settlement of Britain by Homo sapiens sapiens' *Antiquity* 74: 513–18.

Janes, Robert R. (1973) 'Indian and Eskimo contact in southern Keewatin: An ethnohistorical approach' *Ethnohistory* 20(1):39–54.

Jones R.L. and D.H. Keen (1993) *Pleistocene Environments of the British Isles*, London: Chapman & Hall.

Keeley, Lawrence H. (1996) *War Before Civilization*, Oxford: Oxford University Press.

Kelly, Robert L. and Lawrence C. Todd (1988) 'Coming Into the Country: Early Paleoindian Hunting and Mobility' *American Antiquity* 53(2):231–44.

Kitagawa, H. and J. van der Plicht (1998) 'Atmospheric Radiocarbon Calibration to 45,000 yr BP: Late Glacial Fluctuations and Cosmogenic Isotope Production' *Science* 279:1187–90.

Krech S. III 1979 'Inter ethnic relations in the lower MacKenzie River region' *Arctic Anthropology* 16(2):102–22.

Larsson, Lars (ed.) (1996) *The Earliest Settlement of Scandinavia and its relationship with neighbouring areas*, Stockholm: Almquist & Wiksell International.

Lowe J.J. and M.J.C Walker (1987) *Reconstructing Quaternary Environments*, Harlow: Longman Scientific & Technical.

MacGregor, J.G. (1998) *Peter Fidler: Canada's Forgotten Explorer 1769–1822*, Calgary: Firth House Ltd.

Ray, Arthur J. (1984) 'Periodic Shortages, Native Welfare and the Hudson's Bay Company 1670–1930', in Shepard Krech III (ed.) *The Subarctic Fur Trade: Native Social and Economic Adaptations*, Vancouver: University of British Columbia Press.

Richards, M. and P.A. Mellars (1998) 'Stable isotopes and seasonality of the Oronsay middens' *Antiquity* 72:178–83.

Richards, M.P. and R.E.M. Hedges (1999a) 'Stable Isotope Evidence for Similarities in the Types of Marine Foods Used by Late Mesolithic Humans at Sites Along the Atlantic Coast of Europe' *Journal of Archaeological Science* 26:717–22.

—— (1999b) 'A Neolithic revolution? New evidence of diet in the British Neolithic' *Antiquity* 73:891–7.

Richards, M.P., R.E.M. Hedges, R. Jacobi, A. Current and C. Stringer (2000) 'FOCUS: Gough's Cave and Sun Hole Cave Human Stable Isotope Values Indicate a High Animal Protein Diet in the British Upper Palaeolithic' *Journal of Archaeological Science* 27:1–3.

Smith, Christopher (1997) *Late Stone Age Hunters of the British Isles*, London: Routledge.

Smith, Christopher and Stan Openshaw (1990) 'Mapping the Mesolithic', in Pierre M.Vermeersch and Philip van Peer (eds) *Contributions to the Mesolithic in Europe*, Leuven: Leuven University Press.

Smith, James G.E. (1976a) 'Introduction: The Historical and Cultural Position of the Chipewyan' *Arctic Anthropology* XIII (no. 1):1–5.

—— (1976b) 'Local Band Organization of the Caribou Eater Chipewyan' *Arctic Anthropology* XIII (no. 1):12–24.

Smith, James G.E. and Ernest S. Burch Jr (1979) 'Chipewyan and Inuit in the Central Canadian Subarctic, 1613–1977' *Arctic Anthropology* XVI (no. 2):76–101.

Surovell, T.A. (2000) 'Early Paleoindian Women, Children, Mobility and Fertility' *American Antiquity* 65(3):493–508.

Thommessen, T. (1996) 'The early settlement of northern Norway', in L. Larsson (ed.) *The Earliest Settlement of Scandinavia*, Stockholm: Almquist & Wiksell International.

Tolan-Smith, Christopher (1998) 'Radiocarbon chronology and the Lateglacial and early Postglacial resettlement of the British isles', in B.V. Eriksen and L.G. Straus (eds) *Quaternary International* 49/50, 21–7.

Tolan-Smith, Christopher (in press) 'Social interaction and settlement patterns in hunter-gatherer societies – applications of the "amity–enmity" model', in Lynne Bevan and Jenny Moore (eds) *Peopling the Mesolithic in a Northern Environment*, Oxford: British Archaeological Reports.

Tolan-Smith, Christopher with Clive Bonsall (1999) 'Stone Age studies in the British Isles: the impact of accelerator dating', in Evin, Jacques *et al.* (eds) *14C and Archaeology Acts of the 3rd International Symposium* (Lyon 6–10 April 1998) Mémoires de la Société Préhistorique Française Tome XXVI, 1999 et Supplément 1999 de la Revue d'Archéometrie Rennes: Université de Rennes.

Woodburn, James (1980) 'Hunters and gatherers today and reconstruction of the past', in Ernest Gellner (ed.) *Soviet and Western Anthropology*, London: Duckworth.

8

"WHERE DO WE GO FROM HERE?"

Modelling the decision-making process during exploratory dispersal

James Steele and Marcy Rockman

Human habitat use: what factors determine ease of access to resources?

The first peopling of the Americas provides us with a unique insight into the effects of human habitat preferences on dispersal rates. As colonizers entered the Americas from the high-latitude environments of Beringia, initial dispersal would have been south-ward – and, for the terrestrial biomes, up gradients of increased resource productivity. The habitats of the New World span the whole range from Arctic tundra to tropical rainforest. By mapping the archaeological record of the settlement prehistory of each such ecoregion, we can begin to evaluate different models of human habitat selection.

"Habitat" is defined as the sum of the specific resources that are needed by organisms for survival and reproductive success (Krausman 1999). "Habitat selection" refers to an active behavioural process in which an animal searches for features within an environment that are directly or indirectly associated with the resources that it would need to survive and reproduce. Habitat selection occurs at different time- and space scales: first-order selection of the species' geographical range, second-order selection of the home range of an individual or social group, and lower-order selection of foraging areas within the home range, and of resources to exploit within those areas. "Habitat preference" is the consequence of habitat selection, whereby animals spend a disproportionate amount of their time in specific locations favourable to their resource needs (Krausman 1999). The focus of this paper is on human habitat preferences, human adaptability, and the implications for hunter-gatherer dispersals.

Innate biases and intrinsic properties of environments

As organisms, we are the products of our evolutionary history. Human genetic diversity is very limited, reflecting the late Middle Pleistocene age of our last common ancestor (as estimated by geneticists using the molecular clock). It is therefore reasonable to assume that we all share some cognitive constraints, and that these evolved in some ancestral hominid population prior to the great diaspora of anatomically modern human hunter-gatherers. We might then also expect that human dispersal into unfamiliar regions would have been biased by a preference for the kinds of Pleistocene habitats that were most densely populated by ancestral human groups.

Gamble (1993) has argued that at a large time- and space scale it was the innate accessibility of the resources of a given type of habitat (based on Kelly's (1983) study of primary and secondary biomass productivity and accessibility) that determined the rate at which that habitat is settled and exploited by Pleistocene hunter-gatherers. Gamble observes that during the Pleistocene, "the two easiest habitats – tropical savannahs and temperate grasslands – are colonized first, with the difference in time apparently due to the barrier created by the intervening Sahara Desert" (1993: 11). It has also been suggested that humans have an innate visual preference for savannah-style landscapes, reflecting the sub-Saharan African environment of evolutionary adaptedness (Balling and Falk 1982; Orians and Heerwagen 1992). People "prefer environments in which exploration is easy and which signal the presence of resources necessary for survival", and where the likelihood of detecting danger in the form of "predators or unfriendly conspecifics" is high (Orians and Heerwagen 1992: 557). From a less extreme adaptationist perspective, Kaplan and Kaplan (1982, as summarized by Gimblett 2002) argue that humans have evolved the mental and perceptual capabilities for processing adaptively relevant environmental information: environmental cognition is mediated by mental models which are constantly being updated, and which in turn inform decisions. People should prefer landscape scenes having qualities that facilitate comprehension of the landscape, and should show aversion to scenes that are ambiguous and so hard to identify, or that place very high processing demands on the observer.

Learned historical biases and niche construction

A more culture-historical approach is implied by the work of Potts (1998), who has proposed that we should think of human evolution as the product of "variability selection". This process is characterized by the appearance of "complex structures or behaviours that are designed to respond to novel and unpredictable adaptive settings" (Potts 1998: 85). In this approach, we might expect adaptability to have its evolutionary signature in human cultural and social variability and rapid adaptation to the whole range of available habitats and landscape types. We can infer that the principal determinants of variable dispersal rates should be not just the innate characteristics of each habitat, but also the degree of similarity of the new habitat to that to which a colonizing population is already culturally adapted. Humans will disperse across habitat boundaries at rates determined by the learning time required to adapt to the new habitat's resource structure. This in turn should be determined both by the innate legibility (or accessibility) of the resource structure of the new habitat and by the similarity of that resource structure to that of the habitat from which people are dispersing.

We can extend this perspective to emphasize the active role of organisms in modifying the resource structure of their environments, which – if such a role persists across generations in some predictable way – can actually modify natural selection pressures on the organisms. This is most familiar in anthropology as gene–culture co-evolution

(Durham 1991), although Laland *et al.* (2000) suggest that such niche construction is a much more widespread evolutionary process. It is a truism that humans modify their habitats by technological means to make them more favourable for habitation. Such active strategies may serve, for example, to enhance navigation through hard-to-read landscapes (maps, cairns); to mitigate the effects of seasonality on food availability (storage); to mitigate the effects of diurnal or seasonal temperature fluctuations on well-being (fire, clothing, shelter); to improve the accessibility of food resources and to increase extractive efficiency (food capture and processing technology); or to modify the patch structure of the landscape (controlled burning, game drives, lithic place-provisioning). Agriculture and herding are forms of habitat modification which lie further along a continuum that also contains such hunter-gatherer strategies.

In this perspective, variation in human dispersal rates may be determined by the extent to which the new habitat needs to be modified to become favourable for habitation, and by the ease or difficulty with which a dispersing group can move from its existing set of technological solutions to those required by the new landscape. The initial search costs are not only those of learning to read the new landscape, but also those of moving across a "technology landscape" (Kauffman *et al.* 1998) whose fitness function varies with the environmental problems that the technologies must solve.

Habitat preference and the peopling of the Americas

Kelly and Todd (1988) have proposed an elegant model of the initial phase of adaptation of the first peoples of the New World, which emphasizes the efficacy of a focus on hunted animal resources. Their model derives from expectations of the difficulty of accessing more regionally specialized resources with limited knowledge of resource geography. We shall focus on a complementary issue, namely that of the "cultural pre-adaptations" of America's first settlers, and the possibility of recovering evidence of their decisions during exploratory dispersal. No-one comes to a new landscape devoid of expectations. These expectations will be shaped by the traditional environmental knowledge of the peoples from whose lands the settlers and their immediate ancestors have come. Can we guess at the rules of thumb that guided these pioneers' route-finding across unfamiliar landscapes, and can we test our guesses using archaeological data?

We shall begin by considering the probable cultural pre-adaptations of the first peoples to reach the Americas south of the ice sheets. They were lateglacial hunter-gatherers from Beringia – the tract of "mammoth steppe" connecting northeast Siberia and Alaska across the Bering land bridge. Today, this environment is characterized by extreme seasonal variation in air temperature and by low mean summer temperatures (Figure 8.1). In other words, the environment has a very low value on the index of effective temperature (ET) (Figure 8.2).

In the late last glacial, this situation could only have been amplified. Modern hunter-gatherers in environments with low ET (therefore with a low primary productivity and short growing season) tend not to depend on plant foods for their diets; they hunt or fish (Figure 8.3). The first peoples to reach the Americas south of the ice sheets would have come from environments represented at the left-hand

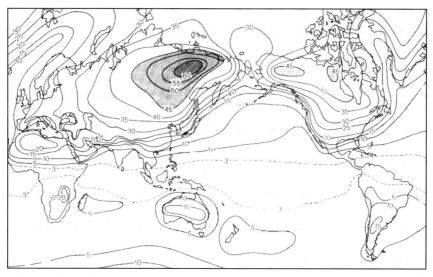

Figure 8.1 Annual range of air temperature (°C), showing differences between the means for
January and July (after Goudie 1984)

extreme of these scatterplots. Men tend to do a larger share of the subsistence work in
environments with a low ET (Figure 8.4a). Modern hunter-gatherers in high latitudes
tend to be "technology specialists", even when they do not depend on marine resources

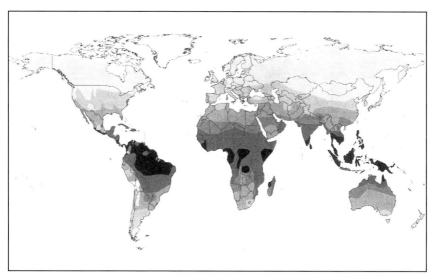

Figure 8.2 Effective temperature (annual mean data), from Binford (2001). Effective temperature
is a compound measure of the intensity and seasonality of solar radiation at different
locations (see e.g. Kelly 1995: 66)

133

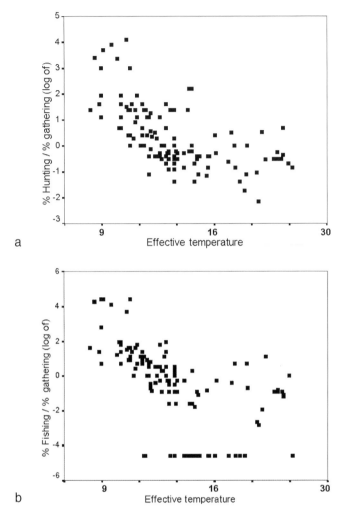

Figure 8.3 The ratio of hunting and gathering (a) and the ratio of fishing and gathering (b) as a function of effective temperature, for a sample of hunter-gatherer societies (data from Kelly 1995)

for living (Table 8.1). And when hunting of terrestrial animals plays a key role in the diet, people need to be more mobile across a larger annual range (Figure 8.4b).

We can now make some predictions about the probable "cultural pre-adaptations" of a high-latitude population from northeast Asian or Beringia for the first peopling of the Americas. The economy had a focus on animals, the culture was that of "technology specialists", men made a relatively large subsistence contribution, and – if these populations were specialists in hunting land mammals – they were used to high annual mobility over very extensive ranges.

Table 8.1 Correlations of aspects of hunter-gatherer technology with latitude (controlled for % dependence on aquatic resources)

Aspect of technology	Correlation (r) with latitude
Diversity of untended facilities	0.49
Diversity of toolkit	0.47
Diversity of weapons	0.45
Complexity of toolkit	0.28
Diversity of tended facilities	0.24

Source: Bamforth & Bleed (1997), who analysed data on 20 hunter-gatherer groups from Torrance (1983) and Murdock (1967)

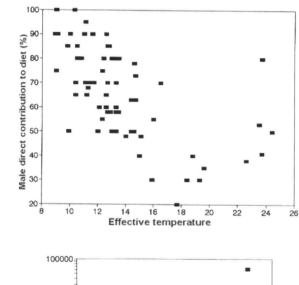

a

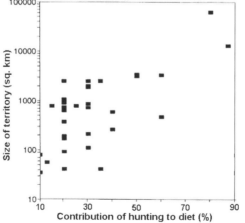

b

Figure 8.4 Male contribution to diet as a function of effective temperature (a) and territory size as a function of dependence on hunting (b) for a sample of hunter-gatherer societies (data from Kelly 1995)

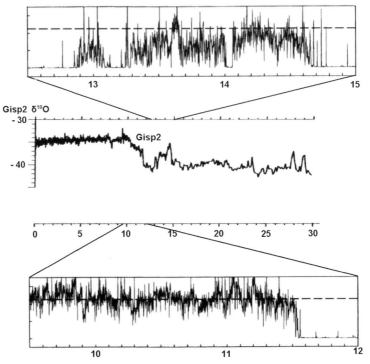

Figure 8.5 Lateglacial climatic variability, as indicated by aeolian dust concentrations in the GISP2 ice core (after Taylor *et al.* 1993). The central chart shows oxygen isotope variability, while the upper and lower charts show variance in conductivity (an independent proxy measure of climate, but with higher chronological resolution). Horizontal scale in kyr BP.

But we can say more than that, if we consider the temperature evidence from the GISP2 ice core (Figure 8.5). The upper and lower graphs show conductance across the ice core at successive levels, indicating the amount of windborne dust in the ice layers (and thus of aridity, a marker for climatic cooling). The upper and lower graphs are separated in time by the Younger Dryas (*c.*12.8–11.6 kyr), reflected here in high dust levels and consequent very low ice core conductance. The upper graph shows fluctuations in conductance in the 12.5 kyr to 15 kyr interval, encompassing the Bolling-Allerod interstadial (and the Clovis-age Paleoindian archaeological record in North America). The lower graph shows fluctuations in conductance in the 12 kyr to 9.5 kyr interval, from the end of the Younger Dryas into the Early Holocene. If we contrast the range and amplitude of short-term climate fluctuations during the Bolling-Allerod interstadial with those of the Younger Dryas or the Early Holocene, we see that in the Bolling-Allerod period there was wild fluctuation between the two extremes (on an interannual and interdecadal timescale). What might that have meant for the adaptations of contemporary hunter-gatherers? Maybe we can get some clues from looking at

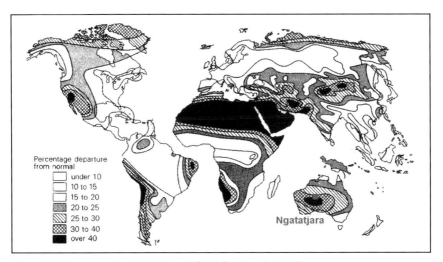

Figure 8.6 Interannual variability in rainfall (after Goudie 1984)

foragers in modern environments with high interannual variance in rainfall, and thus in primary productivity (Figures 8.6 and 8.7). For instance, Gould (1991) observed that the Ngatatjara of the Australian Western Desert deploy "strategy switching":

"in order to minimize risks imposed by droughts, the Ngatatjara responded in their movements and group composition by means of two alternative strategies: drought escape and drought evasion. Drought escape involved

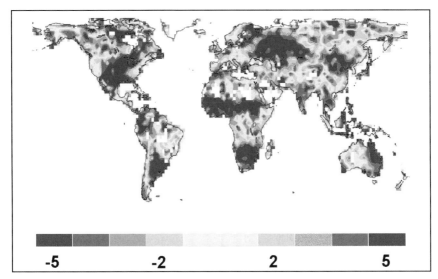

Figure 8.7 Magnitude and direction of El Niño timescale variations in rainfall (after Dai *et al.* 1997)

temporary abandonment of entire areas by individual households or by individuals to distant, better-favoured areas. Drought evasion involved retreat by small family groups into areas within their 'home' country where relatively dependable water resources were available."

Lateglacial hunter-gatherers lived in a time when the climatic pulse was beating more wildly than it does today. Modern ethnographic data suggest that this might be associated with a cultural propensity for strategy switching and a flexible attitude to annual ranges. Thus we can add to our list of probable cultural pre-adaptations of a high-latitude, northeast Asian/Beringian source population that they were used to the more flickering pulse of lateglacial climate, which might suggest a more flexible attitude to territories and to annual mobility strategies.

How can we predictively model exploratory dispersal at the landscape scale?

Having established a set of expectations concerning the cultural pre-adaptations of a high-latitude, northeast Asian/Beringian source population, we turn now to modelling dispersal routes during the pioneer phase. We will use GIS techniques to address the questions of how people found their way around newly colonized landscapes and what they were looking for as they made their route choices.

Anderson and Gillam (2000) recently calculated the routes between possible points of entry and a series of early sites south of the ice sheets. Their route-finding algorithm is one that minimizes slope (using least-cost path routines). For our own exercise in

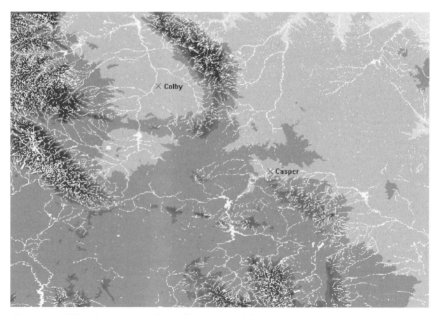

Figure 8.8a Wyoming: topography and permanent lakes and watercourses

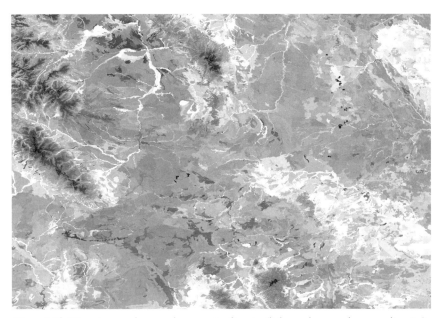

Figure 8.8b Wyoming: modern vertebrate species diversity (lighter colour equals greater diversity)

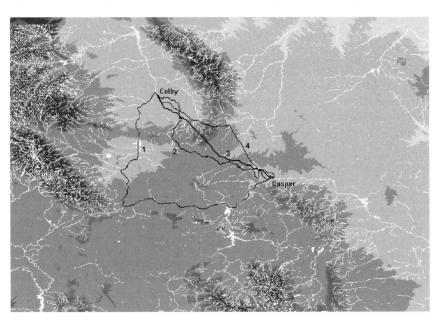

Figure 8.8c Wyoming: least-cost paths from Casper to Colby (path 1 maximizes proximity to permanent lakes and watercourses, path 2 minimizes slope, path 3 maximizes viewshed, and path 4 maximizes vertebrate species richness)

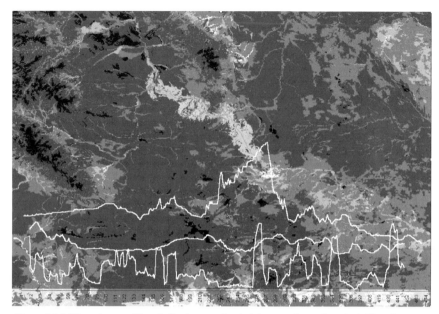

Figure 8.8d Wyoming: profiles of affordances of path 4 (see text for explanation) (data for maps a, b, and c from Wyoming Internet Map Server http://www. wims.uwyo.edu/)

modelling route choice, we focus on the state of Wyoming. As a modelling exercise, we ask how pioneers might have made their way from Casper (next to the North Platte River, just north of the Laramie Mountains) to Colby, in the Bighorn Basin (Figure 8.8). Casper is a Hell Gap (Late Paleoindian) site, but it yielded an isolated Clovis point as well. So we know that early Paleoindians did indeed pass that way. Colby is a Clovis-age mammoth kill site. So, once again, we know that early Paleoindians did indeed pass that way. To illustrate our methods we use digital information about modern topography (digital elevation model, or DEM) and hydrology (permanent lakes and watercourses). We also use information about the modern distribution of vertebrate species richness, as derived from the national GAP survey and conservation programme.

We have used GIS least-cost path algorithms to map routes from Casper to Colby which each optimize one of four different parameters. One maximizes encounter rates with areas of high vertebrate-species richness, one maximizes viewshed (within a 10 arc-minute effective viewing radius), one minimizes slope, and one maximizes proximity to lakes and permanent watercourses. The different rules of thumb that people might use as they decide in which direction to proceed in each step produce very different routes across the landscape. We can begin to map something of the experience of moving along these paths across the landscape.

Figure 8.8d shows (in light grey in the contour of the map – see Figure 8.8c path 4) the cumulative viewshed within a 10 arc-minute effective viewing radius for all the steps along that path from Casper to Colby that maximizes encounter rates with areas of highest vertebrate biodiversity. It also shows the profiles along that path for a series

140

Figure 8.9 Wyoming bedrock geology, reclassified in terms of its potential to yield raw materials for stone tools (on a scale of 1–6, where 6 indicates a high potential): 1 = igneous/ metamorphic, or unclassified; 2 = unconsolidated deposits, gravels, drift; 3 = sandstones, shales, other sedimentaries; 4 = non-cherty limestones and dolomites; 5 = agate or petrified wood-bearing; 6 = chert-bearing (original geology data from Wyoming Internet Map Server, http://www.wims.uwyo.edu/). The least-cost paths from Figure 8.8d are overlaid.

of affordances (moving from Casper, at left, to Colby, at right). The uppermost line is an elevation profile along the path (vertically exaggerated). The lowermost line is a profile showing how much new area becomes visible (within a 10 arc-minute effective viewing radius) in successive steps, as you move along that path. The middle line shows the mean value for vertebrate biodiversity in the newly visible area in successive steps, as you move along the path. About halfway along the path, you might well stop and turn back – it's getting steeper (you are climbing the Bighorns), you can't see much that is new, and what little you can see (in terms of resource quality) is just getting worse.

How might we test our predictions of the exploratory wayfinding routines of America's first settlers? Maybe we can use archaeological data. Figure 8.9 shows Wyoming's bedrock geology, reclassified in terms of its potential to yield raw materials for stone tools. The different paths across the landscape would bring people into proximity with very different rock formations. If we can source the rocks these settlers used to make their first stone tools, we may be able to track their movements across the landscape between actual sites, and thus establish how they learned their landscape.

This exercise simply demonstrates that we can begin to predict where people would have walked, according to the rules of thumb they applied in exploratory wayfinding, and that we can use GIS techniques to explore the experience of moving across a landscape in these ways. However, when we don't know the origins and termini of possible paths, we must characterize the whole landscape in terms of its locally varying affordances to colonizers. This means taking account of not just local values for some quality (e.g. edible biomass), but also the connectedness and accessibility of every such locale.

Integrating predictions of cultural pre-adaptations with models of exploratory mobility

What might our predictions about the probable "cultural pre-adaptations" of a high-latitude, northeast Asian or Beringian source population for the first peopling of the Americas suggest about exploratory route finding during the dispersal phase? Our predictions are similar to those of Kelly and Todd's (1988) model, although derived for different reasons. In their model of the initial dispersal phase, limited local knowledge favours an economy with an animal focus, and in which periodic shortages of game are dealt with by range relocation. There would be high residential and logistic mobility and high range mobility. The archaeological signatures would include low regional variation, a locational strategy involving short-term, redundant use of "known places" even when these are not optimally located, and a technology focused on portable artefacts with a generalized function, a long life of use and made from high-quality raw materials. To this we would add that such a strategy is very consistent with the probable pre-adaptations of a high-latitude source population. Additionally, we would note that the typically large male contribution to subsistence effort in such ethnographically documented societies could contribute to the potentially rapid reproductive rates that Surovell's analysis (2000) suggests were sustainable, given high residential mobility.

Such expectations of cultural pre-adaptation (themselves testable against the archaeological record of Beringia) suggest that we should model exploratory wayfinding as guided by the need to track rich patches of mobile fauna and the need to locate high-quality raw materials for bifacial tools. A predictive model of rates of discovery of locations and their affordances in the lateglacial and earliest Holocene New World should therefore focus on the reconstruction of lateglacial faunal distributions and on the classification of bedrock geology in terms of the potential for yielding high-quality knappable rock.

Acknowledgments

The GIS analysis of paths and path profiles was greatly facilitated by Mark Lake's viewshed routines for Grass Y.Z. we thank him for making these public and for his support in their application here.

References

Anderson, D.G. and J.C. Gillam (2000) 'Paleoindian colonization of the Americas: implications from an examination of physiography, demography, and artifact distribution.' *American Antiquity* 65:43–66.

Balling, J.D. and J.H. Falk (1982) 'Development of visual preference for natural environments.' *Environment and Behavior* 14(1):5–28.

Bamforth, D.B. and P. Bleed (1997) 'Technology, flaked stone technology, and risk.' In G. Clark and M. Barton (eds) *Rediscovering Darwin: Evolutionary Theory and Archaeological Explanation.* Archaeological Papers of the American Anthropological Association, no. 7, pp. 109–39.

Binford, L.R. (2001) *Constructing Frames of Reference. An Analytical Method for Archaeological Theory Building Using Ethnographic and Environmental Data Sets*. Berkeley: University of California Press.

Dai, A., I. Y. Fung and A. D. Del Genio (1997) Surface observed global land precipitation variations during 1900–1988. *J. Climate* 10:2943–62.

Durham, W. (1991) *Coevolution: Genes, Culture and Human Diversity*. Palo Alto, CA: Stanford University Press.

Gamble, C. (1993) *Timewalkers: the Prehistory of Global Colonization*. Stroud: Alan Sutton.

Gimblett, R. (2002) *Background to Evolutionary Approaches of Aesthetics to Landscape*. http://www.srnr.arizona.edu/~gimblett/rec_lec2a.html

Goudie, A.S. (1984) *The Nature of the Environment*. Oxford: Blackwell.

Gould, R.A. (1991) 'Arid land foraging as seen from Australia – adaptive models and behavioral realities.' *Oceania* 62:12–33.

Kaplan, S. and R. Kaplan (1982) *Cognition and Environment: Functioning in an Uncertain World*. New York: Praeger.

Kauffman, S.A., J. Lobo and W.G. Macready (1998) 'Optimal search on a technology landscape'. Santa Fe Working Paper 98–10–091 (http://www.santafe.edu/sfi/publications/wpabstract/199810091).

Kelly, R.L. (1983) Hunter-gatherer mobility strategies. *Journal of Anthropological Research* 39:277–306.

—— (1995) *The Foraging Spectrum: Diversity in Hunter-Gatherer Lifeways*. Washington, DC: Smithsonian Institution Press.

Kelly, R.L. and L.C. Todd (1988) 'Coming into the Country: Early Paleoindian hunting and mobility.' *American Antiquity* 53:231–44.

Krausman, P.R. (1999) 'Some basic principles of habitat use.' In K.L. Launchbaugh, K.D. Saunders and J.C. Mosley (eds), *Grazing Behavior of Livestock and Wildlife*, pp. 85–90. (Idaho Forest, Wildlife and Range Experiment Station Bulletin 70). Moscow, ID: University of Idaho.

Laland, K.N., F.J. Odling-Smee and M.W. Feldman (2000) 'Niche construction, biological evolution and cultural change.' *Behavioral and Brain Sciences* 23:131–46.

Murdock, G. P. (1967) *Ethnographic Atlas*. Pittsburgh, HRAF Press.

Orians, G.H. and J.H. Heerwagen (1992) 'Evolved responses to landscapes.' In L. Cosmides and J. Tooby (eds) *The Adapted Mind*, pp. 555–79. New York: Oxford University Press.

Potts, R. (1998) 'Variability selection in hominid evolution.' *Evolutionary Anthropology* 7:81–96.

Surovell, T. A. (2000) 'Early Paleoindian women, children, mobility, and fertility.' *American Antiquity* 65:493–508.

Taylor, K.C., G.W. Lamorey, G.A. Doyle *et al.* (1993) 'The "flickering switch" of late Pleistocene climate change.' *Nature* 361:432–6.

Torrence, R. (1983) 'Time budgeting and hunter-gatherer technology.' In G. Bailey (ed.) *Hunter-gatherer economy in prehistory*, pp.11–22. Cambridge: Cambridge University Press.

9

DEERSLAYERS, PATHFINDERS, AND ICEMEN

Origins of the European Neolithic as seen from the frontier

Stuart J. Fiedel and David W. Anthony

Thirty years ago, Ammerman and Cavalli-Sforza (1971) presented an elegant and initially convincing model explaining the spread of Neolithic farmers from the Near East into Europe. They observed that the dates for fifty-three European sites with early occurrences of wheat or barley showed a pattern of radiation westward from a Near Eastern point of origin (taking Jericho, Çayönü, Ali Kosh, or Jarmo as the hypothetical starting point yielded the same result in each case). The rate of expansion averaged about 1 km per year. The "wave of advance" model that they applied to the radiocarbon and spatial data was explicitly derived from Fisher's (1937) mathematical/genetic model of the spread of a beneficial allele through a population. It required no human motivation, intentionality, or agency:

> It has been shown mathematically ... that if such an increase in population coincides with a modest local migration activity, random in direction (comparable to a Brownian motion), a wave of population expansion will set in and progress at a constant radial rate. This is just what we have observed with the measured rate for the European data.
>
> (Ammerman and Cavalli-Sforza 1971: 687)

Ammerman and Cavalli-Sforza were careful to distinguish the kind of cumulative short-distance movements they envisioned ("a form of colonization without colonists" [1984: 68]) from long-distance, planned colonization or migration. Popular presentations of the wave-of-advance model emphasized that the Neolithic expansion was gradual, random, and largely unconscious. Thus, John Pfeiffer (1977: 271) wrote (all emphases are our own),

> It all happened on a purely local basis, the result of decisions made within and among families. People moved always so as to stay as close to friends and

144

relatives as possible, always settling themselves five to ten miles from the nearest community. *There was no plan or large-scale migration.* But there was a general trend, a tendency to avoid going east where the population centres were and to move in a northwesterly direction.

In a similar vein, Ruth Whitehouse (1976: 146–7) stated:

> The movements of people that spread the farming economy across Europe were *presumably not deliberate* campaigns to colonise new land, but rather what has been called a "wave of advance" of population, representing the *gradual expansion* of an increasing population … . Such population movements are random in that they are not given a deliberate direction by the moving population; the direction of movement and the area occupied are, however, restricted by environmental factors and it is these limiting factors that give *an appearance of conscious colonization* to the settlement of Europe by early farmers.

We first examined the radiocarbon dates that formed the underpinning of the wave-of-advance model in a 1976 student paper for a graduate seminar at the University of Pennsylvania. A revised version was presented in 1979 at a conference of Southeast European archaeologists (one of the "Hleb i Vino" conferences hosted by Bernard Wailes and Ruth Tringham). The spatial pattern of the dates appeared to indicate a punctuated and directional rather than regular radial expansion of agricultural populations (Figure 9.1). Punctuated directionality further suggested that Neolithic people had migrated into new territories intentionally, with foreknowledge.

We introduced the concept of "leap-frog" migration to describe this inferred behavior. Initial migrants moved long distances to colonize selected locations that met specific ecological and social criteria ("patches," in ecological terminology). This process left large uninhabited areas that were filled in only after population increase within the initial settlements. Initially, we adopted an eco-functionalist explanation for leap-frog behavior: we assumed that people gathered accurate information about their destination and then moved to the most favorable ecological patches. This assumption reflected the dominant paradigm of 1970s' Americanist archaeology, but it seemed logical. Long-distance migration is always risky – you can get lost or robbed on the way, and you are a stranger in a strange land after you arrive. People would have taken such risks only after they acquired accurate and detailed information about routes and destinations. Later, Anthony (1990, 1997) recognized that this information need not be accurate – it need only be believed. He suggested (1997) that long-distance migrations were governed not just by ecological-demographic factors, but also by social inequalities and beliefs. But from the beginning, we both recognized that the architecture of the flow of information – its source, its diffusion from the source to a specific audience, and its spread from that audience to other groups in the home society – would strongly affect the size, composition, and destination of any long-distance migration. We hypothesized that the information source for European Neolithic farmers could have been a marginal frontier population interacting with

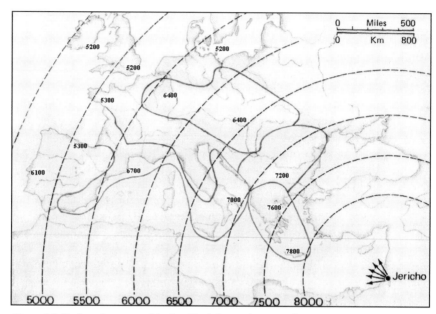

Figure 9.1 Radiocarbon ages of the first Neolithic settlements of Europe, as contrasted with the predictions of the Ammerman and Cavalli-Sforza model (dotted radial lines). The spatial pattern of the dates appears to indicate a punctuated and directional rather than regular radial expansion of agricultural populations

both the intrusive farmers and the indigenous Mesolithic hunter-gatherers – like the hunters and trappers of the early North American frontier. These frontiersmen perhaps subsisted by obtaining forest resources such as furs or honey and exchanging them with more sedentary villagers to the south and east. They may have conveyed to farmers their intimate knowledge of the European interior and the dispositions of its native inhabitants. We called this the "Natty Bumppo" model, after the hero of James Fenimore Cooper's classic, *Leatherstocking Tales.*

For various reasons, our 1979 conference paper never was published and subsequently has been cited only once (Anthony 1990: 910). However, similar ideas have since circulated within the archaeological community, and frontier-interaction theories have been articulated, e.g. by Zvelebil (1986; Zvelebil and Lillie 2000) and van Andel and Runnels (Runnels and van Andel 1988; van Andel and Runnels 1995). The concept of leap-frog migration, further developed in Anthony's 1990 article on migration processes, has proven particularly influential. In European Neolithic studies, a current variant is the "enclave colonization" model (e.g. Zilhão 2000, 2001; Bogucki 2000). Anderson and Gillam (2000) have modeled Paleoindian peopling of North America as a leap-frog process (a modification of Martin's [1973] wave-of-advance or "blitzkrieg" model); and Jochim *et al.* (1999) have used the same ideas to explain the Magdalenian colonization of southern Germany.

It seems that this may be a model with considerable explanatory power in other archaeological applications, and one reason for resurrecting the original paper is to clarify its genesis. Another reason is the accumulation of new data over the intervening period, which can be tested against the predictions we made twenty-five years ago. A vigorous debate now rages over the role of the indigenous Mesolithic European natives: were they displaced or absorbed by intrusive Near Eastern colonists, or did they remain in place and borrow agriculture, or even develop it independently (e.g. Dennell 1983; Zvelebil and Zvelebil 1988; Ammerman 1989)? Many recent discussions (e.g. Donahue 1992; Whittle 1996; Halstead 1996; Zvelebil and Lillie 2000) present "indigenist" interpretations of the archaeological record. Recent analyses of mitochondrial DNA (mtDNA) and Y-chromosome distributions in extant European populations ostensibly support the indigenist position (e.g. Richards *et al.* 1996, 2000; Semino *et al.* 2000). However, some geneticists (e.g. Chikhi *et al.* 1998; Barbujani and Bertorelle 2001) continue to assert that genetic data instead delineate a wholesale population replacement or swamping by intrusive Near Eastern farmers, as originally envisioned by Ammerman and Cavalli-Sforza (1984).

We believe that a re-evaluation of the Neolithic expansion as a migration process along a shifting frontier will be a useful contribution to the ongoing debates. This chapter may be a step toward the eventual formulation of a SPIWA ("staged population-interaction wave of advance") model for the European Neolithic, as recently advocated by Renfrew (2001).

Chronological problems with the wave-of-advance model

The wave-of-advance model for the European Neolithic expansion has become steadily less convincing as new data have come in. The metaphor of a gradually moving wave does not accurately describe the patterning of the radiocarbon dates (Zilhão 2001). Even when we first examined the problem in 1976 the dates appeared to cluster spatially in a manner suggestive of several sequential rapid migratory pulses. Radiocarbon assays published since then have only reinforced this pulse-like pattern (see Figure 9.1). The first cluster of dates demarcates initial Neolithic settlement of Thessaly just before 7,600 rcbp (*c.*6,500 cal BC) (Perlès 2001: 94). After a pause of four or five centuries, cereal agriculture moved into Macedonia and the southern Balkans *c.*7,200 rcbp (6,000 cal BC). At the same time, there was a rapid movement by colonists carrying domesticated animals and Cardial-impressed pottery along the Mediterranean coast (*c.*7,100 rcbp in Dalmatia and southern Italy, 6,700 rcbp in southern France and Aragon, Spain, and 6,300 rcbp in Portugal) (see now Zilhão 2001). After a long pause in Hungary, farmers of the Linearbandkeramik (LBK) culture moved over the Carpathians and northwest through Central Europe, beginning at 6,400 rcbp (5,400 cal BC), and reaching The Netherlands and Belgium in less than a century. After another long delay, groups on the northern and western fringes (northwest France, northern Spain, Britain, Ireland, Denmark and southern Scandinavia) adopted farming around 5,200 rcbp (4,100 cal BC). These dates suggest a punctuated equilibrium model for the spread of farming through Europe, with rapid advances followed by long pauses and in-filling of settlement. This pattern is typical of migrating pioneer farmers moving into new territories (Lefferts 1977: 44).

Biological evidence for a Neolithic migration

The long-distance migration of a substantial number of people into a new environment can be tracked archaeologically through the study of changes in either material culture or biological remains. Biological proof of a Neolithic migration into Europe would require identification of biological (skeletal or genetic) traits that distinguish the ancestral Near Eastern farming groups unambiguously from European Mesolithic populations.

In Europe, the appearance of agriculture is generally coincident with a shift from robust, Cro-Magnon-like skeletal and cranial morphology to a more gracile "Mediterranean" type. This change is clearly documented, for example, at the transition from Lepenski Vir II (a distinctive epi-Mesolithic encampment) to III (a typical Starčevo Neolithic community) (Nemeskeri 1972). But some see evidence for an in situ microevolution of these new physical traits (y'Ednyak and Fleisch 1983). The earlier shift to Mesolithic foraging ways had already engendered a tendency toward skeletal gracility and size reduction (perhaps linked to use of the bow) (Brues 1959; Frayer 1981; Jackes *et al.* 1997). So the Mesolithic people who may have adopted agriculture, particularly along the Mediterranean rim, perhaps were not very distinctive physically from farmers of Near Eastern epi-Paleolithic descent. Given this ambiguity, some analysts will see replacement at the Mesolithic/Neolithic boundary where others see continuity (e.g. see Lalueza Fox [1996] and Zilhão [2000] versus Jackes *et al.* [1997] on the early Neolithic in Portugal).

Ammerman and Cavalli-Sforza (1984: 84), while recognizing that human biological traits constituted the best data set for testing the fit of their "demic diffusion" model, lamented that "Genetic markers, unfortunately, cannot be obtained at the present time from skeletal material." As a proxy for ancient genes, they examined the genetic patterns of modern Europeans, although they realized that these may have been altered by post-Neolithic migrations and natural selection. Cavalli-Sforza's analyses of classic genetic markers have been supplemented in recent years by studies of mtDNA and Y-chromosome distributions. Some geneticists have interpreted the new data as revealing a surprising continuity of regional populations since the Upper Paleolithic, with only minor input (*c.*20 percent) from Neolithic immigrants (e.g. Richards *et al.* 1996, 2000; Semino *et al.* 2000). According to Richards *et al.* (2000), only mtDNA haplogroups J and T1, accounting for 8.3 percent of the European population, are of "Neolithic" age. Haplogroups H, H-16304, T, T2, and K (occurring in nearly 50 percent of Europeans), are all "Late Upper Paleolithic," with estimated origin dates of about 12,000 to 15,000 years.

These dates are probably too old. Not only are allele origin dates always somewhat older than the time of dispersal of the groups bearing them (Barbujani and Bertorelle 2001), but many mtDNA-based origin dates in other regions are much older than the archaeological evidence for human dispersals would indicate (Fiedel 2001). The hypothesized Upper Paleolithic expansion northward out of southern European refugia in response to Bølling warming at 12,500 cal BC could well be an erroneous back-dating of the much better documented Neolithic colonization. One marker of the suggested Upper Paleolithic expansion, mtDNA haplogroup V, is thought to have originated *c.*15,000 BP in Iberia (Torroni *et al.* 1998). But this is a dubious statistical inference; in fact, haplogroup V is absent from Neolithic and Bronze Age tooth samples from the Basque region (Izagirre and de la Rua 1999). The mtDNA haplotype identified in a 14,000 year-old skeleton from the Italian Alps is not found in any contemporary Europeans. The latter finding raises "the possibility of a lack of continuity between the Mesolithic and present-day European gene pools" (Benedetto *et al.* 2000). In the near future, progress in extraction, PCR amplification and identification of ancient DNA may provide a clearer picture of the genetics of Neolithic Europeans.

However, the interpretation of genetic data may not become any less equivocal. As Renfrew (2001) observed, if Mesolithic and Neolithic gene frequencies were similar at the outset of colonization, a wave of advance could have occurred without leaving any discernible trace in modern haplotype distributions. Genetic analysts typically assume that the modern haplogroup frequencies of Turkey and the Levant approximate the gene pool of the Anatolian and Levantine Neolithic. This need not be true. Turkic invasions from Central Asia, which began in the eleventh century AD, account for about 30 percent of the modern Anatolian gene pool (Benedetto *et al.* 2001). The effects on that gene pool of the earlier intrusions of Hittites, Phrygians, Ionian Greeks, Cimmerians, and Galatian Celts remain difficult to assess. It would be helpful to assemble a data base of ancient DNA from Anatolian Neolithic skeletons, perhaps starting with the many well-preserved remains from Çatal Hüyük (a pilot study of Çatal Hüyük DNA is now in progress [R. Malhi, personal communication, October 2001]).

Finally, there is the fundamental problem that the people of the Neolithic, whether indigenous Mesolithic foragers or intrusive Anatolian farmers, certainly exchanged genes with each other. Ethno-linguistic frontiers do exist, and in some places (England and Wales, German and French parts of Switzerland, the four dialect and folk-culture regions [Fischer 1989] of eastern North America) have been remarkably stable for many centuries – but even in these places people have moved freely across cultural frontiers. Ethno-linguistic frontiers rarely coincide with sharply defined genetic boundaries. Anthropology suffers from a peculiar theoretical schizophrenia in which ethno-linguistic boundaries are reduced to merely "imagined" constructs if people can move freely across them – a confusion of culture with biology that undermines the very concept of *cultural* difference. According to Eric Wolf (1982: 167–9; 1984: 394), the Iroquois did not exist as a culturally distinct, bounded tribe, because much of their population consisted of adopted Delaware, Nanticoke, Mohegan, etc. – in spite of the fact that all such adoptees dressed, spoke, and lived cultural lives that were fully Iroquoian (Richter 1992: 68–73). Anthropology insists that culture and biology are utterly separate categories, but Wolf and many others consistently confuse cultural identity with genetic identity. Cultural frontiers can be very robust in spite of constant movement across them, if the people who move adopt the language and culture of those on the other side. The cultural frontier between early European foragers and farmers certainly was robust – forager and farmer cultures remained archaeologically (culturally) distinct for millennia after the initial contact. But it also witnessed a lot of back-and-forth movement: trading trips, negotiations, borrowed labor, and marriage. Very likely it was genetically porous. We can agree with Bogucki (1988: 110) that "It is a short step from providing protein and labour to providing sons and daughters as mates." He suggested that LBK villages eventually absorbed neighboring Mesolithic groups, after centuries of interchange between visibly distinct cultures. If the movement of marriage partners across a porous frontier was the norm, "it is doubtful whether future DNA-based research will pick up clear patterns of genetic descent" (Whittle 1996: 44).

Archaeological evidence for immigrant farmers and the indigenous Mesolithic

Recognizing that the relevant biological data are likely to remain equivocal for some time, we can turn, with caution, to archaeological evidence for the expansion and displacement of cultures. Substantial discontinuity in numerous cultural elements – house shapes and alignments, stone tools, ceramics, ornaments, burials, etc. – can indicate the arrival of an intrusive population, particularly if very similar and earlier assemblages occur in another region where clearly antecedent cultures are known. In the case of the initial Southeast European Neolithic, the most probable homeland for an intrusive population of farmers would be Anatolia. So the introduction of recognizably Anatolian cultural traits should accompany the beginning of farming in Greece and the Balkans.

While we should be able to recognize the Anatolian origin of immigrant material culture, we should not expect to find an exact reproduction of Anatolian material culture in Greece, because long-distance migration usually has a transforming effect on social identities. Colonists do not represent a random sample of all parts of their homeland, but instead tend to recruit from quite specific places and social segments, so they depart carrying just a subset of the homeland's dialects and material culture. When they arrive in a new place after a long-distance migration, they are intensely dependent on each other to survive, and they come under the social influence of the first effective settlers. The first families or migrant groups to establish a viable foothold in the new land usually claim the best territories, establish ritual or religious primacy for their own cults and ceremonies, and give loans and advice to later migrants. Under these circumstances, the customs of these "apex" families (Alvarez 1987) become targets for new behaviors.

Linguists have long recognized the rapid leveling of differences between dialects among long-distance colonists, and the consequent appearance of a more homogeneous way of speaking (Chambers and Trudgill 1990: 104–9; Hock and Joseph 1996: 361–5). Similar processes of simplification (in comparison to the home region) and leveling (adoption of a standardized form) have been noted in the material culture of migrants – notably in domestic architecture and the organization of settlements (Upton and Vlach 1986; Noble 1992). Long-distance migration typically creates communities that are initially relatively homogeneous, in language and material culture; it provides conditions for the rapid emergence of apex families, usually the families of the first-comers; and the cultural hegemony of these families tends to set the rules that guide future generations' behavior, which perpetuates the inordinate cultural influence of the first effective settlers.

The Anatolian intruders

The artifact assemblages of the earliest farming communities in Greece contain a wide array of items that are known in earlier Anatolian or broader Near Eastern cultural traditions and that are not documented in native European Mesolithic traditions. These include:

- bone belt-hooks (Nea Nikomedeia, Sesklo – also at Çatal Hüyük, Hacilar);
- stone studs or labrets (a very visible modification of the face and mouth, therefore likely to be a signal of identity);
- antler-handled sickles (Azmak – also at Hacilar VI);
- polished stone axes (earliest at Mureybet in Syria *c.*9,600 rcbp and Çayönü in Turkey *c.*9,300 rcbp);
- baked clay stamp-seals and slingstones;
- female figurines;
- stone frog figurines (Nea Nikomedeia, Achilleion Ib, Anza II, Azmak – also at Hacilar VI);
- mud-brick rectangular houses;
- carved stone vessels; and
- both monochrome and red-and-white painted pottery.

Two broad artifact categories, ceramics and lithics, are basic to almost all archaeological definitions of prehistoric cultural difference. Both categories show a discontinuity between the Greek Mesolithic (no pottery, quite variable flint tools) and Neolithic (pottery, blade tools, ground and polished stone tools). The Greek Neolithic forms are similar to those of Neolithic Anatolia. Near Eastern sites exhibit a slow development and adoption of pottery over centuries, beginning with poorly fired, chaff-tempered wares. In contrast, Greek and Southeast European sites generally manifest either a brief "aceramic" phase (which actually contains ceramic artifacts in most assemblages said to be "aceramic") or a short phase of well-made monochrome ware followed quickly by the florescence of finely made painted pottery (Proto-Sesklo in Thessaly, Anza I in Macedonia, Starčevo II in Yugoslavia, Karanovo I in Bulgaria). Interestingly, there is no significant cline in the radiocarbon dates for painted ceramics; they first appear around 7,600 rcbp in Hacilar VI in southwestern Turkey, and almost simultaneously, about 7,600–7,400 rcbp, in Thessaly (Achilleion phase Ib, Sesklo) and Macedonia (Nea Nikomedeia). Given the general similarities in shape, color, and technology between Anatolian and Greek ceramics, the dates suggest a rapid transmission through unknown intermediaries between Anatolia and Greece.

Perlès' (1988, 2001) re-analysis of aceramic Greek Neolithic lithic assemblages has highlighted the difference between Mesolithic and Neolithic tool technologies. Greek Mesolithic assemblages from Franchthi Cave and Sidari, for example, consist of large numbers of markedly microlithic irregular flakes; only a few pieces are geometric or regular in form, and some of these have retouched edges. In contrast, the lithic assemblages from aceramic Neolithic levels contain well-made geometric microliths in triangular and trapezoidal shapes, along with larger blade and truncated-blade tools (Sordinas 1970; Jacobsen 1973: 79; Milojcic *et al.* 1962). In parts of Europe where an indigenous Mesolithic adoption of the Neolithic economy is clearly demonstrated (e.g. the Bug-Dniester region in the Ukraine and the Limburg region in Holland), continuity of lithic forms is quite marked (Tringham 1971; Newell 1972). In Greece there is, instead, discontinuity in lithic technology.

The Greek Early Neolithic looks Anatolian not just in artifact types and technology, but also in subsistence. The subsistence economy of Greek Neolithic societies was largely derived from the Near East, probably through Anatolia. Previous claims to the contrary (e.g. Dennell 1983) have been rendered untenable by accumulating archaeological and genetic data. The Neolithic complex was based on the cultivation of cereals and legumes, and the breeding of sheep, goats, pigs, and cattle. Sheep and goats, which predominated among the domestic stock of the earliest farmers in Greece and Southeast Europe, must have been imported from the Near East or Anatolia, because the wild ancestral species were not native to Southeast Europe. Wild goats have been tentatively identified among the fauna in the Upper Paleolithic zone of Franchthi Cave, but they are absent from the Mesolithic levels. The domestic sheep (*Ovis orientalis*) and goat in the Early Neolithic at Franchthi Cave were not of local origin (Jacobsen 1976). Although it was formerly believed that the earliest sheep in the western Mediterranean might have been domesticated from the indigenous mouflon, the latter has now been shown to be a feral form (Donahue 1992). Wild cattle and pigs were indigenous to Europe, but there are no Early Neolithic sites where domestic forms occur separately from the imported ovicaprids. The former inference of an early independent domestication of cattle in Greece was based on bone-derived radiocarbon dates of questionable accuracy (Protsch and Berger 1973; Perlès 2001: 88). The earliest known domesticated cattle come from Pre-Pottery Neolithic B (PPNB) villages in northern Syria, dated to *c.*7,700 cal BC (*c.*8,700 rcbp) (Cauvin 2000: 217). A recent genetic analysis shows that European cattle are of Near Eastern origin (Troy *et al.* 2001).

The staple crops of Southeast Europe included several varieties of wheat – einkorn, emmer, and hexaploid (bread) – and barley – two-row and six-row forms – as well as legumes. Of these plants, only the native range of wild einkorn seems to have extended to Southeast Europe. However, recent genetic analysis indicates that einkorn was first cultivated on the flanks of the Karacadag Mountains in Turkey, and spread into Europe from that region (Heun *et al.* 1997). Emmer wheat (*Triticum dicoccum*), a more ubiquitous type than einkorn in early European Neolithic sites, is a definite Near Eastern import (Renfrew 1973). Emmer wheat and sheep appear as important elements of the earliest Neolithic economies at Knossos (Evans 1968), Argissa (Milojcic *et al.* 1962), Nea Nikomedeia (Rodden 1962), Anza (Gimbutas 1972), and Obre (Benac 1973).

In Greece, the appearance of a Neolithic economy was accompanied by an abrupt discontinuity from the earlier Mesolithic in subsistence economy, settlement locations, domestic architecture, rituals, and technology (Perlès 2001). Moreover, the pattern of change matches that expected from a migration. The first Neolithic settlers in Greece planted wheat and raised imported livestock, but they lived in crude, temporary pit-houses, discarded a very restricted range of material culture, and occupied just a few sites – the places where the "aceramic" phase is found. In long-distance migration, there is always a group of "scouts" – explorers, mercenaries, migrant laborers, or perhaps, in this case, fishermen – who bring back information about their travels, usually just to their families and co-residents. Their limited knowledge of other places and equally limited personal social relations at home tend to focus narrowly both the destination and the social composition of the resulting migration stream. But if any negative conditions prevail at home, among any social segment, and the scouts tell good stories about the destination, a migration stream can easily follow. That second phase of migration, the first real surge of effective settlers, normally includes a wider range of people – including, importantly, entire families – who first establish a functioning society. That expectation is met by the appearance of the ceramic Greek Neolithic, with its substantial mud-brick houses and pottery.

A similar two-stage process of scouting camps followed by more permanent settlements has been recognized in the Magdalenian re-colonization of northern Europe (Jochim *et al.* 1999; Housley *et al.* 1997) and in the colonization of Cyprus by PPNB-related farmers and herders from the Levant around 9,300 rcbp (8,600 cal BC) (Peltenburg *et al.* 2000). The latter brought with them sheep, goats, cattle, pigs, and fallow deer. Peltenburg *et al.* infer a long period of exploration by hunters preceding this colonial venture. The earliest hunting forays may have caused the demise of the pygmy hippopotami on Cyprus around 10,600 rcbp (Simmons *et al.* 1999, but cf. Binford 2000). The Neolithic colonization of Cyprus had to be a carefully planned undertaking. The later (*c.*8,000 rcbp) colonization of Crete by pre-ceramic villagers, probably from Anatolia, was also well planned. Judging from the minimum number of animals that must have been ferried across to ensure a successful breeding stock, the voyage required a veritable flotilla of oared longboats (Broodbank and Strasser 1991). When the second stage of colonization began in Greece, a similar substantial population of people and animals would have been required to ensure viability. The need for sufficient stocks of seed and animals made Neolithic migrations different in their organizational requirements from all earlier migrations by foraging societies.

The Mesolithic people of Southeast Europe did not develop an indigenous agricultural complex through independent experimentation or stimulus diffusion. The new economy, along with an idiosyncratic material culture of clear Anatolian heritage, was imported wholesale in a two-stage sequence that correlates with the scouts-and-settlers pattern expected in a long-distance migration.

The indigenous Mesolithic population: the marine coast

One might still argue (implausibly), as Whittle seems to (1996: 43–4), that the local Mesolithic population simply adopted the Near Eastern agricultural economy, moved to places in the Greek landscape where they had never lived before, invented new house forms, artifact types, and technologies, and suddenly underwent a massive population explosion. But even this unlikely drama requires a cast to perform it, and most of Greece and Southeast Europe seems to have been curiously empty of humans during the late Mesolithic (Chapman 1989: 505). Only a few Mesolithic sites have been found in Greece (Perlès 2001: 20–37), and at only one, Franchthi Cave, was a Neolithic occupation stratified above the Mesolithic. No other Greek Neolithic site occupies a place in the landscape that was lived in during the Mesolithic. From the Peloponnese north all the way to the Danube there are just a half-dozen well-documented late Mesolithic sites: Franchthi and Sidari in Greece, and Crvena Stijena and several others in Yugoslavia (Theocharis 1973: 24; Tringham 1971: 52–7; Perlès 2001: 20–37; Srejovic 1972: 10). A female burial is reported in association with a microlithic assemblage in Theopetra Cave in Thessaly – the only evidence for Mesolithic habitation in a region that has more than 120 Early Neolithic farming settlements (Whittle 1996: 23). North of the Danube there are another half-dozen sites within the curve of the Carpathians, e.g. Subotica, Szodliget, Eger, and Sered (Brukner 1974; Dobosi 1976; Kalicz and Makkay 1972). Even if undated surface scatters of geometric microliths are included, the total number of Mesolithic sites in interior Southeast Europe is surprisingly low in comparison to Western Europe, Poland, Ukraine, Russia, or the Levant.

Only two environments in Southeast Europe seem to have attracted more than a few scattered Mesolithic inhabitants: the Iron Gates region of the Danube (see below); and the marine coast and its adjacent mountains, including some islands. Several Mesolithic bands moved seasonally between the shores of the Adriatic and the karst coastal mountains in Croatia (Miracle *et al.* 2000). Greece's Mesolithic sites are concentrated on the south and southwest coasts. The Mesolithic population of Bulgaria is documented only on the south coast (Gatsov 1989) and in the Pobiti Kamini Hills near the Black Sea. The Mesolithic population of southern Yugoslavia was coastal (Srejovic 1989). In the Cyclades, allegedly Mesolithic burials and dwellings are reported from 1996 excavations at Maroulas on the island of Kythnos (but Perlès [2001: 22] assigns these remains to a later period). In the northern Sporades, a Mesolithic occupation, dated *c.*11,000 to 8,000 rcbp, has been investigated in the cave of Cyclope on the now uninhabited island of Yioura (Sampson 1998a, b). Fish bones, shells of mollusks and land snails, and bird and mammal remains indicate seasonal occupations by mobile, seafaring foragers. Fish were caught using bone hooks. Domesticated animals are reported from the "upper" Mesolithic of Cyclope cave, with obsidian from Melos. Perhaps the animals were obtained from the seafaring pioneer farmers who had colonized Cyprus about 8,600 rcbp. Despite the proximity of Yioura to the mainland of Thessaly, it is noteworthy that the microlithic industry bears little resemblance to the contemporaneous late Mesolithic assemblages from mainland Greek sites, such as Franchthi and Klisoura. Instead, the trapezoidal and lunate microliths from the island cave resemble epi-Paleolithic tools from sites near Antalya, in southwestern Anatolia.

More indigenous Mesolithic: the Iron Gates

The Greek archaeological record suggests an encounter in which immigrant farmers initially had very little interaction with what seems to have been a very thin population of coastal fisher-foragers. Only after the immigrants established an effective society and their descendants began to move north through the Macedonian forests toward the Danube basin did they encounter their first substantial native population: the foragers of the Iron Gates.

The peculiar riverine sites in the Iron Gates region of the Danube, including Lepenski Vir, Padina, Vlasac, Schela Cladovei, and Icoana, have been described as Mesolithic, but radiocarbon dates show them to be contemporaneous with the Greek Neolithic and its earliest northern offshoot, the Starčevo Neolithic (c.7,400–6,600 rcbp, or 6,250–5,700 cal BC). Moreover, pottery was found in all levels at Padina in association with "Mesolithic" trapezoidal houses, and it also occurs in the supposed "pre-ceramic" Level I at Lepenski Vir (Srejovic 1972: 134; Jovanovic 1973; Garasanin and Radovanovic 2001). The unique cultural features of these sites – standardized trapezoidal houses, monumental stone sculpture, extended burials near hearths, and heavy dependence on fish – do effectively differentiate them from the Neolithic immigrants. These peculiarities may well have resulted from the indigenous development of a local Mesolithic culture adapted to an ecological niche of great abundance. However, one must ask why this adaptation did not develop much earlier. Chapman (1989) suggests that the riverine focus developed in response to colonization of the Danube by fish as the climate and environment changed, around 8,300–7,500 rcbp. Sedentism, ceremonial activities and construction, and perhaps some status differentiation, may have begun in the context of competition between local forager bands, jostling for access to the riverine fishery. However, even if this rivalry was the initial spur to creation of small-scale sacred ceremonial centers along the river, the local foragers soon encountered an exogenous challenge.

The pottery in Lepenski Vir I and II clearly demonstrates interaction with Neolithic neighbors of the Anza I and Early Starčevo cultures (Garasanin and Radovanovic 2001). If the pottery was obtained by trade, the Mesolithic bands must have offered something in exchange – perhaps processed fish and furs (Voytek and Tringham 1989). Their former dispersed settlement pattern may have been modified to facilitate more regular trading contact with the intrusive farmers. The grotesque fish–human images carved on boulders at Lepenski Vir may have had two social functions. First, as components of funerals and other communal rituals, they enhanced group solidarity in the face of a threatening new socioeconomic system (Chapman 1989; Whittle 1996: 44–6); second, as permanent visible fixtures at the river edge, they signaled to the Neolithic intruders the natives' prior claim to this territory. The Iron Gates

(Djerdap) was an apt place to make this assertion of ownership. With his trained military eye, Mortimer Wheeler (1972: 8) observed of the Iron Gates:

> It is indeed the veritable gateway between the lower Danube and the Near East on the one hand and the great Hungarian plains, with their vital mid-European arteries, on the other. From early historic times its strategic value has been sufficiently manifest on more than one occasion.

It should be noted that, only a short time after establishment of the fully Neolithic Lepenski Vir III settlement on the ruins of the Mesolithic camp, the location was abandoned for millennia. This may indicate that the Neolithic farmers were less concerned with securing a good local fishing place than with winning control of this nexus of indigenous social and ideological resistance. Once they accomplished their goal, they had little further interest in this agriculturally marginal area.

Targeted migration: the pull of known environments

To some extent, conflict between the indigenous and intrusive populations may have been minimized by their differing land-use preferences. Early Neolithic sites in Southeast Europe are not usually located in the same areas where Mesolithic sites are found. Mesolithic sites occur on sand dunes between the lower Danube and the Tisza, on similar dunes in the Pobiti Kamini hills in Bulgaria, in the karst limestone mountains of Bosnia, and along the low sandy banks of rivers. Early Neolithic sites tend to be located on heavier soils in river bottoms and, as one moves north, on loess soils (Jarman *et al.* 1982).

The first farmers in Greece were drawn to the broad floodplains of Thessaly – an environment unique in all of Greece (van Andel and Runnels 1995). Abandoned levees and fan deltas offered the farmers well-drained locations for settlement and easily worked loam, annually refreshed with floodwater and new silt, for planting their crops. As Neolithic farmers pushed northward, they sought out similar locations. Körös sites in the Great Hungarian Basin were preferentially established on the crests of natural levees in the floodplains of rivers and lakes (Kosse 1979). In southern Yugoslavia, the Early Neolithic sites are typically located in large *poljes* (basins with fluctuating lakes) or on levees in riverine valleys (Barker 1975). Settlers in southern Bulgaria also favored riverine settings (Dennell and Webley 1975). The composite floodplain of the Tavoliere in southeast Italy – the focus of dense Early Neolithic settlement – resembled the basins of Thessaly (van Andel and Runnels 1995). All these European landscapes share key attributes with the Anatolian regions from which Early Neolithic settlers probably originated. When Çatal Hüyük was inhabited, the Konya Plain was a broad floodplain (Roberts *et al.* 1996). In fact, a recent re-analysis of the paleobotanical evidence suggests that *Scirpus* (bulrushes), collected in the wetlands, may have been a significant carbohydrate source for the residents (Hastorf and Near 1998). The margins of lakes in the Beyşehir-Sugla basin provided a similar setting for Neolithic villages such as Suberde and Erbaba. It appears that Anatolian emigrants to southern Europe were looking for microenvironments that closely replicated their homeland.

The rational selectivity evident in Early Neolithic settlement locations has posed a problem both for proponents of demic diffusion and for indigenist critics of the colonization model. "Unless one grants these early farmers a phenomenal amount of good luck and even better judgment, it is hard to see how pioneering immigrants had such detailed knowledge of the area they were colonizing" (Dennell 1983: 158; cf. Whittle 1996: 61). Van Andel and Runnels (1995: 498) ask, "How did these migrants locate the Thessalian plains which high mountains shield from view by land and sea?" They speculate that Thessaly had been explored previously by "wandering seafarers" and obsidian traders. This inference seems to be substantiated by the recent discovery in the northern Sporades, an island chain off Thessaly, of intermittent visits by Mesolithic fishermen with cultural links to western Anatolia (Sampson1998a, b).

Push factors: population pressure and social inequality

One question raised by indigenists is the motivation for emigration of hypothetical Neolithic colonists. Ammerman and Cavalli-Sforza (1971, 1984) assumed that population pressure was the root cause of migration. In 1979, we spoke vaguely of "population pressure, local soil exhaustion, a desire for 'elbow room,' or any combination of these." However, as Whittle (1996: 43) correctly observed, "the Neolithic presence in Turkey, both in western Anatolia and in European Turkey, is itself so far very weak," and there is no evidence that settlement density in the Konya basin increased through the early Neolithic. The situation in Anatolia has improved recently with the discovery at Hoca Cesme, on the Aegean coast, of numerous levels with monochrome Early Neolithic pottery of Central Anatolian type, stratified below a layer with painted pottery resembling Sesklo and Karanovo I types (Özdoğan 1995). This find at least substantiates the presence of Neolithic communities on the western fringe of Anatolia, even if it does not demonstrate any pressure on local resources.

Population pressure

Generally, it is difficult to correlate people's culturally mediated perceptions of regional carrying capacity with objective criteria. At what level of density did early Neolithic farmers of Anatolia and Greece begin to feel crowded? It may be futile to seek archaeological evidence of pressure in increasing site density in a hypothetical ancestral area such as the Konya Plain. The availability of migration to marginal or distant lands as a safety valve may actually have permitted maintenance of a constant density in the home region for an extended period. Archaeological evidence of increased density may only signal the closing off of the migration option. In Thessaly, recent survey data (Gallis 1992, van Andel *et al.* 1994) indicate only a minor increase in the number of sites from the Early to Middle Neolithic, but a sharp increase in numbers, as well as growth in the size of individual sites, in the Late Neolithic, after 5,500 cal BC. Emigration might be expected to surge as density rose. Indeed, van

Andel and Runnels (1995: 498) suggest that "It may be no coincidence that the first settlements in Yugoslavian Macedonia and southern Bulgaria date to c. 7800 BP [5,800 cal BC], implying that a new spillover had begun [from Thessaly]."

One indirect sign of population pressure might be the appearance of new, density-dependent diseases. Density-dependent or animal-hosted pathogens may have accompanied the shift to farming and herding (Groube 1996). Some of the children's skulls at Abu Hureyra in Syria displayed cribra orbitalia, a thickening and pitting of the eye sockets that is ascribed to anemia caused by long-term parasite infection. Jackes *et al.* (1997) observed the same condition in their Portuguese Neolithic sample. Porotic hyperostosis occurred in Neolithic skulls from Çatal Hüyük, Franchthi Cave, and Nea Nikomedeia, suggesting that thalassemia had already evolved in defense against malarial parasites (Angel 1972). If this interpretation of Neolithic anemia is correct (we must caution that similar conditions can result from other infections and from nutrient deficiencies [Holland and O'Brien 1997]), it raises two intriguing possibilities: first, that Neolithic intruders carried malarial plasmodia or other parasites into the midst of naive Mesolithic populations lacking defense mechanisms; and second, that perceptions of endemic disease may have been a factor periodically inducing Neolithic villagers to seek new locations for settlement.

Social push factors

But it is a mistake to focus exclusively on population pressure or its frequent companion, disease. People do not stay where they are until pushed away by starvation and density-dependent epidemics. In many cases, migration is a response to other kinds of negative pushes – particularly social problems (Anthony 1997). Kopytoff (1987) examined the strong fissioning tendency among African societies, which he attributed partly to the widespread custom of associating status with age. Older brothers occupy ceremonial offices and make decisions, denying younger brothers opportunities for prestige and social advancement. Ambitious younger brothers have frequently migrated to a new place where they could attract followers and establish their own rights and privileges (Kopytoff 1987: 18–19). A similar migratory tendency of younger siblings is documented among the aristocratic lineages of ancient Rome (Fustel de Coulanges 1956), the Hopi clans of the American Southwest (Schlegel 1992), and the ruling lineages of the Maya (Fox 1987). The critical push factor in these cases was not overpopulation, but social regulations that favored some kin segments or siblings over others. In societies where the rules of inheritance and the customary distribution of privileges favor some individuals or groups unequally, those who are disfavored often migrate. Migration is not just an instinctive response to overcrowding, but instead is a consciously thought-out social strategy through which kin groups improve their access to prestige, power, and resources. Is there any reason to suppose that the Neolithic occupants of Anatolia and the Near East were encouraged to migrate by increasing social inequalities at home?

Larger families

The growth of population after the Neolithic transition, particularly after pottery was widely adopted by farming populations, may itself have generated entirely new social strains and competition. In a comparative study of Mesolithic and Neolithic human remains from Portugal, Jackes *et al.* (1997) observed that fertility increased dramatically after the transition; the average number of births per woman rose from four to six. Angel (1971) calculated that the average number of births per woman at Çatal Hüyük was 4.2. At Tell Abu Hureyra in Syria, there is skeletal evidence of an immediate effect of the introduction of pottery (at the surprisingly late date of *c.*7,300 rcbp or *c.*6,200 cal BC in this case) on population. A much higher proportion of the skeletons from the ceramic levels are those of infants, compared to the preceramic period (Molleson 1994). Molleson hypothesizes that pottery was used to soak and cook grains for porridge. This new, easily chewed foodstuff allowed earlier weaning and increased the fertility of women by boosting their carbohydrate intake, thus resulting in a reduced interval between births. The larger families of the post-pottery period would have meant increased social competition among siblings.

The tyranny of the elders

Molleson's analysis of the Abu Hureyra skeletons showed that pottery and porridge also had implications for adult health and longevity. Although caries began to appear, tooth wear decreased markedly. Molleson cites the particular case of a woman with an unhealed broken jaw, who could not have survived without easily chewable gruel. Longer survival of toothless older adults may have had the side-effect of fostering a more rigid, gerontocratic social organization. Old people may have held on longer to the social positions of highest status (clan leader, priest, etc.), thus closing off opportunities for social advance by ambitious younger people (particularly men). Ancestor cults flourished in the Near East during the PPNB period, when the skulls of selected ancestors were reverently decorated and placed in special crypts inside houses. Could the concentration of power and prestige among clan or lineage elders have led to young men seeking opportunities in less restrictive environments on the frontier?

Domus *and* agrios

We would hesitate to endorse Gimbutas' (1974, 1991) elaborate reconstruction of the pantheon of Neolithic goddesses. Nevertheless, the preponderance of female depictions in the figurines of early Neolithic Anatolia and Southeast Europe, as well as the legacy of ancient matrilineal institutions in western Anatolia and the Aegean, as dimly viewed through Classical Greek literature (Thomson 1949, Harrison 1922), imply that female-centered domestic cults and inheritance rules might go back to the Neolithic. Houses with shared walls or neatly arranged in rows are suggestive of a tightly regulated society, and the omnipresent figurines and domestic shrines imply that the domestic order was maintained by a powerful communal ideology. Hodder

(1990, 2001) probably is correct in his reconstruction of a female-centered domestic ideology for the first Neolithic societies. Recently, Jacques Cauvin (2000) has taken this observation a step farther. He suggests that ideological changes associated with domesticity, residential stability, and the growing social power of women were responsible both for the origins of agricultural economies and for the later expansion of agricultural populations. In his scheme, the outward movement of agricultural populations during PPNB (8,300–7,000 cal BC) was caused by an ideological shift away from a female-centered universe to a virile, expansive, outward-striving, male-centered community psychology. He ignores other push factors, and his explanation of the supposed symbolic shift is vague. But we agree that gender may have played a role in Neolithic migrations.

Cross-cultural research by Divale (1974) suggests that a pattern of heightened male involvement in external activities (war, hunting, trade) may be inherent in matrilocal social organizations. The Iroquoians of the northeastern United States provide an ethnohistoric case of long-distance raiding and hunting by males in a matrilocal society. Few legitimate outlets for male aggression or status-striving exist in communities where related women are the residential core within households and occupy the principal status positions in descent group ceremonies. Young males with limited prospects in Neolithic villages may have felt compelled to seek alternative personal advancement through warfare or trade on a distant frontier.

Hunting seems to have retained social and ideological importance for Neolithic men for centuries after the availability of domestic animals had reduced its dietary significance. The Neolithic colonizers of Cyprus and Crete carried fallow deer across the sea, along with their domestic stock, presumably to stock the forest with their favorite game. Fallow deer were also brought into Greece by the Neolithic settlers (Hubbard 1995). At Çatal Hüyük, at 6,700 cal BC, cattle had already been domesticated for centuries; but in "shrine" A.III.1, paintings on adjacent walls show men hunting red deer on one wall and a bull on the other (Mellaart 1967: 174). Mellaart noted (1967: 176) that this Level III shrine was not rebuilt in Level II, and he took this to show the decline of hunting: "Sometime during the fifty-eighth century BC [uncalibrated] agriculture finally triumphed over the age old occupation of hunting and with it the power of woman increased: this much is clear from the almost total disappearance of male statues in the cult." We don't want to put too much weight on this subjective interpretation of the evidence, but we must note the near-perfect synchrony of the postulated decline in hunting (a male status activity) in central Anatolia and the establishment of frontier Neolithic colonies in Thessaly.

Some male burials in the earliest LBK settlements (e.g. at Schwanfeld, in Franconia, directly dated to c.5,500 cal BC) were accompanied by trapezoid arrow points. Gronenborn (1999: 177) suggests that this standardized treatment may demarcate

> a subgroup within Earliest LBK society which devoted itself to the traditional tasks of hunting and fighting … . Associations of hunter-warriors could have been a vital part of Earliest LBK society. For example, they might have played an important role in the expansion of LBK, as young hunters, who

had already travelled to distant territories, may have led groups out of the core region to settle in new lands. Thus, the interpretation of the Schwanfeld burial as the founder of the settlement seems possible. The founders might have become group leaders, and eventually the lineage of community leaders descended from them.

In early Greek and Balkan Neolithic sites, where faunal assemblages are dominated by domestic animals, a small proportion of the bones usually represent wild game, including fur bearers. Level III at Lepenski Vir – the Starcevo component that replaced the Mesolithic community – yielded bones of brown bear, wolf, lynx, marten, beaver, wild cat, and fox (Bökönyi 1970: 187). Bones of wild cat were found in Phase I at Achilleion, and fox bones were recognized in later phases (Bökönyi 1989). In the Earliest LBK at Bruchenbrücken (c.5,400 cal BC) bones of otter, fox, and beaver are common (Gronenborn 1999: 163), and beaver bones occur at LBK sites in France (Hachem 2000). In the Near East, around 7,000 cal BC, murals at Çatal Hüyük depict men (perhaps members of a sodality) wearing leopard skins (Mellaart 1967). Onagers were hunted near Umm Dabaghiyah, and their hides were processed at the site (Kirkbride 1974). Numerous fox bones were found in PPN Jericho (Clutton-Brock 1969). These finds seem to demonstrate the existence of a demand for furs and hides in farming communities to the south and east, which might have provided the impetus for entrepreneurial males to venture into the woodlands of Southeast Europe.

While we recognize that the market forces of global capitalism that drove the North American fur trade in the seventeenth and eighteenth centuries have no close counterpart in the Neolithic Near East or southern Europe, an analogy may be drawn with respect to the symbolic role of shell beads in both systems. In North America, wampum beads, manufactured from clam and conch shell by coastal natives, became the premier exchange medium in the early fur trade. Perhaps, *Spondylus* shell beads served the same function in early Neolithic Europe. *Spondylus* beads were already being manufactured outside of Franchthi Cave in the Early Neolithic, c.7,500 rcbp (Jacobsen 1976). They were still being made in Greek Middle Neolithic sites (Halstead 1993). They were traded from the Aegean coast deep into the European interior, where they occur at Starcevo sites and later (6,400 rcbp) in the earliest LBK villages (e.g. Vedrovice in Moravia [Gronenborn 1999: 172]). Some valued commodities – furs and hides, perhaps – must have passed down the line from northern frontier communities in exchange for the *Spondylus* beads that were coming up from the Greek coast.

The pushes that impelled Neolithic migrations could have included local outbreaks of disease; larger family sizes with more competition between siblings; the development of ancestor cults that increased the power and tyranny of elders; the elaboration of female-centered domestic cults and descent groups that restricted male positions of power within the *domus;* and the growing market in overhunted agricultural regions for furs, fish, and more exotic tokens from distant places.

The Iceman and other Bumppos

In 1979, we did not expect that archaeological documentation of the activities of our hypothetical pathfinding, beaver-trapping deerslayers would ever be found. Given the nature of animal fur preparation, skinning and initial dressing probably would have been carried out at or near kill sites, which would be very difficult for the archaeologist to find, and only a few bones of the exploited species would appear in settlements to bear witness to these activities. Under normal circumstances of preservation, the hides and fur, of course, will have disappeared from the record (Groenman-van Waateringe *et al.* 1999).

Remarkably, in 1991, a Natty Bumppo-like individual emerged from melting ice in the Tyrolean Alps (Barfield 1994). The Iceman dates from about 3,200 cal BC (Late Neolithic in western Europe). He may have been a shepherd taking his flock to mountain pastures, or an itinerant trader. He was probably a craftsman, too; arsenic in his hair suggests that he smelted copper, and he carried a copper axe. His last meal was probably an unleavened wafer made of einkorn wheat grown in one of the valley-bottom villages of northern Italy. Someone shot him in the back with an arrow a few hours before he lay down, exhausted and bleeding, in a hollow between the rocks of a high mountain slope. Whatever his relationship to the lowlanders, he was prepared to live off the land in the mountains, and he carried a diverse tool-kit to maintain his self-sufficiency. His gear included a back-pack, a stone knife, a flint scraper, flake, an awl, a stone-retouching tool, two birch-bark containers, a net (for bird-catching?), an unfinished bow, and a quiver of arrows. His clothing – leggings, a cap, a breechcloth, and a coat – was made of fur and leather from red deer hide. He wore an outer cape made of woven reeds. A few pieces of ibex bone show that he had hunted that mountain denizen. In Whittle's view (1996: 316–7), the Iceman "was a knowledgeable individual, carrying out routine movement high in the mountains," who "neatly illustrates the continuing theme of mobility." His "allegiances may have been … ambiguous … . An individual like a mountain shepherd could have seen himself as belonging to and in contact with several different worlds." Hodder (1999: 144) interprets the Iceman as symbolic of the Late Neolithic transition toward a more male-focused, individualistic, and aggressive lifeway and ideology "antithetical to societies based on a corporate sense of lineage and dependency and symbolized by the domestic hearth." But, he also observes (1999: 141) that "there may always have been people on the margins of society, independent hunters and travellers."

We see the Iceman as a nearly timeless, archetypical frontiersman. Apart from his copper axe, and the grains of einkorn in his colon, the Iceman's accoutrements would not be out of place in the Mesolithic. But hand him a musket, and he could be up in the Rockies in the 1830s, setting beaver traps.

Summary

The Neolithic colonization of Europe was a complicated process that took more than 2,500 years to unfold. Analysis of calibrated radiocarbon dates reveals a series of punctuated, rapid expansions, interrupted by periods – 500 to 1,000 years long – of stasis and in-filling. The earliest colonists in Southeast Europe sought out floodplains and lake basins that were close analogues to familiar ancestral habitats in Anatolia and optimal for their farming practices. The two-stage structure of the Early Neolithic expansion and the selectivity of initial settlement locations imply carefully planned colonizing ventures, based on detailed prior knowledge of the landscape. The second-stage farmers may have derived this vital geographic information from fishing groups that initially created settlement facilities on the Greek coast to support long-distance fishing trips. These frontiersmen probably shifted opportunistically from hunting and fishing, to herding, to trading.

Unlike the cases of hunter-gatherer expansion into uninhabited landscapes that are discussed in some other chapters in this volume, colonization by farmers required substantial logistical planning and gathering of resources for the movement of a viable population not just of people, but also animals and seed-corn. This live baggage increased the risks of the movement and heightened the importance of the information obtained from the scouts. The risks were greatly increased by the fact that the initial movement was almost certainly by boat across the Aegean Sea, a truly remarkable undertaking.

Later Neolithic expansion into Europe had to confront long-entrenched indigenous foragers. In addition, as farmers moved north beyond the Mediterranean climate zone, they encountered new soil types and seasonal patterns of temperature and precipitation to which they and their domesticated plants and animals had to adapt. As the frontier shifted northward and westward, interactions between farmers and indigenous Mesolithic foragers took varied forms: avoidance through habitat partition, symbiotic coexistence, expropriation, violent resistance and aggression, exchange of subsistence and prestige items, intermarriage, alliance, acculturation and incorporation. No single model of expansion can incorporate all of these events, but our understanding of them will improve when we expand our dichotomous conception of farmers and foragers to include the frontier populations that moved back and forth between them.

References

Alvarez, R. R., Jr. (1987) *Familia: Migration and Adaptation in Baja and Alta California, 1800–1975*, Berkeley: University of California Press.

Ammerman. A. J. (1989) "On the Neolithic Transition in Europe: A Comment on Zvelebil and Zvelebil," *Antiquity* 63:162–5.

Ammerman, A. J. and L. L. Cavalli-Sforza (1971) "Measuring the Rate of Spread of Early Farming in Europe," *Man* 6:674–88.

—— (1984) *The Neolithic Transition and the Genetics of Population in Europe*, Princeton, NJ: Princeton University Press.

Anderson, D. G. and J. C. Gillam (2000) "Paleoindian Colonization of the Americas: Implications from an Examination of Physiography, Demography, and Artifact Distribution," *American Antiquity* 65(1):43–66.

Angel, J. L. (1971) "Early Neolithic Skeletons from Çatal Hüyük: Demography and Pathology," *Anatolian Studies* 21:77–98.

—— (1972) "Ecology and Population in the Eastern Mediterranean," *World Archaeology* 4: 88–105.

Anthony, D. W. (1990) "Migration in Archaeology: The Baby and the Bathwater," *American Anthropologist* 92:895–914.

—— (1997) "Prehistoric Migration as a Social Process," in J. Chapman and H. Hamerow (eds) *Migrations and Invasions in Archaeological Explanation*, Oxford: British Archaeological Reports, International Series 664.

Barbujani, G. and G. Bertorelle (2001) "Genetics and the Population History of Europe," *Proceedings of the National Academy of Sciences* 98:22–5.

Barfield, L. (1994) "The Iceman Reviewed," *Antiquity* 68:10–26.

Barker, G. (1975) "Early Neolithic Land Use in Yugoslavia," *Proceedings of the Prehistoric Society* 41:85–104.

Benac, A. (1973) *Obre I and II*, Sarajevo: Wissenschaftliche Mitteilungen des Bosnisch-Herzegowinischen Landes Museum, No. 3a.

Benedetto, G. di., I. S. Nasidze, M. Stenico, *et al.* (2000) "Mitochondrial DNA Sequences in Prehistoric Human Remains from the Alps," *European Journal of Human Genetics* 8(9): 669–77.

Benedetto, G. di., A. Erguven, M. Stenico, *et al.* (2001) "DNA Diversity and Population Admixture in Anatolia," *American Journal of Physical Anthropology* 115:144–56.

Binford, L. R. (2000) "Review of Faunal Extinction in an Island Society: Pygmy Hippopotamus Hunters of Cyprus, by Alan H.Simmons and Associates," *American Antiquity* 65: 771.

Bogucki, P. (1988) *Forest Farmers and Stockherders: Early Agriculture and its Consequences in North-Central Europe*, Cambridge: Cambridge University Press.

—— (2000) "How Agriculture Came to North-Central Europe," in T. D. Price (ed.) *Europe's First Farmers*, Cambridge: Cambridge University Press.

Bökönyi, S. (1970) "Animal Remains from Lepenski Vir," *Science* 167:1702–4.

—— (1989) "Animal Remains. In Achilleion: A Neolithic Settlement in Thessaly, Greece, 6400–5600 BC," in M. Gimbutas, S. Winn, and D. Shimabuku (eds) *Monumenta Archaeologica* 14:315–325, Los Angeles: Institute of Archaeology of University of California.

Broodbank, C. and T. F. Strasser (1991) "Migrant Farmers and the Colonization of Crete," *Antiquity* 65:233–45.

Brukner, B. (1974) "Paleolit I Mesolit," in B. Brukner, B. Jovanovic, and N. Tasic (eds) *Praistorija Vojvodine*, Novi Sad, Yugoslavia (publisher unknown).

Brues, A. M. (1959) "The Spearman and the Archer," *American Anthropologist* 61:457–69.

Cauvin, J. (2000) *The Birth of the Gods and the Origins of Agriculture*, Cambridge: Cambridge University Press.

Chambers, J.K. and P. Trudgill (1990) *Dialectology*, Cambridge: Cambridge University Press.

Chapman, J. (1989) "Demographic Trends in Neothermal South-East Europe," in C. Bonsall, (ed.) *The Mesolithic in Europe*, Edinburgh: John Donald.

Chikhi, L., G. Destro-Bisol, G. Bertorelle, V. Pascali, and G. Barbujani (1998) "Clines of Nuclear DNA Markers Suggest a Largely Neolithic Ancestry of the European Gene Pool," *Proceedings of the National Academy of Sciences* 95:9053–8.

Clutton-Brock, J. (1969) "Carnivore Remains from the Excavations of the Jericho Tell," in P. Ucko and G. Dimbleby (eds) *The Domestication and Exploitation of Plants and Animals*, Chicago: Aldine.

Dennell, R. (1983) *European Economic Prehistory: A New Approach*, London: Academic Press.

Dennell, R. and D. Webley (1975) "Prehistoric Settlement and Land Use in Southern Bulgaria," in E. S. Higgs (ed.) *Palaeoeconomy*, Cambridge: Cambridge University Press.

Divale, W. T. (1974) "Migration, External Warfare, and Matrilocal Residence," *Behavior Science Research* 9:75–133.

Dobosi, V. T. (1976) "Prehistoric Settlement at Demjen-Hegyeskoberc," *Folia Archaeologica* 27:9–40. Budapest.

Donahue, R. E. (1992) "Desperately Seeking Ceres: A Critical Examination of Current Models for the Transition to Agriculture in Mediterranean Europe," in A. B. Gebauer and T. D. Price (eds) *Transitions to Agriculture in Prehistory*, Monographs in World Archaeology 4, Madison: Prehistory Press.

Evans, J. D. (1968) "Knossos Neolithic, Part II: Summary and Conclusions," *British School at Athens Annual* 63:267–76.

Fiedel, S. J. (2001) "Clocks or Crocks? Biomolecular Chronology Versus Archaeology." Paper presented at 66th annual meeting of Society for American Archaeology, New Orleans, April 19.

Fischer, D. H. (1989) *Albion's Seed: Four British Folkways in America*, New York: Oxford University Press.

Fisher, R. A. (1937) "The Wave of Advance of Advantageous Genes," *Annals of Eugenics* 7:355–369.

Fox, J. W. (1987) *Maya Postclassic State Formation*, Cambridge: Cambridge University Press.

Frayer, D. W. (1981) "Body Size, Weapon Use, and Natural Selection in the European Upper Paleolithic and Mesolithic," *American Anthropologist* 83:57–73.

Fustel de Coulanges, N. D. (1956) *The Ancient City: A Study of the Religion, Laws, and Institutions of Greece and Rome*, New York: Doubleday.

Gallis, K. I. (1992) *Atlas Proistorikon Oikismon tis Anatolikis Thessalikis Pediadas*, Larisa: Eteria Istorikon Erevnon Thessalias.

Garasanin, M. and I. Radovanovic (2001) "A Pot in House 54 at Lepenski Vir," *Antiquity* 75:118–25.

Gatsov, I. (1989) "Early Holocene Assemblages from the Bulgarian Black Sea Coast," in C. Bonsall (ed.) *The Mesolithic in Europe*, Edinburgh: John Donald.

Gimbutas, M. (1972) "Excavation at Anza, Macedonia: Further Insight into the Civilization of Old Europe, 7000–4000 B.C.," *Archaeology* 25(2):112–23.

—— (1974) *The Gods and Goddesses of Old Europe, c. 7000–3500 BC*, London: Thames and Hudson.

—— (1991) *The Civilization of the Goddess*, San Francisco: Harper.

Groenman-van Waateringe, W., M. Kilian, and H. van Londen (1999) "The Curing of Hides and Skins in European Prehistory," *Antiquity* 73:282.

Gronenborn, D. (1999) "A Variation on a Basic Theme: The Transition to Farming in Southern Central Europe," *Journal of World Prehistory* 13(2):123–210.

Groube, L. (1996) "The Impact of Disease upon the Emergence of Agriculture," in D. R. Harris (ed.) *The Origins and Spread of Agriculture and Pastoralism in Eurasia*, Washington, DC: Smithsonian Institution Press.

Hachem, L. (2000) "New Observations on the Bandkeramik House and Social Organization," *Antiquity* 74:308–312.

Halstead, P. (1993) "*Spondylus* Shell Ornaments from Late Neolithic Dimini, Greece: Specialized Manufacture or Unequal Accumulation?" *Antiquity* 67:603–9.

—— (1996) "The Development of Agriculture and Pastoralism in Greece: When, How, Who, and What?" in D. R. Harris (ed.) *The Origins and Spread of Agriculture and Pastoralism in Eurasia*, Washington, DC: Smithsonian Institution Press.

Harrison, J. E. (1922) *Prolegomena to the Study of Greek Religion*, Cambridge: Cambridge University Press.

Hastorf, C. and J. Near (1998) "Archaeobotanical Analyses," *Catal News* 5 (http://www.catalhoyuk.com).

Heun, M., R. Schafer-Pregl, D. Klawan, *et al.* (1997) "Site of Einkorn Wheat Domestication Identified by DNA Fingerprinting," *Science* 278:1312.

Hock, H. H. and B. D. Joseph (1996) *Language History, Language Change and Language Relationship*, Berlin: Mouton de Gruyter.

Hodder, I. (1990) *The Domestication of Europe*, Oxford: Blackwell.

—— (1999) *The Archaeological Process: An Introduction*, Oxford: Blackwell.

—— (2001) "Symbolism and the Origins of Agriculture in the Near East," *Cambridge Archaeological Journal* 11(1):107–12.

Holland, T. D. and M. J. O'Brien (1997) "Parasites, Porotic Hyperostosis, and the Implications of Changing Perspectives," *American Antiquity* 62(2):183–93.

Housley, R. A., C. S. Gamble, M. Street, and P. Pettitt (1997) "Radiocarbon evidence for the Lateglacial Human Recolonization of northern Europe," *Proceedings of the Prehistoric Society* 63:25–54.

Hubbard, R.N. L. B. (1995) "Fallow Deer in Prehistoric Greece, and the Analogy between Faunal Spectra and Pollen Analyses," *Antiquity* 69:527–38.

Izagirre, N. and C. de la Rua (1999) "An mtDNA Analysis in Ancient Basque Populations: Implications for Haplogroup V as a Marker for a Major Paleolithic Expansion from Southwestern Europe," *American Journal of Human Genetics* 65:199–207.

Jackes, M., D. Lubell, and C. Meiklejohn (1997) "Healthy but Mortal: Human Biology and the First Farmers of Western Europe," *Antiquity* 71(273):639–58.

Jacobsen, T. (1973) "Excavations in the Franchthi Cave, 1969–1971," pts. 1 and 2. *Hesperia* 42:45–88, 253–83.

—— (1976) "17,000 Years of Greek Prehistory," *Scientific American* 234(6):76–87.

Jarman, H. N., D. W. Bailey, and M. Jarman (eds) (1982) *Early European Agriculture: Its Foundations and Development*, Cambridge: Cambridge University Press.

Jochim, M. A., C. Herhahn and H. Starr (1999) "The Magdalenian Colonization of Southern Germany," *American Anthropologist* 101(1):129–42.

Jovanovic, B. (1973) "The Early Neolithic Architecture of Djerdap (Iron Gate) Gorge," *Proceedings of the Eighth International Congress of Prehistoric and Protohistoric Sciences* 10:290–3. Belgrade.

Kalicz, N. and J. Makkay (1972) "Probleme des fruhen Neolithikums der nordlichen Tiefebene," in *Die Aktuellen Fragen der Bandkeramik*, Székesfehérvár, Hungary (publisher unknown).

Kirkbride, D. (1974) "Umm Dabaghiyah: A Trading Outpost?" *Iraq* 36:85–92.

Kopytoff, I. (1987) "Internal African Frontier: The Making of African Political Culture," in I. Kopytoff (ed.) *The African Frontier: The Reproduction of Traditional African Societies*, Bloomington: Indiana University Press.

Kosse, K. (1979) *Settlement Ecology of the Early and Middle Neolithic Körös and Linear Pottery Cultures in Hungary*, Oxford: British Archaeological Reports.

Lalueza Fox, F. C. (1996) "Physical Anthropological Aspects of the Mesolithic-Neolithic Transition in the Iberian Peninsula," *Current Anthropology* 37(4):689–95.

Lefferts, H. L., Jr. (1977) "Frontier Demography: An Introduction," in D. H. Miller and J. O. Steffen (eds) *The Frontier, Comparative Studies*, Norman, OK: University of Oklahoma Press.

Martin, P. S. (1973) "The Discovery of America," *Science* 179:969–74.

Mellaart, J. (1967) *Çatal Hüyük, a Neolithic Town in Anatolia*, New York: McGraw-Hill.

Milojcic, V., J. Bressneck, and M. Hopf (1962) *Die Deutschen Ausgrabungen auf der Argissa-Magula in Thessalien*, vols. I and II, Bonn: Rudolf Habelt.

Miracle, P., N. Galanidou, and S. Forenbaher (2000) "Pioneers in the Hills: Early Mesolithic Foragers at Sebrn Abri (Istria, Croatia)," *European Journal of Archaeology* 3(3):293–329.

Molleson, T. (1994) "The Eloquent Bones of Abu Hureyra," *Scientific American* (August): 70–5.

Nemeskeri, J. (1972) "The Inhabitants of Lepenski Vir," in D. Srejovic (ed.) *Europe's First Monumental Sculpture: New Discoveries at Lepenski Vir*, New York: Stein and Day.

Newell, R. R. (1972) "The Mesolithic Affinities and Typological Relations of the Dutch Bandkeramik Flint Industry," in *Die Aktuellen Fragen der Bandkeramik*, Székesfehérvár, Hungary (publisher unknown).

Noble, A. G., (ed.) (1992) *To Build in a New Land: Ethnic Landscapes in North America*, Baltimore: Johns Hopkins Press.

Özdoğan, M. (1995) "The Beginning of Neolithic Economies in Southeastern Europe: An Anatolian Perspective in View of Recent Evidence." Paper presented at the Second Neolithic Seminar, Ljubljana, 3–5 March 1995.

Peltenburg, E., S. Colledge, P. Croft, A. Jackson, C. McCartney, and M. A. Murray (2000) "Agro-Pastoralist Colonization of Cyprus in the 10th Millennium BP: Initial Assessments," *Antiquity* 74:844–853.

Perlès, C. (1988) "New Ways with an Old Problem: Chipped Stone Assemblages as an Index of Cultural Discontinuity in Early Greek Prehistory," in E. B. French and K. A. Wardle (eds) *Problems in Greek Prehistory*, Bristol: Bristol Classical Press.

—— (2001) *Early Neolithic Greece*, Cambridge: Cambridge University Press.

Pfeiffer, J. E. (1977) *The Emergence of Society*, New York: McGraw-Hill.

Protsch, R. and R. Berger (1973) "Earliest Radiocarbon Dates for Domesticated Animals," *Science* 179:235–9.

Renfrew, C. (2001) "From Molecular Genetics to Archaeogenetics," *Proceedings of the National Academy of Sciences* 98(9):4830–2.

Renfrew, J. (1973) "Agriculture," in D. Theocharis (ed.) *Neolithic Greece*, Athens: National Bank of Greece.

Richards, M., H. Corte-Real, P. Forster, *et al.* (1996) "Paleolithic and Neolithic Lineages in the European Mitochondrial Gene Pool," *American Journal of Human Genetics* 59:185–203.

Richards, M., V. Macaulay, E. Hickey, *et al.* (2000) "Tracing European Founder Lineages in the Near Eastern mtDNA Pool," *American Journal of Human Genetics* 67(5):1251–76.

Richter, D. (1992) *The Ordeal of the Longhouse: The Peoples of the Iroquois League*, Chapel Hill, NC: University of North Carolina Press.

Roberts, N., P. Boyer, and R. Parish (1996) "Preliminary Results of Geoarchaeological Investigations at Çatalhöyük," in I. Hodder (ed.) *On the Surface: Çatalhöyük 1993–95*, McDonald Institute for Archaeological Research/British Institute of Archaeology at Ankara Monograph 22.

Rodden, R. J. (1962) "Excavations at the Early Neolithic Site at Nea Nikomedeia," *Proceedings of the Prehistoric Society* 28:267–8.

Runnels, C. N. and T. H. van Andel (1988) "Trade and the Origins of Agriculture in the Eastern Mediterranean," *Journal of Mediterranean Archaeology* 1:83–109.

Sampson, A. (1998a) "From the Mesolithic to the Neolithic, New Data on the Aegean Prehistory," http://www.geocities.com/athens/forum/8635/sampson.html

—— (1998b) "Cave of Cyclope, Youra, Alonnessos," http://www.culture.gr/2/21/214/21403e/e21403eb.html

Schlegel, A. (1992) "African Political Models in the American Southwest: Hopi as an Internal Frontier Society," *American Anthropologist* 94(2):376–97.

Semino, O., G. Passarino, P. J. Oefner, *et al.* (2000) "The Genetic Legacy of Paleolithic *Homo sapiens sapiens* in Extant Europeans: A Y Chromosome Perspective," *Science* 290:1155–9.

Simmons, Alan H. and Associates (1999) *Faunal Extinction in an Island Society: Pygmy Hippopotamus Hunters of Cyprus*, New York: Kluwer Academic/Plenum.

Sordinas, A. (1970) "Stone Implements from Northwestern Corfu, Greece," *Memphis State University Anthropological Research Center Occasional Papers 4*.

Srejovic, D. (1972) *Europe's First Monumental Sculpture: New Discoveries at Lepenski Vir*, New York: Stein and Day.

—— (1989) "The Mesolithic of Serbia and Montenegro," in C. Bonsall (ed.) *The Mesolithic in Europe*, Edinburgh: John Donald.

Theocharis, D. (1973) *Neolithic Greece*, Athens: National Bank of Greece.

Thomson, G. D. (1949) *Studies in Ancient Greek Society*, London: International Publishers.

Torroni, A., H-J. Bandelt, L. D'Urbano, *et al.* (1998) "mtDNA Analysis Reveals a Major Late Paleolithic Population Expansion from Southwestern to Northeastern Europe," *American Journal of Human Genetics* 62(5):1137–52.

Tringham, R. (1971) *Hunters, Fishers and Farmers of Eastern Europe, 6000–3000 BC*, London: Hutchison University Library.

Troy, C. S., D. E. MacHugh, J. F. Bailey, *et al.* (2001) "Genetic Evidence for Near-Eastern Origins of European Cattle," *Nature* 410:1088–91.

Upton, D. and J. M. Vlach (eds) (1986) *Common Places: Readings in American Vernacular Architecture*, Athens, GA: University of Georgia Press.

Van Andel, T. H. and C. N. Runnels (1995) "The Earliest Farmers in Europe," *Antiquity* 69:481–500.

Van Andel, T. H., K. Gallis, and G. Toufexis (1994) "Early Neolithic Farming in a Thessalian River Landscape, Greece," in J. Lewin *et al.* (eds) *Mediterranean Quaternary River Environments*, Rotterdam: Balkema.

Voytek, B. and R. Tringham (1989) "Rethinking the Mesolithic: The Case of South-East Europe," in C. Bonsall (ed.) *The Mesolithic in Europe*, Edinburgh: John Donald.

Wheeler, M. (1972) "General Editor's Preface," in D. Srejovic (ed.) *Europe's First Monumental Sculpture: New Discoveries at Lepenski Vir*, New York: Stein and Day.

Whitehouse, R. (1976) "Later Prehistory," in D. Collins (ed.) *The Origins of Europe*, New York: Crowell.

Whittle, A. (1996) *Europe in the Neolithic: The Creation of New Worlds*, Cambridge: Cambridge University Press.

Wolf, E. (1982) *Europe and the People Without History*, Berkeley: University of California Press.

—— (1984) "Culture: Panacea or Problem?" *American Antiquity* 49(2):393–400.

y'Ednyak, G. and S. Fleisch (1983) "Microevolution and Biological Adaptability in the Transition from Food-Collecting to Food-Producing in the Iron Gates of Yugoslavia," *Journal of Human Evolution* 12:279–96.

Zilhão, J. (2000) "From the Mesolithic to the Neolithic in the Iberian Peninsula," in T. D. Price (ed.) *Europe's First Farmers*, Cambridge: Cambridge University Press.

—— (2001) "Radiocarbon Evidence for Maritime Pioneer Colonization at the Origins of Farming in West Mediterranean Europe," *Proceedings of the National Academy of Science* 98(24):14180–5.

Zvelebil, M. (1986) "Mesolithic Prelude and Neolithic Revolution," in M. Zvelebil (ed.) *Hunters in Transition: Mesolithic Societies of Europe and Their Transition to Farming*, Cambridge: Cambridge University Press.

Zvelebil, M. and M. Lillie (2000) "Transition to Agriculture in Eastern Europe," in T. D. Price (ed.) *Europe's First Farmers*, Cambridge: Cambridge University Press.

Zvelebil, M. and K. V. Zvelebil (1988) "Agricultural Transition and Indo-European Dispersals," *Antiquity* 62:574–583.

10

ENTERING UNCHARTED WATERS

Models of initial colonization in Polynesia

Atholl Anderson

Reflecting on the discovery of the Marquesas Islands in AD 1595, the Portuguese navigator Pedro de Quiros first set down the 'problem of the Polynesians': 'the embarkations of the natives are adapted for short voyages. For which reason it is to be sought, what could be believed to be the manner how they could go to distant parts' (quoted in Parsonson 1963: 12). During the subsequent 400 years, the 'manner' has been pondered abundantly in research of formidable diversity. Yet some additional insight may be available in considering it as a problem of learning about an unfamiliar landscape, in exploring the ways in which predictability of landscape qualities may have underwritten processes of initial colonization. The possibilities are broad, and I shall confine attention here to some propositions about how pioneering settlers accommodated two levels of Pacific landscape. One consisted of the ocean and its pattern of islands, a two-dimensional landscape to be mapped on the sea, and mirrored in the night sky; the other, the resource landscapes of Oceanic islands, which were the targets of dispersal. Successful settlement depended on effective means to cross the former and behavioural flexibility in relation to the constraints of the latter.

The frontier of human colonization reached the western edge of Polynesia (Tonga, Samoa) about 2800 BP, in the Lapita expansion (3300–2800 BP), which first carried people, pottery, cultigens (taro, yam, banana, etc.) and domestic animals (pig, dog, fowl) into Remote Oceania (Figure 1).[1] The early significance of agriculture and the degree to which voyaging continued after initial settlement are uncertain, but the broad narrative of Lapita dispersal is widely agreed (Kirch 1997; Sand 1997; Burley 1998; Anderson and Clark 1999). What happened after it is just as widely debated, a contrast reflecting both the strain which an increasingly oceanic environment eastward places on models of early seafaring and the absence in aceramic East Polynesia of a distinctive horizon-marker of initial colonization comparable to Lapita pottery. There was a minor phase of renewed migration about 2000 BP, during which islands close to Fiji and Tonga were settled (Niue, Rotuma Pukapuka), but the major expansion was into East Polynesia at a time, and in a manner, which remain widely debated. This region is the main focus of discussion here.

East Polynesia covers an area equivalent to the north Atlantic from the equator to Arctic Circle. About 99.5 per cent of it is ocean, across which are scattered 15

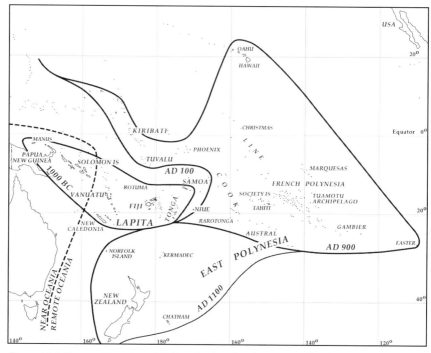

Figure 10.1 Remote Oceania and Polynesia, showing the major archipelagos

archipelagos with a total land area of only 291,000 km^2, and 92 per cent of that is in New Zealand. To an extent beyond any other prehistoric dispersal, the colonization of the region was dependent, therefore, upon long-distance voyaging, searching for unknown lands in unknown seas. Passages between even some of the central archipelagos were as long as between Britain and Iceland, while passages out to the marginal archipelagos and islands were equivalent to crossing the north Atlantic. How did Polynesians learn to get about in this barren landscape?

Exploratory strategies

In the modern orthodox, or neo-traditional, hypothesis of voyaging, it is assumed that long before the settlement of Polynesia there existed a well-developed sailing technology in western Oceania. It included large, fast (a mean speed of 4–6 knots), weatherly voyaging canoes that could be navigated by stellar techniques and dead reckoning, amongst other methods (Finney 1979; Lewis 1994). As exploration moved towards and into Polynesia, sailing followed a cautious long-term strategy which proceeded first into the direction of the prevailing wind. As navigational experience accumulated and islands became occupied, passages were made across the prevailing wind direction and, later still, downwind. Voyaging was a continuous activity, leading to substantial continuity in discovery. As the area of ocean to be searched increased eastward, so did the rate of voyaging, which maintained the rate of discovery. Hundreds of years could separate discovery from colonization (Irwin 1992, 1998), but the settlement frontier moved incrementally, developing, with return voyaging, extensive spheres of interaction (Kirch 1986) – broad 'seascapes' (Gosden and Pavlides 1994) of social and economic relationships.

In this model a sophisticated maritime technology contrasts with a blind or questing approach to exploration of a landscape regarded as unpredictable. Exploration proceeded by searching in all directions within a wide upwind-to-crosswind arc from each island. With a rapidly increasing area of ocean to be searched toward the east in order to find scarcer and smaller islands, geography continuously stretched both the length and the span of the 'windscreen wiper' exploration arc, slowing discovery and requiring developments in navigational ability. Islands were found only according to their relative visibility and accessibility, determined by size, height, target angle, direction in relation to prevailing wind, etc. This is a biogeographical approach which is unmodified for human behaviour, except to the extent that the location of islands was fixed retrospectively into an expanding geography by return voyaging.

One of the more obvious drawbacks to the model is that the strategic argument at its core cannot be tested. Potential island targets are neither randomly nor regularly distributed across the Pacific, so it is impossible to tell whether colonization of islands upwind had bypassed similar islands at similar distances in crosswind directions, or downwind islands in crosswind colonization. In fact, leaving aside Hawaii and New Zealand, both of which lie within different wind systems, the actual distribution of Pacific islands is just about as inconvenient for such a test as it could possibly be. The main trend of their distribution is northwest to southeast, with practically none in the tropics to the south or north of the main band except at a considerable distance away. Consequently, successful colonization must have proceeded directly into the prevailing southeast trade winds, irrespective of the voyaging strategy (or indeed whether the process was merely stochastic and colonization occurred by drifting, as studied by Levison *et al.* 1973), since that is where undiscovered islands were continually found to be nearest and most numerous. Continuing in this direction would be encouraged by its constant reward (Keegan and Diamond's (1987) 'autocatalysis'). Prudent sailing may be proposed as an effect of this process but does not need to be invoked as its cause.

Computer simulations incorporating progressively more complex sailing capabilities show, predictably, if not redundantly, that simple one-way voyaging has lower rates of success than return voyaging and that more sophisticated strategies of the latter kind have the highest success rates. Irwin (1992) thinks these results indicate the necessity of improved voyaging capability as colonization proceeded into increasingly barren ocean, but that depends, inter alia, on whether rates of discovery were known, or even mattered. No inter-archipelagic voyages were observed historically, and no coherent navigation methodology was recorded in Polynesia, so there is no ethnographic benchmark, nor any other, against which to choose between the simulated strategies; nor is it possible to define the levels of voyaging failure which may have been acceptable in prehistory. In any particular case, discovery might have occurred after few

171

voyages using more capable strategies or after more voyages using less capable strategies. Furthermore, increased voyaging success rates, if they occurred at all, might have owed less to strategic changes than improvements in boat building or food storage at sea, or through selection of voyagers according to physiological ability to survive long passages (Houghton 1996), to mention some other possibilities.

It is worth considering, therefore, whether a more realistic hypothesis could be developed, and on what basis. Historical observation of Polynesian sailing canoes suggests an alternative approach.

A new historical model

All modern propositions about colonization voyaging in Polynesia (Irwin 1992; Lewis 1994; Finney 1979, 1994; Anderson 1996) have drawn on the performance data of the 'replica' voyaging canoes, especially *Hokule'a*, but these are of doubtful validity. None of the voyaging canoes are replicas of any early historical Polynesian vessel. *Hokule'a* incorporates design features chosen from throughout Polynesia, in the belief that the original prehistoric voyaging canoe was not represented by any of the early historical types. Modern materials and design were used in her construction, including plywood and fibreglass hulls, buoyancy chambers, laminated beams, and synthetic lashings, rigging and ocean-going sails (Finney 1979). Drawing assumptions from *Hokule'a* about the performance parameters or sea-keeping of prehistoric voyaging canoes is thus open to question.

The most striking difference between modern experimental and early historical vessels lies in their standing rigging and the size of sails. There are no early sail measurements, but a general impression can be obtained from historical drawings, subject though they are to draughting skill and other vagaries of representation. Using the size of human figures as a guide, it is possible to estimate, very approximately, waterline length and sail dimensions. Results (Figure 10.2) show that while *Nalehia*, built to replicate a nineteenth-century Hawaiian canoe, fits the general run of historical data, *Hokule'a* and *Hawai'iloa* which were built on the combined-features principle have ratios of sail area to length that are about twice that expected (Anderson 2001b).

Sailing across the wind, and especially upwind, on a large vessel requires a fixed mast, normally with substantial standing rigging, and those qualities were scarce in eighteenth-century East Polynesian designs. The Tahitian boom-sprit rig had that capability, but double canoes in Hawaii were commonly paddled as an auxiliary means of propulsion. The crab-claw rig, held up by light stays, is frequently shown on larger vessels with the curved leech forward of the mast, in downwind mode, and it could only have been sheeted aft of the mast to enable upwind sailing by re-rigging to an extent difficult at sea. In New Zealand certainly, and perhaps in the Marquesas (where the early data are ambiguous), the sailing rig was a simple Oceanic spritsail held transversely across the hulls by a forestay from each spar fixed to the prow of the corresponding hull. There were no shrouds, so the sail was held up only by wind pressure against sheets held aft. These vessels could only sail off the wind and had to be paddled in any other direction (Anderson 2000a; Beattie 1994).

172

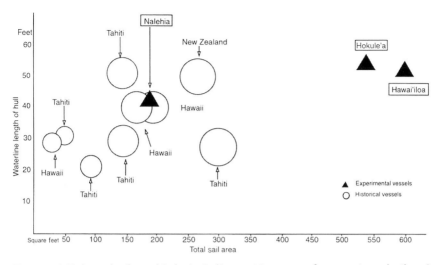

Figure 10.2 Estimated sail area (circle size indicates ±20 per cent of mean estimated sail area) and waterline length: comparison of East Polynesian double-canoes appearing in historical drawings with modern "replica" double-canoes (additional references in Anderson 2001b)

The early prehistoric sailing rig, therefore, may have been an unstayed or lightly stayed simple Oceanic spritsail, which, sailed in the offwind arc with small sails, could not have approached the 4 knots mean passage speed derived from modern experimental voyaging. Ethnographic measurements pertinent to this point are scarce, but Lauer's (1976) observations of ocean passages in Amphlett Islands (New Guinea) outrigger vessels fitted with *Pandanus* leaf lateen sails recorded average sailing speeds, excluding periods of calm, of about 2.5 knots, with the figures falling to less than 2 knots on most of the longer passages. Downwind sailing, drifting with rig lowered in contrary winds, and paddling in calms (Horvath and Finney (1976) showed experimentally that about 50 km per day was possible by paddling) may have produced mean passage speeds of about 1 knot on long East Polynesian passages in prehistoric double canoes.

In short, these considerations suggest that colonization voyages were much more difficult and slower than envisaged by orthodox opinion. Long passages to the marginal islands would have depended on infrequent periods of persistent fair winds, such as winter westerlies to get to Easter Island and summer easterlies to get to New Zealand. Return voyaging may have been possible navigationally but in practice was probably too arduous to be undertaken over the longer passages, except very occasionally. This model (detailed in Anderson 2000a) reverses the neo-traditional perspective by suggesting that maritime technology was fairly simple and return voyaging very uncommon, so that colonization was coincident with discovery, and interaction between archipelagos was limited in extent. It could be assumed that voyaging was not a continuous activity and that colonizers baulked relatively readily at sea gaps that were awkward to cross. This would produce a discontinuous pattern of colonization.

However, it is also possible that technological constraints were to some extent lifted by landscape learning, i.e. that initial colonists, instead of merely probing across a broad front of the unknown, sought to find and generalize landscape patterning that helped to refine a successful predictive capacity in exploration. Oceania exhibits some landscape regularity of a kind which could have been recognized sufficiently early in the discovery sequence to make it a useful basis for prediction.

There is a very noticeable 'grain' in the disposition of land masses, and this grain occurs at two spatial scales. Overall, there is the northwest-to-southeast trend to the broad band of islands from New Guinea to Easter Island. At the individual archipelagic level the same trend is apparent. Tropical Pacific archipelagos, plotted as anonymous patches (Figure 10.3), look like lakes in a heavily glaciated landscape, and for an analogous reason: over nearly all of Polynesia the expanding Pacific plate moves like an immense continental glacier, subducting at its western contact with the Indo-Australian plate. Hot spots in the mantle produce volcanic activity, and each island or seamount is then carried away to the northwest as another forms in its place – Hawaii is the classic example. The frequency of this orientation (Figure 10.4) may not have been very apparent to Lapita voyagers, but it was more pronounced to the east, and it could have impressed prehistoric explorers as a reliable exploration pointer. Consequently, they had three landscape features with which to build a search strategy: prevailing

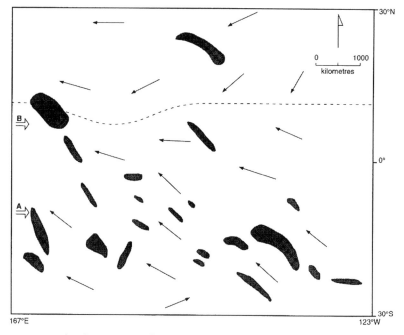

Figure 10.3 Archipelagos in tropical Remote Oceania plotted as patches. Broad arrows A and B show the Melanesian and Micronesian routes in the region, respectively. Thin arrows are prevailing wind directions, and the dotted line is the inter-tropical convergence zone.

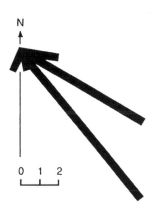

Figure 10.4 Frequency of archipelago orientation (bar length by number of cases) in Remote
Oceania

wind directions, continuity of the broad band of islands to the southeast, and northwest–southeast orientation of individual archipelagos. Although archipelagos are
fewer in East Polynesia, colonists may also have come to assume that new islands
would be found less than a week's voyaging (500–700 km) distant on offset courses, as
in the cases of voyages from the southern Cook Islands to the Society Islands, the Societies to the southern Line Islands, the Gambiers to the Australes, the Gambiers to
Rapa and the Tuamotus to the Marquesas.

A productive strategy would have been to keep moving toward the southeast while
also searching regularly at right angles to intercept each new archipelago across its long
axis, where the target angle was broadest (Figure 10.5). Unlike the laborious search
pattern in the orthodox model, this alternative strategy is effectively reduced to a
simple axis of sailing directions – southeast, with offsets to southwest and northeast –
and it required sailing across the prevailing wind direction from the beginning, using
suitable tail winds as these occurred. Relatively few voyages would have found all the
islands in the main band quite quickly. Once exploration had reached well to the
southeast, the discovery of the marginal archipelagos, though more difficult, may have
been simply in continuation of that strategy, with Hawaii and, later, New Zealand
being found by interception voyages that travelled further than usual in easterlies. In
any event, it was probably the opening up of broad-reaching angles of attack, or better,
that enabled the discovery of those archipelagos – in other words, to go northwest or
southwest depended on first going far enough east.

This hypothesis of an exploratory system implies no long-term strategic change in
voyaging behaviour. If longer passages were mostly one-way, then later voyages probably sailed from the margins of the broad island band into regions of the Pacific that
were barren in habitable land, with consequent high loss rates. This may have been
unknown to the communities at origin, and it would not affect the overall sequence,
because nearly all islands that could have been colonized had already been discovered.

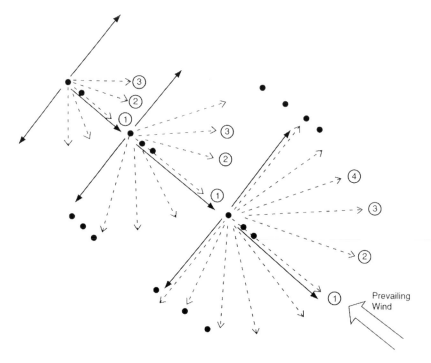

Figure 10.5 The orthodox "windscreen wiper" pattern of searching throughout the upwind arc (dotted lines), compared with upwind and offset searching (solid lines) according to prediction of the distribution of islands (dots)

Historical observation of Polynesian sailing vessels and a reconsideration of the geography of East Polynesia thus suggest a new model of voyaging. One of the few means by which the relative plausibility of this model can be measured against that of the orthodox hypothesis, or any other, is by considering its chronological implications in relation to the evidence of initial colonization. But which evidence is that?

The pattern of initial colonization

Opinions differ as to how the chronological record of initial colonization, in Oceania as elsewhere, should be legitimately constituted. One issue is whether it should include all radiocarbon results in a 'generalist' approach that seeks to perceive the broad pattern underlying individual variation. Characteristically disclosed is a 'tail' of data that extends beyond the period when the existence of people can be shown by other methods (e.g. Hunt and Holsen 1991), and this has encouraged partitioning of the chronological record into phases of increasing archaeological visibility, correlated with discovery, colonization and settlement (e.g. Graves and Addison 1995). But treating all radiocarbon dates alike risks ascribing a spurious validity to those with poor provenance, inadequate laboratory pretreatment, high inbuilt age or of non-archaeological origin, which may, indeed, account wholly for the putative phase of discovery (Anderson 1995). In contrast, a 'particularist' approach vets each radio-carbon determination in terms of sample type, provenance, pretreatment, consistency with comparable results and so on, in order to discard poor chronological data ('chronometric hygiene', e.g. Anderson 1991; Spriggs and Anderson 1993). There is a risk of eliminating poor dates that may actually represent the earliest stage of coloniza-tion, but this approach provides, at least, a chronology that is based on good data and isolates the cases which need further testing.

In fact, many of the latter cases have been re-examined recently, and they have produced a consistent pattern of younger radiocarbon ages. In Hawaii, South Point had dates up to 2200 BP, which have been re-analysed as indicating an age not exceeding 500 BP (Dye 1992), and Bellows Beach, though more difficult to interpret, was not occupied earlier than about 1200 BP, and possibly later (Tuggle and Spriggs 2000). In the Marquesas, the critical sites at Ha'atuatua and Hane, which dated to about 2000 BP, are now dated as no earlier than about 900 BP (Rolett and Conte 1995; Anderson and Sinoto 2002). The same change has occurred in the chronology of Anapua; and a more recent site with extinct fauna, at Hanamiai, has a similar age (Rolett 1998). In Easter Island, the only site containing significant remains of extinct fauna dates to about 1000 BP (Steadman *et al.* 1994). In the Society Islands, the two famous sites, Vaito'otia-Fa'ahia and the Maupiti cemetery, estimated as the earliest in the archipelago at about 1400 BP, are now shown to date to about 1000–1100 BP (Anderson and Sinoto 2000) and 500–700 BP (Anderson *et al.* 1999), respectively. In New Zealand, the most important early site is Wairau Bar, now dated to about 700 BP (Higham *et al.* 1999), and there are similar ages for comparable sites containing abun-dant remains of extinct fauna the length of the country (Anderson 1991). In addition, newly found archaeological sites of Polynesian colonization in the subantarctic islands (Anderson and O'Regan 2000) and Norfolk Island (Anderson and White 2001) also date to 700–800 BP.

It cannot be shown that any of these are sites of initial occupation, although some might be, but they are the earliest cultural sites for which there are robust radiocarbon chronologies, and some contain remains of vulnerable fauna that did not long survive the arrival of people. As a group, these sites appear quite suddenly. There is no preceding phase of stratigraphic phenomena, such as an increasing incidence of char-coal in sedimentary sequences, which might be construed as an indication of earlier cultural habitation. Consequently, they suggest that the colonization era in tropical East Polynesia did not begin until about 1100 BP (Figure 10.6).

A second difference of perspective exists in the interpretation of palaeoenviron-mental data which purport to record anthropogenic perturbations dated up to 2500 BP in East Polynesia. One much-debated case is from Mangaia, southern Cook Islands, where different investigations have set the age of initial human contact between 1,600 and 2,500 years ago (Kirch and Ellison 1994; adopted by Irwin 1998, 2000), and similar arguments have been advanced for colonization of French Poly-nesia by 1600 BP (Parkes and Flenley 1990), New Zealand by 1700 BP (Sutton 1987),

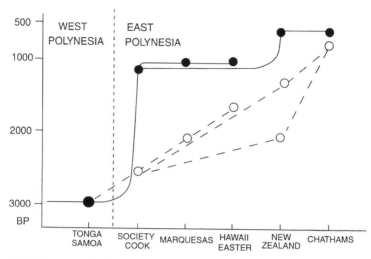

Figure 10.6 Two views of Polynesian colonization chronology: the orthodox pattern (dotted lines and open circles), based on palaeoenvironmental and older archaeological data; the alternative pattern (solid line, filled dots), based on critical review of palaeoenvironmental data and new series of radiocarbon ages for archaeological sites

Hawaii by up to 2500 BP (references in Spriggs and Anderson 1993) and Easter Island by 1700 BP (Flenley 1996).

However, in each of these regions there are problems in distinguishing anthropogenic from natural perturbations in the pollen spectra. Pollen from introduced taxa are vanishingly scarce, and vegetation changes dated to earlier than archaeologically demonstrated human occupation are within the range of natural variation. Chronologies depend on interpolation from sedimentary rates that are anchored by few radiocarbon dates; and those, in turn, are seldom consistent between comparable cases and often involve samples of mixed isotopic composition (Anderson 1995, 2001c). The potential significance of the critical radiocarbon issue is demonstrated by recent comparative research in New Zealand. McGlone and Wilmshurst (1999) showed that, whereas radiocarbon dates on the inception of continuous deforestation recorded in ombrogenous peat bog strata are characteristically late (younger than 900 BP), much earlier dates on the same horizon (older than 1500 BP) came from sediments recovered in lakes and swamps that are susceptible to in-washing of old soil carbons. In tropical Polynesia there are virtually no lowland ombrogenous mires. Palynological data are exclusively from lake and swamp cores, and their radiocarbon dating is, therefore, similarly suspect. Where the most careful dating has occurred, palynological evidence does not support propositions of colonization earlier than about 950 BP in Hawaii (Athens *et al.* 1999) or 700 BP in New Zealand (Newnham *et al.* 1998; McGlone and Wilmshurst 1999) – i.e., at the same time as the early archaeological sites.

The argument of relatively late colonization of Hawaii is supported by carbon-14 AMS ages on bones of the small Pacific rat, *Rattus exulans* (Athens *et al.* 1999), which was carried, deliberately or not, on voyaging canoes. In New Zealand, similar data have been much more variable, some suggesting that rats arrived up to 2,200 years ago (Holdaway 1999); and this evidence, like that of the early palynological perturbations, has been taken to support notions of early discovery rather than late colonization. However, a recent analysis of the radiocarbon dates shows a strong correlation between sample age and the laboratory sequence of processing. For example, thirty of the first thirty-two dates processed on rat bone from the Rafter Laboratory (GNS) in New Zealand ranged from 1100 to 2200 BP, whereas twenty-five of the next twenty-eight dates were younger than 900 BP, even though many of them were from the same provenances as the earlier samples. It remains unclear how the laboratory problems arose, but the results are unacceptable (Anderson 2000b).

Turning to the exploration models, the orthodox hypothesis predicts a continuous rate of discovery. It is compelled logically to do so because a sophisticated maritime technology could not be held up for long at the 800 km crossing between West and East Polynesia, having already made similar crossings in the southeast Solomons and from New Caledonia or Vanuatu to Fiji within not much more than a century. Thus Kirch (1986) and Kirch and Hunt (1988) suggested settlement of the central archipelagos of East Polynesia by 2200 BP to 3000 BP. Hunt and Holsen (1991) thought Hawaii was colonized by 2000 BP. Irwin (1992: 216) proposed settlement of the Cook Islands by 2700 BP, the Societies by 2600 BP and the Marquesas by 2100 BP, with Hawaii and Easter Island colonized by 1700 BP, New Zealand by 1200 BP and the Chathams by 700 BP – a full 2,000-year span of colonization voyaging. This lengthy process, compared with only a few hundred years for the earlier Lapita dispersal, was attributed by Irwin (1992) to the increasing need to search vast areas of ocean, plus greater variation in wind and sea conditions away from the tropics. This model has appealed to the palaeoenvironmental data as indicating early discovery and to the older archaeological data as indicative of early colonization. But the manifest unreliability of current palaeoenvironmental evidence, coupled with strong evidence that a substantial pause occurred between the colonization of West and East Polynesia – a proposition also supported by arguments from historical linguistics (Pawley 1996) – clearly contradicts the chronological implications of the orthodox model.

In summary, the predictions of the orthodox model fail against the current evidence in the following particulars. First, early (>1500 BP) crosswind sailing should have found some of the archipelagos lying north or south of the main Oceanic island band, such as New Zealand, the Kermadecs, the Line and Phoenix Islands etc., but these were actually found much later in the sequence (Anderson 1991, Anderson *et al.* 2000). The order of colonization shown by current radiocarbon data – West Polynesia, central East Polynesia, marginal East Polynesia (Hawaii, Easter Island) and South Polynesia (New Zealand etc.) – is better predicted by a downwind sailing model that requires no strategic variation in sailing behaviour. Second, the chronological evidence of a strongly episodic colonization sequence comprising extensive, rapid bursts of dispersal contradicts the orthodox assumption of continuity in discovery (and there is no evidence of separate phases of discovery and colonization) and also removes the necessity of inferring a continually increasing rate of voyaging activity. Third, the orthodox proposal of increasingly sophisticated maritime technology is also contradicted by evidence of relatively limited interaction. Lithic sourcing studies show that, while small quantities of basalt were exchanged between East and West Polynesia, and some interaction occurred between the central East Polynesian archipelagos and the Mangareva and Pitcairn groups, the marginal archipelagos of Hawaii, Easter Island and the New Zealand region all lay beyond post-discovery contact with central East Polynesia, or each other, in the colonization era (Weisler 1997; Anderson 2000c).

If, therefore, long-distance seafaring in Remote Oceania was more difficult over the long term than neo-traditional views make it appear, then particular emphasis is lent to two pertinent questions. What was it that prompted or initiated episodes of discovery voyaging? And, once voyaging was under way, what factors maintained the momentum of an initial colonization phase?

Initiation of Oceanic colonization

One fundamental factor in setting off movement into Remote Oceania was probably the arrival of suitable sailing vessels. The late Pleistocene settlement of west Pacific islands has encouraged a view that sailing technology was already quite sophisticated, using sails and involving return voyaging (Irwin 1992; Horridge 1986) on ocean passages of 40–70 km towards the Solomons and of 180 km to Manus (Papua New Guinea), by about 20,000 BP. The latter case, however, is instructive. Archaeological investigations show that obsidian came from Lou Island to mainland Manus, about 30 km away, but no obsidian was taken out of the archipelago until the late Holocene. People got to Manus but they were unable to develop any kind of return or systematic voyaging.

They probably had neither sails nor outrigger canoes. Both of these are plausibly mid-Holocene developments, as suggested by the transfer by sea of stone adzes in the Taiwan Strait about 4500 BP (Rolett *et al.* 2000). Sails are mentioned in Chinese records about 3,500 years ago (Needham 1971), and sewn-plank, inserted-frame boat construction goes back worldwide to a similar period. Words for outrigger canoes appear in reconstructed Malayo-Polynesian languages (Pawley and Pawley 1994), and the Lapita expansion probably depended on outrigger sailing vessels powered by demountable Oceanic spritsails. Terms referring unequivocally to double canoes, however, have an exclusively eastern Pacific distribution, which Blust (1997) argues is evidence of their original development in the Fiji and West Polynesia area, from where they carried migration into East Polynesia (and, incidentally, also back into the western Pacific in the second millennium AD, to the 'Polynesian outliers').

Implicit in these conjectures is the idea that progress in sailing technology involved a series of responses to ill-defined stimuli, including the need to sail increasingly further between islands as colonization moved eastward. For example, the double-hulled canoe had a much higher load capacity than the outrigger canoe. This enabled it to stay at sea longer and transport a viable founding group, so that a single vessel could be a long-range, self-contained colonization packet. But whether there was a conscious process of development, or merely recognition of technical advantages when these appeared, is unknown.

Another important initiating factor in Remote Oceanic colonization may have been climatic variation. Suggestions that Polynesian voyaging took advantage of periods of climatic stability or El Niño-derived wind shifts have been canvassed before (Bridgman 1983; Finney 1985), and the general significance of El Niño/Southern Oscillation (ENSO) events to cultural change in the late Holocene Pacific has been widely discussed (e.g. Grove and Chappell 2000; Anderson *et al.*, in press). However, intriguing data are now emerging that document a long-term pattern in which the main periods of migration were also those of the highest frequency of El Niño events. The data are yet sketchy, but particularly strong and frequent El Niño events seem to have occurred around approximately 3100–2900 BP and 1150–1000 BP, at the time of the main Oceanic migration phases, with no events of comparable severity in the period between (R. Grove, personal communication, 2000). Increased meteorological instability may have caused a significant rise in accidental voyaging generally, including to the Polynesian outliers in the west. The potential significance of such events to colonization is twofold. First, El Niño conditions weaken the dominant trade wind flow and induce a higher frequency of westerly winds. For vessels sailing downwind, these conditions increased the probability of sailing to the east, whether deliberately or by accident. Second, El Niño conditions in the Pacific increase humidity to the east while causing drought to the west. Successively poor growing seasons in western islands may have favoured emigration as a solution, while unusually lush conditions on newly discovered eastern islands may have reinforced the attraction of voyaging in that direction. In combination, these effects could have been influential in creating the periodicity of colonization in Remote Oceania.

The propulsion of Oceanic colonization

The dynamics of colonization is a topic of more complexity than can be entered into here, but it is worth discussing the main explanations that have been offered in the Oceanic case, particularly as they construct perceptions of landscape. The underlying theme, not unexpectedly in the case of islands, is the role of resource stress.

According to traditional accounts, common in Polynesia, colonization voyages were often undertaken, one-way and under duress, by the losers in competition between clans for political supremacy. Given the constant reworking of clan traditions to shape lineage histories for contemporary advantage (e.g. Sissons *et al.* 1987; Anderson 1998), the specific traditions which were collected in the nineteenth century need not be regarded as literal chronicles, but they exhibit a common pattern. Competition was often expressed in disputes over land and access to resources. Given the small size of most central East Polynesian islands, it is not difficult to imagine that experiences of socio-economic stress lay behind many such events, and that either actual resource depletion or population growth, or both, gave rise to those perceptions. This leads to a broad hypothesis of causation in Remote Oceanic colonization: that it arose from resource stress.

The argument has two faces. One relates colonization to a pristine but fragile abundance of indigenous faunal resources, naive to human predation, while its obverse notes a paucity of indigenous plant foods and emphasizes the necessity of agriculture. In turn, these imply alternative perceptions of island landscapes by initial colonists: either as sufficiently abundant in native resources or as relatively barren but potentially productive through cultural intervention.

The strandlooper model

As initially conceived by Groube (1971) in relation to the Lapita colonization of West Polynesia, the 'strandlooper' model (named for a South African analogy) argues that expectations of rich reserves of unexploited marine fauna, especially shellfish, drew colonization ahead of the dispersal of an agricultural economy. More generally, it is argued that there was an initial emphasis on native faunal resources, irrespective of whether the first colonists also brought some or all of the Oceanic domestic plants and animals (Anderson 1996). Certainly, early archaeological sites in tropical Remote Oceania characteristically disclose evidence of a greater reliance on hunting and fishing than in later sites. Remains of seabirds and of flightless land birds, as well as of turtles, marine mammals, large reef fish and large species of shellfish, are particularly prominent. In the temperate islands of New Zealand huge wingless birds (moas: *Dinornithiformes*) and many other flightless taxa were abundant in the dry eastern forests and were supplemented around the coasts by substantial breeding colonies of seals. Sites of the colonization era were evidently situated to exploit these resources and, for the most part, were located south of the growth limits of Polynesian cultigens.

Although quantitative estimates are restricted to New Zealand (e.g. Anderson 1989; Caughley 1989), the initial biomass of accessible native fauna on many Pacific islands may have been able to sustain years of human settlement before substantial investment was required in agriculture or renewed colonization was compelled by resource stress. In fact, the rate of colonization in Remote Oceania generally may have been related to the distribution of opportunity to exploit faunal resources. The large islands between Vanuatu and Samoa were colonized relatively slowly, over perhaps 200–300 years in the Lapita expansion, possibly because several generations of sustained foraging could be absorbed in each archipelago before depletion became obvious. By that stage, investment in local social and economic systems, including in developing agriculture, may have reduced an interest in renewed colonization to a small sector of an established population. In central East Polynesia, however, absolutely lower levels of accessible biomass, and less diversity of indigenous resources on much smaller islands, offered an earlier inducement to move on, and so colonization moved faster. It is possible that in many cases the whole population, or much of it, moved after only a few years and that some early sites on different islands, or even archipelagos, represent the same colonizing propagule rather than the settlements of different communities.

Integral to this scenario is rapid population growth. The well-known data from the early nineteenth-century colonizing population on Pitcairn Island show a rate of increase of 3.7 per cent per annum during the first few generations, and this case suggests a general proposition. Both the nutritional advantages inherent in an initial richness of native resources and a strong social imperative of rapid reproduction could have sustained comparable rates over several hundred years in East Polynesia as colonization proceeded from island to island. Population doubling times would have been equal to generational replacement rates (about 20 years), so that even a small founding population of, say, 100 (gender-balanced and in the fertile age range) arriving by 1100 BP in East Polynesia could have produced sufficient descendants over the next 100 years to found viable colonies of 50–100 people in each of the main archipelagos and islands. The assumption here is that as soon as population pressure on resources came to be felt, a colonizing movement of Keegan's (1995) type A ensued. It also follows, of course, that as initial abundance declined, so too did rates of population growth, perhaps precipitously. This is the situation inferred by Anderson and Smith (1996) for southern New Zealand when seal and moa populations crashed through overhunting, and it was probably common in Polynesia generally.

The agriculturalist model

In the expansion of Neolithic culture out of Southeast Asia, the existence of agriculture has been held as indispensable to island colonization. Thus, Spriggs (1997) suggests that agriculture provided a means of overcoming significant limitations in the availability of native food plants east of the Solomon Islands. As agriculture developed in Remote Oceania, and populations increased in the absence of endemic malaria, there was an eventual renewal of migration, carrying colonists into East Polynesia.

In considering this hypothesis it is necessary to distinguish between the undoubted importance of agriculture in the long-term growth of Oceanic populations, through the eventual creation of domesticated or 'transported' landscapes (Kirch 1997), and the role of agriculture in initial colonization. In regard to the latter, the assumption that because Remote Oceanic islands could not be colonized without agriculture, colonization was not attempted prior to its arrival, is teleological. If no other restriction had existed than an absence of agriculture, then there should have been numerous attempted colonizations of Remote Oceania over the 30,000 years that human settlement stood at the Solomon Islands frontier, but evidence exists of none. Furthermore, agriculture had clearly existed for more than a millennium in West Polynesia before the colonization of East Polynesia, so its availability was not a critical factor in initiating migration.

The difficulty of survival of settlements in Remote Oceania before the availability of agriculture may be overstated. Although comparatively impoverished, Remote Oceania still supported various minor and 'emergency' food plants, and at least two of the more important plant taxa had preceded people into the region by natural dispersal: *Pandanus* species and the coconut. The critical issue is what proportion of nutritional requirements had to be obtained from plants, and that depends on the availability of alternative sources. Southern Maori and Moriori survived very well without agriculture and with few plant food sources, through an abundance of fat-rich fauna. Other Oceanic peoples had wider choices of native food plants and they could have obtained additional carbohydrates from shellfish amongst other animal sources

(Anderson 1981). Fat-rich protein sources included seabird colonies (chicks and eggs), turtles, lizards, crocodiles, dugong and dolphin – not to mention cannibalism. Coconut flesh could also have been processed in large quantities to produce an oil-rich cream. Provided that colonization groups stayed in a 'skimming' mode, taking the rich food resources from one island then moving quite soon to the next, non-agricultural colonization should have presented no insuperable difficulty. After some time – which may have varied, depending on island size and type, from a few to some hundreds of years on tropical islands and sooner on the subtropical islands (Anderson 2001a) – agricultural production was needed to ensure long-term settlement stability at high population densities. However, that requirement needed neither to have been apparent to the initial colonists nor to have deterred them.

On the substantive issue of whether agriculture was, in fact, brought by initial colonists the data are uncertain. No horticultural structures or tools can be identified definitively in early Lapita sites in Remote Oceania, and no remains of cultigens are recorded, but then there are no suitable early Lapita sites for plant preservation. Of the domestic animals, the fowl seems to have arrived in the Lapita era but probably not the dog, and a recent reassessment of the status of pig remains in early Lapita sites in West Polynesia suggests that it too may have been absent (Smith 1999). An effectively foraging economy still seems the most probable case (Best 1984; Anderson 1996; Burley 1998).

It has been convenient to discuss these various hypotheses individually, but it is more realistic to imagine that episodes of colonization were initiated and sustained by more complex sequences of causation. For example, in the movement from West to East Polynesia climatic instability may have precipitated renewed migration as a response to developing resource stress. At about the end of the first millennium AD, a phase of mound building began in Tonga and Samoa, and monumental structures and fortifications began to appear by the twelfth century throughout the island land-scapes. If these features represent the development of resource competition expressed in inter-group aggression and 'superfluous behaviours' (Graves and Sweeney 1993), then migration could have appealed as a solution. It may not be too fanciful to suggest that it was in this competitive context that the double canoe developed, not initially as a vehicle for migration, but as a large, stable platform chiefly for display of maritime power and warfare. This was, at least, a primary function of that vessel type in eigh-teenth-century Tahiti.

Conclusions

No consensus yet exists on the timing, manner and motivations of initial colonization in Polynesia, or in Remote Oceania generally. Two broad models are in contention. The orthodox or neo-traditional model envisages navigated voyages by fast, weatherly sailing vessels using a pattern-searching strategy that resembles an advancing-front mode of dispersal and seeks to explain colonization as driven by replication of the intensively agricultural societies or 'transported landscapes' of ethnographic description. The emphasis is on technical specialization in both mobility and subsistence adaptations, and the preferred chronology of slow movement through East Polynesia would be consistent with a density-dependent or type K mode (Keegan 1995) of dispersal.

In contrast, it can be argued that technology of mobility and subsistence was relatively generalized. It is not necessary to propose a sophisticated sailing capability, nor is it consistent with pertinent historical evidence or data indicative of limited interaction between many archipelagos. Patterning in the distribution and shape of archipelagos could have been used to predict the location of island targets and to reduce colonizing voyages to narrow directional sectors, as in a linear or streaming mode of dispersal. Colonization may have been propelled by a positive-feedback relationship of rapid population growth in conditions of unexploited reserves of terrestrial and marine fauna, the easy depletion of which drove continuing migration at low population density. This is essentially Beaton's (1991) 'transient explorer' or Keegan's (1995) type A mode of dispersal. It can be assumed that growth rates dropped rapidly in the non-migratory remnant of each population after faunal collapse.

These models are, perhaps, better regarded less as alternative descriptions of initial colonization behaviour than as phases in the larger colonization process. Rapid linear movement, based on active landscape prediction and high population growth in conditions of abundant faunal resources, is proposed in other cases of initial colonization (e.g. Steele *et al.* 1998), whereas incremental or demic expansion and more specialized technologies are regarded as succeeding modes of adaptation. If that view is taken, then it is worth noting that the exploratory phase is quite visible in the archaeological record of Polynesia, which is a particular advantage of using island records to study processes of colonization in general.

Note

1 The settlement of Micronesia had certainly begun by 2000 BP; but how much earlier people had reached its western islands, and the timing and direction of dispersal elsewhere, remain uncertain (Rainbird 1994).

References

Anderson, A.J. (1981) The value of high latitude models in south Pacific archaeology: a critique. *New Zealand Journal of Archaeology* 3:143–60.

—— (1989) *Prodigious Birds: moas and moahunting in prehistoric New Zealand.* Cambridge University Press, Cambridge.

—— (1991) The chronology of colonization in New Zealand. *Antiquity* 65:767–95.

—— (1995) Current approaches in East Polynesian colonization research. *Journal of the Polynesian Society* 104:110–32.

—— (1996) Adaptive voyaging and subsistence strategies in the early settlement of East Polynesia. In T. Akazawa and E. Szathmary (eds) *Prehistoric Dispersal of Mongoloids,* 359–74. Oxford University Press, Oxford.

—— (1998) *The Welcome of Strangers: an ethnohistory of southern Maori, AD 1650–1850.* University of Otago Press, Dunedin.

—— (2000a) Slow Boats from China: issues in the maritime prehistory of the Indo-Pacific region. In S. O'Connor and P. Veth (eds) *East of Wallace's Line: studies of past and present maritime cultures of the Indo-Pacific region*. *Modern Quaternary Research in Southeast Asia* 16:13–50.

—— (2000b) Differential reliability of ^{14}C AMS ages of *Rattus exulans* bone gelatin in south Pacific prehistory. *Journal of the Royal Society of New Zealand* 30:243–61.

—— (2000c) Implications of prehistoric obsidian transfer in South Polynesia. *Indo-Pacific Prehistory Association Bulletin* 20(4):117–23.

—— (2001a) No meat on that beautiful shore: prehistoric colonisation of the subtropical islands. In A.J. Anderson and B.F. Leach (eds) *Archaeozoology of Oceanic Islands*. Special volume of the *International Journal of Osteoarchaeology* 11:14–23.

—— (2001b) Towards the sharp end: The type and performance of prehistoric Polynesian voyaging canoes. *Pacific 2000: Proceedings of the Fifth International Congress on Easter Island and the Pacific*, 29–37. Los Osos: Easter Island Foundation.

—— (2001c) The colonization chronology of French Polynesia. In C.M. Stevenson, G. Lee, F.J. Morin (eds) *Pacific 2000: Proceedings of the Fifth International Congress on Easter Island and the Pacific*, 247–53. Los Osos: Easter Island Foundation.

Anderson, A.J. and G. Clark (1999) The Age of Lapita Settlement in Fiji. *Archaeology in Oceania* 34:31–9.

Anderson, A.J. and G. O'Regan (2000) To the final shore: prehistoric colonisation of subpolar Polynesia. In A.J. Anderson and T. Murray (eds) *Australian Archaeologist: collected papers in honour of Jim Allen*, 440–454. Coombs Academic Press, ANU, Canberra.

Anderson, A.J. and Y.H. Sinoto (2002). New radiocarbon ages of colonization sites in East Polynesia. *Asian Perspectives* 41:242–57.

Anderson, A.J. and I.W.G. Smith (1996) The transient village in southern New Zealand. *World Archaeology* 27:359–71.

Anderson, A.J. and J.P. White (eds) (2001) The Prehistoric Archaeology of Norfolk Island, Southwest Pacific. *Records of the Australian Museum*, supplement 27.

Anderson, A.J., Conte, E., Clark, G., Sinoto, Y.H. and F.J. Petchey (1999) Renewed excavations at the Motu Paeao site, Maupiti Island, French Polynesia: Preliminary results. *New Zealand Journal of Archaeology* 21:47–66.

Anderson, A.J., Wallin, P., Martinsson-Wallin, H., Fankhauser, B. and G. Hope (2000) Towards a first prehistory of Kiritimati (Christmas) Island, Republic of Kiribati. *Journal of the Polynesian Society* 109:273–93.

Anderson, A.J., Gagan, M. and J. Shulmeister (in press). Mid-Holocene cultural dynamics and climatic change in the western Pacific. In K.A. Maasch and D.H. Sandweiss (eds) *Climate and Culture Change*.

Athens, J.S., Ward, J.V., Tuggle, H.D. and D.J. Welch (1999): *Environment, vegetation change and early human settlement on the 'Ewa plain: a cultural resource inventory of Naval Air Station, Barber's Point, O'ahu, Hawai'i. Part III: Paleoenvironmental investigations*. International Archaeological Research Institute, Honolulu, HI.

Beaton, J. M. (1991) Colonizing continents: some problems from Australia and the Americas. In T. Dillehay and D. Meltzer (eds) *The First Americans: Search and Research*, 209–30. CRC, Boca Raton.

Beattie, J. H. (1994) *Traditional Lifeways of the Southern Maori: The Otago University Museum Ethnological project, 1920*. University of Otago Press, Dunedin.

Best, S. (1984) Lakeba: the prehistory of a Fijian island. Unpublished PhD thesis, University of Auckland, Auckland.

Blust, R. (1997) Subgrouping, circularity and extinction: some issues in Austronesian comparative linguistics. *Papers for the Eighth International Conference on Austronesian Linguistics*, Academia Sinica, Taipei: 1–54.

Bridgman, H.A. (1983) Could climatic change have had an influence on the Polynesian migrations? *Palaeogeography, Palaeoclimatology, Palaeoecology* 41:193–206.

Burley, D.V. (1998) Tongan archaeology and the Tongan past, 2850–150 B.P. *Journal of World Prehistory* 12:337–92.

Caughley, G. (1989) New Zealand plant-herbivore ecosystems past and present. *New Zealand Journal of Ecology* 12 (supplement): 3–10.

Dye, T. (1992) The South Point radiocarbon dates thirty years later. *New Zealand Journal of Archaeology* 14:89–97.

Finney, B.R. (1979) *Hokule'a: The Way to Tahiti*. Dodd, Mead and Co., New York.

—— (1985) Anomalous westerlies, El Niño, and the colonization of Polynesia. *American Anthropologist* 87:9–26.

—— (1994) *Voyage of rediscovery: a cultural odyssey through Polynesia*. University of California Press, Berkeley.

Flenley, J.R. (1996) The palaeoecology of Easter Island, and its ecological disaster. In S.R. Fischer (ed) *Easter Island Studies: contributions to the history of Rapanui in memory of William T. Mulloy*, 27–45. Oxbow Books, Oxford.

Gosden, C. and C. Pavlides (1994) Are islands insular? Landscape vs. seascape in the case of the Arawe Islands, Papua New Guinea. *Archaeology in Oceania* 29:162–71.

Graves, M.W. and D.J. Addison (1995) The Polynesian settlement of the Hawaiian archipelago: integrating models and methods in archaeological interpretation. *World Archaeology* 26:380–99.

Graves, M.W. and M. Sweeney (1993) Ritual behaviour and ceremonial structures in eastern Polynesia: changing perspectives on archaeological variability. In M.W. Graves and R.C. Green (eds) *The Evolution and Organisation of Prehistoric Society in Oceania*, 106–25. New Zealand Archaeological Association Monograph 19, Auckland.

Groube, L.M. (1971) Tonga, Lapita pottery and Polynesian origins. *Journal of the Polynesian Society* 80:278–316.

Grove, R. and J. Chappell (eds) (2000) *El Niño – History and Crisis*. Studies from the Asia-Pacific Region. White Horse Press, Cambridge.

Higham, T.G., Anderson, A.J. and C. Jacomb (1999). Dating the First New Zealanders: the chronology of Wairau Bar. *Antiquity* 73:420–7.

Holdaway, R.N. (1999). A spatio-temporal model for the invasion of the New Zealand archipelago by the Pacific rat *Rattus exulans. Journal of the Royal Society of New Zealand* 29:91–105.

Horridge, G.A. (1986) The evolution of Pacific canoe rigs. *Journal of Pacific History* 21: 83–99.

Horvath, S.M. and B.R. Finney (1976) Paddling experiments and the question of Polynesian voyaging. In B.R. Finney (ed.) *Pacific Navigation and Voyaging*, 47–64. Polynesian Society Memoir 39, Wellington.

Houghton, P. (1996) *People of the Great Ocean: Aspects of human biology of the early Pacific*. Cambridge University Press, Cambridge.

Hunt, T.L. and R.M. Holsen (1991) An early radiocarbon chronology for the Hawaiian islands: a preliminary analysis. *Asian Perspectives* 30:147–61.

Irwin, G.J. (1992) *The Prehistoric Exploration and Colonisation of the Pacific*. Cambridge University Press, Cambridge.

—— (1998) The colonisation of the Pacific Plate: chronological, navigational and social issues. *Journal of the Polynesian Society* 107:111–43.

—— (2000) No man is an island: the importance of context in the study of the colonisation and settlement of the Pacific islands. In A.J. Anderson and T. Murray (eds) *Australian Archaeologist: collected papers in honour of Jim Allen*, 393–411. Coombs Academic Press, Australian National University, Canberra.

Keegan, W.F. (1995) Modeling dispersal in the prehistoric West Indies. *World Archaeology* 26:400–20.

Keegan, W.F. and J.M. Diamond (1987) Colonization of Islands by Humans: A Biogeographical Perspective. In M.B. Schiffer (ed.) *Advances in Archaeological Method and Theory*, vol. 10, 49–92. Academic Press, San Diego.

Kirch, P.V. (1986). Rethinking East Polynesian Prehistory. *Journal of the Polynesian Society* 95:9–40.

—— (1997) *The Lapita Peoples: ancestors of the Oceanic world*. Blackwell, Oxford.

Kirch, P.V. and J. Ellison (1994) Palaeoenvironmental evidence for human colonization of remote Oceanic islands. *Antiquity* 68:310–21.

Kirch, P.V. and T.L. Hunt (eds) (1988) *Archaeology of the Lapita cultural complex: a critical review*. Thomas Burke Memorial State Museum Research Report 5, Seattle.

Lauer, P.K. (1976) Sailing with the Amphlett Islanders. In B.R. Finney (ed.) *Pacific Navigation and Voyaging*, 71–89. Polynesian Society Memoir 39, Wellington.

Levison, M., Ward, R.G. and J.W.Webb (1973) *The Settlement of Polynesia. A Computer Simulation*. University of Minnesota Press, Minneapolis.

Lewis, D. (1994) *We, the Navigators: the ancient art of landfinding in the Pacific*. University of Hawaii Press, Honolulu.

McGlone, M.S. and J.M. Wilmshurst (1999) Dating initial Maori environmental impact in New Zealand. *Quaternary International* 59:5–16.

Needham, J.W. (1971) *Science and Civilisation in China*, vol. IV. Cambridge University Press, Cambridge.

Newnham, R.M., Lowe, D.J., McGlone, M.S., Wilmshurst, J.M. and T.G.F. Higham (1998) The Kaharoa tephra as a critical datum for earliest human impact in northern New Zealand. *Journal of Archaeological Science* 25:533–44.

Parkes, A. and J.R. Flenley (1990) *The Hull University Moorea expedition, 1985: final report*. Department of Geography, University of Hull.

Parsonson, G.S. (1963) The settlement of Oceania: an examination of the accidental voyage theory. In J. Golson (ed.) *Polynesian Navigation. A symposium on Andrew Sharp's theory of accidental voyages*, 11–63. The Polynesian Society, Wellington.

Pawley, A. (1996) On the Polynesian subgroup as a problem for Irwin's continuous settlement hypothesis. In J. Davidson, G. Irwin, F. Leach, A. Pawley and D. Brown (eds) *Oceanic Culture History: Essays in honour of Roger Green*, 387–410. New Zealand Journal of Archaeology Special Publication, Dunedin North.

Pawley, A. and M. Pawley (1994) Early Austronesian terms for canoe parts and seafaring. In A.K. Pawley and M.D. Ross (eds) *Austronesian Terminologies: continuity and change*, 329–61. Pacific Linguistics C–127, Australian National University, Canberra.

Rainbird, P. (1994) Prehistory in the Northwest Tropical pacific: The Caroline, Mariana and Marshall islands. *Journal of World Prehistory* 8:293–349.

Rolett, B.V. (1998) *Hanamiai: prehistoric colonization and cultural change in the Marquesas Islands (East Polynesia)*. Yale University Publications in Anthropology 81, New Haven.

Rolett, B.V. and E. Conte (1995) Renewed investigation of the Ha'atuatua Dune (Nuku Hiva, Marquesas Islands): a key site in Polynesian prehistory. *Journal of the Polynesian Society* 104:195–228.

Rolett, B.V., Chen, W-C, and J.M. Sinton (2000) Taiwan, neolithic seafaring and Austronesian origins. *Antiquity* 74:54–61.

Sand, C. (1997) The chronology of Lapita ware in New Caledonia. *Antiquity* 71:539–47.

Sissons, J., Wi Hongi, W. and P. Hohepa (1987) *The Puriri Trees are Laughing: a political history of Nga Puhi in the inland Bay of Islands.* The Polynesian Society, Auckland.

Smith, A. (1999) An assessment of the archaeological evidence for cultural change in early West Polynesian prehistory. Unpublished PhD thesis, La Trobe University, Melbourne.

Spriggs, M. (1997) *The Island Melanesians.* Blackwell, Cambridge MA.

Spriggs, M. and A.J. Anderson (1993) Late colonization of East Polynesia. *Antiquity* 67:200–17.

Steadman, D, Vargas, P. and C. Cristino (1994) Stratigraphy, chronology and cultural context of an early faunal assemblage from Easter Island. *Asian Perspectives* 33:79–96.

Steele, J., Adams. J. and T. Sluckin (1998) Modelling Paleoindian dispersals. *World Archaeology* 30:286–305.

Sutton, D.G. (1987). Time-place systematics in New Zealand archaeology: the case for a fundamental revision. *Journal de la Société des Oceanistes* 84:23–9.

Tuggle, H.D. and M. Spriggs (2000). The age of the Bellows dune site O18, O'ahu, Hawai'i, and the antiquity of Hawaiian colonization. *Asian Perspective* 39:165–88.

Weisler, M.I. (ed.) (1997) *Prehistoric Long-distance Interaction in Oceania: an interdisciplinary approach.* New Zealand Archaeological association monograph 21, Auckland.

11

THE WEATHER IS FINE,
WISH YOU WERE HERE,
BECAUSE I'M THE LAST ONE ALIVE

"Learning" the environment in the
English New World colonies

Dennis B. Blanton

Western European colonies in the New World offer a valuable context in which to explore the influence of environment on colonizing efforts. In this chapter I explore the example of Jamestown in English "Virginia," especially during the crucial first decades of colonization between 1607 and 1680, when the matter of learning the environment – or not – is a key element of the story. From practically the moment of arrival of the English, there has been considerable speculation over why they suffered as they did in the midst of a virtual Eden, brimming with natural resources, including native foods. Mortality rates were startling in the first years, typically exceeding 50 percent, with many deaths explicitly attributed to starvation. Their failure to become comfortable – to learn – mystified the Indians, who variably treated the struggling English with pity or scorn. What we discover is a lethal combination of ethnocentrism, ignorance, and misplaced priorities in their interaction with the environment, but over the long run they developed a more viable though still imported mode of existence.

All the best intentions

By the mid-sixteenth century knowledge of a new world on the far side of the Atlantic was well established among western Europeans. Spain in particular had extracted several fortunes from South and Central America, and Spanish enclaves, especially missions, were established across southern North America. Meanwhile, the French were especially aggressive in the northern latitudes and secured their claim with missions and trading posts. Relatively brisk travel between the colonies and homelands brought considerable knowledge of conditions along the North American Atlantic coast, knowledge that was constantly augmented as ships of all flags coasted up and down the continent, probing harbors, taking on provisions, and spying and pirating.

It was a far from perfect knowledge, however, and an accurate appraisal of the mid-Atlantic margin of North America was particularly lacking. The vantage point of passers-by from the water or shoreline allowed only for sketchy evaluation, and the standard, very brief layover provided a sense of conditions in one place for only one season or maybe only for a given day. Thus, sweeping and commonly inaccurate generalizations were made from these limited views. As historian Karen Kupperman has pointed out, this was still a time of imperfect geographical knowledge, and extrapolations based on climate and environment at a specific latitude were often erroneous (Kupperman 1982).

The question of motivation is a place to begin for anyone evaluating the degree of English success in adapting to Virginia. In general, the Jamestown colony was an overly ambitious business venture endorsed by a government seeking to compete with other European successes in the New World. At home, the practical matters of crowding and lack of opportunity for the populace were real concerns, and a Virginia colony was an attractive safety valve. Commerce mattered a great deal, especially if it gave some independence in trade, and for the first seventeen years the colony was the project, literally, of the Virginia Company. Thus, straining for relief and striving for respect, the English could easily rationalize launching the "Virginia adventure." The risks involved appear to have been recognized by many of the principals, but the potential costs were expected to be worth the return.

Moreover, there was not far below the surface an attitude of Divine Right, even the obligation of better men to bridle the wilds of the New World (Redman 1999: 19, 21). Captain John Smith apparently embraced this justification, writing:

> Many good religious devout men have made it a great question, as a matter in conscience, by what warrant they might goe to possesse those Countries, which are none of theirs, but the poore Salvages. Which poore curiosity will answer it selfe; for God did make the world to be inhabityed with mankind ... there is so much of the world uninhabited, as much more in other places, and as good, or rather better than any wee possesse, were it manured and used accordingly.
>
> (Kupperman 1988: 284–5)

One, thus, discovers a mindset among these colonists that it was their rightful place, even duty, to make the Virginia environment a productive one, which in their view usually meant imposing an English model.

Balancing commerce with survival

The commercial interests of the Virginia Company channeled the energies of the new colonists toward identifying, collecting, and exporting commodities of value in Europe. Compliance with these profit-motivated goals came at the expense of their obvious need for better food and shelter. It was in this mode, however, that a great deal of the landscape learning occurred. Long-distance expeditions and local reconnoitering provided information sufficient to draft reasonably accurate maps of the major landscape features. Captain John Smith's famous 1612 map (Figure 11.1) depicted the major rivers and many lesser tributaries, the extent of Chesapeake Bay, major and minor Indian settlements, and, based on interviews with local Indians, the approximate location of mountains to the west and north (Smith 1986). Other maps, such as a Dutch chart made from information gathered by 1617, were more concerned with navigation, but landscape features near the shore were not omitted (Stephenson and McKee 2000: 41; Kelso *et al.* 1997).

Smith made it his business to explore widely on behalf of the colony, seeking first to take stock of potential commercial resources, but also to gather intelligence that mattered to the immediate concern for safety and sustenance. Part of the grand plan was to "truck" for corn with the Indians, and determining the sources and quantities available was crucial. Smith set out to explore the nearest major tributary of the James River and the many native villages along its shore with this in mind. Well upstream and attended only by two other Englishman and two Indian guides, Smith was taken captive by a large Indian hunting party, and he completed this landscape learning experience as a hostage (Kupperman 1988: 57–8). Never the one to miss an opportunity, Smith gained considerable knowledge of the territory and the people in it as he

Figure 11.1 Captain John Smith's 1612 map of Virginia. Reproduced with permission from *Virginia, Discovered and Discribed by Captain John Smith. Graven by William Hole. 1606.* 8th State. [Ca. 1624]. From John Smith, *The Generall Historie of Virginia, New England, and the Summer Isles.* London: Printed by I.D. and I.H. for Michael Sparkes, 1627. [LVA Maps: Voorhees Collection.] Archives Research Services, The Library of Virginia, Richmond, VA.

was carried around as a trophy on the 100-mile trek from settlement to settlement. And thanks to Pocahontas, so the myth goes, he lived to learn from it.

Others of Smith's expeditions were more ambitious and twice involved exploration of the Chesapeake Bay by boat, "searching every inlet, and Bay, fit for harbours and habitations" (Kupperman 1988: 85–90). Together with about a dozen men he traveled several hundred miles in about three months during the summer of 1608, turning back finally at the head of the bay in present-day Maryland. His account of this adventure provides ample evidence of the bounty of the natural environment and how much he marveled over it. In one description he says, "here are mountaines, hils, plaines, valleyes, rivers and brookes, all running most pleasantly into a faire Bay compassed but for the mouth with fruitfull and delightsome land" (Kupperman 1988: 212). It was as early as the first year, too, that the naming of familiar or important places began. To this day, for example, a headland bearing the name Stingray Point denotes the place Smith was barbed by a stingray in the summer of 1608.

In the end, the fish, lumber, medicinal plants, and minerals that Smith listed as useful export commodities never significantly added to the company or government coffers. He argued strongly for the value of the local fishery, especially sturgeon, and estimated that the lumber of walnut and cypress trees, with the proper investments, would be extremely marketable (Kupperman 1988: 218, 214). Well known was the stronger interest among most of the immigrants and the company in strikes of precious metal and perhaps iron ore. They squandered considerable effort in the desperate search for gold and silver, only to learn that the "guilded" stones were worthless flecks of mica and quartz. Indeed, Smith constantly expressed his aggravation at the so-called "Refiners," saying, "these that tooke upon them to have skill this way, tooke up the washings from the mounetaines and some moskered shining stones and spangles … flattering themselves in their own vaine conceits to have bin supposed what they were not" (Kupperman 1988: 218). Thus, the wealth of information collected by Smith and others about local resources never translated into ready stores of food during the early years.

Inexperience

Simple inexperience took time to overcome and itself put the colony at risk. The age of sail thrust colonizing parties into strange environments very abruptly. Not only were these small English parties adjusting to landfall after months at sea, but they were also confronted with a land that was for all practical purposes unfamiliar. They were not making the gradual adjustments and processing information in the way that overland parties could. The irony, again, is that despite their recognition of the obvious potential of the environment in Virginia, they simply did not know at first how to take advantage effectively of the natural bounty. Europe at the time was largely a cultural landscape of fields, towns, and cities connected by a network of relatively good roads and improved waterways. Virginia was the opposite in their eyes, described by Smith as "a plaine wildernes as God first made it" (Kupperman 1988: 213), implying that extracting a living from such a primeval place in short order was a challenge indeed.

Anything approaching a comprehensive knowledge of the eastern Virginia land-scape took decades to obtain, and it was over a century before the western reaches of what is now Virginia were charted accurately. Smith's explorations of the rivers and bay in the first few years established the basic spatial parameters of the region and a sense of potential commodities and natural resources, but the limits of this knowledge were very real and largely recognized at the time. He was emphatic on this point, saying, "being sent more to get present commodities, then knowledge by discoveries for any future good, I had not power to search as I could," and, therefore, "As for the goodness and true substances of the Land, wee are for the most part yet altogether ignorant of them" (Kupperman 1988: 209). Smith, in fact, was careful to mark the extent of his personal travel with Xs so as to qualify the information on his map.

A sense of frustration is palpable in the early accounts, as food on the wing and the hoof and in the waters was plainly visible to the hungry colonists but far from easy to put on the table. The English were far more familiar with matters of animal husbandry than they were stalking deer, trapping fish, and downing waterfowl. Two quotations capture this helplessness well. One is from Smith:

> Now although there be Deere in the woods, Fish in the rivers, and Fowles in abundance in their seasons; yet the woods are so wide, the rivers so broad, and the beasts so wild, and wee so unskilfull to catch them, wee little troubled them nor they us.
>
> (Kupperman 1988: 282)

The other, from George Percy, was, "There was never Englishmen left in a forreigne Countrey in such miserie as wee were in this new discovered Virginia" (Billings 1991: 34).

The colonists' plan hinged in large measure on establishing populations of livestock and poultry rather than hunting game, but this did not happen overnight. We can look to recent archaeology in the fort at Jamestown for a measure of the risks in this strategy. Several large pits dating from between 1607 and 1610 have yielded very large samples of food bone. The assemblages consist mainly of the bones of imported domesticates and native wild fauna (Bowen and Trevarthen Andrews 1999). The native fauna represented is unusual in the incidence of small mammals and reptiles – "vermin," as the English admitted (Earle 1979: 109) – as opposed to the preferred high-yield game animals of the Indians, such as deer and turkey. The domesticates include cow, pig, and poultry, but rats, horses, cats, and dogs in the mix are testament to some extraordinary circumstances leading to dietary stress. In short, the colonists were bottom feeding from the natural world, being somewhat parasitic of Indian produce, and resorting to consuming their own non-food, usually taboo, animals, in part because they were unable or unwilling to master the hunting and fishing methods of the Indians. Furthermore, the most extreme and thankfully rare example of desperation is a couple of cases of cannibalism during the "Starving Time" of 1609–10. In one instance it is reported that, "so great was our famine, that a Salvage we slew, and buried, the poorer sort tooke him up againe and eat him" (Kupperman 1988: 130).

To complete the perspective, the regional faunal studies of Henry Miller (1988) and Bowen and Trevarthen Andrews (1999) have charted adjustments over the ensuing century that reveal a genuine pattern of learning, but one best characterized as subsistence compromise. The truly anomalous diet of commensal and taboo animals of all sorts in the first years is replaced on later sites with a patterned co-occurrence of wild game (up to 30–40 percent) and domesticates. In this period, from about 1620 to 1660, fish, waterfowl, small mammals, and deer are all commonly represented, but along with equal or greater proportions of domestic beef, pig, and sheep bones. It is notable that Anglo-Americans in the mid-Atlantic never relied on large-game hunting (deer and turkey) as a major food option, but more as sport – much as it had been in their homeland. Though clearly committed to an agrarian pattern, the often large volume of fish and waterfowl in pre–1660 contexts is testament to adaptation to the rich Chesapeake estuary and a reliance on both traditional European and Native American methods. The tendency at this time was to embrace local fish, fowl, and staple grains such as maize, but to reject less familiar native root and nut foods. After 1660, wild game is a minor element of faunal assemblages, replaced almost entirely by domesticated animals. This reflects successful implementation of a plantation system and the negative effect that associated broad-landscape alterations had on game animals.

English inexperience also made them oblivious in the beginning to environmental extremes and ways to deal with them. Together with University of Arkansas climatologists, I was able to establish that a period of severe drought coincided with the first six years of the Jamestown-era settlement (Blanton 2000; Stahle *et al.* 1998). With no experience to tell them what was normal or abnormal in Virginia, it was not clear at all to the English that climatic extreme was accounting for much of the native maize shortfall and poor water quality in wells and the brackish river. Smith recorded direct and indirect comments by the Indians that a dry spell was under way, but there was no basis for him to evaluate the comments. It was not until about twenty years after arrival that a sense of the local climate patterns was gained and noted in colonial records, and most importantly a better notion of the limiting factors the Virginia environment imposed on their plans.

One of the better known symptoms of adjustment was a mysterious "seasoning" period (Earle 1979). We are told that new arrivals did better in the local climate after surviving the first year or at least one warm season. What this really meant is not altogether unclear, but it probably does not mean a crude selection by disease where survivors gained some immunity. Kupperman (1979) argues persuasively that the symptoms of apathy, inactivity, and anorexia were derived from a combination of psychological and physiological ailments. Malnutrition, in her words, "interacted with the psychological effects of isolation and despair and each intensified the other," a situation, she reported, that had been documented among twentieth-century prisoners of war (Kupperman 1979: 39). In a companion article, Kupperman (1984) describes the anxiety among seventeenth-century English about traveling in warm climates, or the "torrid zone" as they called certain latitudes. The received wisdom under the ancient medical theory of the four humors was that these were unhealthy places where extreme and prolonged heat would unbalance the system. To be sure, a period of acclimation was required for the newly arrived, but it was probably prolonged by "a distaste for an environment so different from their own" (Kupperman 1984: 228). By about 1650, however, the incidence of death from seasoning had all but ceased (Bridenbaugh 1980: 47).

Proud Englishmen

A distinct strain of ethnocentrism runs through the contemporary English accounts, which translated at the very least into rather extreme cultural conservatism. Fresh off the boat as they were from England, it would take some time for the colonists to adjust and adapt to the new home. It is not clearly evident, however, that there was ever an expectation of making significant adjustments according to the dictates of the local conditions. Instead, there seems to have been every intention of recreating England in Virginia, which meant finding ways of modifying the landscape rather than submitting to it.

Perhaps one can point to the military character of the first period as a barometer of the damn-the-torpedoes mentality. Armament and fortification, prominent in the written and archaeological records, indicate an intent to take the place by storm if necessary and, again, with the goal of imposing an English stamp on the place (Noel Hume 1994; Kelso *et al.* 1997). Further, the brief list of site-selection criteria they brought with them served short-term, preconceived military and commercial needs well enough, but would prove inadequate over the long run for sustaining a small urban center. It was the strategic asset of defensibility and the commercial asset of a deep-water landing that strongly influenced the initial choice, much more so than drinking-water quality, soil quality, etc. The flaw in their choice was recognized by the Indians, and the shortcomings of the Jamestown location for long-term settlement were succinctly described by a Powhatan chieftain when he referred to the place as "a little waste ground" (Barbour 1969: 141).

The sense of frustration that came from literally carving out a colony from the wilderness was expressed. For instance, Smith tells us, "there was nothing in the country but what nature affordeth" (Kupperman 1988: 115). And he went on to say, "and every thing of worth is found full of difficulties, but nothing so difficult as to establish a Common-wealth so farre remote from men and meanes" (Kupperman 1988: 83).

We also see a certain aversion to native foods that occurred in abundance and served the Indians as seasonal staples. We learn from their accounts that losing familiar provisions "did drive us all to our wits end," and "those wild fruits the Salvages often brought us ... would not fulfill the unreasonable desire, of those distracted Gluttonous Loytereres" (Kupperman 1988: 115–16).

Over the long run, when it was decided that the demand for local commodities was not sufficient to mean quick profit, attention was turned to other options, which included exotic ones. What turned the fortunes of the foundering colony around, in fact, were introduced types of tobacco from the West Indies. This well-known experiment of John Rolfe's, culminating in a shipment of tobacco to England in 1614, created a sensation. Returns were great enough that tobacco cultivation was extended at the expense of most everything else, including food crops. Samuel Argall was alarmed, for

196

instance, to discover in 1617 that the plants were being planted in the very streets of Jamestown (Noel Hume 1994: 353). This is an example of agricultural engineering at this early stage, as opposed to steady, thoughtful learning and adjustment.

Parenthetically, the successes of John Smith during his brief period of leadership speak to us of the difference individuals can have on the outcome of colonizing efforts. He was enough the anthropologist, military strategist, and leader to implement a plan of dispersal, trade, and defense which staved off starvation. He was quick to brag that, "This order [to "billett" with the Indians], many murmured, was very cruell. But it caused the most part so well bestir themselves that of 200 men (except they were drowned), there died not past 7 or 8" (Tyler 1946: 187). Smith organized the colonists in this brief period to gather native foods but was mystified that, "But such was the most strange condition of some 150, that had they not beene forced nolens volens perforce to gather and prepare their victuall, they would all have starved, and have eaten one another" (Tyler 1946: 186).

Confinement

Exploring the environment in the first years at Jamestown involved real risk. The English did not enter an unoccupied territory but located themselves squarely within a Native American paramount chiefdom, which also happened to be at the margins of Spanish claims. A concern for safety, both from Spanish marauders and local Indians, limited the extent the English could go to explore the area. The mandate of the company instructions to find a location that was 100 miles up a navigable stream and easily defensible, a place that was strong and fertile, and one where there was no conflict with the Indians (Noel Hume 1994: 130) carried a military tone for these reasons. On the face of it, Jamestown Island met the landscape criterion of a strong yet "wholesome and fertile place," but history witnesses that it hardly satisfied the requirements for long-term, successful settlement. In 1699, the Jamestown site was all but abandoned, and the colonial capital moved to the more desirable site of present-day Williamsburg.

The English were probably most intimidated by the prospect of Indian attack outside the confines of their fortified settlements. Much of their early commentary speaks to this concern. The fear was not always overstated either, as from the beginning they learned the real risks that went with excursions and explorations on foot, even within sight of the fortified compound. In and around the new fort in the first months, Smith says, "many were the assaults, and Amubscadoes of the Salvages, and our men by their disorderly stragling were often hurt" (Noel Hume 1994: 144). One solution was to limit their overland travels and rely heavily on water travel. Though effective, the view from the water was limited and a full assessment of the landscape and natural resources delayed.

Table 11.1 Archaeological correlates of colonial Virginia landscape learning

Hallmarks	Landscape learning curve	Potential archaeological correlates
1607–1618 Exploration and hardship period		
Male-dominated popul	Minimal land clearance	Nucleated, fortified settlement
Nucleated settlement	Minimal infrastructure	High mortality/physical stress
Nucleated, fortified sites	Minimal agriculture	Military gear
Military character	High mortality	Anomalous subsistence evidence
High mortality	Faulty environmental	Strongly male-oriented
Much native trade	knowledge	Impermanent architecture
Regular native conflict		
1618–1680 Initial expansion period		
Settlement dispersal	Dispersed settlements	Dispersed, diverse settlements
Settlement hierarchy	Extensive land clearance	Environmental impact/
Domestic farmsteads	Emergent infrastructure	degradation
Internal economy	Acclimation (lower	Agriculture-oriented subsistence
Architectural adaptation	mortality)	Introduced plants and animals
Technological adaptation	Reproducing population	Domestic orientation
Acclimation	New technologies and	Agricultural success
Emergent infrastructure	architecture	Specialized facilities
System of government	Technological adaptation	Landscape segmentation
External commerce	Architectural adaptation	Frontier outposts
Forced labor	Environmental knowledge	
	Frontier exploration	
1680–1750 Emergent Chesapeake society period		
Expanding settlement	Agricultural improvements	Unique landscape modification
Expanded commerce	Crop development	Unique architectural styles
Hierarchical society	Sophisticated resource	Unique subsistence pattern
Local culture	extraction	Unique technologies
	Frontier expansion	Environmental degradation
		Settlement abandonment

Archaeological correlates

It is clear that the first decade or so of English colonization was one of limited success in coping with the Virginia environment. The record of adaptation improved over time, however, such that the colony came to thrive and, by the end of the century, a distinctive "Chesapeake culture" emerged that was based on a blend of traditional English, Native American, and African influences. As Cronon (1983) describes, the choice was not a forced one between learning to live in different landscapes – native, "Indian", or modified English – but choosing between two ways of living, or belonging to the New World landscape. I suggest that the first century of this colonial history can be subdivided into three periods, reflecting the degrees of success and rates of landscape learning (Table 1). Under this scheme, one can propose a number of archaeological correlates. A great many of these have been confirmed in the Chesapeake region, and the scheme may prove worthwhile for model-building in other locations. While there is ample evidence that even in the English New World – the New England, Mid-Atlantic, and Southern colonies – adaptive modes were quite varied along a broad spectrum (Murrin 1990), it will be useful to explore what common elements are present across this broad region.

Summarizing the Jamestown case, we recognize an initial, decade-long period during which poor planning and extreme resistance to change, among other factors, created a lethal context which more than once brought the new colony to the verge of collapse. This was the most intensive learning period, however, and it took forced adjustment to local conditions to secure the future of the enclave. This spell is characterized by strains of "maladaptation," when decision-making was dangerously hampered by limited experience of Virginia (Redman 1999: 47–8).

In the succeeding period of about two generations, commercial success and incremental adaptation led to explosive expansion. This was still a distinct period of learning but one characterized more by deliberate experimentation, as well as incidental change based on long-term local experience. During this span women came to make up a larger share of the population (Morgan 1971), as did enslaved Africans, and it is probably worthwhile to contemplate the extent to which these segments of the population accelerated parts of the learning process.

By the end of the seventeenth century, the cumulative effect of adaptation was emergence of a distinctive regional culture. In recent years, the development of a distinctive local pattern has been explained as a creolization process, with selective borrowing of subsistence, technology, and other elements of the several contributing cultures (Mouer 1993). An important aspect of the new stability was the fact that the colonial population finally turned the corner to sustained, natural growth, increased life expectancy, and balanced sex ratios (Murrin 1990).

References

Barbour, P. L. (ed.) (1969) *The Jamestown Voyages Under the First Charter, 1606–1609*, 2 vols, London: Cambridge University Press for Hakluyt Society.

Billings, W. M. (1991) *Jamestown and the Founding of the Nation*, Gettysburg, PA: Thomas Publications.

Blanton, D. B. (2000) "Drought as a Factor in the Jamestown Colony," *Historical Archaeology* 34(4):74–81.

Bowen, J. and S. Trevarthen Andrews (1999) "The Starving Time at Jamestown: Faunal Analysis of Pit 1, Pit 3, the Bulwark Ditch, Ditch 6, Ditch 7, and Midden 1," technical report submitted to the "Jamestown Rediscovery" project, Jamestown Island, VA: Association for the Preservation of Virginia Antiquities.

Bridenbaugh, C. (1980) *Jamestown, 1544–1699*, New York: Oxford University Press.

Cronon, W. (1983) *Changes in the Land: Indians, Colonists, and the Ecology of New England*, New York: Hill and Wang.

Earle, C. (1979) "Environment, Disease, and Mortality in Early Virginia," in T. W. Tate and D. L. Ammerman (eds) *The Chesapeake in the Seventeenth Century: Essays on Anglo-American Society*, Chapel Hill, NC: University of North Carolina Press.

Kelso, W. M., N. M. Lukketti, and B. A. Straube (1997) *Jamestown Rediscovery II*, Jamestown, VA: Association for the Preservation of Virginia Antiquities.

Kupperman, K. O. (1979) "Apathy and Death in Early Jamestown," *Journal of American History* 66:24–40.

—— (1982) "The Puzzle of the American Climate in the Early Colonial Period," *American Historical Review* 87(5):1262–89.

—— (1984) "Fear of Hot Climates in the Anglo-American Colonial Experience," *William and Mary Quarterly*, 3rd Series, vol. XLI: 213–40.

—— (1988) *Captain John Smith: A Select Edition of His Writings*, Chapel Hill, NC: University of North Carolina Press.

Miller, H. M. (1988) "An Archaeological Perspective on the Evolution of Diet in the Colonial Chesapeake, 1620–1745," in L. G. Carr, P. D. Morgan, and J. B. Russo (eds) *Colonial Chesapeake Society*, Chapel Hill, NC: University of North Carolina Press.

Morgan, E. S. (1971) "The First American Boom: Virginia 1618–1630," *William and Mary Quarterly*, 3rd Series, vol. XXVIII, No. 2:169–98.

Mouer, L. D. (1993) "Chesapeake Creoles: The Creation of Folk Culture in Colonial Virginia," in T. R. Reinhart and D. J. Pogue (eds) *The Archaeology of 17th-Century Virginia*, Richmond, VA: Dietz Press.

Murrin, J. M. (1990) "Beneficiaries of Catastrophe: The English Colonies in America," in S. P. Benson, S. Brier, and R. Rosenzweig (eds) *The New American History*, Philadelphia: Temple University Press.

Noel Hume, I. (1994) *The Virginia Adventure: Roanoke to Jamestown, An Archaeological and Historical Odyssey*, New York: Alfred A. Knopf.

Redman, C. L. (1999) *Human Impact on Ancient Environments*, Tucson, AZ: University of Arizona Press.

Smith, Captain J. (1986) "A Map of Virginia, With a Description of the Countrey, the Commodities, People, Government and Religion [1612]," in P. L. Barbour (ed.) *The Complete Works of Captain John Smith (1580–1631)*, Chapel Hill, NC: University of North Carolina Press.

Stahle, D. W., M. K. Cleaveland, D. B. Blanton, M. D. Therrell, and D. A. Gay (1998) "The Lost Colony and Jamestown Droughts," *Science* 280:564–7.

Stephenson, R. W. and M. M. McKee (2000) *Virginia in Maps: Four Centuries of Settlement, Growth, and Development*, Richmond, VA: Library of Virginia.

Tyler, L. G. (ed.) (1946) *Narratives of Early Virginia, 1606–1625*. Original Narratives of Early American History series, reprint of 1907 edition, New York: Charles Scribner's Sons, Barnes & Noble.

Part III

ADVANCES IN THEORY AND METHOD

12

COLONIZING NEW LANDSCAPES
Archaeological detectability of the first phase

Lee Hazelwood and James Steele

Radiocarbon dating has often been used to estimate the origination time, location, and rate of spread of cultural innovations and of expanding or migrating populations (e.g. Ammerman and Cavalli-Sforza 1984; Roper 1985; Kuzmin and Tankersley 1996; Glass *et al.* 1999). Diagnostic artefacts are often also used as proxy markers of the diffusion of populations or of novel economic strategies. A related spatial demographic measure is 'cumulative occupancy'. This is the total number of person/years lived at a given location over a given period, and will reflect the duration of occupation, the initial rate of increase to carrying capacity, and the absolute value of that carrying capacity. A slow expansion in a uniform habitat will lead, in time, to the situation where people are living at the same densities everywhere, but where the most person/years have still been lived near the origin of the expansion. Sometimes it is assumed that the diffusion must have originated in the places where such early cultural indicators are found at greatest densities, in the expectation that they have been recovered there in greatest densities because they had been used and discarded there for the longest time.

However, quite frequently these archaeological 'meters' give confusing readings. The peopling of the Americas is a case in point. The ages of the earliest radiocarbon-dated early sites do not obviously reduce as we move south and east from the assumed Beringian origin of this population expansion (Dillehay 1999). The recorded areas of greatest densities of Paleoindian fluted points are not located close either to the southern end of the ice-free corridor or to the southwestern margin of the Cordilleran ice sheet that would have been circumvented on the coastal migration route (Anderson and Faught 2000). These paradoxes have led some to conclude that the Americas were colonized much earlier than the weight of evidence seems to suggest (Dillehay 1999). Others have argued that no coherent spatial signature of a lateglacial expansion is visible because the data we have are so contaminated by modern sampling biases (Shott 2002).

In this paper, we shall analyse the conditions under which we might reasonably expect to find such gradients (in dates and in density of artefact discards) pointing back up to the origin of the dispersal. We shall argue that such a pattern will only survive in the modern archaeological record when some rather narrow conditions are met for the demographic parameters that determined the original population expansion. We will suggest that these conditions may well not have been met during the lateglacial colonization of the Americas. Finally, we will demonstrate that the lack of a clear spatial pattern to the dated sites and the discarded artefact densities may in fact be very informative about what actually happened at that time.

Continuum modelling of population expansions

In order to understand the spatial and radiocarbon signatures of diffusion processes (including demic expansions), we need first to build models of such processes. Any attempt to describe the aggregated behaviour of a system with large numbers of interacting elements will involve some simplifying assumptions. Ours are at two levels. Firstly, we shall make a population-level description of the demographic characteristics of demic expansion (in other words, we shall do some continuum modelling). Secondly, in describing these characteristics at the population level we shall make no special assumptions about any predominant direction of movement. Each of these assumptions raises philosophical issues that cannot be addressed here. Our position is simply that such simplifying assumptions are necessary as a first step if we are to begin to make sense of the archaeological records both of initial human dispersal and of subsequent waves of migration and of cultural diffusion.

Let us discuss in slightly more detail what is meant by these assumptions. First, we require that any model that describes the time evolution of some populations must contain information about each individual, such as the timing of its birth and death, and the distance and direction of its dispersal. This information can be included directly for each individual or through a population-averaged quantity. An understanding of the most natural quantity can be seen by considering the two following scenarios. For a population composed of a small number of individuals, it is clear that that each birth or death produces a marked difference in the total population (Figure 12.1a). The dispersal pattern that results from the simple strategy in which there is no predominant direction leads to many distinct dispersal patterns, as shown in Figure 12.2. When presented with such dispersal data it is often impossible to interpret the underlying dispersal strategy. For example, the pattern of Figure 12.2b could result by

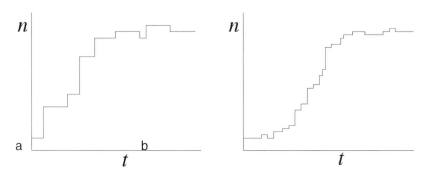

Figure 12.1 Growth curve for (a) small and (b) large populations, with reproduction at random intervals

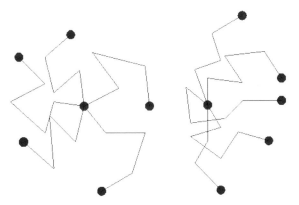

Figure 12.2 Small population dispersing at random: two instances

chance from a strategy with no predominant direction or from one that is generated by a strategy with directionally biased movement.

By contrast, for a large reproducing population, such chance variation among individuals in their reproductive histories and in their total movements over a life span is not expected to have a significant influence on the patterns observed at the level of the total population (Figures 12.1b and 12.3). With increasing numbers of individuals the change in the population density in time and space appears as almost continuous. By mathematically averaging the behaviour of individuals it becomes possible to move from an individual-based description to a continuously changing population-density function in time and space. Identifying the underlying dispersal strategy becomes straightforward now that we have averaged out the chance variations. Clearly the pattern in Figure 3a is the result of a dispersal strategy with no predominant direction

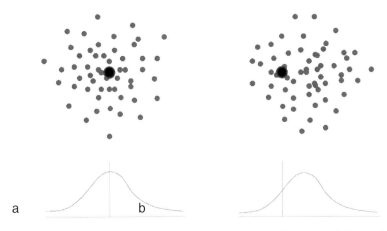

Figure 12.3 Large population dispersal with (a) no predominant direction and (b) a predominant direction

205

and that in Figure 3b is the result of a dispersal strategy with directed movement. This mathematical averaging is the basis by which continuum mathematical models of population dispersal are constructed.

The Fisher–Skellam model

Continuum-based models incorporating population reproduction/death rates and dispersal were first applied by Fisher (1937) in the study of an advantageous gene and then by Skellam (1951) in the theoretical study of population dispersal. This model, now generally referred to as the Fisher–Skellam (F-S) model, is well known for producing an advancing population front (or travelling wave solutions). We have considered the application of the Fisher–Skellam model to hominid dispersal in previous works (Steele *et al.* 1996, 1998). Here we shall quickly review the model before drawing attention to the main results required for this chapter.

Essentially, the F-S model comprises two parts: a population growth term and a population dispersal term, written mathematically as

$$\frac{\partial n}{\partial t} = f(n, \alpha, K) + D\nabla^2 n$$

where n (r,t) denotes the population density at time t and at position $\mathbf{r} = (x,y)$. D is the diffusion constant affecting the rate at which the population moves from regions of higher density to those of lower density, and ∇^2 is the Laplacian operator. $f(n, \alpha, K)$ is the population growth function, which is usually taken to be the logistic growth law proposed by Verhulst (1838) and is widely used in theoretical population biology (Murray 1993). This function describes a self-limiting density-dependent population increase and is given by

$$f(n, \alpha, K) = \alpha n \left(1 - \frac{n}{K}\right)$$

where α is the intrinsic maximum population growth rate and K is the carrying capacity, related to local environmental factors.

The crucial biological parameters for the model are the so-called Malthusian growth parameter α, the carrying capacity K and the diffusion constant D. D represents the degree of mobility of an individual (e.g. Ammerman and Cavalli-Sforza 1984). In general individuals will move from their birthplace a distance λ during their generation time τ. The square of this distance will in general be proportional to the time available; the constant of proportionality is the diffusion constant D:

$$D = \frac{\lambda^2}{4\tau}$$

This version of D assumes that there is no predominant direction of individual movements, when aggregated at the population level. This minimalist assumption is a modelling convention: we would not want to track the movements of all individuals, but we can still describe regularities in the redistributions of ensembles of individuals probabilistically (and then deterministically using a diffusion term). The assumption of undirected movement is one that we would make where we have insufficient prior knowledge of either the environmental cues or the behavioural rules that could have produced correlated decisions (and thus directionality of movement) at the population level (Turchin 1998).

General results for a homogeneous K-surface

Solutions to the F-S equation can in general only be obtained numerically. An example of the travelling population wave in one spatial dimension can be seen in Figure 12.4. Although changing the parameters α, D and K leaves the generic shape of the wave profile unchanged it will affect the wave front width and the wave velocity (as we discuss in detail below).

The wave front region, over which the density of the population changes from high to low, can be shown through dimensional arguments to be dependent on D and α and to have an intrinsic spatial scale

$$\xi \approx \sqrt{\frac{D}{\alpha}}$$

A more useful measure of the wave width L can be estimated using the maximum gradient (see Murray 1993) to be $L = 8\xi$. Notice that small values of α relative to those of D correspond to large transition regions (wave widths), as shown in Figure 12.5 and the converse to small transition regions.

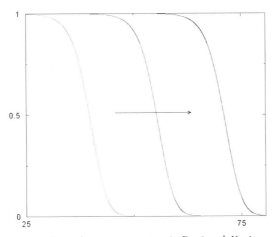

Figure 12.4 Wave propagation using parameters $\alpha = 1$, $D = 1$ and $K = 1$

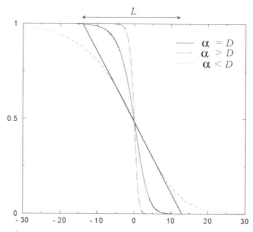

Figure 12.5 Effects of α and *D* on wave width

The wave speed (v) is also a very important quantity for population dispersal. It can be shown that the speed the wave front travels is also related to α and *D*, tending asymptotically to approach $v = \sqrt{D\alpha}$ (Kolmogoroff 1937). The relationship between the wave velocity v and wave width can be seen in Figure 12.6a. The wave profile's dependence on the carrying capacity *K* can be seen in Figure 12.6b and simply steepens the maximum gradient of the wave front by

$$\frac{dn}{dx} = -\frac{K}{L}$$

Finally, if we integrate the population density over time at a particular location we can obtain the 'cumulative occupancy' (n_{cum}). The cumulative population density corresponding to the travelling wave in Figure 12.4 can be seen in Figure 12.7. Notice that when the carrying capacity is uniform in space the cumulative density always decreases away from the origin of dispersal. The resulting spatial gradient can be calculated to be

$$\frac{dn_{cum}}{dx} = -\frac{K}{v}$$

General results for a heterogeneous K-surface

What happens to the propagation of travelling waves over a heterogeneous carrying capacity surface? The wave characteristics such as wave width and velocity are unaffected. However, the varying population densities at points in space are determined in some way by the *K*-surface. Provided that the *K*-surface changes on spatial scales greater than the wave width *L*, the population density follows this *K*-surface precisely.

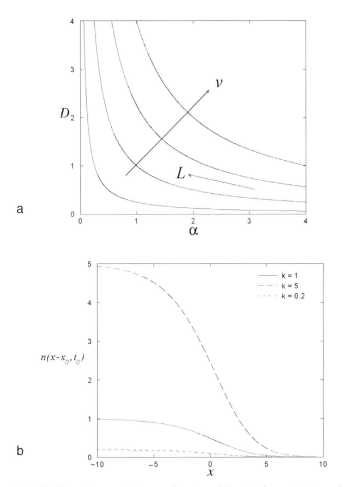

Figure 12.6 (a) Isolines of wave velocity as a function of D and α for $v = 1, 2, 3,$ and 4; (b) effect of changing the carrying capacity K

By contrast, if the surface changes on spatial scales shorter than L, then the resulting population density follows some average state (Figures 12.8a and b).

While the variations to the travelling population wave are easy to predict, the effects on the cumulative density can be much more difficult to interpret. Consider for example a uniformly increasing K-surface: the travelling wave follows the increasing gradient of K in a clear way (Figure 12.8c). By contrast, the cumulative population resulting from such a wave is no longer the simple monotonic decay from the origin (Figure 12.8d). It is now difficult to interpret the origin of these waves without a perfect knowledge of the K-surface.

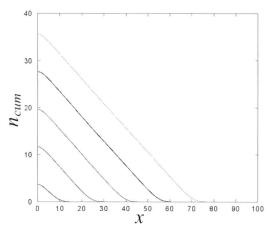

Figure 12.7 Advancing cumulative population profiles

Archaeological detection

Having summarized the properties of Fisher–Skellam models of population expansion, we now return to the conditions for their archaeological detection. Validating modelling results with experimental field data can often prove difficult. In situations where experiments can be reproduced, it is easy to obtain the data required to validate or invalidate the models. By contrast, in situations where experiments are difficult or impossible to reproduce, we are restricted by the available data. These restrictions may rule out modelling completely, if the available control data are too poor to make this worthwhile, or they may simply restrict the range of modelling parameters that can be used to validate the models.

Archaeology is a prime example of a discipline in which models are weakly constrained by surviving control data. In an ideal situation we would expect to be able to determine the origin of an expansion in space and time, the velocity of expansion in different directions, and the reproductive rates and movement rates that drove that expansion. Recent attempts to derive these values for prehistoric dispersals have tried to extract the information from variation in the radiocarbon dates of early sites, and from the variable densities of discarded early artefacts (Housley *et al.* 1997; Steele *et al.* 1998, 2000; Gkiasta *et al.* 2003). We shall now consider the intrinsic limitations on this kind of inference.

Radiocarbon dating

Radiocarbon dating is based on the ability to measure the carbon isotopic composition of an organic sample today and to compare it with the estimated isotopic composition of the same sample when it was part of a living organism fixing carbon in its tissues. By quantifying the 'missing fraction' of the unstable radioisotope carbon-14, whose decay rate is known, it is possible to estimate the time elapsed since the organism's death. Known variation in the past isotopic composition of the atmospheric and

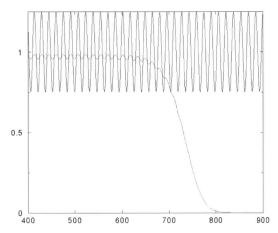

Figure 12.8a Quickly varying *K*-surface

marine carbon reservoirs requires calibration of raw isotope measurements to derive an estimate of the organism's true age. However, even before calibration the measurement is subject to counting error or uncertainty, such that the carbon-14 content (when translated into an uncalibrated age) is quoted as a mean with standard deviation, $t \pm \sigma$ (where $\pm \sigma$ indicates the range covered by 68.3 per cent of the probability distribution for the date).

This error is largely an artefact of measurement precision, and the error in accelerator mass spectrometry (AMS) dates is usually of the order of 50–100 years (although it may be greater with very small or very old samples). However, error can sometimes be further reduced by making multiple determinations of the age of a single event and

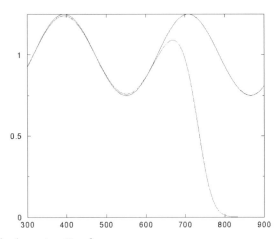

Figure 12.8b Slowly varying *K*-surface

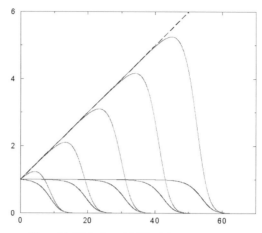

Figure 12.8c Wave profiles with $\nabla K = 0$ and $\nabla K = 0.1$

averaging them – either by replicate dating of the same sample or by averaging the radiocarbon ages of different samples which are assumed a priori to derive from the same past event (Bowman 1990). We shall consider the idealized case in which the date is characterized by a modal age, with error variance distributed symmetrically about that mean. Calibration, insofar as it changes the modal age and the size of the standard error, is still compatible with this approach. We shall not consider here the asymmetrical and irregular aspects of calibrated probability distributions, since they introduce further and significant complications into the analyses proposed below. Commonly we want to estimate the velocity of a travelling wave, using this probabilistic dating technique.

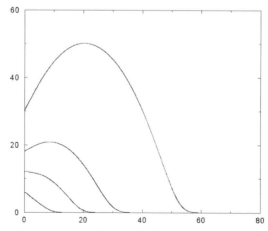

Figure 12.8d Cumulative population density for $\nabla K = 0.1$

212

How do we calculate the velocity of the advancing population front from radio-carbon dates? Consider two points A and B separated by a distance Δx. Radiocarbon determinations date first occupation at A to $t_A \pm$ uncertainty δt_A, and at B to $t_B \pm$ uncertainty δt_B. The velocity of expansion between these two locations is simply the slope of the curve in Figure 12.9 and is calculated by

$$v_{RC} = \frac{\Delta x}{\Delta t_{RC}}$$

where $\Delta t_{RC} = t_B - t_A$. Including the errors in the dates increases the range of possible velocities (see Figure 12.9), calculated to lie in the range

$$\frac{\Delta x}{\Delta t_{RC} + \sum \delta t} \leq v \leq \frac{\Delta x}{\Delta t_{RC} - \sum \delta t}$$

where $\delta t = \delta t_A + \delta t_B$. Using a Taylor expansion in δt we find this is more conveniently expressed as an approximate range $v_{RC} - v_{error} < v < v_{RC} + v_{error}$, where

$$v_{error} = v_{RC} \frac{\delta t}{\Delta t_{RC}}$$

Intuitively one realizes that calculating velocities when errors in δt are the same order as the time between events is incorrect. To obtain accurate calculations $\delta t << \Delta t_{RC}$, with the percentage error given by

$$\text{relative error} = \frac{v_{error}}{v_{RC}} = \frac{\delta t}{\Delta t_{RC}} = \frac{\delta t}{\Delta x}$$

Detection of a founding population wave using radiocarbon data

In this section we bring together the quantitative measures described in the previous sections to determine the conditions necessary for the detection and modelling of an advancing founding population wave. The key results were the wave width L and wave speed v and the range of velocities predictable from imprecise radiocarbon determinations.

Let us first look at the leading edge or first detection of an archaeological marker. The model predicts a population density wave that is at the carrying capacity K, decreasing to infinitesimally small value ahead of the population front. The first question that arises is at what population density we would expect to detect the arrival of the population. We might therefore assign a population cut-off n_c below which we are unlikely to detect the first arrival (an interesting situation arises if n_c is greater than the estimated carrying capacity K. In this case we would never expect the initial population wave to be detected).

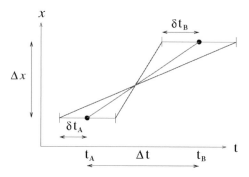

Figure 12.9 Velocities of an advancing population front calculated from radiocarbon dates

Secondly, the wave width *L* can have important consequences for archaeological inter-pretation. To reconstruct the passage of the population travelling front we must look on length scales or spatial separations Δ*x* greater than the wave width *L* if we are confidently to determine whether the population front had reached a given point at a given time.

Intuitively, we would expect that steep and slow waves (low *L* and low *v*) will be the best for detecting population advance, as shown in Figure 12.10a. By contrast, with shallow and fast waves it will be more difficult to determine whether we are detecting pioneer or established phase occupation (Figure 12.10b). It is trivial to show for a given wave width *L* and velocity *v* that waves will be indistinguishable for a time δ *t_fi*:

$$\delta t_{fi} \approx \frac{2L}{v} \approx \frac{8}{\alpha}$$

where α is the population growth rate defined earlier.

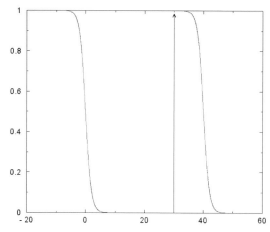

Figure 12.10a Steep and slow waves are easy to distinguish

214

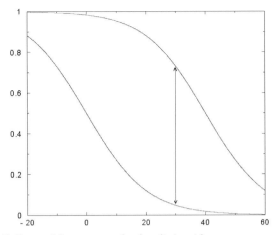

Figure 12.10b Shallow and fast waves are hard to distinguish

We can now define criteria that must be met if we are to determine the characteristics of an expanding population front from archaeological data. The requirements are that the spatial separation between sites must obey $\Delta x \gg L$ and that the temporal separation between sites must obey $\Delta t \gg |\delta t_{RC}| + |\delta t_{fs}|$.

Detecting a founding population wave from time-averaged archaeological find densities.

In this section we consider the problems encountered when attempting to match modelled and archaeological data for cumulative occupancy. The simplest case occurs when the carrying capacity remains approximately constant over the region of interest. In this case it is easy to show that the calculated cumulative occupancy gradients tend quickly to

$$\frac{dn_{cum}}{dx} = -\frac{K}{v}$$

as was illustrated earlier. Defining the minimum gradient that may be detected archaeologically requires a clear understanding of spatial scales and resolution. This problem becomes even more complex for heterogeneous K-surfaces as we have demonstrated for a simple linearly increasing K-surface (Figure 12.8).

While we cannot at this time define the archaeological conditions for such detection, we proceed by estimating the period during which this spatial information, if extractable, would remain before being washed out by the heterogeneous K-surface. We can estimate this time by constructing the following simple ansatz with waves that are relatively steep (low L) and that travel at a velocity v from sites A to B. The difference in cumulative density can then be simply estimated to be

215

$$\frac{\Delta n_{cum}}{\Delta x} = (K_B - K_A)\frac{t}{\Delta x} - \frac{K_B}{v}$$

where t is the time elapsed from the initial migration. It is easy to show that if site B possesses a larger carrying capacity than site A, then any gradient in cumulative occupancy pointing back towards the origin of the dispersal will be washed out (due to the difference in carrying capacities), in a time

$$t_{wash} = \frac{K_B}{K_B - K_A}\frac{\Delta x}{v}$$

After this time the cumulated occupancy or population density surface begins to be indistinguishable from the carrying capacity surface.

Applications

We have demonstrated that demic expansion as modelled using the Fisher–Skellam equations is a travelling wave process, in which the wave width and speed are determined by population-averaged reproductive and dispersal rates. We have also demonstrated that radiocarbon dating (an inherently probabilistic technique, with an absolute limit to its precision) can only reveal gradients in the ages of sites along an axis of colonization subject to an upper limit for both wave speed and wave width. Some recent models have, in effect, created a dichotomy between population expansions with high α and low D (small L) and those with low α and high D (large L) (Table 12.1). The absence of a clear spatial gradient in initial dates of the first peopling of the Americas indicates that the expansion was of the second type. It was, by implication, rapid (a high v, cf. Glass *et al.* 1999; Steele *et al.* 2000). Another implication is that the wave speed was determined more by unusually high exploratory mobility than by exceptionally rapid reproductive increase (i.e. there was a high ratio of D to α, giving a broad and shallow wave profile – a large L). We have seen in the previous sections that such a combination of high values for v and L makes it difficult to discern, just from its date and location, whether a site is from a pioneer or established phase. It is probable that if we are to identify pioneer-phase occupancy, we must use some additional archaeological criteria. Various two-phase models of the colonization process are summarized in Table 12.2, and these may provide such supplementary forms of evidence.

In a previous study, we applied Fisher–Skellam modelling to human dispersal into North America south of the ice sheets (Steele *et al.* 1998). Archaeologically, in such cases we may wish to take numbers of sites or of discarded artefacts (such as the fluted projectile points of the early colonizers of North America) as markers of cumulative occupancy (Steele *et al.* 1998; Anderson and Faught 2000) – an appropriate conflation when the large-scale record is time-averaged across both initial and established phases of settlement, when the original per capita/per year discard rates can be

Table 12.1 Dichotomous models of colonization strategy

Beaton (1991): 'Transient explorers' vs 'Estate settlers'

	Transient explorers	*Estate settlers*
Demography		
Budding threshold	Low	High
Group composition	Stable	Slightly fluid
Inbreeding	High	Low
Fecundity	Low	High
Extinction probability	High	Low
Economy		
Different ecological zone tolerance	High	High
Estate	Unconstrained	Bounded
Archaeology		
Site forms	Very similar	Varied
Tool inventory	Generalized conservative	Specialized inventive
Range of activity/site	Repetitive	Varied
Strategy	Forager/pursuer	Searcher/collector
Colonizing logic		
Diet breadth	Narrow	Wide
Geometry	Lineal	Bow-wave/radial
Ecology	Patch-similar	Cross-patch

Davies (2001) on 'Push' versus 'Pull' stimuli for population dispersal

	Rapid, directional dispersal	*'Wave of advance'/fission dispersal*
Territory/mobility	No territorial structures (groups highly mobile and at low densities)	Territorial structures; colony formation by group fissioning
Technocomplex interstratification	Possible, since group ranges can overlap	None - territories preclude group range overlap
Habitat preferences affecting rates and directions of spread	Possible	Possible
Initial occupation pattern	Initial random scatter of pioneer sites, followed by gradual in-filling	Short latency to landscape packing behind colonizing frontier
Clines of pioneer occupation dates	Evident	Evident

reasonably assumed to have been constant in space and time, and when the record has been sampled in an unbiased manner today. These simplifying assumptions are very large and naive, but they do enable us to begin to model the archaeological signature of a dispersal process using archaeological data (time-averaged artefact and site densities) as our indicators.

Table 12.2 Two-phase models of hunter-gatherer dispersals and their archaeological
signatures

*Kelly and Todd's (1988) model of population expansion into unfamiliar but highly productive
landscapes (the late glacial/Holocene Americas)*

	Initial phase	*Second phase*
Landscape knowledge	Limited local knowledge	Extensive local knowledge
Economy		
Resource focus	Animal focus, periodic shortages dealt with by range relocation	Broad-spectrum, intensive, periodic shortages dealt with by diversification, storage and trade
Mobility strategy	High residential and logistic mobility, high range mobility	Highly differentiated settlement systems, increased organizational links between sites
Archaeology		
Regional variation	Low	High
Locational strategy	Short-term, redundant use of 'known places' even when these are not optimally located; kill sites may not make best use of local topography	Territorial; specialized activity locations (e.g. permanent drive lines, weirs, prepared hearths); efficient use of local topography (e.g. large kill sites located at arroyos, cliffs and sand dunes)
Technology	Portable, high-quality raw materials, generalized function, long use-life	More use of task-specific and/or expedient tools
Storage strategy	Range mobility substitutes for storage	Seasonal food storage

*Davies' (2001) model of colonization of unfamiliar but productive landscape (Aurignacian/amHs
colonization of Europe)*

	Pioneer	*Developed*
Artefact assemblages	Relatively simple and small, fewer tool-types	Larger, more differentiated: wider range of activities apparent
Statigraphic position	Underlying/pre-dating 'Developed' phase assemblages in site or region	Overlying 'Pioneer' phase assemblages, or constituting basal unit with no 'Pioneer' assemblages present
Location	Scattered, possible riparian/coastal focus	Denser, more evenly distributed, possibly spanning wider range of ecotones
Density	Low	High (and groups less mobile)
Raw material use	Local, possibly expedient	Local, but possibly also more exotic materials used
Artefact/raw material caching	Limited evidence	Possibly greater evidence
Symbolic activity	Little or none evident	Frequent, evident

(continued on the next page)

Housley et al. *(1997)'s model of recolonization of a deglaciating landscape (late glacial northern Europe)*

	Pioneer phase (400–600 years)	*Residential base phase*
Seasonality of occupation	One season only (seasonal/logistic use)	More than one season (possibly permanent use)
Faunal assemblages	Small	Large
Species focus	Reindeer dominant	Reindeer, horse and bovid dominant
Artefact assemblages	Small/medium, refits between sites	Large as well as small, refits within sites only
Site type	Open air hearths, tents	House structures, tents, pits
Art	Poor	Rich
Burials	In caves, usually males	Open site burials, both sexes

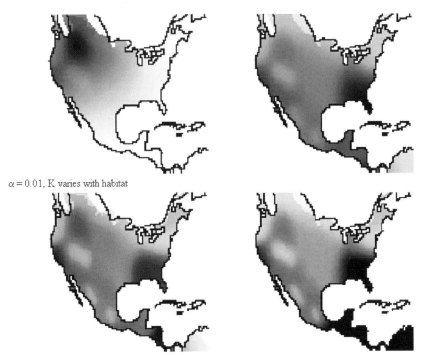

$\alpha = 0.01$, K varies with habitat

$\alpha = 0.03$, K varies with habitat

Figure 12.11 Cumulative occupancy of North America by a colonizing population over the first 1,000 years and over the first 2,000 years, for two different values of α. All model runs assumed an initial population originating at the southern end of the ice-free corridor, expanding across a heterogeneous K-surface reconstructed from paleoecological indicators. Grey-scale values are autoscaled within each map to maximize contrast and do not conform to a single absolute scale of values across the series (from Steele *et al.* 1998).

219

We have previously shown that where this dispersal process involved movement up gradients of carrying capacity (as in dispersal towards the southeast from a possible origin in Alberta), the cumulated density of evidence for human occupation would be greatest in the more productive environments – and the initial pioneer gradient washed out – when the indicator artefact maps have been time-averaged over a thousand years or more (Figure 12.11). Substituting the model values used by Steele *et al.* (1998) ($D = 900$, K ranging from ~1 person per 100 km^2 at the origin to ~7 persons per 100 km^2 in the southeast, cf. Figure 12.11) into the equation for t_{wash} (above), we find indeed that, over a distance $\Delta x = 5,000$ km, a cumulative occupancy gradient pointing back to the origin will wash out after ~1,000 years for $\alpha = 0.01$, and after ~500 years for $\alpha = 0.03$. We have now shown analytically why this pattern, which matches observed gradients in density of recorded Paleoindian fluted points, is in fact consistent with a lateglacial Beringian origin for the dispersal.

Acknowledgment

We would like to thank Tim Sluckin for his assistance during the preparation of this paper.

References

Ammerman, A.J. and Cavalli-Sforza, L.L. (1984) *The Neolithic Transition and the Genetics of Populations in Europe*. Princeton: Princeton University Press.

Anderson, D.G. and Faught, M.K. (2000) 'Palaeoindian artefact distributions: Evidence and implications.' *Antiquity* 74:507–13.

Beaton, J.M. (1991) 'Colonizing continents: some problems from Australia and the Americas.' In T.D. Dillehay and D.J. Meltzer (eds), *The First Americas: Search and Research*, pp. 209–30. Boca Raton, FL: CRC.

Bowman, S. (1990) *Radiocarbon Dating*. London: British Museum Press.

Davies, W. (2001) 'A very model of a modern human industry: new perspectives on the origins and spread of the Aurignacian in Europe.' *Proceedings of the Prehistoric Society* 67:195–217.

Dillehay, T.D. (1999) 'The Late Pleistocene cultures of South America.' *Evolutionary Anthropology* 7:206–16.

Fisher, R.A. (1937) 'The wave of advance of advantageous genes.' *Annals of Eugenics* 7: 353–69.

Gkiasta, M., Russell, T., Shennan, S. and Steele, J. (2003) 'The Neolithic transition in Europe – the radiocarbon record revisited.' *Antiquity* (in press).

Glass, C., Steele, J. and Wheatley, D. (1999) 'Modelling spatial range expansion across a heterogeneous cost surface.' In Procs. CAA 97, Birmingham. *British Archaeological Reports (International Series)* 750:67–72.

Housley, R. A., Gamble, C. S., Street, M. and Pettitt, P. (1997) 'Radiocarbon evidence for the Lateglacial human recolonisation of Northern Europe.' *Proceedings of the Prehistoric Society* 63:25–54.

Kelly, R.L. and Todd, L.C. (1988) 'Coming into the country: Early Paleoindian hunting and mobility.' *American Antiquity* 53:231–44.

Kolmogorov, A. N., Petrowski, I. and Piscounov, N. (1937) 'Etude de l'équation de la diffusion avec croissance de la quantité de matière et son application à un problème biologique.' *Moscow University Bulletin of Mathematics* 1:1–25.

Kuzmin, Y.V. and Tankersley, K.B. (1996) 'The colonization of Eastern Siberia: An evaluation of the Paleolithic Age radiocarbon dates.' *Journal of Archaeological Science* 23:577–85.

Murray, J.D. (1993) *Mathematical Biology*. 2nd, corrected edition. Heidelberg: Springer-Verlag.

Roper, D.C. (1985) 'Spatial dynamics and historical process in the Central Plains Tradition.' *Plains Anthropologist* 40:203–21.

Shott, M.J. (2002) 'Sample bias in the distribution and abundance of Midwestern fluted bifaces.' *Midcontinental Journal of Archaeology* 27:89–123.

Skellam, J.G. (1951) 'Random dispersals in theoretical populations.' *Biometrika* 38:196–218.

Steele, J., Sluckin, T.J., Denholm, D.R. and Gamble, C.S. (1996) 'Simulating the hunter-gatherer colonization of the Americas.' *Analecta Praehistorica Leidensia* 28:223–7.

Steele, J., Adams, J. and Sluckin, T. (1998) 'Modelling Paleoindian dispersals.' *World Archaeology* 30:286–305.

Steele, J., Gamble, C. and Sluckin, T. (2000) 'Estimating the rate of Paleoindian expansion into South America.' In T. O'Connor and R. Nicholson (eds), *People as Agents of Environmental Change*, pp. 125–133. Oxford: Oxbow Books.

Turchin, P. (1998) *Quantitative Analysis of Movement*. Sunderland, MA: Sinauer Associates.

Verhulst, P.F. (1838) 'Notice sur la loi que la population suit dans son accroissement.' *Corr. Math. et Phys.* 10:113–21.

13

LESSONS IN
LANDSCAPE LEARNING

David J. Meltzer

For those of us who worry about colonization, this is a most welcome volume. Too often in the past, the question of how colonizing groups new to a place learned that landscape has rarely been addressed, or if addressed, only in the simplest of ways. In my own world, for example, deceptively complex simulation models have been crafted to show that initial colonizers could move with breathtaking speed through a continent as vast, unknown, increasingly exotic (as they moved south), and highly diverse (in both space and time) as North America, by focusing their subsistence efforts on big-game animals. In these models megafauna serves as keystone taxa, enabling people to override ecological boundaries without having to learn much more about resources and place than how to track mastodons in the forest, once their distant cousins on the Plains – mammoths – were left behind.

To be sure, the initial colonizers in the Americas *could* have focused their subsistence attention on big game. However, actual archaeological evidence for such is meager, and invoking that undemonstrated assumption in order to make a colonization model work borders on the teleological. More to the point, in these models learning is virtually ignored: hunting technologies and strategies brought from elsewhere, and imposed on the new continent (or imposed serially on new taxa and new habitats within that continent), are implicitly assumed sufficient to provide what learning there was.

And yet, we know that within a few centuries of their initial appearance in the New World the descendants of the first Americans became remarkably knowledgeable about their place and its resources. Clearly, a whole lot of landscape learning was going on during the centuries and millennia after initial colonization that we have not been thinking about or talking about – which is not surprising, I suppose, since landscape learning is not something that has garnered much anthropological attention. This was a process rarely witnessed or recorded in the ethnographic accounts of foragers, whose landscapes were normally well known and thoroughly mapped by the time ethnographers arrived on the scene (making the process of how that information is learned by subsequent generations a primary focus of attention [e.g. Nelson 1969: 374–6; Richerson and Boyd 1992: 70–1]). As Kelly (Chapter 3) notes,[1] we have no analogies to call upon in the matter of landscape learning. Modern hunter-gatherers have substantial knowledge of their landscape – not complete knowledge (no group ever has that [Smith 1988:

222

250]) – but knowledge sufficiently deep that it can reduce forager uncertainty, and make it possible to gamble for higher stakes on risky strategies and, in general, maximize returns (Smith 1988: 231–2). They, ethnographers, could see the product of the process (landscape knowledge), could appreciate its vital importance (and, to be sure, its importance was appreciated), but could not see how it developed in the first instance.

What does emerge from the anthropological literature, however, are important insights into the use and transmission of information. Kaplan and Hill argue (1992: 186–7; also Kelly 1995: 151; Stephens and Krebs 1986: 103), for example, that the greatest effort in information acquisition should occur in patchy environments that vary temporally and in large scale – effectively the ecological situation in which virtually all colonizing groups initially found themselves. (That situation would change over time, presumably, as these groups accumulated knowledge of the environment and resources.) Indeed, there are reasons to think that on such an unknown landscape selection would favor rapid and extensive exploration, and intense episodes of landscape learning (Orians and Heerwagen 1992: 557). In principle, this ought to be true but would depend on whether the group is there to settle, say, or has a more specialized purpose (e.g. mineral extraction), though of course the scope and scale of such exploration and learning may vary.

So I, for one, very much welcome the discussion and ideas in this very interesting volume, which has sought to probe an aspect of colonization that has been underdeveloped in archaeology – certainly in terms of the peopling of the Americas, but evidently in regard to the archaeology of other times and places as well. It is not a matter that lends itself to easy archaeological answers, however, since the landscape learning process we seek to understand took place in real time, and involved such intangible matters as knowledge and information. Its traces are not readily detectable in the archaeological record, which only records its secondary material consequences, and at vastly greater temporal spans. Despite this, the papers in this volume, which range widely over times and places and topics, make some considerable headway in the matter and raise important issues and ideas. I see some common themes and many useful insights emerging from them which I would like to discuss, starting with some organizing and house-cleaning.

I tend to think of colonization and landscape learning as taking place on empty landscapes, by which I mean landscapes utterly devoid of other people. It is a parochial bias, I know, but one almost unavoidable in considering the initial peopling of the Americas; after all, at some point, likely before Late Glacial Maximum (LGM) times, this hemisphere had literally no human occupants. For the first ones to arrive, the landscape was truly unknown. It was not unknowable or necessarily difficult to learn, of course, but it was unknown.

Yet, not all landscape learning takes place in such a context. In some instances, there are (or were) native peoples on the landscape. Even at times after the initial arrival of humans in the Americas – or, for that matter, any other part of the world – landscapes once occupied (or initially colonized) can become devoid of people. This can be either in a literal sense, as when there has been broad-scale regional abandonment (obviously, partly a matter of scale), or in a figurative sense, as when new groups come into a landscape already occupied, but by peoples with whom the newcomers may have limited or no interaction (or may not even consider human). In those cases the landscape may seem relatively or effectively empty, so far as a wave of colonists might perceive it, but it will not be entirely unknown, at least not to all the players on the stage, who might be expected to interact at some level with one another. Indeed, as we know from the ethnographic record, where all peoples have neighbors, near or distant, they rely on those neighbors (to some varying degree) for information (acquired directly or indirectly), resources, and even potential mates, and against whom they may also compete or whose presence otherwise affects the decision-making calculus of moving about the landscape and utilizing its resources.

Thus, like Rockman (Chapter 1), I think it useful to think of colonization and learning as taking place in two broad contexts: one in which a resident population is absent, the other in which a resident population is present (Figure 13.1). Within those broadly defined categories, however, are divisions and gradations. Absence, as implied above, can be conceived of in two ways: humans were either never present on that landscape, as in the Americas in pre-LGM times or Europe prior to 1 mya, or humans were once present but had disappeared by the time of the arrival of the colonizers in question, as in the case of the recolonization of post-LGM northern Europe. Presence, similarly, can be conceived of in several different ways, arrayed along a continuum of interaction. At one extreme is the situation in which there is no interaction (possibly the case of early modern humans arriving in Europe). Then there is limited, or possibly hostile, interaction, as in the case in North America of the Norse (c. AD 1000) or various European groups (fifteenth to seventeenth centuries). At the other end of the continuum are those settings where there is complete and (relatively) peaceful interaction (few instances of this readily come to mind, but perhaps the incoming Neolithic farmers of Europe interacting with Mesolithic groups or the *Bounty* mutineers and the Pitcairn Islanders can serve as cases in point). The presence of a resident population completely changes the calculus of the learning equation from that experienced by groups on a people-less landscape.

In the least complicated case (in the sense of having the fewest variables) – that of the very first colonization of an island or a continent – all learning must be done de novo by the colonists. As a consequence, the rate of learning will be slower than in cases in which native groups are or were once present (all other things being equal). This is so simply because there is so much more to learn and no help in the learning process. This is possibly the most challenging learning situation a colonist might encounter: how challenging depends on the degree to which the newly entered landscape differs from the one left behind – a matter in which the colonization of Oceanic islands, for example, may differ from that of continents the size and diversity of the Americas. While the learning challenge might be formidable, there are nonetheless benefits to being first, not the least being a naive native fauna and essentially unfettered mobility (save, of course, for natural barriers, be they topographic, ecological, or geographic).

By contrast, in situations in which a population is present at the time another group arrives, the rate of learning can be faster. In fact, one might surmise that even if prior native groups are no longer physically present in the region, their traces on the landscape (e.g. material remains on their archaeological sites; water holes) may provide ready clues to the structure and nature of available resources. If native groups are present, the rate and shape of the learning process will be more or less rapid (or steep),

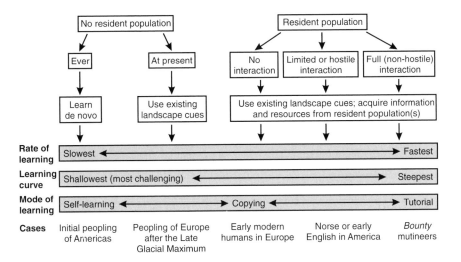

Figure 13.1 Patterns of landscape learning on occupied and unoccupied lands

depending on the nature and degree of the interaction; that is, whether learning takes place by copying from a distance, say, or by direct tutorial. Of course, one can easily conceive – and Blanton's English colonists in Chapter 11 provide an example – of cases where stubborn disinterest in native adaptations, and inappropriate imposition of knowledge of prior landscapes (rather than learning the new landscape), actually slow the learning process. Moreover, native peoples on the ground create a social environment that one must also learn (Rockman), and that can substantially complicate the colonization process. A relevant example in this instance, as Hardesty describes (Chapter 5), are mining rushes, in which colonists are moving into an area for a specialized purpose (in these cases, seeking gold or other minerals), for brief periods of time, using knowledge, methods, and technologies that are not strongly place-dependent, and relying on long-distance supply lines for food and other critical resources.

There are also, as one can readily surmise, obvious benefits to not being first: namely, that the time-intensive and longer-term process of learning about the behavior and distribution of, for example, different plant and animal resources in different areas and under different climatic and ecological circumstances can be acquired in very short order, without requiring long periods of observation or experimentation, or without having directly to explore and encounter the resources or landscape. The knowledge barriers (Rockman's term) are lower.

Categories of learning

And what is (or must be) learned? The papers in this volume discuss all manner of learning processes and products, but they can readily be sorted into three broad categories: learning about routes, regimes (primarily climatic), and resources. Table 13.1 describes several components of the learning process in each: the cognitive base and initial conditions brought to the process, which includes the hardware and software humans use to experience their world, as well as their prior knowledge; some of the cues and parameters they might be able to take from the environment and landscape; and how that particular process might play out over time and space. These components are not intended to be comprehensive but merely suggestive of the processes and patterns. They might also help in considering the archaeological implications of the various processes.

Each of these categories entails different learning strategies; they vary in their degree of difficulty, and they involve different actions taking place at different scales (all of which, of course, is further dependent on whether the learning is for purposes of long-term settlement or for purposes of short-term resource extraction – all things being equal, the learning required for the former is much greater).

Routes

Learning routes, what Golledge (Chapter 2) refers to as "wayfinding," is, of course, essential to any newcomer on a landscape. In the absence of maps and in the face of an utterly unknown landscape, colonizers use a variety of topographic markers, environmental cues, and generic knowledge, as well as the cognitive software that humans have developed over evolutionary time (such as a sense of direction, the ability to store information, and the ability to integrate time and motion and relative position in real time as one moves across space), to move themselves across space without getting lost, while maintaining their awareness of position relative to their starting point (Table 13.1). Both Golledge's and Kelly's chapters discuss the specific entailments of wayfinding, mostly as it is practiced on landscapes that are known, have native guides, or at least are not entirely unfamiliar (see also Orians and Heerwagen 1992).[2]

It is of interest that, in spite of the relative familiarity with the landscape that characterizes these cases, Golledge nonetheless observes that ineffectiveness and inefficiency seem to characterize the movement of people across space. While the consequences nowadays may be little more than socially awkward moments (late arrivals to a dinner party, for example), in times past and on unknown landscapes the penalties may have been more severe – as when, perhaps, hunting parties became lost and failed to retrace their steps back to their group, or ocean-going colonists were not as prudent as they needed to be (as Anderson describes in Chapter 10). Being lost on land was not always fatal, of course, nor did it always carry the same costs. In the tropics it would hardly matter if groups became lost: they are surrounded by food.[3] In the desert, and in the High Arctic, the costs were much higher, and groups would take measures to avoid the risk of getting lost (e.g. Nelson 1969: 99–104) and rarely got lost except when ill (as in cases where food supplies were low and they were forced to survive predominantly on dried meat [L. Binford, personal communication, 2001]) or because of bad weather (Nelson 1969).

From these discussions, several points of archaeological interest emerge in regard to wayfinding on unknown landscapes. First, initial responses to an unknown landscape are typically made to features of that landscape that are rather general, including

Table 13.1 Components of landscape learning

	Wayfinding	Tracking weather and climates	Mapping resources
Cognitive base and initial conditions	Sense of direction Ability to store information Ability to integrate time, motion, and position while moving Generic navigation knowledge (celestial markers, etc.)	Generic climate knowledge (seasonal changes, etc.) Ability to store or capture information Human generation time	Generic knowledge of geology, hydrology, plants and animals Ability to store information Ability to relocate resource occurrences
Cues and parameters	Prominent landmarks Geographic features (rivers, mountain chains, etc.) Spatial patterning to natural features	Scale of climate change relative to generation or residence time (detectability) Duration, periodicity, and amplitude of climate changes (predictability) Variability of climate (stability)	Relative movement of the resource (fixed/not fixed) Relative stability and availability of resource (reliability) Abundance, behavior, and/or distribution of resources (predictability)
Learning patterns in time and space	Begins at the most general landscape features, then becomes more spatially specific and refined over time ("megapatch" to "patch") Begins on landscapes easiest to traverse and navigate, then later on landscapes that impede travel or wayfinding May involve artificial signage/waypoints (caches)	Begins with specific features (local weather), then becomes more general and cumulative over time (climate) Predictability increases with residence time, depending on periodicity and stability of climate Learning may have upper limits, depending on detectability, residence time, and capture capacity (cannot "see" a glacial period)	Early, redundant use of fixed, permanent resources (stone) Learning begins at general level (animals of same size class; plants of same family or genera), and becomes more specific Knowledge increases with residence time, but may also require experimentation May have gender correlates, depending on relative labor investment in hunting versus gathering

prominent landmarks, rough spatial configurations, and major topographic and geographic features (linear mountains, major rivers, coastlines), as well as to major features or regularities of the seascape (Anderson; see also Orians and Heerwagen 1992: 563). Arguably, the less familiar the forager is with an area, the greater the size of the canvas being mapped and the coarser the resolution of that map (Anderson; Kelly). Initially, it is more critical or advantageous to outline the broad boundaries of a new region than it is to focus on a small area in detail. This would suggest that initial pathways will follow distinctive topographic features. Ultimately, however, the cognitive maps we humans construct are at the other end of the spatial scale, and often comprise named, highly specific referents to particular places, their characteristics, use, and identity (social, geographic, history, etc.) (Golledge; Kelly; also Silberbauer 1981). This obviously brings up the issue of scale and the relative size of the spatial units that are first encountered and learned on new landscapes – a matter I deal with in more detail below.

Second, as with Roebroek's bees (Chapter 6), wayfinding might be a staged process, initially involving scouting activities (possibly embedded in hunting forays) across the new landscape. Unlike Tolan-Smith (Chapter 7), I am not convinced that the deployment of logistical parties across the landscape necessarily implies "extant, pre-existing knowledge about the landscape." This suggests that the first archaeological appearance of colonizing groups in an area may not represent the first colonization-leading-to-settlement of that area.

Third, because not all landscapes are alike in terms of their structure, complexity, available resources, or legibility (Golledge's term), not all landscapes will necessarily attract exploration and colonization or be as easy to learn (Golledge; Kelly; Rockman). In some instances, travel is impeded, while wayfinding is not (e.g. tundra, mountainous terrain); in other cases, travel is unimpeded, while wayfinding is difficult (vast, flat, featureless plains [Silberbauer 1981: 98]); in still other cases, both travel and wayfinding can be complicated (in heavy forests, for example). In these last cases, wayfinding and travel strategies might involve the use of landscape features such as rivers to ease travel and movement (Kelly). In all cases, of course, it is pattern on the ground that matters. An order or predictable spatial patterning to natural features – as, for example, in the distribution of Oceanic archipelagos (Anderson) – will certainly ease the process of wayfinding. The key, as Orians and Heerwagen observe (1992: 560), is that:

> safe movement through the environment requires a great deal of skill and knowledge. Landscapes that aid and encourage exploration, wayfinding, and information processing should be more favoured than landscapes that impede those needs.

For this reason, there is certainly little reason to expect a priori that an initial colonizing group will immediately fan out across a continent or land mass in a wave-like or advancing front pattern (Rockman).[4]

Finally, in addition to the many and often highly visible or prominent natural features humans may use as landmarks to increase environmental legibility (features to place on their emerging cognitive maps of the landscape), human groups also create artificial landscape markers or signage systems to facilitate their wayfinding (Golledge). Signage can be, as Golledge notes, distinctive enough to mark group identity and boundaries. Signs, symbols, or names would be increasingly important on geographically more monotonous landscapes (Kelly), which would in turn select for artificial sign posts.

Climatic regimes

While the English who came to Virginia experienced severe climatic shock on arrival (Blanton), more often than not colonists expanding into new ranges are less likely to move as quickly into climatic situations that are foreign to their prior experience. Even so, shifts in latitude or altitude, movement into regions climatically controlled by different air masses, expansion into interior areas from coastal areas, or any of a host of positional changes on a large land mass (or island-hopping across an ocean area) can change climatic parameters in subtle, and sometimes not so subtle, ways. Leaving aside for the moment the consequences of such differences for the flora and fauna of a region, these climate patterns are part of the essential environmental stage on which colonization is played out, and they must be learned (Table 13.1).

The many aspects of climate – be they temperature, precipitation, evaporation, length of growing season, storm frequency, annual snowfall, and so on – are not static in space or time (though I'll confine the comments that follow to temporal variability). Periodic and quasi-periodic climatic cycles and changes occur at multiple temporal scales simultaneously. Those occurring on a seasonal or annual basis, and perhaps those occurring on decadal scales (e.g. drought episodes, El Niño/Southern Oscillation [ENSO] events), can be directly experienced during an individual's lifetime. Those occurring on scales of centuries or millennia or over longer periods (e.g. Bond cycles, Dansgaard-Oeschger events, glacial–interglacial cycles) certainly cannot be experienced by any single individual. However, it may be possible for climatic extremes that occur over, say, the course of a century or more to be experienced and subsequently "recorded" in the corpus of group knowledge (of which, more below).

Of course, colonists new to a landscape haven't the knowledge base to predict climatic patterns or variation much longer than those that might occur on an annual or seasonal basis. Their predictive ability increases with the time spent on the landscape, but that depends too on the amplitude, periodicity, duration, and variability of climatic change in the area. Where seasonal climatic variability occurs in a short wavelength, and follows a roughly periodic function (either of high [seasonal] or low [equable] amplitude), the pattern can in principle become apparent and predictable in a relatively short period of time (e.g. Orlove *et al.* 2000). Occasional departures from that pattern, depending on their frequency, will be much more difficult to anticipate or predict. Such departures may seem random or – depending on their scale – may appear to be a monotonic trend, but may actually be part of a larger cycle (that is, periodic over an even longer time period). Longer wave functions, whether periodic or non-periodic, occurring on a scale of several decades, centuries, or greater time periods, will – as noted – be the most difficult to detect (and likely impossible to

predict), quite simply because the larger patterns will not be visible to a single generation, which may only experience the peak or trough of a particular oscillation (which
may outlast that generation).

All of this means that where a climate is more variable or unstable (across space and
time, at whatever scale), more of it has to be experienced before it can become predictable and less uncertain (McGovern 1994: 149). Colonists new to a landscape, or colonists who may have arrived at a time of rapid climate change (occurring on a scale
detectable to humans) or extreme weather events (unusually heavy rainfall, long
periods of drought) can find themselves severely disadvantaged (Epstein 1999), and
may lack any clear sense of whether the pattern they are experiencing will be short- or
long-lived, typical or unusual, or predictable or not. One such example is the severe
drought in which the early English colonists in Virginia found themselves (Blanton;
also Stahle *et al.* 1998). This climatic instability may be a particularly relevant factor
for colonizers moving about in glacial periods – as opposed to interglacial times – for
in general (and all other things being equal), climatic instability is more pronounced
during glacial times, when its effects may also be amplified (McManus *et al.* 1999). Of
course, such changes need not be deleterious: there are examples of climatic changes
which made possible the dispersal of colonists into a new area, possibly including an El
Niño-triggered eastward expansion of Oceanic groups – expansion which Anderson
suspects may have been as much accidental as deliberate. And other examples include
the Thule movement across the maritime region of northernmost North America, *c.*
AD 1000, and the Norse expansion into Greenland, Iceland, and Newfoundland
about the same time – though the subsequent climatic reversals, which came in a
matter of centuries, shook the tentative hold those European groups had in their new
lands.[5] The take-home lesson here, as Crumley notes, is that:

> Local and regional knowledge about the environment, transmitted through
> culture, can be the source of appropriate adaptive strategies in times of
> marked environmental change. Conversely, unfamiliarity with environmental
> parameters can lead to disastrous choices and actions.
>
> (Crumley 1994: 240)

But how is such knowledge gained? Obviously, in the absence of instrumentation
and historic records, duration of residence on the landscape is critical. Gunn (1994:
84–7) introduces the useful term "capturing" to describe the manner in which individuals and groups recognize and incorporate climatic and environmental information on different scales. As he argues, there is likely an upper temporal limit to
capturing among non-literate groups, controlled partly by the wave length, amplitude,
and periodicity of the climatic changes, but mostly by the time period over which
those conditions are experienced, the cognitive abilities of human individuals and
groups to store and retain information (there is an information decay over time), and
the continuity of the cultural traditions in that particular locality. Practically speaking,
for mobile colonists in many parts of the world the capture of information on climate
is likely to have a very low upper limit of, say, several decades. Capture time will

increase to centuries, and perhaps millennia, as mobility is reduced and colonization grades into long-term settlement.[6]

Unfortunately, as Gunn points out, little of that process of information capture may be visible archaeologically, as much of it will reside in the non-material realms of folklore, storytelling, and ritual (as is the case among modern hunter-gatherers [e.g. Nelson 1969]) and "stored cognitively as a landscape or mental map, with attendant adaptive behaviour" (Gunn 1994: 89). Herein, however, we see the intersection and integration of routes and regimes.

Resources

Learning resources (Table 13.1) will vary in difficulty with the relative spatial fixity of the resource on the landscape, its relative permanence or impermanence (reliability), and the predictability of its abundance, behavior, and distribution. Fixed, permanent resources like outcrops of stone suitable for artifact manufacture, or sources of precious metals (as discussed by Hardesty), for example, are spatially and temporally permanent, and once those sources were located they became known and predictable points on a landscape. My sense is that outcrops of stone are relatively easy to find (compare Rockman and Tolan-Smith), the process involving little more than following alluvial gravels or glacial moraines upstream to the outcrop. Surely colonists of even moderate competence had that basic prior knowledge of geology and hydrology. As Hardesty shows, prior geological knowledge – rudimentary as it was – proved quite effective in many of the mining rushes. It was hardly flawless, however, and as the local geological landscape was learned, the miners had to tweak both their geological knowledge and their extraction technologies, to adapt better to the local conditions and maximize their returns.

In contrast, impermanent resources such as plants and animals (to varying degrees – after all, relative to the human lifetime many trees are "permanent") had to be identified, initially to determine whether resources not yet in the diet should be. Moreover, their properties or behaviors, habitat, location, and short- and long-term patterns in abundance and distribution – as these varied over time and space – had to be learned. This is particularly the case in regard to animals, for unless encounter rates on the landscape in question were very high, locating animal prey required knowledge of the spatial and temporal and landscape behavior of animal prey, which will vary by the animals' age, sex, group size and composition, season, competitive relationships, available water sources, physiological stage (breeding, pregnancy, lactation), grazing sequences, species composition, and heterogeneity of the vegetation community, topography, and exposure to predation, among other factors (see also Roebroeks), all of which had to be observed and learned (Silberbauer 1981: 291–2). Thus, while I appreciate and partly agree with the argument of Kelly (Chapter 3; also Kelly and Todd 1988) that groups new to a landscape would have to rely on a generalized and transferable knowledge of animal behavior that could be extrapolated from one area to another, it must be cautioned that even if those hunter-gatherers were foraging across a class of animals the same size (large animals, say),[7] and using the same generalized hunting technology, different animals within that class can behave very differently across the landscape – depending on all those conditions just noted.

Learning a native flora,[8] particularly one as large and complex as that on a continent – North America has 20,000 species of plants, and nearly 30,000 if one counts subspecies and varieties – was surely no easy task. And yet that learning was accomplished, ultimately, with astonishing success: as Moermann observes (personal communication, 2000), "no one has ever found a plant native to North America with any medicinal value not known to and used by native Americans" (Moermann estimates the number of those medicinal plants at about 2,700; see also http://www.umd.umich.edu/cgi-bin/herb). How that was done or how long it took is not known. It is surmised that the process was based on "astute and accurate observation that could only have been elaborated on the basis of many years of explicit empirical experimentation" (Berlin and Berlin 1996: 53).

Well it might have been, but the mechanics are unclear: did groups scan flora independently each generation? That seems unlikely, given the vast number of plants to scan. One would suppose, instead, that broad classes of plants (say, genera, or families, in our Linnean system) would be identified (oaks, for example), along with the general properties of that taxon. Then it was merely a matter of learning the specific properties of the different local species of oak. Knowledge at a more general taxonomic level would be easier to capture (there are only about 290 families of plants in North America) and transmit to subsequent generations, especially if the taxon in question was a long-lived perennial (Moermann, personal communication, 2000). Knowledge learned at this level would give colonists an entrée into new habitats in which the specific flora might be alien to their experience, but where they would at least recognize the plant as a familiar one. Conceive of this as a generalized rather than a specialized learning strategy – thereby enabling gathering of the sort Kelly and Todd (1988) envision for hunting.

The process of learning about specific plants – whether they had food, medicinal, or other value – almost surely involved some degree of observation (to see whether other animals ate them) and experimentation (to detect effects of ingesting them). In Moermann's view, intense periods of plant resource research (the term is not inappropriate in this context) would likely occur under two conditions: when new diseases appear, and when there is a substantial environmental transformation. Obviously, moving into a new landscape is a case of the latter.

Learning resources will not have, in all instances, a distinctive archaeological signature. Kelly and Roebroeks both note, rightly, that redundancy in stone sources may be an indicator of a lesson learned. Of course, redundancy may occur for reasons beyond the possibility that no other suitable stone sources are known. As to learning the less permanent resources, the archaeological record may in the end prove ambiguous. For example, the sharp rise from the late Pleistocene into the Early Holocene on the North American Plains of the number of bison kill sites, and the number of individual bison killed per site, cannot be interpreted strictly as a by-product of having learned more effective (and lower-risk) strategies for killing bison. While some of that surely was taking place, it was also the case that bison numbers were increasing dramatically, the consequence of competitive release following the extinction of the major grazers among the Pleistocene megafauna (*c*.10,500 BP). Once bison had the Plains to themselves, they increased in number and spread out into this increasingly large habitat (the grassland itself was changing in ways advantageous to their foraging). That increase, and the increase in human predation, was a co-evolutionary process in which hunters' learning how better to disadvantage the animals was no doubt critical to the process. Beyond that general statement, however, it is not clear how much more might be said about the learning process.

Matters are even less apparent when dealing with plants, and here I can do little more than offer the caveat that the first significant use of a plant in an area is not necessarily a signal of learning results. Knowing what properties a plant possesses or what it might provide is a necessary but not sufficient condition for its use. At some point(s) in prehistory, it was determined how to remove the tannic acid from oak acorns, enabling their use as a food source. But the adoption for use as a food source of this or of any other plant occurs for a variety of reasons (e.g. Gremillion 1996), in most instances quite unrelated to when its properties were first detected.

Obviously, those agricultural groups who are traveling with food resources – "transported landscapes," Kirch (1997: 218) calls them – can dispense with much of the learning process. Such is obviously relevant in the case of the colonization of Neolithic Europe, and perhaps of Oceania (Anderson; but cf. Kirch 1997).

Who's learning what? Gender and landscapes

Several of the authors in this volume (e.g. Golledge; Kelly) note that wayfinding and resource procurement are not gender-neutral among hunter-gatherers (for that matter, wayfinding is not gender-neutral among modern, Western groups [see Lawton 1996: 141]). Working on the assumption of an evolutionarily derived division of labor, in which males predominantly hunted and females foraged,[9] they (and others: see Meltzer [in press]; Silverman and Eals 1992: 534–5) point out that there are – or ought to be – correlates or differential patterning in wayfinding skills, foraging knowledge, and the scale of foraging. This is argued to be so because tracking and killing animals entail different kinds of spatial problems than does foraging for edible plants (Silverman and Eals 1992: 534–5). Because of the mobility of animals, hunting requires the ability to orient oneself in relation to distant points on a landscape (either visible or not), and to be able constantly and accurately to update position and location during movement ("homing," in Golledge's term). In contrast, gathering involves locating immobile food resources within complex spatial arrays of vegetation, and this entails the ability to recognize and recall spatial configurations of objects and track that position over time (seasonal changes in plant distributions), as well as possess an incidental memory for objects and their locations (Silverman and Eals 1992: 535).

From this, we can infer that landscape learning – of routes and resources – was similarly gender-linked. Much of the "local" knowledge of resources (plants and small animals) and their spatial/temporal patterns and distributions was likely learned, acquired, and accumulated by women (and young children). Broader-scale ("macroenvironmental") landscape knowledge – and this includes both routes and resources – would result from men's more extensive, long-distance logistical hunting forays across the area (also Binford 1983: 40). That mating distances similarly tend to be greater in males than females (MacDonald and Hewlett 1999) is likely a correlate of this pattern, which has interesting and (so far) largely unexplored implications for the genetic diversity and structure of a fast-moving, far-flung colonizing population (but see Seielstad *et al.* 1998).

The role of prior knowledge

Few colonizers enter a landscape that is completely and utterly foreign to them. Those that do, for example the English colonists of the early seventeenth century, were put in that position by virtue of having crossed vast distances in relatively brief periods of time (Blanton). Had the first Americans somehow made the traverse directly from Siberia to tropical South America, then indeed the learning challenge would have been formidable. But they did not. Instead, they, as well as the post-glacial colonists of northern Europe (Tolan-Smith), the Lapita wayfarers of the Pacific (Anderson), and other groups (perhaps except the ethnocentric seventeenth-century English! [Blanton]), were all moving into settings in which they could apply their prior knowledge to the new place and resources. At least initially.

That said, on the ground learning was nonetheless critical, not just as a consequence of extending ever farther from a point of origin (and thus into less familiar climatic and ecological settings), but also because even when dealing with roughly familiar resources the specific availability, distribution, abundance, and predictability of those resources will vary according to the climatic, geological, topographic, and ecological conditions of the local landscape. As I noted earlier, even miners – armed with highly specific applied knowledge and on the ground strictly for resource extraction – nonetheless had to adjust their prior knowledge (Hardesty). Learning those conditions was a matter of time, and experience – particularly in the absence of local informants or role models.

As generic knowledge figures in learning across all these domains (Golledge, Kelly), it is appropriate to add a word on the negative side of such learning. The accumulation of environmental knowledge is never complete, comprehensive, or accurate. Under the circumstances, applying misinformation – presumptions about what a landscape might be like that are based on already suspect intelligence about prior, seemingly similar environments – is a risky strategy. Indeed, one of the characteristics of colonizers who fail (the Norse, the early English) is the use of what McGovern (1994: 149) terms "false analogy," by which he means that the "managers' cognitive model of ecosystem characteristics (potential productivity, resilience, stress signals) may be based on the characteristics of another ecosystem whose similarities mask critical threshold differences from the actual local ecosystem."

By relying too heavily on pre-existing knowledge (or, better, expectations), colonizers run the risk of applying (perhaps faulty) preconceived models to a landscape, and in so doing fail to consider the actual patterns on that landscape, leading them to make false predictions and disastrous responses to anticipated changes. This might prove particularly disadvantageous to colonists, for reliance on generic knowledge will assuredly be greatest during the early phases of movement into a region, and it is at those points in the colonization process, Orians and Heerwagen note (1992: 562–3), that snap judgments about a landscape or habitat are often made: "responses at this stage are known to be highly affective, to occur almost instantly, and are believed to represent subsequent actions." Making a snap judgment with imperfect knowledge can be detrimental (and economically unfortunate to the luckless post-Comstock miners who missed gold deposits that occurred in areas outside their sphere of geological understanding, as Hardesty observes).

Learning in time and space

All of which raises the question, how quickly can colonizers learn the routes, regimes, and resources of a landscape – particularly a landscape the size of, say, a continent? The authors in this volume have plenty of opinions on the matter. Few of them necessarily agree on the details, but all agree that learning is a long process (Kelly; also Nelson 1986). Blanton gives a figure of twenty years as the time it took the English in Virginia to gain a sense of the local climate patterns and over a century to develop accurate charts. Rockman puts the compilation of socially and ritually preserved forms of environmental information at 200–400 or more years. Tolan-Smith suspects it may have taken a couple of thousand years for groups to adjust to the postglacial ecology of the British Isles. Golledge merely observes that the process of making an environment legible is "a function of time of exposure and familiarity," without being more specific. I think all are likely correct, given the varying scales of information acquired (information comes in time-stamped and time-packaged units). There is, as I noted earlier, presumably an upper limit to the temporal scale of processes that can be observed and learned: it is unlikely, for example, that climatic patterns that occur at a very low frequency – such as a glacial cycle – could be tracked through many hundreds of human generations over the tens of thousands of years it took to play out. The longest detectable cycles might be those that occur on a scale closer to one or a few human generations.

Although learning was done in real time, it would be readily extended over many generations. Group size, as Kelly observes, plays a determining role in learning and (perhaps more important) information storage capacity; that is, learning is done by individuals, but it rapidly transcends them as social learning (see Richerson and Boyd 1992: 70ff) across space and through inter-generational time (the elder to the younger), and moving beyond the local group to encompass larger units – as Roebroeks stressed (also Meltzer, in press). Social learning is critical because over time information can be shared and compounded to include large areas not seen by all, and record events and conditions otherwise only experienced by a few individuals.

And here, unexpectedly, is where landscape learning may have archaeological correlates, as the process of information exchange would have involved interaction between scattered colonizers, such as aggregation or long-distance social and exchange networks (as discussed by Roebroeks). Obviously, we'll never see information being exchanged archaeologically, but we can potentially see the context in which it occurred, and possibly the spatial scale at which it was taking place.

As to the spatial scale of learning (and this seems true of learning routes, regimes or resources), several of the authors are in agreement that one begins learning at the coarsest, broadest scale. Using Beaton's handy if ill-defined concept of a "megapatch," I have argued elsewhere (Meltzer [in press]) that initial colonizers in a new world will have a relatively low level of landscape and resource resolution. As a consequence, resources will appear patchy and out of phase relative to the forager groups, leading to larger range sizes. And given the larger size of their settlement range, and attendant limitations on their ability to track variation and changes in resource availability (a result of relatively small population numbers and low density on the landscape), colonizing groups will likely be associated with or (better) track gross habitat types. While Beaton calls them megapatches, the same notion appears independently here under several different guises, including macroenvironments (Golledge) or macro-oceanic island patterns (Anderson) or large-scale features (Blanton). It would be interesting to explore this in the case of Neolithic Europe and to see if this is one of the axes along which hunter-gatherers and agriculturalists diverge significantly. This may also have a bearing on the shape of colonizing expansion, whether an advancing front or stream/path.

Conclusions

Let me conclude with some general lessons that emerge from this volume, with an eye on those of archaeological relevance (Table 13.1). Landscape learning is vital, regardless of whether other people are present. On people-less landscapes, learning is dominated by geographic and ecological concerns that are derived and framed by the paths or initial conditions from which these colonizing pulses derive. When other people are already there, landscape learning is still critical and necessary, particularly in those instances where incoming groups have very different adaptive strategies. Yet, the calculus of the learning curve is arguably going to be much more complicated, for now there is a complex social landscape to navigate, which in some instances can be advantageous to colonizers and in other cases a decided hindrance – the latter usually because of overt hostility or mutual distrust and avoidance.

Landscape learning (especially of routes and resources) takes place from the general to the specific in terms of space (starting with megapatches or macroenvironments, working toward ever smaller units of space – patches or microenvironments). In contrast, learning extends from the specific to the general in terms of time, particularly in the case of climatic regimes (which are initially observed on a daily basis). This implies, archaeologically, that we should see over time a shift from an initial exploitation of large areas to the use of progressively smaller regions.

Not all landscapes are alike in terms of their colonization potential. If we possessed fine enough chronological resolution, then we should see differences in habitat use over time. On a gross scale, we do see this: the high Andes, for example, were occupied relatively late in the South American cultural sequence. Whether we will ever reach the point where it might be possible to tease apart and test whether there was a difference in the timing of entry into, say, the eastern forests of North America, as opposed to the open western grasslands, is anyone's guess.

Because not getting lost is a critical aspect of moving about an empty landscape, we can hope to see archaeologically the artificial signposts established to help find the way out – and back. I have argued (Meltzer 2002) that stone tool caches in Clovis times (of which there are now a dozen or more) may have helped serve that function.[10] Obviously, natural landmarks (both permanent ones such as mountain peaks and river junctions and impermanent ones such as game trails), if they served such roles, and they surely did (Golledge; Kelly; Zedeño and Stoffle), cannot be so easily assigned such a function long after the fact.

As several chapters suggest, on an unknown landscape selection would favor rapid and extensive exploration (Kaplan 1992: 585; Orians and Heerwagen 1992: 557): hunting parties or scouts go ahead and send back information, like Roebroeks' bees orienting themselves before foraging. That information is gathered by individuals in quick time and for small areas, but its contents and utility can extend over longer periods and encompass larger areas, in so far as the information is shared widely within the group, and pertains to more permanent or predictable landmarks, environmental features, or resources. Whether we will be able to see or, better, recognize such real-time processes, given the resolution of the archaeological record, is unclear.

Almost certainly, the farther back in time or the coarser the chronological resolution, the less likely we are to see anything that we can reasonably and securely assign to such a process – as several authors note (e.g. Roebroeks; Tolan-Smith). Roebroeks gives the example of archaeological resolution in Middle Pleistocene Europe on the order of 50,000 to 100,000 years, involving sites which may represent palimpsests of thousands of years. It is not unreasonable to ask, as he does, "How can we distil information about landscape learning from such a huge palimpsest? What, if anything, can we do?" Legitimate questions!

But there is reason to suspect there may be some archaeological correlates to all this. One, of course, is in the patterning of expansion. Not all landscapes are alike. They differ in their yield of food, water, and other resources, as well as in their relative danger (from the physical or biological environments). Humans have the behavioral flexibility to select settings which provide the highest benefit-to-risk ratios, according to current conditions and needs (Orians and Heerwagen 1992: 561). This can be reflected in the differential use of space, or a stutter-step movement in time (Tolan-Smith's notion of a "standstill" phase, which has an analogue in the "long pause" in the colonization of Oceania, as Anderson notes). Ultimately, teasing out differential use of landscapes in space and time is a scale issue that may or may not be resolvable in a particular instance (Anderson; Roebroeks). If it is, we may be able to say something about the modal shape of movement – whether in streams, leap-frogging, waves, etc. (Rockman).

As both Kelly and Roebroeks note, repeated use of a particular locality may reflect in part the process of landscape learning and wayfinding. Better to return to the same spot than to risk not finding a vital resource elsewhere. The regular and repeated use of distinctive stone sources in North American Paleoindian times may be evidence of this practice.

Landscape learning is a collective enterprise, and for that reason when dealing with small groups colonizing large landscapes we expect to see aggregation sites in the archaeological record – these are the contexts within which information was exchanged. Following this line still further, one can argue that groups are in learning "mode" when we have in evidence large-scale social systems on that landscape (Lourandos 1997).

Finally, the obvious point: landscape learning is critical to the ultimate success of colonization. Colonizers, as several papers noted, bring with them a knowledge base, social intelligence, and a set of adaptive and technological strategies to new lands and places (and here I am speaking specifically of colonists who come to settle: not explorers or other specialized task groups). All of that can get a group very far indeed. But if they do not expand their knowledge base, adjust their thinking, or adapt their old strategies to new conditions, they can fail as colonists. The near-disaster of the English in Virginia in the early 1600s, and the hasty retreat of the Norse from Newfoundland six centuries earlier and (later) from Greenland, are perhaps only the most spectacular and best-known examples. Tellingly, the archaeological evidence for Norse–Inuit contact is "strangely one-sided" (McGovern 1994: 140). Norse artifacts are much more common in Inuit sites than the reverse. If the flow of material culture is in any way a manifestation of the flow of information (it need not be, of course, but in this record instance it appears to be so [McGovern 1994: 146–8]), then the Norse were learning very little from the native peoples of the lands they sought to colonize, and it was to their disadvantage.

In the case of the English colonists, the lessons from their misery are clear and link many of the above issues: it is easier to shift niches than it is to make a wholesale change in subsistence strategies. It is better to walk your way into a new landscape than disembark onto it (the Oceania example is the exception that proves the rule, for the remote islands being colonized had naive and easily trapped and exploited fauna, and were at least climatically similar to those left behind, allowing imported crops to do well). Existing populations do you no good if they are hostile, or even if you think they are or find them beneath you. Finally, it is best not to be confused about your mission. If it is strictly economic, as in the sixteenth-century Spanish model (where the goal was to conquer or convert the natives and capture their wealth), one moves across the landscape feeding on the native larder. Since settlement is not a goal, there is little need to learn the landscape. If settlement is the goal, one has to learn the local resources and adapt extant procurement strategies and technologies. Unfortunately for these early English colonists, their goals were a confused combination of the two, and tactical decisions driven by an effort to maximize economic returns had unfortunate consequences for efforts at settlement. The lesson here: one can learn the wrong parts of the landscape, and one can squander one's learning chances on the chase of gold, and not the goal of filling cupboards.

Almost certainly in the prehistory of other times and places over the grand sweep of the human diaspora, other poor learners living on new and unknown landscapes, perhaps in relatively small, isolated groups, disappeared without issue or note in marginal environments or in the face of natural events beyond their capacity to cope (Butzer 1977: 579).

Notes

1 I have responded here to all the papers in this volume that were available at the time of preparing this commentary. The papers by Fiedel and Anthony (Chapter 9), Steele and Rockman (Chapter 8), and Hazelwood and Steele (Chapter 12) were not forwarded to me in time for consideration in this review. (All citations without dates or pagination refer to chapters in this book.)

2 Golledge observes, in this regard, that even today people tend to rely more on their cognitive maps than on instrumentation or technical aids in wayfinding. He attributes this to the fact that most trips tend to be in familiar environments. But perhaps it may also be a vestige of our evolutionary history, and of how we as a species learned to navigate space – the end product of a learning process that, of course, took place without instruments.

3 This is not universally true, as Gonzalo Pizarro's near-fatal encounter with the tropics in the upper Amazon in 1540-2 shows.

4 Of course, this is not the only reason to doubt that human groups will move across space in a wave-like pattern.

5 Which is not to say that climatic change was responsible for the expansion or the subsequent contraction of these groups – only that it played a part in the process.

6 From this, however, one should not assume that sedentary farmers, for example, will always have an advantage, for other variables – such as duration of residence on the landscape – remain just as critical components of the equation. The massive failure of farmers on the American Plains during the Dust Bowl period of the 1930s is evidence of that. They had arrived on the Plains 20 years earlier, during a relatively wet period, and decades after the first Euroamerican settlers on the Plains had been driven off by drought. The lack of continuity between the earlier and later occupations meant there was little appreciation for the inevitability of drought on that landscape and little questioning of the wisdom of dry farming in that setting (Webb 1931).

7 One can assume that large animals will be highly ranked resources, as they routinely are amongst hunter-gatherer groups. That they were highly ranked does not mean, of course, that these were the sole resources exploited by these groups; only that, if encountered, they would be pursued. Demonstrating that there was specialized use of these resources is a separate matter. It might be added that this does not necessarily include the largest animals, for hunting such animals carries a substantially greater cost in terms of risk. Not all hunter-gatherers hunt elephants (see e.g. Lee 1979: 217; Silberbauer 1981: 293).

8 My thinking on this matter is very much influenced by email correspondence with Daniel Moermann and through our collaboration on a proposal addressing the question of how knowledge of plants might have been acquired over time and on new landscapes.

9 While there is a substantial literature on the subject of why that division exists, it can perhaps be best summed up simply by noting that hunting – especially hunting of large game – had high survivorship costs. Women, who tend to be risk-aversive (and perhaps carrying children) avoided such activities; men, less so (Borgerhoff Mulder 1992: 363; Foley 1988: 218-20; Kelly 1995: 269; Silberbauer 1981: 93).

10 I recognize, of course, that not all caches may have had that function, or even that all Paleoindian caches did – only that at this time and place in prehistory, caches may have served in the creation of a landscape map.

References

Berlin, E. and B. Berlin (1996) *Medical ethnobiology of the Highland Maya of Chiapas, Mexico: the gastrointestinal diseases.* Princeton: Princeton University Press.

Binford, L.R. (1983) "Long term land use patterns: some implications for archaeology," in R.C. Dunnell and D.K. Grayson (eds) *Lulu Linear Punctated: essays in honor of George Irving Quimby.* University of Michigan Anthropological Papers 72:27–53.

Borgerhoff Mulder, M. (1992) "Reproductive Decisions," in E. Smith and B. Winterhalder (eds) *Evolutionary Ecology and Human Behavior.* New York: Aldine de Gruyter.

Butzer, K. (1977) "Environment, culture, and human evolution," *American Scientist* 65:572–84.

Crumley, C. (1994) "Epilogue," in C. Crumley (ed.) *Historical ecology.* Santa Fe, NM: School of American Research Press.

Epstein, P.R. (1999) "Climate and health," *Science* 285:347–8.

Foley, R. (1988) "Hominids, Humans, and Hunter-Gatherers: An Evolutionary Perspective," in T. Ingold, D. Riches, and J. Woodburn (eds) *Hunters and Gatherers: History, Evolution, and Social Change.* Oxford: Berg.

Gremillion, K. (1996) "Diffusion and adoption of crops in evolutionary perspective," *Journal of Anthropological Archaeology* 15:183–204.

Gunn, J. (1994) "Global climate and regional biocultural diversity," in C. Crumley (ed.) *Historical ecology.* Santa Fe, NM: School of American Research Press.

Kaplan, H. and K. Hill (1992) "The evolutionary ecology of food acquisition," in E. Smith and B. Winterhalder (eds) *Evolutionary ecology and human behavior.* New York: Aldine de Gruyter.

Kaplan, S. (1992) "Environmental preferences in a knowledge seeking, knowledge using organism," in J. Barkow, L. Cosmides, and J. Tooby (eds) *The adapted mind: evolutionary psychology and the generation of culture.* Oxford: Oxford University Press.

Kelly, R.L. (1995) *The foraging spectrum: diversity in hunter-gatherer lifeways.* Washington, DC: Smithsonian Institution Press.

Kelly, R. L. and L.C. Todd (1988) "Coming into the country: early Paleoindian hunting and mobility," *American Antiquity* 53:231–44.

Kirch, P.V. (1997) *The Lapita peoples: ancestors of the Oceanic World.* Cambridge, MA: Blackwell.

Lawton, C. (1996) "Strategies for indoor wayfinding: the role of orientation," *Journal of Environmental Psychology* 16:137–45.

Lee, R.B. (1979) *The !Kung San: Men, Women, and Work in a Foraging Society.* Cambridge: Cambridge University Press.

Lourandos, N. (1997) *Continent of hunter-gatherers: new perspectives in Australian prehistory.* Cambridge: Cambridge University Press.

MacDonald, D. and B. Hewlett (1999) "Reproductive interests and forager mobility," *Current Anthropology* 40(4):502–23.

McGovern, T. (1994) "Management for extinction in Norse Greenland," in C. Crumley (ed.) *Historical ecology.* Santa Fe, NM: School of American Research Press.

McManus, J.F., D. Oppo, and J. Cullen (1999) "A 0.5 million-year record of millennial scale climatic variability in the North Atlantic," *Science* 283:971–5.

Meltzer, D.J. (2002) "What do you do when no one's been there before? Thoughts on the exploration and colonization of new lands," in N. Jablonski (ed.) *The First Americans: the Pleistocene Colonization of the New World.* San Francisco: California Acadamy of Sciences.

—— (in press) "Modeling the initial colonization of the Americas: issues of scale, demography, and landscape learning," in G.A. Clark and C. Michael Barton (eds) *Pioneers on the Land: the Initial Human Colonization of the Americas.* Tucson, AZ: University of Arizona Press.

Nelson, R.K. (1969) *Hunters of the northern ice*. Chicago: University of Chicago Press.

—— (1986) *Hunters of the northern forest*. Chicago: University of Chicago Press.

Orians, G. and J. Heerwagen (1992) "Evolved responses to landscapes," in J. Barkow, L. Cosmides, and J. Tooby (eds) *The adapted mind: evolutionary psychology and the generation of culture*. Oxford: Oxford University Press.

Orlove, B.S., J. Chiang, and M. Cane (2000) "Forecasting Andean rainfall and crop yield from the influence of El Niño on Pleiades visibility," *Nature* 403:68–71.

Richerson, P. and R. Boyd (1992) "Cultural inheritance and evolutionary ecology," in E. Smith and B. Winterhalder (eds) *Evolutionary ecology and human behavior*. New York: Aldine de Gruyter.

Seielstad, M., E. Minch, and L. Cavalli-Sforza (1998) "Genetic evidence for a higher female migration rate," *Nature Genetics* 20:278–80.

Silberbauer, G. (1981) *Hunter and habitat in the central Kalahari Desert*. Cambridge: Cambridge University Press.

Silverman, I. and M. Eals (1992) "Sex differences in spatial abilities: evolutionary theory and data," in J. Barkow, L. Cosmides, and J. Tooby (eds) *The adapted mind: evolutionary psychology and the generation of culture*. Oxford: Oxford University Press.

Smith, E.A. (1988) "Risk and uncertainty in the 'original affluent society': evolutionary ecology of resource-sharing and land tenure," in T. Ingold, D. Riches, and J. Woodburn (eds) *Hunters and gatherers. 1: History, evolution and social change*. Oxford: Berg.

Stahle, D., M. Cleaveland, D. Blanton, M. Therrell, and D. Gray (1998) "The Lost Colony and Jamestown droughts," *Science* 280:564–7.

Stephens, D. and J. Krebs (1986) *Foraging theory*. Princeton: Princeton University Press.

Webb, W.P. (1931) *The Great Plains*. Lincoln, NE: University of Nebraska Press.

INDEX